Implementing Semantic Web Servi

T0280424

Dieter Fensel · Mick Kerrigan · Michal Zaremba
Editors

Implementing Semantic Web Services

The SESA Framework

 Springer

Dieter Fensel
Mick Kerrigan
Michal Zaremba

STI Innsbruck
ICT – Technologie Park
Technikerstr. 21a
6020 Innsbruck, Austria

dieter.fensel@sti2.at
mick.kerrigan@sti2.at
michal.zaremba@sti2.at

ISBN: 978-3-642-09575-7   e-ISBN: 978-3-540-77020-6

ACM Computing Classification (1998): H.3.5, H.4, D.2.12, I.2.1, J.1, K.4.4

Cover design: KünkelLopka, Heidelberg

Printed on acid-free paper

9 8 7 6 5 4 3 2 1

springer.com

To all Semantic Web and Semantic Web Services (SWS) researchers:
Let's make it real!

Preface

Motivation

Computer science appears to be in a period of crisis. The globalization trend is moving programming jobs to low-labor countries. This appears to place computer science research and departments at risk of being considered as working on obsolete technology. However, the opposite is true. Computer science is on the verge of a new generation of computing that is leading to innovation not only in computing but also in business, science, and all other endeavors that depend on computing.

Times of crisis are also times of innovation and can lead to paradigm shifts. Computer science is entering a new generation. The previous generation was based on abstracting from hardware. The emerging generation comes from abstracting from software and sees all resources as services in a Service-Oriented Architecture (SOA). A SOA is essentially a collection of services and these services can communicate with each other. The communication can involve simple data passing or it could involve multiple services coordinating some activity. In a world of services, users are concerned only about the services and not about any software or hardware components that implement the service. To this end, service-oriented computing has become one of the predominant factors in current IT research and development efforts over the last few years.

Standardization in this area has already made its way out of the research laboratories into industrial-strength technologies and tools. Again, Web technologies prove to be a good starting point: *Web Services* seem to be the middleware solution of the future for enabling the development of highly interoperable, distributed software solutions: the new technologies subsumed under this common term promise easy application integration by means of languages such as XML, and a common communication platform by relying on widely used Web protocols.

A service-oriented world will have in the future an "uncountable" number of services. Computation will involve services searching for services based on functional and nonfunctional requirements and interoperating with those that they select. However, services will not be able to interact automatically and SOAs will not scale without signification mechanism of service discovery, negotiation, adaptation, composition, invocation, and monitoring as well as service interaction which will require further data, protocol, and process mediation. Hence, machine processable semantics are critical for the next generation of computing – SOAs – to reach its full potential. Only with semantics can critical subtasks can be automated leaving humans to focus on problem solving.

This book presents a comprehensive Semantically Enabled Service-oriented Architecture (SESA) framework which aims to augment the worldwide movement to service orientation with semantics in the context of evolving industrial standards and technologies. Several promising results from numerous recent EU projects and efforts within standardization bodies such as OASIS and W3C show the direction for further developments and commercialization of semantic-based technologies.

Goals

The goal of this book is to provide an insight into and an understanding of the problems faced by Web Services and SOAs. Considering current Web service technologies, there is a large amount of human effort required in the process of finding and executing Web Services. This book lays the foundation for understanding the Semantic Web Services infrastructure, aimed at eliminating human intervention allowing for seamless integration of information system. It focuses on a particular infrastructure, which is currently the most advanced Semantic Web Services infrastructure, namely, SESA, and its related efforts such as the Web Services Execution Environment (WSMX) activities and the Semantic Execution Environment (OASIS SEE TC) standardization effort.

With the present book we want to give an overall understanding of SESA and show how it can be applied to the problems of SOAs. Industry, which plans to commercialize semantic solutions, is searching for examples and literature that guide it in the development of the end-to-end applications and systems that use semantics. This book targets professionals and researchers who want to improve their understanding of how semantics can be applied in execution engines to enable interoperability between distributed information systems. While such systems are already in the process of being developed and standardized in the open source community, the lack of appropriate literature prevents the wider popularization of these technologies. That is to say that while prototypes of such systems are already available, the commercialization of these technologies remains in its infancy. This book aims to bridge this gap and bring existing prototypes closer to commercial exploitation.

Intended Audience

The book is suitable for professionals, academic and industry researchers working on various aspects of semantics, who have knowledge of integration aspects gained from their past experiences using traditional integration technologies. Through this book they will learn how to apply the Semantic Web Services infrastructure to automate and semiautomate tasks, which until now have required a lot of human intervention, while using existing integration technologies. This book is also suitable for novice readers, such as advanced graduate students enrolled in courses covering knowledge management, the Semantic Web, and engineering and semantics in information systems. This book will educate them about grounding technologies for Semantic Web Services, but will also explain the more generic issues related to integration of information systems.

Organization of This Book

We have divided the book into four main parts.

Part I provides an introduction to the field and its history. We cover basic Web technologies, Web Services and their predecessors, and the state of research and standardization in the Semantic Web field.

Part II presents SESA – the architecture aiming to enable the execution of Semantic Web Services. We describe the building blocks and show how they are consolidated into a coherent software architecture that can be used as a blueprint for implementation.

Part III gives more insight into middleware services. The architecture defines the necessary conceptual functionality that is imposed on the architecture through the underlying principles. Each such functionality is realized (totally or partially) by a number of so-called middleware services.

Part IV shows how SESA can be applied to real-world scenarios and provides an overview of compatible and related systems.

Acknowledgements

The work presented in this book has been funded by the European Commission under SWWS (IST-2001-37134), DIP (FP6-507483), Knowledge Web (FP6-507482), TRIPCOM (FP6-027324), and SUPER (FP6-026850) projects. In addition, contributions came from several Austrian-based projects, namely, SEMBIZ (812525), GRISINO (810805/5512), RW2 (809250), and TSC (809249). The work presented in this book was funded as well through the Lion project supported by Science Foundation Ireland under grant no. SFI/02/CE1/I131. Additionally we would like to acknowledge US National Science Foundation grants CCR-0311512 and IIS-0534419. The majority of the research that is described in this publication must be accredited to the tireless efforts of the SEE, WSMO, WSML, WSMX, and WSMT working groups, to whom we remain gratefully indebted for their valuable discussion and helpful advice.

The editors, January 2008

Contents

Part I Foundations

1   From Web to Semantic Web 3
  1.1 The Web – A Familiar Starting Point 3
  1.2 Architectural Principles of the World Wide Web 5
  1.3 The World Wide Web Consortium – W3C 7
  1.4 Spawning the Semantic Web 9
  1.5 The Semantic Web 14
  1.6 The Semantic Web – Future Prospects 24
  1.7 Summary 25

2   Semantic Web Services 27
  2.1 Behavioral Perspective of the World Wide Web 27
  2.2 Web Services 34
  2.3 Semantic Web Services: The Future of Integration! 37
  2.4 The Ideal World 40
  2.5 Summary 41

3   WSMO and WSML 43
  3.1 The Web Service Modeling Ontology 43
  3.2 The Web Service Modeling Language 53
  3.3 Summary 65

Part II SESA Environment

4   Introduction to Semantically Enabled Service-oriented Architectures 69
  4.1 SESA Background 69
  4.2 Service Orientation 70
  4.3 Execution Environment for Semantic Web Services 74
  4.4 Governing Principles 76

4.5   SESA Vision – Global View 76
4.6   SESA Roadmap 82
4.7   SESA Research Areas and Goals 83
4.8   Summary 97

5   **SESA Middleware** 99
5.1   Services Viewpoint 100
5.2   Technology Viewpoint 112
5.3   Summary 117

6   **SESA Execution Semantics** 119
6.1   Motivation 120
6.2   Proposed Description Formalism 121
6.3   Mandatory Execution Semantics 122
6.4   Case Study Example of SESA Execution Semantics 126
6.5   Technical Perspective on Execution Semantics 131
6.6   Summary 134

Part III SESA Services

7   **Reasoning** 137
7.1   Reasoning Requirements 137
7.2   Logical Background 140
7.3   Reasoning Tasks 144
7.4   Reasoning Within SESA 155
7.5   A Generic Framework for Reasoning with WSML 156
7.6   Rule Interchange Format 162
7.7   Conclusion 164

8   **Discovery** 167
8.1   A Conceptual Model for Discovery 167
8.2   Web Services at Various Levels of Abstraction 168
8.3   Keyword-Based Discovery 169
8.4   Discovery Based on Simple Semantic Descriptions 174
8.5   Discovery Based on Rich Semantic Descriptions 182
8.6   Summary 191

9   **Selection** 193
9.1   Introduction 193
9.2   Nonfunctional Properties 194
9.3   Selecting Services 201
9.4   Related Work 207
9.5   Summary 208

10   Mediation 211
    10.1 Preliminaries 211
    10.2 Ontology-Based Data Mediation 214
    10.3 Behavioral Mediation 223
    10.4 Summary 231

11   Storage and Internal Communication 233
    11.1 Introduction to Triple Space Computing 234
    11.2 Triple Space Kernel 237
    11.3 Role of Triple Space Computing in SESA 247
    11.4 Evaluation 255
    11.5 Summary 256

Part IV SESA Application and Compatible Systems

12   SESA Application 261
    12.1 Case Scenario: B2B Integration 261
    12.2 Case Scenario: Voice and Data Integration 270
    12.3 Summary 284

13   Compatible and Related Systems 285
    13.1 The Internet Reasoning Service 285
    13.2 Other WSMO-Compatible Tools 293
    13.3 Tools Based on OWL-S 294
    13.4 METEOR-S 296

14   Conclusions and Outlook 303
    14.1 Why SOA? 303
    14.2 Future Work 305
    14.3 Commercialization 306

References 307

Index 319

List of Contributors

Jos de Bruijn – Chapter 3
Faculty of Computer Science, Free
University of Bozen-Bolzano,
Piazza Domenicani 3, 39100 Bolzano,
Italy
debruijn@inf.unibz.it

Christoph Bussler – Chapter 2
Cisco Systems, Inc., San Jose, CA, USA
ChBussler@aol.com

Emilia Cimpian – Chapter 10
STI Innsbruck, Leopold Franzens
Universität Innsbruck, ICT – Tech-
nologie Park, Technikerstrae 21a, 6020
Innsbruck, Austria
emilia.cimpian@sti2.at

Dieter Fensel – Chapters 1–14
STI Innsbruck, Leopold Franzens
Universität Innsbruck, ICT –
Technologie Park, Technikerstrasse 21a,
6020 Innsbruck, Austria
dieter.fensel@sti2.at

Graham Hench – Chapter 1
STI Innsbruck, Leopold Franzens
Universität Innsbruck, ICT –
Technologie Park, Technikerstrasse 21a,
6020 Innsbruck, Austria
graham.hench@sti2.at

Uwe Keller – Chapter 7
STI Innsbruck, Leopold Franzens
Universität Innsbruck, ICT –
Technologie Park, Technikerstrasse 21a,
6020 Innsbruck, Austria
uwe.keller@sti2.at

Mick Kerrigan – Chapter 3
STI Innsbruck, Leopold Franzens
Universität Innsbruck, ICT –
Technologie Park, Technikerstrasse 21a,
6020 Innsbruck, Austria
mick.kerrigan@sti2.at

Michael Kifer
Department of Computer Science, State
University of New York at Stony Brook,
Stony Brook, NY 11794-4400, USA
kifer@cs.sunysb.edu

Holger Lausen – Chapter 8
STI Innsbruck, Leopold Franzens
Universität Innsbruck, ICT –
Technologie Park, Technikerstrasse 21a,
6020 Innsbruck, Austria
holger.lausen@sti2.at

Adrian Mocan – Chapter 10
STI Innsbruck, Leopold Franzens
Universität Innsbruck, ICT –
Technologie Park, Technikerstrasse 21a,
6020 Innsbruck, Austria
adrian.mocan@sti2.at

Matthew Moran – Chapter 5
DERI Galway, National University of
Ireland Galway, IDA Business
Park, Lower Dangan, Galway, Ireland
matthew.moran@deri.org

Barry Norton – Chapter 13
Knowledge Media Institute, Open
University, Walton Hall, Milton
Keynes MK7 6AA, UK
b.j.norton@open.ac.uk

Carlos Pedrinaci – Chapter 13
Knowledge Media Institute, Open
University, Walton Hall, Milton
Keynes MK7 6AA, UK

Dumitru Roman – Chapter 9
STI Innsbruck, Leopold Franzens
Universität Innsbruck, ICT –
Technologie Park, Technikerstrasse 21a,
6020 Innsbruck, Austria
dumitru.roman@sti2.at

Omair Shafiq – Chapter 11
STI Innsbruck, Leopold Franzens
Universität Innsbruck, ICT -
Technologie Park, Technikerstrasse 21a,
6020 Innsbruck, Austria
adrian.mocan@sti2.at

Nathalie Steinmetz – Chapter 7
STI Innsbruck, Leopold Franzens
Universität Innsbruck, ICT –
Technologie Park, Technikerstrasse 21a,
6020 Innsbruck, Austria
nathalie.steinmetz@sti2.at

Ioan Toma – Chapter 9
STI Innsbruck, Leopold Franzens
Universität Innsbruck, ICT –
Technologie Park, Technikerstrasse 21a,
6020 Innsbruck, Austria
ioan.toma@sti2.at

Jana Viskova – Chapter 12
Department of Information Networks,
University of Zilina, Zilina, Slovakia
viskova@kis.fri.utc.sk

Tomas Vitvar – Chapters 5, 12
DERI Galway, National University of
Ireland Galway, IDA Business
Park, Lower Dangan, Galway, Ireland
tomas.vitvar@deri.org

Zhixian Yan – Chapter 5
STI Innsbruck, Leopold Franzens
Universität Innsbruck, ICT –
Technologie Park, Technikerstrasse 21a,
6020 Innsbruck, Austria
zhixian.yan@sti2.at

Maciej Zaremba – Chapter 6
DERI Galway, National University of
Ireland Galway, IDA Business
Park, Lower Dangan, Galway, Ireland
maciej.zaremba@deri.org

Michal Zaremba – Chapter 5
STI Innsbruck, Leopold Franzens
Universität Innsbruck, ICT –
Technologie Park, Technikerstrasse 21a,
6020 Innsbruck, Austria
michal.zaremba@sti2.at

Part I

Foundations

1

From Web to Semantic Web

Although the targeted audience of this book is professionals and researchers who are presumably somewhat familiar with the current state of the art when it comes to the Internet, World Wide Web, Web programming, semantic technologies, etc., this chapter will provide a very brief background of the history of the World Wide Web and its current relevant technologies essential to semantically enabled service-oriented architectures. Second, to bring the reader "up-to-speed" and to establish a common ground to base the rest of the chapters on, this chapter will emphasize the limits of the current Web technologies in order to clearly motivate the need for the technological advancements proposed in this book. The chapter's twofold purpose is then to provide sufficient background information and to prove that the technologies of the Semantic Web provide the foundation on which Semantically Enabled Service-oriented Architecture (SESA) is able to functionally operate.

1.1 The Web – A Familiar Starting Point

For the context of this book, we will provide a short look at the origins of the World Wide Web. Our story actually begins with Tim Berners-Lee's first visionary outline of the Semantic Web, thoroughly presented in the keynote session at the XML 2000 conference;[1] however, such a story necessitates some minimal background.

The final decade of the twentieth century proved to be quite pivotal in the evolution of the Internet and the World Wide Web. One significant precursor to this progressive decade was in 1983, when ARPANet – originally a mere network of four connected servers which spurred the development of technologies such as e-mail, FTP, and Telnet (more or less the grandfather of the Internet as we know it today) – made the official host protocol transition from NetWare Core Protocol (NCP) to Transmission Control Protocol/Internet Protocol (TCP/IP – the two main communication protocols on which the Internet currently runs). The 1980s closed with the decommissioning of ARPANet, in celebration of its 20th anniversary, and the path was set for the World Wide Web to take over [134].

---

[1] http://www.w3.org/2000/Talks/1206-xml2k-tbl/Overview.html

By the end of 1990, Tim Berners-Lee and Robert Cailliau, while working together at the European Organization for Nuclear Research, more commonly known as CERN, had begun to develop what is now accredited as the first Web browser, editor, server, and line-mode browser, whose name resultantly coined the term World Wide Web. Originally spelled without spaces, the *WorldWideWeb* was a tool which provided the first way to view the Web although at the time the "Web" only consisted of a single Web server and Web page, and the system was limited to text only (embedded graphics were not initially supported). The WorldWideWeb, later renamed *Nexus* in order to save confusion between the program and the abstract information space, was a distributed hypertext-based system which originally set out to resolve the challenges of information management within CERN. Alternatively, by basing the system on three simple and extremely extensible elements, hereafter referred to as the World Wide Web's enabling protocols (a standard protocol, globally unique identifiers, and a standardized format specification for publishing which strives to provide the internationalization of documents; all of which are later thoroughly discussed), the foundation for the world's most successful distributed information system was in place.

Tim Berners-Lee and his colleagues at CERN were not the only ones who recognized the dire need to categorically organize networked information, as well as to make documents and resources remotely available, in order to allow for efficient search and retrieval (management) of shared information. *Gopher*, a distributed document search and retrieval network protocol, was designed in 1991 by a group of researchers lead by Mark McCahill at the University of Minnesota. Gopher essentially set out to achieve the same overall goal as what was accomplished at CERN; however, its design was too rigid and limiting compared with the Berners-Lee hypertext-based model (although Gopher also used a similar link-based model). Like the WorldWideWeb, it is a client–server model. Both systems involve multiple remote servers, where any server can point to a document on any other server. Both systems allow the user to essentially jump from one server to another by simply reading a screen of text (Gopher had a more rigid hierarchy of folders and documents), making a selection, and resultantly receiving another screen of information allowing for further selection, and so on. Gopher, however, guides you through one menu followed by another until you are able to locate the desired document or resource. The WorldWideWeb, on the other hand, allowed the user to directly link from one document to the next.

While the WorldWideWeb had a graphical interface, and it is rightly recognized as the first graphical user interface for browsing the Web, the first graphical Web browser, *Mosaic*, was developed by Marc Andreessen and Eric Bina at the National Center for Supercomputing Applications (NCSA) in 1993. Mosaic provided a browser which supported both the World Wide Web enabling protocols and Gopher protocols, in addition to several other protocols. It came storming upon the then still relatively immature Web-centric community and was quickly crowned as the Internet's first *killer application*. Whether this is true may still be debatable, however what is clear is that is was merely an application. The true power under the hood was the combination of the Web's enabling protocols and the resultant hypertext-based model as laid out by Berners-Lee.

Today, Gopher refuses to go down without a fight. Hobbyists and archivists still manage to maintain a handful of servers, though even the die-hard enthusiasts admit they have no expectations of Gopher ever overtaking the Web, although they passionately expect it to continue to exist. Through an adventurous series of IP conflicts and licensing battles, Mosaic would go on to spawn what would later be referred to as the *browser wars*. Yet in hindsight, Gopher is already a geriatric protocol and Mosaic simply proved to be the first necessary interface required to bring the Web to the nonexpert user. There were of course several other players in the infant years of the Web; however, the context of this book does not allow us to properly treat other important contributions. For the sake of brevity, we focus on the essential standardized *building blocks* which proved to be of far greater importance than other combined singular efforts: these aforementioned Web-enabling protocols became the fundamental architectural principles of the Web [111, 199].

1.2 Architectural Principles of the World Wide Web

The fundamental architectural principles of the World Wide Web that enable its universality are the standardizations of identification, interaction, and format. Identification is probably the most essential of these three fundamental principles since it is its global uniqueness which allows resources to be identified via hypertext links regardless of where they are located on the Web. After these resources have been identified, a standardized interaction protocol is required in order to quickly and efficiently traverse between hypertext links via simple client–server interactions in a stateless request–response manner. This allows the user to navigate through the available resources. Lastly, given the correct identifier and valid interaction protocol, a standardized format for the data transmitted is required in order to provide an easy-to-use layout language for the Web [17]. The combination of the protocols is shown in Fig. 1.1.

Identification – Uniform Resource Identifiers

Uniform Resource Identifiers (URIs) follow the very simple but effective identification principle, whereby global naming leads to a global network. Originally coined "Universal Resource Identifier," the idea (as an official standard) dates back to June of 1994 when it was first mentioned in an Internet Engineering Task Force (IETF) RFC.[2] Since, URIs have become understood as "uniform" and have been distinguished between Uniform Resource Locators (URLs) and Uniform Resource Names

---

[2] Historically, the original term the author used was Universal Document Identifier in the WWW documentation. In discussions in the IETF, there was a view expressed by several people that "universal" was too strong, in that it could or should not be a goal to make an identifier which could be applied to all things. The author disagreed and disagrees with this position. However, in the interest of expediency at the time he bowed to peer pressure and allowed "uniform" to be substituted for "universal" in RFC2306. He has since decided that that did more harm than good, and he now uses "universal" to indicate the importance to the Web architecture of the single universal information space [18].

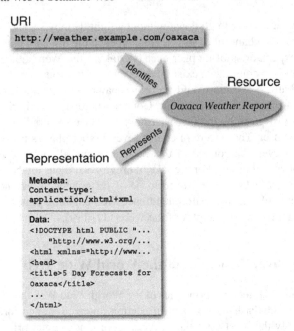

Figure 1.1. Architectural principles of the World Wide Web. (Reproduced from [110])

(URNs), although there are both classical and contemporary views of their differing semantics. Generally, URLs were conceived as addresses of a dereferencable resource, whereas URNs are not necessarily dereferencable. Much of the motivation for the Semantic Web comes from the value locked in relational databases and legacy systems. To release this value, objects must be exported to the Web as first-class objects and therefore must be mapped into a system of URIs [192].

Interaction – Hypertext Transfer Protocol

The most commonly used interaction protocol is the `http://` scheme (Hypertext Transfer Protocol, HTTP). In most cases this is a server or domain name which has the practical side effect that domains indeed belong to legal entities. The HTTP URIs are resolved into the addressed document by splitting them into two halves. The first half is applied to the Domain Name Service to discover a suitable server, and the second half is an opaque string which is handed to that server.

A feature of HTTP is that it allows a client to specify preferences in terms of language and data format. This allows a server to select a suitable specific object when the URI requested was generic. This feature is implemented in various HTTP servers but tends to be underutilized by clients, partly because of the time overhead in transmitting the preferences, and partly because historically generic URIs have been the exception. This feature, known as format negotiation, is one key element of independence between the HTTP specification and the HTML specification.

Format – Hypertext Markup Language

The hypertext pages on the Web are written using the Hypertext Markup Language (HTML), a simple language consisting of a small number of tags to delineate logical constructs within the text. Unlike a procedural language such as postscript, HTML deals with higher-level constructs such as "headings," "lists," "images," etc. This leaves individual browsers free to format text in the most appropriate way for their particular environment.

The earliest versions of HTML were deliberately kept very simple, allowing browser developers a fair amount of leeway when deciding how to display the formatted data. Although most Web browsers are able to communicate using a variety of protocols, such as FTP or Gopher, HTML caters to HTTP. In order to give the fast response time needed for hypertext applications, a very simple protocol which uses a single round trip between the client and the server is used [77].

Combination of All Three Principles: The World Wide Web

Berners-Lee was insistent that only these three protocols were required, and nothing more. Simplicity was key. "What was often difficult for people to understand about the design was that there was nothing else beyond URIs, HTTP, and HTML. There was no central computer 'controlling' the Web, no single network on which these protocols worked, not even an organization anywhere that 'ran' the Web. The Web was not a physical 'thing' that existed in a certain 'place.' It was a 'space' in which information could exist [19]."

At first look, these architectural principles do not appear exactly groundbreaking, nor complex – actually, perhaps their most attractive feature is outright simplicity (as an efficient, high-level architecture should be). Second to their simplicity is their consistent widespread *acceptance* and *usage* (or *consensus*). And this was again due to Berners-Lee's genius and foresight. Had the enabling protocols been restricted under proprietary licenses,[3] and left under the complete jurisdiction of Berners-Lee and his close colleagues, then they never would have been allowed to evolve into the foundational building blocks upon which the Web is set. Berners-Lee realized it was not possible to propose a universal space and simultaneously keep control of it; in order for the Web to become universal, it was necessary for it to be an open system, and this was the most groundbreaking characteristic of the architectural principles of the Web.

1.3 The World Wide Web Consortium – W3C

Of course such an open system did not come without consequence. The world had been invited to experiment with these easily extendable standards and the danger of fragmentation quickly arose. With so many diverse contributors, the Web faced the

---

[3] In April of 1993, CERN agreed to allow anyone to use the Web protocol and code royalty-free [20].

threat of developing in multiple directions, resulting in an overabundance of hetero-geneous data; the paramount problem the Web sought to resolve in the first place. Thus, the *openness* of the open system showed potential signs of being its own demise. Berners-Lee realized this necessitated a protagonist that would prove to be even more influential than his voice alone: the World Wide Web Consortium (W3C). In October of 1994, W3C was founded as an international consortium consisting of member organizations and a full-time staff with the goal of developing and maintain-ing Web standards. W3C's mission is: *To lead the World Wide Web to its full potential by developing protocols and guidelines that ensure long-term growth for the Web.*

W3C was by no means the first consortium which set out to develop open tech-nical specifications; the IETF, for example, predates W3C by almost a decade. However, unlike the IETF, W3C maintains a full-time staff to help design and de-velop code, and, since its inception, the W3C membership has been more open and diverse (accepting both government- and non-government-associated organizations, industrial and academic groups). While the IETF has evolved in a similar direction, W3C reaped these benefits from its beginning. Lastly, W3C chose to limit its influen-tial arm to simply "recommending" (officially "W3C Recommendations"), wary of using the term "standardizing" since this would slowly defeat the initial open policy behind the Web itself.

Officially, W3C pursues its mission statement by engaging in education and out-reach, and by promoting and developing software. Yet its greatest contribution re-mains the *open* forum where a properly established consortium can discuss, argue, and agree on how to move forward *together*. Without such a forum, achieving "Web interoperability" (the effective umbrella goal of W3C) would not be possible. And so as utopian as it may sound, the successful tale of the Web sits on the idealistic pillars of *openness* and *togetherness*.

As with all great developments of human history, the World Wide Web was not built in a day either; however, its crowning moment of established maturity (or foun-dation for) can be narrowed down to three days. December 14, 1994 marks a culmi-nating point in the development of the Web and W3C. It was the date of the first W3C consortium meeting at MIT. The following day, Netscape Communications Corpo-ration released a commercial version of Mozilla (the direct descendent of Mosaic), renamed Navigator 1.0; perhaps Mosaic was the first to bring the Web to nonexpert users, but Navigator was the first to actually attract a mass number (and market ma-jority) of users. This achievement has a twofold accreditation: firstly, Netscape was released over the Internet, rather than the traditional model of actually purchasing software at a computer store; secondly, Navigator was available free of charge. Marc Andreessen (one of the original developers of Mosaic, cofounder and then Vice Pres-ident of Technology for Netscape Communications Corporation) and founding part-ner James H. Clark were indeed following the same release trend set by other Web software developers; however, they were the first commercial company to offer their product "free of charge!" Practically overnight, Andreessen and Clark had set a mar-ket model to be followed: distribute software online – free of charge (at the very least, beta versions) – which allows for cheap and quick release cycles; profit is then gained through advertisements and additional (charged) services which are presented to the user when he/she visits the Web site where the product is offered ("downloadably"). Though perhaps unintentionally (since they originally attempted to only provide trial versions without charging), Andreessen and Clark had stumbled upon both this new business model and the realization that the Web provided a more profitable platform for a service company than a software company (a realization that will be further developed and capitalized upon throughout this book). A slew of Web marketing strategies and profitable business models would follow; however, these aspects are slightly beyond the scope of this book.

The final move in the elaborate game leading up to the concrete establishment of the Web and W3C's dominant authority came on the December 16. Owing to budget adjustments which directly reflected CERN's focus on high-energy physics rather than Web development, CERN was forced to resign as a W3C host. While this could be considered a temporary setback to the solidification of W3C, a new replacement was quickly found: The French National Institute for Computer Science and Control (INRIA). INRIA already had a credible reputation and proved to be a suitable replacement.[4] Although it was never CERN's intention, this replacement quickly showed that the W3C was indeed a consortium rather than an organization solely driven by its bigger members [19].

So the pieces were set in place. In addition to these culminating three days, 1994 was the year the Web successfully edged out Telnet as the most popular service on the Internet, second to FTP. The following decade would be incredibly fast-paced as W3C would attempt to always remain one step ahead of the world of developers it attempts to somehow guide in a general direction. But 1994 had come to a triumphant close and for the 20-odd members who attended W3C's first Advisory Committee meeting that December; one can be sure that their New Year's resolutions were hopeful to say the least. As Berners-Lee affectionately puts it, "That bobsleigh I had been pushing from the starting gate for so long was now cruising downhill [19]."

1.4 Spawning the Semantic Web

Our Web timeline now reaches an introspective point, whereby the potential of the foundations already in place required evaluation and an analytical synopsis of their limits. Though the underlying Web infrastructure was still young, the visionaries behind its creation already foresaw its prospective drawbacks. Essentially, and in perhaps rudely general terms, the Web at this point had only fulfilled one part of Berners-Lee's two-part vision of what it should become. The Web was now a capable platform for sharing information between two remote human users – what is referred to as human-to-human communication. The real challenge was to enable the same communication, but between two machines (and optimistically without any dependency upon human interaction): machine-to-machine communication. The resulting

---

[4] INRIA had already developed a browser/editor that would later become Amaya, W3C's flagship Web editor [19].

exemplary Web will be a combination of both these parts, resulting in a paradigm where "the whim of a human being and the reasoning of a machine coexist in an ideal, powerful mixture [19]."

The key to enabling machine-to-machine communication is semantics. Semantics, in this context, is not limited to its definition in the field of linguistics (referring to the study of meaning of linguistic expressions) nor to its prior understanding in computer science (e.g., referring to the study of the formal semantics of a programming language); it is an extension of both. Semantics is machine-useable content, and the Semantic Web is the next generation of the World Wide Web which includes (and of course utilizes) such content. This simple statement opens up an entirely new paradigm in computer science, one which serves as the cornerstone of the ideas presented in this book [210].

One particularly important event not mentioned in the previous section was the first international World Wide Web conference held in Geneva, Switzerland, in September of 1994. Right out the gate, months before the first W3C meeting (its formation was in fact officially announced at the conference), Berners-Lee was already bringing the term "semantics" to the floor. At this early stage, still 6 years prior to his laid-out vision of the Semantic Web, and the succeeding article in *Scientific American* (which effectively coined the term for the general public), Berners-Lee addressed the need for semantics in order for machines to move between the Web of links and nodes in the same fashion as the human user.

1.4.1 Enter XML

As ingenuitive as the foundational protocols of the Web are, they did not quite meet the "semantic" requirements needed to enable machine-to-machine communication. A first step in the right direction was the introduction of the Extensible Markup Language (XML), which successfully arose to supersede the Standard Generalized Markup Language (SGML) upon which HTML is based. With arbitrary SGML tags, we could begin to indicate the meaning of particular data directly within the document source – this was exactly what was required to successfully share structured data across different information systems (in contrast to HTML, which can be considered relatively unstructured/less rich owing to its lack of expressivity, i.e., well-defined content). XML is simply a SGML subset tailored for the World Wide Web which imposes certain restrictions (such as closed tags and case-sensitive names) while still allowing user-defined tags.

User-defined tagnames and attributes in XML allow for easier machine processing; however, such allowance for subjective definitions again opened the door to the threat of fragmentation. As with all expressive and extensible languages, each time new tags are introduced within a certain company or research group, for example, they will only be understood within that certain company or research group. This would prove to be a hurdle reserved for semantic languages to be later layered on top of XML, but regardless XML still provided a common, structured format which allows machines to share data – a standard representational format for documents beyond HTML, including typical office documents such as calendars and spread-sheets (which previously had no widely used standardized interoperable formats).

The official W3C recommendation, XML 1.0, defined as "a system for defining, validating, and sharing document formats on the Web," springs us ahead to February of 1998[5]. Around the same time came the development of the Resource Description Framework (RDF), a language specifically designed for representing information about resources in the World Wide Web. While XML provided the stepping stones towards *machine-processable*, RDF attempted to lay the bridge towards *machine-understandable*

Again, XML is a common, structured format which allows machines to share data; however, it still does not hold any true semantic meaning. It remains simply a syntactic language. While it does provide a stricter separation between content and layout, RDF was necessary in order close in on real machine-processable Web content and interoperable services. Unlike other references in the literature, we do not include XML per se as a particular language of the "Semantic Web," but instead consider the family of standards around XML an intermediate step towards a real machine-processable Web infrastructure [77].

1.4.2 Enter RDF

RDF turns out to be an excellent complement to XML, providing a language for modeling its semistructured building blocks: *metadata*. Metadata is simply "data about data," or more specifically, in the context of the Web, metadata is "data describing Web resources."[6] RDF uses such metadata to make statements about Web resources (even those resources which are perhaps not retrievable, but which are identifiable thanks to URIs) in the form of subject–predicate–object expressions as shown in Fig. 1.2.

These subject–predicate–object triples, commonly written as P(S,O), serve as the basis of the RDF metadata model. In accord with English grammar, the subject denotes a resource and the predicate denotes certain properties of this particular resource (the subject), which resultantly expresses a relationship between the subject and the object (which also denotes a particular resource, literal, or blank node). An object of a triple can in turn function as the subject of another triple, yielding a directed labeled graph, where resources (subjects and objects) correspond to nodes and predicates correspond to edges. Furthermore, RDF allows a form of reification (a statement

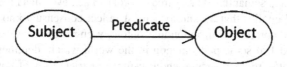

Figure 1.2. RDF graph data model. (Reproduced from [127])

---

[5] http://www.w3.org/Press/1998/XML10-REC

[6] http://www.w3.org/Press/1999/RDF-REC

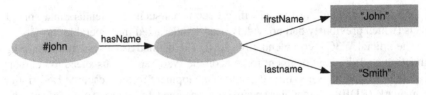

Figure 1.3. Example RDF graph. (Reproduced from [77])

```
<rdf:RDF xmlns:rdf="http://www.w3.org/1999/02/22−rdf−syntax−ns#"
        xmlns:ex="http://example.org/#"
        xml:base="http://example.org/">
  <rdf:Description about="#john">
   <ex:hasName rdf:parseType="Resource">
    <ex:firstName>John</ex:firstName>
    <ex:lastName>Smith</ex:lastName>
   </ex:hasName>
  </rdf:Description>
</rdf:RDF>
```

Figure 1.4. Example RDF/XML. (Reproduced from [77])

about a statement), which means that any RDF statement can be used as a subject in a triple. Figures 1.3 and 1.4 show an example RDF graph and its corresponding RDF/XML serialization.

1.4.3 Enter Ontologies

The proclaimed backbone of the Semantic Web, when layered upon RDF and XML, is *ontologies*. In the early 1990s, ontologies had shifted from a philosophical topic ("a theory about the nature of existence, of what types of things exist") [22] to an applicable concept of applied artificial intelligence. In simple terms, the latter case utilizes ontologies as formal structures which facilitate knowledge sharing and reuse. The technical definition is as follows: "An ontology is a formal, explicit specification of a shared conceptualization [90]."

This definition uses *conceptualization* to refer to an abstract model of some phenomenon in the world which identifies the relevant concepts of that particular phenomenon. *Explicit*, in this sense, refers to the restriction of concepts, types, and their usage constraints. *Formal* simply implies that a necessary standardized syntax (with specified semantics) is required in order to achieve "machine-readability." Finally, *shared* implies that an ontology must reflect consensual knowledge rather than simply the opinion of an individual ontology engineer. Thus, an ontology is an abstract model of some phenomenon in the world which identifies the relevant concepts of that particular phenomenon, using a restricted set of concepts, and a specified machine-readable syntax, in order to portray the consensual interpretation of the particular phenomenon [72]. Once again, the most advantageous aspect of an ontology is it is most informal, i.e., the fact that it is a consensual product.

However, as is sufficiently summarized in [72], an ontology is as much a prerequisite for consensus as a result of it. An intersubjective consensus is required in order for agents (be it a user or a program) to exchange semantic information in the first place. And this consensus can only result from a social process (open forum, discussion, debate, and a resulting consensual taxonomy). Such a definition places ontologies is a very unique (but growing) category of computer science; one which heavily depends upon the social sciences, a field which has essentially evolved into what many colleges and universities now refer to as "interdisciplinary studies."

Ontologies proved to be the "missing link" that successfully interwove human and machine understanding. This is achieved via a set of defined terms and relations which can be interpreted by both humans and machines. The meaning for the human is presented by the term itself, which is usually a word in a natural language, and by the semantic relationships between the terms. An example of such a human-understandable relationship is the superconcept-subconcept relationship (often denoted with the term "is-a"). This relationship denotes the fact that one concept (the superconcept) is more general than another (the subconcept). For instance, the concept *person* is more general than *student* or *researcher*. Figure 1.5 shows an example "is-a" hierarchy, where the more general concepts are located above the more specialized concept.

The utility of an ontology stems from two powerful aspects: a set taxonomy and a set of inference rules. The aforementioned "set of defined terms and relations" comprises the taxonomy; or, more specifically, a taxonomy provides a vocabulary of defined classes of objects and relations among them, with which one is able to model a particular domain. Terms such as *class*, *subclass*, and *relations* allow hierarchies to be created between entities, and furthermore, their semantics can be understood by both humans and machines. A taxonomy, however, is only as powerful as its underlying logic: more or less, a collection, or set, of inference rules.

Inference rules in ontologies supply further expressivity; they are what extend ontologies beyond other previous data structures, such as relational databases and legacy system, for these inference rules allow for automated reasoning. Knowledge

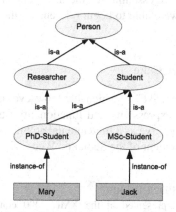

Figure 1.5. Example "is-a" hierarchy taxonomy. (Reproduced from [77])

representation and automated reasoning had long since been exciting topics for artificial-intelligence researchers; however, they had yet to break ground beyond impressive demonstrations. In order for such technologies to realize their full potential, they must be linked into a single global system: the Web.

With the combination of ontologies, layered on top of XML and RDF, and the exponentially growing Web at the turn of the twentieth century, the stage was set for the Semantic Web. And so we again return to Berners-Lee, who again craftfully clustered together the already flourishing results of the W3C – in a fashion quite similar to his simple combination of the Web-enabling protocols – in order to lay out his vision of the Semantic Web, the next generation of the World Wide Web.

1.5 The Semantic Web

> The Semantic Web is not a separate Web but an extension of the current one, in which information is given well-defined meaning, better enabling computers and people to work in cooperation.

The Semantic Web – Scientific American, May 2001

By February of 1999, RDF became an official W3C Recommendation[7] and XML thrived to the point where the XML 2000 conference boasted its status as the historical premier IT event.

It was at this conference, during the "Knowledge Technologies" session that Berners-Lee gave his opening keynote presentation entitled "RDF and the Semantic Web." In short, in accord with the session summary, his simple proposal was that RDF, and its provision of interoperability between applications (machine-to-machine communication), would enable automated processing of Web resources and serve as the foundation for the "Semantic Web." However, this session turned out to be more than a simple proposal. It was, in all its grandeur, the capstone to the already-developing Semantic Web. Berners-Lee clearly laid out the necessary steps and fundamental architecture essential for the next generation of the Web; and for the first time researchers were able to begin referencing the famous "Semantic Web layer cake."

1.5.1 The Semantic Layer Cake

The "Semantic Web layer cake" – which has now evolved into a more precise, oddly stacked layering of expressivity and functionality (its current state shown in Fig. 1.6[8]) – would not only serve as a fundamental architecture, but also as a visionary roadmap to the development of the Semantic Web.

---

[7] http://www.w3.org/Press/1999/RDF-REC

[8] The original layer cake, presented at the XML 2000 conference can be found at http://www.w3.org/2000/Talks/1206-xml2k-tbl/slide10-0.html

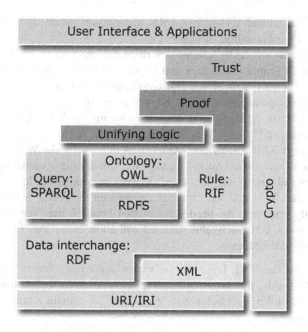

Figure 1.6. The Semantic Web layer cake

Syntactic Foundation

URI/IRI Layer

The bottom layer in the layer cake, the URI/Internationalized Resource Identifier (IRI) layer, sits upon Unicode, which provides a syntactical basis for the Semantic Web languages, allowing machines to process data directly. Unicode provides an elementary character-encoding scheme, which is used by XML, as well as other upper-level languages. The URI standard provides a means to uniquely identify and address documents, concepts, objects, and relations (more generally, resources on the Web) specified in the upper layers and essentially ground them to Unicode. This foundational layer ensures that all concepts used in the languages that complete the cake can be specified using Unicode and are uniquely identified by URIs [192].

XML Layer

As XML progressed as one of the fastest developing Web standards, multiple XML-related recommendations came to the forefront of W3C forum discussions; and the collection of these recommendations, some of which are in fact the core of XML, would comprise the XML layer of the architecture. Some of these recommendations included:

- **Namespaces:** XML namespaces are an integral part of the overall language. Namespaces provide a simple method for qualifying element and attribute names in an XML document. By utilizing URIs, namespaces are able to take full advantage of URI's universality.[9]

- **XML Schema:** An XML schema describes the structure of XML documents. It expresses a shared vocabulary and allows machines to carry out rules made by people. It entails data typing and constrains document structure to maintain predictable computable processing. Beyond explicitly describing the structure of XML documents, XML Schema provides a means for defining the content and semantics as well.[10]
- **XML Query:** XML Query (or XQuery), as defined by the W3C Architecture domain, is a standardized query language for "combining documents, databases, Web pages and almost anything else." XQuery provides flexible query facilities to extract data from real and virtual documents on the World Wide Web; therefore, finally providing the needed interaction between the Web world and the database world. Ultimately, this standard will allow collections of XML files to be accessed like databases.

Conclusively, the XML layer still only provides a basic format for structured documents. And while this layer is of course essential, as its foundational positioning implies, it is still a layer below the "good stuff." It remains a language with no particular semantics.

Semantic Base

Data Interchange Layer: RDF

The data interchange layer provides a basic assertion model which added concepts of assertion (property) and quotation to the layered architecture. In order for assertions to be made, the semantics provided by RDF were necessary. By utilizing the semantics assertions via propositional logic, this layer allows an entity–relationship-like model to be made for data represented and exchanged via the Web. At this level, simple data integration, aggregation, and interoperability are enabled by a collection of RDF standards. An increasing need for interoperability at a more expressive descriptive level is still desired, and so we clamber higher in the layers of the cake.

RDF Schema Layer: RDFS

RDF's limit to expressing simple statements about resources, using named properties and values, required an additional specification in order to define the vocabularies (terms) they intended to use in those statements. More precisely, a schema was required to indicate that they are describing specific kinds or classes of resources, and will use specific properties in describing those resources. This was fulfilled when RDF Schema became a W3C Recommendation in February of 2004.[11] RDF Schema

---

[9] http://www.w3.org/TR/REC-xml-names/

[10] http://www.w3.org/XML/Schema

[11] http://www.w3.org/TR/rdf-schema/

took the basic RDF specification and extended it to support the expression of structured vocabularies. In contrast to an XML schema, which prescribes the order and combinations of tags (the structure) in an XML document, an RDF schema provides information about the interpretation of the statements given in an RDF data model without constraining the syntactical appearance of the RDF description. For a more detailed comparison of XML Schema and RDF Schema we refer the reader to [124]. Essentially, these extensions to the knowledge representation language provided the minimal elements of an ontology representation language; one which the research community quickly adopted and began to further extend [192]. These minimal elements are indeed quite powerful: basic (frame-based) ontological modeling primitives, such as instance-of, subclass-of, and subproperty-of relationships, had been introduced and this allowed for structured class and property hierarchies.

Ontology Layer: OWL

Directly on top of the RDF Schema layer sits the most innovative and effective layer of the cake: the ontology layer – Web Ontology Language (OWL). The XML layer is sufficient for exchanging data between parties who have agreed to definitions beforehand; however, their lack of semantics prevents machines from reliably performing this task given new XML vocabularies. The RDF Schema layer begins to approach this problem by allowing simple semantics to be associated with identifiers. With RDF Schema, one can define classes that may have multiple subclasses and superclasses, and can define properties which may have subproperties, domains, and ranges. In this sense, RDF Schema is a simple ontology language. However, in order to achieve interoperation between numerous, autonomously developed and managed schemas, richer semantics are needed.

The ontology layer adds more vocabulary for describing properties and classes: among others, relations between classes (e.g., disjointness), cardinality (e.g., "exactly one"), equality, richer typing of properties, characteristics of properties (e.g., symmetry), and enumerated classes are incorporated into the semantics of the ontological language. The W3C Web Ontology Working Group that set out to provide a specification for this layer had the following design goals of implementing this layer included:

- Shared ontologies: Ontologies should be publicly available and different data sources should be able to commit to the same ontology for shared meaning. Also, ontologies should be able to extend other ontologies in order to provide additional definitions.
- Ontology evolution: An ontology may change during its lifetime. A data source should specify the version of an ontology to which it commits.
- Ontology interoperability: Different ontologies may model the same concepts in different ways. The language should provide primitives for relating different representations, thus allowing data to be converted to different ontologies and enabling a "Web of ontologies."

- Inconsistency detection: Different ontologies or data sources may be contradictory. It should be possible to detect these inconsistencies.
- Balance of expressivity and scalability: The language should be able to express a wide variety of knowledge, but should also provide for efficient means to reason with it. Since these two requirements are typically at odds, the goal of OWL is to find a balance that supports the ability to express the most important kinds of knowledge.
- Ease of use: The language should provide a low learning barrier and have clear concepts and meaning. The concepts should be independent from syntax.
- Compatibility with other standards: The language should be compatible with other commonly used Web and industry standards. In particular, this includes XML and related standards (such as XML Schema and RDF), and possibly other modeling standards such as UML.
- Internationalization: The language should support the development of multilingual ontologies, and potentially provide different views of ontologies that are appropriate for different cultures [101].

Meeting these requirements was no easy task, but the resulting specification, OWL, provided a new level of semantic expressiveness, one that overshadowed the the primitives of RDF Schema. Owing to their important role in the Semantic Web architecture, Section 1.5.2 provides further background and application of ontologies.

Query and Rule Layers: RIF and SPARQL (and Ontologies)

These two layers are grouped together, not to diminish their necessity or contribution, but rather because the two layers have quite a bit in common, with various overlaps,[12] and both are fairly new (as of June 14, 2007, SPARQL, Query Language for RDF, has reached the status of W3C Candidate Recommendation[13] and as of this publication, the RIF Core Design is only a W3C Working Draft[14]).

SPARQL provides the engine to the the underlying RDF structures; after all, a data language is powerless without a query language. The SPARQL specification defines the syntax and semantics of the SPARQL query language for RDF with the following features:

- Express queries across diverse data sources, whether the data is stored natively as RDF or viewed as RDF via middleware
- Query required and optional graph patterns along with their conjunctions and disjunctions
- Support extensible value testing and constraining queries by source RDF graph
- Provide resolved queries as results sets or RDF graphs

---

[12] Originally, "query" and "rule" were included in the "logic layer" of the Semantic Web layer cake, now replaced by the "unifying logic layer" above the two.

[13] http://www.w3.org/TR/2007/CR-rdf-sparql-query-20070614/

[14] http://www.w3.org/TR/2007/WD-rif-core-20070330/

The rule layer provides an interchange format for different rule languages and inference engines. Rules had long been seen as an important paradigm for representing and reasoning with knowledge on the Semantic Web.[15] In 2005, The Rule Interchange Format W3C Working Group set out with the following motives:

- Rules themselves represent a valuable form of information for which there is not yet a standard interchange format. Rules provide a powerful business logic representation, as business rules, in many modern information systems
- Rules are often the technology of choice for creating maintainable adapters between information systems
- As part of the Semantic Web architecture, rules can extend or complement the OWL to more thoroughly cover a broader set of applications, with knowledge being encoded in OWL or rules or both [100].

The Semantic Web Rule Language (SWRL) [105] is an extension of OWL DL which adds the expressive power of rules (without negation) to OWL; the mentioned uncle example can be expressed in SWRL.

The basic SWRL constructs are Horn-like rules. However, whereas Horn rules have a conjunction of atomic formula in the antecedent (body) of the rule and a single atomic formula in the consequent (head) of the rule, SWRL allows any OWL class description, property, or individual assertion in both the body and the head of the rule. In this way, SWRL diverges from the traditional rules systems which are based on logic programming or deductive databases.

Because SWRL combines the full expressive power of function-free Horn logic with an expressive description logic language, the key inferences tasks (e.g., satisfiability, entailment) are in general undecidable for SWRL.

F-logic [121], and, more specifically, the Horn subset of F-logic extended with negation, has been proposed as an ontology and rule language for the Semantic Web [119]. Rules in F-logic are similar to Horn rules, with the distinction that besides atomic formulae, F-logic rules *also* allow molecules in place of atomic formulae. Note that although the syntax of F-logic seems higher order, the language semantically stays in the first-order framework.

An important concept in F-logic is *object identity* [118]. Each object (e.g., class, instance, method) has a unique object identifier, where an object identifier is in fact a term. In F-logic, classes and methods are interpreted *intentionally*, which means that class identifiers and method identifiers are interpreted by themselves and not directly as sets or as binary relations, as is the case with concepts and roles in description logics. Classes and methods are first interpreted as objects in the domain and these objects are then related to sets of objects and sets of binary tuples, respectively.

The following simple F-logic ontology (Listing 1.1) models the concept person which has an attribute child with type person. The concept parent is a subconcept of person and the rule states that every person with a child is a parent.

---

[15] http://www.ruleml.org/

Listing 1.1. Example F-logic ontology. (Reproduced from [77])

```
person[child =>> person].
parent::person.

X:parent :- X[child ->> Y], X:person.
```

Here it is pertinent to note that in F-logic there is no distinction between classes and instances. An *object identifier* can denote a class, an instance, or an attribute, but there is no separation in the signature Σ for the identifiers denoting either. The advantage of such an overloading object notion is that objects denote classes, instances, and attributes depending on the syntactic context, thereby allowing certain kinds of metastatements.

Both SWRL and F-logic have been proposed as rules languages for the Semantic Web. The main difference between the two proposals is that in SWRL, the rules language is seen as an extension of the ontology language OWL DL, whereas in the F-logic (programming) proposal, ontologies are modeled using rules [77].

Unifying Logic Layer

As laid out in the presentation entitled "The Semantic Web,"[16] as of 2002, the then logic layer was at such a status:

- Universal language for monotonic logic
- Any rule system can export, generally cannot import
- No one standard engine – inference capabilities differ
- Many engines exist (SQL to KIF, Cycl, etc.)
- Any system can validate proofs
- Web assumptions different from closed world

The unifying logic layer turns a limited declarative language into a Turing-complete logical language, with inference and functions. This is powerful enough to be able to define all the rest, and allow any two RDF applications to be connected together. One can see this language as being a universal language to unify all data systems just as HTML was a language to unify all human documentation systems.

Proof, Trust, Crypto, and Application Layers

The proof layer will provide an RDF-based language which allows assertions to be exchanged. These exchanged assertions will allow applications such as access control to use a generic validation engine as the kernel, with very case specific tools for producing proofs of access according to a set of defined agreement. The trust layer is then an extension of this validation; meanwhile, all the semantic languages are effected by the vertical crypto "layer" and the user interface and applications have the obvious seat on top. These final levels of the Semantic Web architecture are still fairly underdeveloped, as their specification and functionality depends entirely upon the further development of the lower, foundational layers.

---
[16] http://www.w3.org/2002/Talks/04-sweb/slide1-0.html

1.5.2 Ontologies and the Semantic Web

A key feature of ontologies is that they, through formal, real-world semantics and consensual terminologies, interweave human and machine understanding [72]. This important property of ontologies facilitates the sharing and reuse of ontologies among humans, as well as machines.

According to [72], "The explicit representation of the semantics underlying data, programs, pages, and other Web resources will enable a knowledge-based Web that provides a qualitatively new level of service." Ontologies provide such an explicit representation of semantics. The combination of ontologies with the Web has the potential to overcome many of the problems in knowledge sharing and reuse and information integration.

These relationships represented in an ontology are fairly easy to understand for the human reader and because the meaning of the relationships are formally defined, a machine can reason with them and draw the same conclusions a human can. These relationships, which are implicitly known to humans (e.g., a human knows that every student is a person) are encoded in a formally explicit way so that they can be understood by a machine. In a sense, the machine does not gain real "understanding," but the understanding of humans is encoded in such a way that a machine can process it and draw conclusions through logical reasoning.

Ontologies – The "Shared" Aspect

In order to accommodate one of the most important characteristic of ontologies, the "shared" aspect, ontologies can be layered upon one another, whereby each layer caters to a different level of generality. Conclusively, domain experts, users, and designers need only agree upon relevant specific domain and application ontologies, as well as upon the higher-level ontologies that are being used, rather than attempt to achieve a global, all-inclusive conceptualization [145].

In the literature [72, 92, 102, 204] we generally find three common layers of knowledge. Based on their levels of generality, these three layers correspond to three different types of ontologies, namely:

- Generic (or top-level) ontologies, which capture general, domain -independent knowledge (e.g., space, time,). Examples are WordNet [71] and Cyc [135]. Generic ontologies are shared by large numbers of people across different domains.
- Domain ontologies, which capture the knowledge in a specific domain. An example is UNSPSC,[17] which is a product classification scheme for vendors. Domain ontologies are shared by the stakeholder in a domain.
- Application ontologies, which capture the knowledge necessary for a specific application. An example could be an ontology representing the structure of a particular Web site. Arguably, application ontologies are not really ontologies, because they are not really shared.

---

[17] http://www.unspsc.org/

The separation between these three levels of generality is not always strict. Although sometimes other types of ontologies, such as representational ontologies or task ontologies, are distinguished, the above three types of ontologies are common in the literature and are in our opinion a useful separation of types of ontologies along the dimension of generality [77].

Expressiveness in Ontologies

Ontologies can also be categorized in accord with their expressiveness. One interpretation of how to distinguish several levels of expressiveness is presented in [144] as such:

Thesaurus: Relations between terms, such as synonyms, are additionally provided. Again, WordNet [71].

Informal taxonomy: There is an explicit hierarchy (generalization and specialization are supported), but there is no strict inheritance; an instance of a subclass is not necessarily also an instance of the superclass. An example is the Yahoo! dictionary.[18]

Formal taxonomy: There is strict inheritance; each instance of a subclass is also an instance of a superclass. An example is UNSPSC.[19]

Frames: A frame (or class) contains a number of properties and these properties are inherited by subclasses and instances. Ontologies expressed in RDF Schema [29], described later, fall in this category.

Value restrictions: Values of properties are restricted. Ontologies expressed in OWL Lite (see the section on ontology language later) fall in this category.

General logic constraints: Values may be constrained by logical or mathematical formulas using values from other properties. Ontologies expressed in OWL DL (see the section on ontology language later) fall in this category.

Expressive logic constraints: Very expressive ontology languages such as those seen in Ontolingua [69] or CycL [135] allow first-order logic constraints between terms and more detailed relationships such as disjoint classes, disjoint coverings, inverse relationships, part–whole relationships, etc. Note that some of these detailed relationships such as disjointness of classes are also supported by OWL DL (and even OWL Lite), which indicates that the borders between the levels of expressiveness remain fuzzy.

History of Ontology Languages

In the areas of knowledge engineering and knowledge representation, interest in ontologies really started taking off in the 1980s with knowledge representation systems such as KL-ONE [27] and CLASSIC [26].

An important system for the development, management, and exchange of ontologies in the beginning of the 1990s was Ontolingua [69], which uses an internal

---

[18] http://www.yahoo.com/

[19] http://www.unspsc.org/

Knowledge Interchange Format[20] (KIF) representation, but is able to interoperate with many other knowledge representation (ontology) languages, such as KL-ONE, LOOM, and CLASSIC.

The languages used for ontologies were determined by the tool used to create the ontologies. Systems like KL-ONE, CLASSIC, and LOOM each used their own ontology language, although the Ontolingua system was capable of translating ontologies between different languages, using the KIF language as an interchange language. We can see the languages and tools as being interdependent, but also as being somewhat orthogonal, where we have the language on one axis and the tool on the other. For example, KL-ONE, CLASSIC, and LOOM all have their basis in description logics [10], while KIF has its basis in first-order logic.

In the early 1990s, KIF could be seen as a standard for ontology modeling. The language was used in prominent tools such as Ontolingua and in important ontology engineering projects, such as Toronto Virtual Enterprise (TOVE) [91] and The Enterprise Ontology [211].

Later on in the 1990s, ontologies began to be applied to the World Wide Web. SHOE [102], for example, used Ontologies to annotate Web pages using formal ontologies embedded in HTML documents. Ontobroker and its successor On2broker [74] use ontologies to not only annotate Web pages, but also to formulate queries and derive answers. Ontobroker and On2broker provide an annotation language which is used to annotate HTML documents with references to ontologies. The ontology, the terminology used by the annotation language, is specified using the representation language, based on F-logic [121]. Finally, Ontobroker uses a query language for the retrieval of documents based on their annotations. This query language is a subset of the representation language. All these languages have their impact on the current languages on the Semantic Web.

Web Ontology Language

OWL [58] is an expressive ontology language which extends RDF Schema. OWL itself consists of three *species* of increasing expressiveness:

1. OWL Lite: The least expressive of the OWL species. Compared with RDF Schema it adds local range restrictions, existential restrictions, simple cardinality restrictions, equality, and different types of properties (inverse, transitive, and symmetric).
2. OWL DL: Compared with OWL Lite, OWL DL adds full support for (classical) negation, disjunction, cardinality restrictions, enumerations, and value restrictions. The name "DL" comes from the resemblance to an expressive description logic language [10], namely, $\mathcal{SHOIN}(\mathbf{D})$.
3. OWL Full: Where OWL Lite and OWL DL pose restrictions on the use of vocabulary and the use of RDF statements, OWL Full does not have such restrictions. Therefore, OWL Full allows both the specification of classes as instances and

---

[20] http://logic.stanford.edu/kif/kif.html

the use of language constructs in the language itself, which thereby modifies the language.

For OWL Lite, it turns out that although there are many syntactic restrictions in the language, the actual expressiveness of the language is very close to the expressiveness of OWL DL [106]. OWL Full is a very expressive language and because of the syntactic freedom which is allowed in the language, key inference problems are undecidable.

1.6 The Semantic Web – Future Prospects

While W3C was busy specifying and recommending, the ever-growing Web user/ developer community was not about to wait in the wings. Entire Web-based communities were beginning to merge. Social networks became the newest trend, and remain thriving as of this publication. New technologies such as wikis, weblogs, Folksonomies, RSS feeds, and sites laden with dynamic, multimedia collections came on the scene without the collaborative efforts and consensual guidance provided for the W3C-promoted technologies. These technologies were grouped together under the umbrella term "Web 2.0" even though there was never any formal update to a previous technical specification.

According to [163], the concept of Web 2.0 began with a conference brainstorming session between O'Reilly and MediaLive International and later spurred the Web 2.0 Summit, the fourth of which was held in October of 2007. Web 2.0 originally focused on the Web as a content platform; the goal was to find a way to present more relevant data to the user. Users quickly bought into this interactive model and Web 2.0 was immediately recognized as a foundation upon which thousands of new forms of business would emerge. Web sites such as Flickr[21] which depend upon users' tagged data began to thrive. Sites such as YouTube[22] do not in fact offer a product; rather they are services which provide a way to view videos uploaded by other users. This was an entirely new business model; one which evolved from simply utilizing the enabling protocols of the World Wide Web. Of course this simple point somewhat jeopardizes the justification of coining the term "Web 2.0" if it is nothing more than an application (or implementation) of the foundational architectural principles laid out back in 1994.

The continued development of the Semantic Web will incorporate the content-laden Web 2.0[23] into its layered architecture and a rumored "Web 3.0" may come into existence; however, at the time of publication the term "Web 3.0" had only just begun to appear in credible computer science magazines. The Semantic Web will begin to fully utilize services provided on the Web, and these Semantic Web Services will prove to be the key elements of SESA.

---

[21] http://www.flickr.com

[22] http://www.youtube.com/

[23] If one concludes they are in fact distinct, or that this "incorporation" has not already been completed.

1.7 Summary

And so our whirlwind Web timeline then breeches upon the close of a decade with the foundations for SESA steadily holding ground. In this chapter we have briefly reviewed the development of the World Wide Web, and its evolution into the Sematic Web. We have surveyed the advance of many essential semantic technologies, languages, and protocols, we have established the necessity of both human-to-human and machine-to-machine communication across the Web, and we have presented a brief outline of the Semantic Web architecture (based on the Semantic Web layer cake).

The goal of this chapter was to provide a brief overview of the essential Web developments leading up to the status quo, because these developments form the foundation upon which SESA sits. Without the specifications and architectural principles that comprise the Semantic Web, SESA is not achievable.

The remaining chapters of this book provide a further detailed look at more expressive semantic languages and higher-level semantic tools, as the building blocks for SESA slowly come together, resulting in a comprehensive analysis of SESA and its components.

2

Semantic Web Services

The Semantic Web transforms the current, syntactic Web into a Web that is aware of and fully utilizes explicit semantics in order to overcome the prevalent mismatches in understanding and integration of data structures and data vocabulary. With a Semantic Web as a fundamental basis it is possible for human users to find meaningful data and to interact with the Web in a semantically defined and precise way. Going beyond data and information processing, Web Services bring the aspect of dynamic and distributed computation into the current Web by making the Web infrastructure a device for distributed computing on a worldwide scale. However, Web Services, like the current Web, are syntactic in nature, making even simple dynamic composition and computation impossible in an automated fashion, let alone real and complex applications. Therefore, it is necessary to combine the Semantic Web and Web Services into a new paradigm named Semantic Web Services that supports not only distributed computation, but also dynamic discovery and computation of services, ultimately leading to goal-based computation that is fully declarative in nature. This chapter motivates the need for Semantic Web Services and outlines the vision of semantic computation.

2.1 Behavioral Perspective of the World Wide Web

The World Wide Web (abbreviated as WWW or Web) originated from the need for human communication and ease of distributed and worldwide data access. Consequently the software technology that was put in place supporting Web pages focused on presenting data syntactically to human users. While initially static data was the focus, later on support for dynamic data was added, ultimately leading to the integration of different Web pages displaying different aspects of dynamic data to the same human user, leading to the need for semantic support for homogenous Web page vocabulary in addition to syntactic data display.

It became quickly clear that the Web infrastructure can be used for computer-to-computer communication too, which does not involve a human element at all. Instead, the machine equivalent of Web pages was designed and enabled in the form of remotely accessible procedures. A prominent domain in this space is Business-to-Business (B2B) and Enterprise Application Integration (EAI) [32] where computer-to-computer communication is central to achieving integration.

In the following, this transition from single syntactic Web pages to dynamic and integrated Web pages requiring semantics and subsequently the support for machine-accessible functionality is outlined in more detail as a precursor to the discussion of Web Services in the next section.

2.1.1 Need for Behavior

Human Web

In the very beginning of the Web a human user could request static data by providing a Universal Resource Locator (URL) to a so-called Web browser which took the URL and accessed the data that the URL identified. The data in the form of a Web page could reside in a local or a remote computer system as URLs can address Web pages for both cases. That data was encoded using HTML in such a way that the data was displayed nicely for human users so that they are able to read it in their specific cultural expectation and setting.

This approach of "static data lookup" was reaching its limits very quickly and the first efforts started right away to include dynamic data that changed more or less frequently. This means that data values are looked up from persistent stores or data feeds rather than being hard coded in a file-based Web pages described with HTML. Human users have an interest in much dynamic data and want to observe the state changes. These include weather reports, stock price lookup, upcoming metro line arrival times, as well as the status a coffee machine to save an unnecessary round trip to the coffee kitchen (which was one of the first research applications), just to name a few.

In more technical terms, whenever a human user requests a Web page the dynamic data is not encoded statically but has to be looked up from a state-keeping system every time the page is retrieved. This can be a database, a file in a file system, a queue implementing a data feed, a function call result, the status of a wireless sensor or RFID tag, and so on. Once the data is derived dynamically it is put into its predetermined place on the Web page before being sent back to the browser of the human user.

In many cases a human user is not interested in all available data in a data set. For example, when looking up the status of a specific flight, a human user is usually interested in a particular flight, not all the existing flights of an airline. In order for a human user to indicate the specific flight, an input field is offered to him where he can provide the flight number or place of origin and destination. That would give him the status of all flights with this particular flight number. Usually this is still too much information and so human users are usually requested also to provide the particular day and/or time of the flight that they wish to look up. These input parameters are then used to qualify the dynamic data lookup and the restricted result set is then added to the Web page before being sent back to the human user.

In fundamental terms this is a functional interface with input and output parameters where the human user is the source of the input parameter and the consumer of the output parameters. Even that proved to be not enough functionality and procedural interfaces for human users were needed too, where input from a human user not only qualifies data lookup but also causes state changes. For example, subscribing to a newspaper is a procedural interface where a user selects the newspaper, subscription terms, and payment method. The publisher of the newspaper then acts accordingly once the funds have been received.

Whenever data is requested from a user some validation is commonly implemented to ensure that the user-provided data is consistent and correct in the context of the function or procedure. Sequencing becomes important too, as in the case of the newspaper ordering payment has to happen first before the delivery of the newspaper is scheduled. Error situations for procedural situations have to be understood so that partial progress can be recovered from when a system failure occurs. In the end, for economically useful applications, the simple Web infrastructure was not adequate and a lot more technology was necessary in order to deal with all relevant aspects. This is even more essential for a Web that deals not only with human users but also with software systems as communicating entities.

Machine Web

The Web infrastructure is not really targeted at human users only, even though human user applications were the first applications to appear. The same infrastructure can be used for software systems to communication with each other, also termed machine-to-machine communication. Essentially, software systems also use procedural interfaces in order to communicate with each other.

The main difference is that the result sets are not constructed for human user consumption, meaning that test layout and graphical elements are completely missing. Once a software system has obtained one or more results from other software systems, it can use these results to do its internal data processing to further use the results. In this sense the Web infrastructure is used as a worldwide remote invocation mechanism of functionality provided anywhere on the Web.[1]

For two software systems to understand each other it is necessary that both agree on the same data types as well as on precisely the same syntax used for exchanging messages. Without an agreement on the exact same structures, the receiving software system will not be able to parse and reconstruct the in-memory representation and the communication fails. This is in stark contrast to human user specific data where imprecise or ambiguous data structures can be compensated for by the human user because of the cognitive ability for error compensation. For example, if a Web page layout is not "nice," a human user can still understand it and interpret it sensibly.

A software system can also combine the results obtained through various remote invocations and display them to a human user, possibly using its own data for further

---

[1] As software does represent data in data structures and not Web pages the term "machine pages" is not used, even though it would be the symmetric equivalent to human user Web pages.

data lookup or modification. In this situation the software combines data from different sources before providing a human user representation of it. For example, the value of stock symbols is displayed not in isolation to a human user, but in context with an investment banking Web page that automatically detects the stock a human user has invested in and displays the value for only those stock symbols. So the business logic that displays the value and holdings of the investment account looks up the prices of the stock symbols remotely for further processing.

Challenges

The human Web and machine Web have specific challenges to overcome. Currently solutions to various degrees of satisfaction exist for those. The main challenges are:

- **Syntax.** For the machine-to-machine communication in the machine Web the syntax that software systems use to exchange messages has to be precisely defined so that the sending software and the receiving software have the precise same syntactical representation. This requires that all software systems involved in a particular remote communication agree on the same exchange syntax.
- **Semantics.** Even if the syntax is precisely defined and agreed upon, the semantic content of data structures can be mismatching between a provider and an invoker (or also termed callee and caller) of functionality. A date data type, if interpreted the wrong way, could, for example, mix up the day and the month value, leading to wrong data (in case of day–month combinations that are both valid like February 3) or system failures (for example, when a day of 17 and the month of May are mixed up). This requires an explicit representation of the semantics of the data values such that a misinterpretation is minimized, if not eliminated completely.
- **Combination of Web pages.** Human users navigate from Web page to Web page. If several Web pages cover different aspects of the same data then it is important that the vocabulary used on the Web pages is coherent across the different Web pages even though those Web pages are not provided by the same provider. For example, if a user navigates between the pages of his investment account, the pages for checking accounts, savings accounts, retirement accounts, and stock investment accounts should at least share the same terminology, even if in the background these different products are provided by different organizations that are distributed across the country or the world. If not, the user is constantly confused about the meaning of a particular entry on a particular Web page. This fundamentally requires transformation between vocabularies in case the various products are based on different ones so that from a user perspective the vocabulary is consistent.
- **Combination of machine functions.** Like human users navigate from page to page, a software system can invoke several functions or procedures in order to obtain the results it needs. In this case it is very likely that each function or procedure is based on its own vocabulary and like in the case of Web pages the combination of the data is only consistent if it is possible to transform the data from one vocabulary into another one.

- **Combination of Web pages and machine functions.** In real software systems there is in the general case always a combination of Web pages and machine functions in order to provide the full required functionality. From a syntactical and semantics viewpoint this does not add any more challenge; however, operationally it does. For example, transaction boundaries and throughput planning become essential in such a combination. However, this is not discussed here as the focus is only on the functional aspects.

2.1.2 Role of Semantics

Industrial and academic computer science dealt with syntax from the very beginning. In contrast, explicit semantics became a mainstream topic only recently with the vision of the Semantic Web put forth by Tim Berners-Lee and the W3C,[2] followed up by key researchers in Europe, the USA, and Asia, today making inroads into the software vendor scene. It is therefore important to look at the role that semantics plays in context of Web applications in more detail.

There are two main areas (amongst others) where semantics plays a key role. One is the semantics of data structures and the other is the semantics of behavior. Other areas, which are not discussed further here, are the semantics of identity of communication and software systems, semantics of transaction models and their combination, semantics of error handling, and so forth. In principle, whenever two software systems communicate, all aspects involved in the communication are potentially semantically mismatching and becoming an area of semantic discrepancy.

Data Semantics

Data semantics deals with the description of data structures and data vocabulary that allows ideally perfect semantic understanding between two or more software systems that exchange data. Data semantics for a single software system is called data model here as no agreement is needed by several software systems in order to establish it. When several software systems exchange data between each other then they need to agree on the structure as well as the content at run time. "Agreement" in this case might mean a true agreement after negotiation or a true agreement by the (organizational) power of the stronger. It is unlikely that a single user would be successful negotiating data structures and content with Amazon.[3]

- **Structure.** The basic foundation for data is syntax. In order to support semantics, the syntax needs to be described and defined too, so that the communicating software systems can parse each other's data when they are transmitted. A popular technology is XML that is currently favored by many, despite its problems regarding verbosity and processing constraints. In the semantic community RDF is favored currently. However, as in all aspects of collaboration and communication, the communicating software systems can agree on different types of syntax

---

[2] See http://www.w3c.org
[3] See http://www.amazon.com

as long as the software systems involved interpret the syntax in the exact same way. As a concrete example, an address can have several syntactic elements like city and street, both of elementary data type string. A real estate Web site could have a slightly different notion of address that includes a price as data type float indicating the price the seller of the property states as the purchase price.

- **Vocabulary.** The vocabulary describes the possible content of the data structure. For example, the city element of an address might be a constraint to only existing cities in the USA. In the real estate example, the price might be a constraint to be positive and within 10% range of comparable properties. The constraint on the content of the data elements at run time helps to gain semantic understanding as the communicating software systems also have to agree on the content, not just on the structure. In the address example, this forces both communicating software systems to agree on the same list of eligible cities, preventing a city being named that one of the software systems has never heard of.

In a human Web scenario it is more and more the case that a human user accesses several pages when dealing with data, for lookup or even input. The goal is that the necessary integration of pages, i.e., a human user going from one page to the next, is a seamless experience. This not only includes the same look and feel, but also the same data structures and the same vocabulary. As a consequence, the human user does not realize or recognize that Web pages might be coming from different providers. A current effort to structure this space is with mash-ups.[4] Mash-ups are an example where the data content from different Web pages (and also Web Services) is integrated and the data from all sources is displayed in homogenous (set of) Web pages to a human user. A widely used mash-up is a real estate site called Trulia[5] where real estate offerings are mashed with Google[6] maps.

Semantics is an essential foundation in order to make this approach work. In an ideal world there would not be an integration problem as all data would be stored in one single homogeneous database, updated in real time as well as accessible in real time. This would ensure that all Web pages involved have the same underlying data source and are homogeneous by construction. However, this situation can almost be considered a corner case as in the majority of situations data is coming from different sources. This immediately poses the problem that data structures as well as data vocabulary are not homogenous at all, but differ from each other, sometimes significantly. For example, one source might use "AV," the other "Avenue" as vocabulary. Structurally one source names a field "price," the other "offer price."

In order to make the integration work, two specific problems have to be solved. First, the data structure and vocabulary must be known from each source that is going to be used for integration. Each Web page or Web site in a mash-up must have a clear definition of the data structures and vocabulary it uses. This is defined and represented in an ontology. Once every source exposes its ontology, the user of

---

[4] See http://www.programmableweb.com
[5] See http://www.trulia.com
[6] See http://maps.google.com

the source knows what to expect and what to provide so that the source can stay semantically correct and consistent.

Second, the data structures and vocabulary of different sources have to be mapped to each other so that all integrated sources only have to provide the data structures and vocabulary according to their semantics. Semantic mismatches that require mapping "AV" to "Avenue" are resolved outside the sources during the act of integration. The next two bullet points provide a summary:

- **Ontology**. External representation of the data model by a data source for collaboration and interaction purposes
- **Mediation**. Semantic preserving mapping between ontologies of different sources

Some additional areas subject to semantics are not specific to the Semantic Web. These include nonfunctional properties and correctness of processing. These requirements are to be addressed in all types of Webs, semantic or nonsemantic or human Web as well as machine Web. However, behavior semantics is very important and discussed next.

Behavior Semantics

Behavior semantics assumes that the data semantics problem is already addressed for the software systems being integrated providing Web pages or machine functions or both. Instead, behavior semantics focuses on the proper exchange sequence of messages or data instances between the software systems.

For example, a real estate Web site has several functions for retrieval of real estate offers. One function looks up real estate for sale by ZIP code and returns a list of identifiers. A second function returns an offer price for a given identifier. A third function returns the address for a given identifier. This means that in order to obtain the address and the offer price for a given property two calls have to be made. A Web site that integrates this data with a spatial map (a mash-up between real estate data and map data), however, assumes that there is only one call necessary to obtain the address and the offer price for a given property. So the mash-up site is prepared to make one call for a given identifier; however, the real estate Web site expects two calls to be made. This is an example of a behavioral mismatch as the two software systems that are to be integrated do not match in terms of the sequence of invocations and data instances to be exchanged.

The example highlights the situation of an exchange sequence mismatch as the caller and the callee expose different communication behavior. This and additional requirements are listed next:

- **Exchange sequence mismatch**. An exchange sequence mismatch exists when either the caller or the callee of a Web page or machine function expects or conducts an invocation that the other software system does not plan to execute. It can be the case that a caller wants to call a function, but the callee does not offer the function. Another case is that a callee requires a specific call, but the caller will not execute the call. A third case is where both previous cases exist at the same time.

- **Data mismatch.** It is possible that the data instances passed back and forth between the software systems are not matching in the sense of a data semantics mismatch in structure and vocabulary as discussed earlier. In this case the data mismatch has to be addressed in addition to the exchange sequence mismatch.
- **Data granularity mismatch.** A specific case in the context of the data mismatch exists where the caller has all the data necessary for the callee, but the callee requires the data be sent in a different granularity. For example, a caller is programmed in such a way that it passes all data in one big data structure, whereas the caller needs the data in several smaller pieces. This means that between the caller and the callee the data needs to be restructured to make it of smaller granularity. The opposite or a mixed case is possible too.
- **Conditional exchange sequence.** The communicating software systems are only aware of their interfaces, not of their internal implementation. This is especially true for conditional behavior. It is possible that a condition inside the caller determines if a specific data instance communication happens or not. The callee, however, might not be able to know in which situation the condition is true or false. As a consequence it needs to be able to receive the call (or not) and deal with both situations equally well.

In summary, data semantics and behavior semantics go hand in hand and both need to be addressed independently of the human or machine Web (or their combination). In any combination the goal of the data semantics and the behavior semantics is to ensure that a homogenous situation exists between the software systems at the time of communication or integration. Human users expect consistent structure and vocabularies as well as behavior that do not get them into a deadlock or lifelock situation. The same is true for machine communication, of course.

The next section will focus on Web Services, currently an approach to address the implementation of behavior. Web Services do not yet address the behavior semantics aspect explicitly in their technology. Therefore a subsequent section will discuss Semantic Web Services.

2.2 Web Services

Web Services are a very prominent area of academic research and industrial development currently. Some say that this is finally "it" in terms of a practical distributed computing infrastructures. Others counter that this is only "one more" in terms of a technology stack for remote invocation. All agree that there is too much discrepancy between the promises like ease of use or interoperability and the real state of affairs. However, whatever the opinions might be, in the following Web Services as a subject of research and development are rationalized from the viewpoint of semantics. Their role is discussed as well as some of the challenges that must be addressed.

2.2.1 What Exactly Are (Web) Services?

While initially Web Services were meant to be a simple object access protocol for accessing methods on objects locally as well as remotely, the intent has changed significantly since then. Currently the common expectation is that Web Services support the provision of functionality independent of its implementation technology and execution location.

The conceptual notion of "object" does not play a role anymore. Instead, the notion of interface took its place. This is visible as conceptual elements of objects like unique object identification, methods, class and instance variables, inheritance, and other concepts are not part of the Web service model at all. Web Services provide the notion of an interface independent of the programming language used to implement this interface. Interfaces consist of operations in the procedural sense with the possibility that the execution of an operation causes side effects. In this sense Web Services provide their own formal language for defining interfaces that are then bound to their implementation.

The same clear abstraction is provided for the transport protocol used to access the interface of a service. Several different synchronous as well as asynchronous transport protocols like HTTP or SMTP can be used to execute the remote invocation of service interfaces and their operations. Web service technology therefore supports a transport protocol abstraction in addition to the service implementation abstraction.

These two fundamental abstractions, namely, interface from implementation and communication from transport, are the source of the expectation that Web Services will support the free composition of business functionality without common assumptions or common restrictions across services. This expectation goes as far as being able to take services from any provider and by composition be able to put together robust, secure, reliable business functionality.

The expectation to compose higher-level functionality from individual services requires that the services involved are completely characterized by their interface without the need to understand their implementation at all, neither their implementation location nor any details regarding execution infrastructure. This not only includes reliability properties, security provisions and availability, but first and foremost the semantics of the data and vocabulary referenced by the interface as well as the behavior semantics. Web service technology today is not able to fulfill this expectation as data structures are defined using XML schemas and behavior semantics is not defined in Web service interfaces at all.

There are several conceptual interpretations of Web Services that have been discussed for quite a while and continue being debated. These different interpretations manifest themselves in various "styles" like REST, XMLRPC, SOAP, and document, to name the most important ones. The REST style follows the principles of URL style communication, the XMLRPC style – as the name says – follows the remote invocation idea, the SOAP style argues for the transport abstraction and the document style puts forward the notion of document instead of data objects. Each style has its pros and cons and which style to use often depends on the particular problem that requires a solution. However, a different view argues that at the end of the day a particular functionality has to be achieved, like looking up the offer prices of a real estate. As the ultimate functionality is the focus, any style has to be able to provide it and make the functionality available. Another viewpoint is that the majority of the IT world thinks in terms of remote invocations; hence, the majority of IT architects and IT engineers will resort to a remote invocation style.

For the purpose of discussing Semantic Web Services in this book a particular style does not provide a significant advantage over another style; therefore the particular styles are not at the center of the discussion.

2.2.2 Role of Web Services

The conceptual model, architecture, and implementation technology of Web Services is a research topic of many academic researchers and at the same time a focus of many software vendors, especially those offering products in the so-called middleware infrastructure category. The complexity of Web Services warrants this focus and effort.

From a semantics viewpoint no support is provided by Web Services, however. In order to support semantics, two main approaches are possible. One approach is to change and extend the model of Web Services in order to support explicit semantics. Another model is to utilize Web service technology as foundation systems. This allows making remote invocation of functionality and data transfer happen as a basic feature and layer semantics support on top of this basic layer. In this sense, Web Services are a syntactical foundation enabling a layer "on top" for the semantics support.

The first approach is taken by W3C and some researchers through the effort of SAWSDL.[7] This approach augments the syntactic definition of Web Services with explicit encoding of semantics in the context of a standards organization.

The second approach is taken by several groups in academia, and later in this book the work achieved as well as future research plans will be reported in detail.

Until Semantic Web Services become mainstream, the correct semantics has to be achieved manually by developers through careful service definition, making sure that Web Services interoperate properly in the sense of data and behavior semantics. It is the developers' decision which Web service is being used and which is composed of more complex ones. The success of semantically correct interoperability depends on the developers' knowledge. A developer needs to know the meaning of data structures, vocabulary, and behavior. In addition, unless a developer is aware of existing services, reuse and composition will not happen. As a consequence it is quite possible that Web Services are developed with a lot of effort because existing ones are not known or or because they cannot be discovered easily. As a consequence, the Web service infrastructure cannot "complain" about mismatching semantics or point out the existence of a service.

---

[7] See http://www.w3.org/2002/ws/sawsdl/

2.2.3 Challenges

The Web Services model and technology are in a state of flux and the expectations are that both will keep changing for quite a while. However, there are several challenges in the context of semantics that are briefly discussed next:

- **Semantics.** The biggest challenge is addressing the missing encoding of semantics. The Web Services' model and technology do not have provisions for explicitly encoding data and behavior semantics in interfaces or protocols. Very initial efforts exist by W3C and other standards organizations like OASIS' Semantic Execution Environment;[8] however, they are very initial and are not yet mainstream.
- **Technology.** Communication is a very complex area. Interfaces of callees that are accessed by callers are only a very tiny aspect that requires resolution. Bigger requirements are persistence and transactionality, error recovery, service level agreement supervision, as well as many other areas. All these areas are "under work" and many standards to address all of these are under development. Currently this is leading to a complex set of standards that needs to fit into an overall picture. The same is true for the underlying execution technology.
- **Model complexity.** In historical terms using Web Services for reliable business operations is still too complex and requires too much understanding of all aspects. The complexity of the model of communication visible to the user of this technology is too high and it must be a goal to reduce the visible complexity with the idea to deal with it in the infrastructure technology.

In the context of this book, the complexity and technology challenges play only a peripheral role. The main focus lies on the semantics challenge and will be addressed by Semantic Web Services. Semantic Web Services focus on the semantics aspect of the data semantics and behavior semantics in fundamental terms. In addition, other important areas like service discovery based on semantic descriptions are introduced.

2.3 Semantic Web Services: The Future of Integration!

Integration of services cannot be machine-supported or automated without the explicit representation of the relevant data and behavior semantics as introduced earlier. The goal of Semantic Web Services is exactly that: to provide a conceptual model as well as languages to describe Semantic Web Services. Example implementations of Semantic Web Services exist in, for example, the effort called Web service Execution Environment (WSMX). The fundamental concept of Semantic Web Services was first introduced in an article by Fensel and Bussler [75]. In the meanwhile, many concrete projects resulted in research prototypes as well as formal languages that will be introduced later in this book in a lot more detail.

---

[8] See http://www.oasis-open.org/committees/tc_home.php?wg_abbrev=semantic-ex

2.3.1 (Semantic Web) Services Versus Semantic (Web Services)

When putting forward a conceptual model of Semantic Web Services a fundamental paradigm decision has to be made in the context of the various "Webs" that exist. There is the current "syntactic" Web and there will be the future "Semantic" Web. While one is in existence today, researchers worldwide are working on the Semantic Web and as soon as business models and the viral effect are worked out it can be expected that the Semantic Web will happen on the same large scale as the current Web and eventually replace it while becoming a lot larger. This does not mean at all that there will be two competing Webs, this development will ensure that the current Web transforms over time into a Semantic Web.

Both Webs in their fundamental structure provide access to data, static data as well as dynamic data. Both Webs will ensure that human as well as machine access is easy to achieve. Semantic Web Services add the dynamic access to functionality to the data dimension. Since there are two Webs, which one will be the basis for Semantic Web Services? So, will it be that the service model is added to the Semantic Web as in "(Semantic Web) Services"? Or will it be current Web Services augmented with semantics as in "Semantic (Web Services)"?

From a pragmatic viewpoint it is necessary to support the current predominant Web and Web Services. It is possible to not only include services that are already encoded in a Semantic Web Services language, but also those that already exist and might not have semantics annotation at all. As the underlying Web transforms from the syntactic Web to the Semantic Web, Semantic Web Services should not require to be redone but should be independent of that transformation. Instead, the transition of the Web should be as seamless as possible and Semantic Web Services must be able to support any combination of services in any Web. Therefore, efforts are being made to connect to both worlds equally well in the context of Semantic Web Services.

2.3.2 Advantages of Semantic Web Services

The advantages of Semantic Web Services – as the name indicates – stem from the fact that semantics is encoded explicitly and formally in the service description and that the execution environment for Semantic Web Services is able to interpret and use the semantics appropriately. This supports direct understanding at design time as well as run time.

If data semantics is encoded properly, a data type mismatch regarding the Japanese Emperor date would be detected at design time and no run-time error will occur because of a data mismatch. A proper design-time environment would detect that, for example, a caller is passing on dates including Japanese Emperor dates. The year 2007 is the 19th year of the current Japanese Emperor and therefore 19 is a valid value for the year in Japan. Japan Railroads uses the Emperor date as one of many companies. The design time would also detect that the called service is not able to use Emperor dates and would not be able to process those, causing run-time errors. Therefore, this mismatch would be detected and immediately the designer would be notified about it. The designer can at this point decide not to use the service or to insert proper data mediation. This is significant as in both cases the year in the data structure could be encoded as a data type integer, meaning that the semantics cannot be seen by examining the data structure alone.

In the context of a larger scope it is possible to use the explicit semantic description to search for appropriate services. For example, if complex business logic like a multicity travel schedule planner requires various services for individual elements like hotels, transfers, flights, ships, and so on, then those can be searched for on the basis of their semantic description. Only those would be detected that can, for example, accept credit card payments that allow a reservation period of 24 hours before booking is necessary, and so on. In these composition scenarios, where business logic is composed of services, the semantic precision is the basis for proper discovery and selection.

In process-oriented integration scenarios the behavior semantics becomes very important. If a service requires multiple interactions for it to function properly, the behavior semantics encodes this properly. Any caller can then determine if it can provide the multiple interactions or not. For example, a service that allows the purchase of electronics goods might have several interactions, including placing the order, confirming the order, and notification that the order has been shipped. Any user of this service must be able to send or receive these three interaction points. If not, the communication will fail, rendering the integration useless. A proper design-time environment understands the calling as well as the invoked service and their behavior semantics, being able to determine if the communication will match or not in all possible execution cases. Only then the run-time behavior will succeed without errors.

2.3.3 Functionality

The main areas of functionality in context of Semantic Web Services are discussed next. For each of those a separate chapter follows subsequently in the book.

- **Conceptual model.** Semantic Web Services introduce a set of concepts that are used to express the intent of the designer, for example, the notion of goal, mediator, and service. These concepts have to be argued for, their relationship has to be discussed as well as their meaning.
- **Modeling language.** While a conceptual model defines and clarifies the concepts of Semantic Web Services, for all practical and pragmatic reasons it is necessary to have a formal language that allows one to define a specific situation or application. For example, the goal of planning a vacation trip or the goal of investing some money needs to be defined and therefore written down formally. A formal language is therefore necessary as an important aspect of Semantic Web Services.
- **Reasoning.** In order to support deductive abilities during execution of Semantic Web Services it is necessary to apply reasoning. This ensures that at execution time derivations can be achieved that do not have to be explicitly defined by a human user, but can be derived from known facts or already achieved deductions. Reasoning is therefore an important aspect of Semantic Web Services.

- **Discovery.** As discussed before, often it is not possible or not desirable for developers or designers to know all the necessary services required for a successful execution of Semantic Web Services. It would be a lot more powerful if the execution environment could detect appropriate services automatically through a mechanism called discovery.
- **Selection.** Once discovery has happened it might be the case that several equally suited services are discovered. However, at run time only one is needed to execute a particular invocation. Hence, a selection process has to happen that allows selection of the most appropriate service for a given situation.
- **Mediation.** The above discussion introduced the need for data and process mediation. Both are essential for a Semantic Web Services system to support service execution.
- **Architecture.** In the end, a software system must be built that implements Semantic Web Services so that services can be defined, composed, discovered, selected, and used in all actuality for specific use. An architecture must therefore provide all necessary functionality in various architecture components. Furthermore, an architecture has to ensure proper execution that requires an appropriate execution semantics that matches precisely with the conceptual model.

All the various concepts discussed so far and all the functionality listed will be discussed in separate chapters throughout the remainder of the book in a lot more detail and in the context of very concrete research and industry work. However, it is easy to lose sight of the ultimate goal as a guiding principle and therefore the grand vision of Semantic Web Services is explicitly outlined next as a description of the ideal world.

2.4 The Ideal World

What would the ideal world look like? As a vision it is often helpful to spend some thoughts on it in order to not lose sight of the final destination.

In the context of Semantic Web Services as a basis, all services would be perfectly described regarding their semantics. All data and behavior would be completely defined so that complete understanding of the services is possible related to their use (invocation). The nonfunctional properties of services would be defined too, like their service level promises, their persistent and transactional behavior, and so on. In short, all necessary aspects, functional and operational, are properly encoded and accessible for any design-time and run-time system.

Furthermore, in an ideal world it is possible to discover services on the basis of their semantics description. It would be guaranteed that if a service with specific properties exists, it would be discovered. No service would go undetected that possesses the desired characteristics, functional or operational. This is the basis for dynamic composition at run time where services are searched for and discovered as needed. It would allow one to do some composition at design time, but also dynamically without human supervision at run time.

The ultimate state, however, would be if the proper composition of services to achieve a specific functionality would become invisible and would be left to the operating infrastructure. Instead, it would be great to only state a goal and on the basis of the goal the proper services are discovered and executed properly. During discovery and execution it might be necessary to obtain more data from the user who set the goal, but this would also be a declarative interaction. This approach would ultimately move services from a procedural design task of explicit composition to a declarative task of stating goals (without worrying about the specific composition details).

An example of this vision would be the goal to visit the International Snow Festival in Sapporo, Japan.[9] For clarification the system would need to know the year the visit should take place. The system can figure out the festival duration (usually 1 week) and it would need confirmation of these dates from the user so that the user can indicate extensions or alternative durations. Once the basic data has been obtained the system would put together a schedule with airport transfer, flights, train in Japan, hotel, as well as cultural activities. At this point the user could refine the trip proposal, selecting specific airlines, flight times, and hotel choices. He also could ask for cultural schedules beyond the Snow Festival itself, maybe including Sapporo or even the whole of Hokkaido. The system would then ensure that all data is available and matches with the schedule, possibly suggesting alternative or extended travel dates.

As this small example shows, the user would only be concerned about the details of his goals. The underlying mechanics of searching schedules, availability, discovery of currency exchange services, and so on are completely hidden from the user.

2.5 Summary

Semantic Web Services are a very powerful paradigm to transform the current syntactic Web into a dynamic, semantic and goal-oriented system that exposes goal orientation as the main mechanism of achieving functionality. This requires a tremendous effort from academia as well as industry to provide all the mechanisms needed to accomplish this. These include semantic descriptions of data and services, dynamic discovery and composition, goal resolution, and goal decomposition, all supported by underlying base functionality like reasoning. This book introduces the main research efforts in context of the Web Service Modeling Ontology (WSMO), Web Service Modeling Language (WSML) as well as Web Service Execution Environment (WSMX).

---

[9] See http://www.snowfes.com/english/

3

WSMO and WSML

As introduced in the previous chapter Semantic Web Services offer a mechanism for enabling dynamic integration of services by providing explicit descriptions of the function of services, the data they describe, and the mechanisms to interact with them. In order for Semantic Web Services to be successful it is necessary to define a conceptual model that contains all those elements needed to successfully describe Semantic Web Services and on the basis of this conceptual model to provide a modeling language through which Semantic Web Services can be actually described. Within the context of the book the Web Service Modeling Ontology (WSMO) and its formalism the Web Service Modeling Language (WSML) are used in these two roles to successfully describe Semantic Web Services. This chapter provides an introduction to these two technologies, providing the reader with the key foundational knowledge needed for the rest of the book, as well as a reference source that the reader can browse when needed.

3.1 The Web Service Modeling Ontology

In order to totally or partially automate the process of integrating many services into a Service-Oriented Architecture it is necessary to semantically describe all aspects related to services that are available through a Web service interface. The WSMO [77] provides a conceptual model for creating such descriptions of services. WSMO has its conceptual basis in the Web Service Modeling Framework (WSMF) [75], which it extends and refines to provide an ontological specification of the core elements of Semantic Web Services. WSMO brings together the ongoing work in the fields of the Semantic Web and Web Services and thus must also bring together the design principles of the Web, the Semantic Web, and distributed service-oriented computing. The design principles of WSMO are as follows:

- *Services vs Web Services*: A Web service is a computational entity that is able to provide some functionality to the user by invoking it. A service, in contrast, is the actual value provided by the invocation. WSMO is designed as a means to describe Web Services and not to replace services.

- *Description vs implementation*: WSMO makes a firm distinction between the description of elements of Semantic Web Services and executable technologies. WSMO aims at providing an ontological description model for the former and to be compliant with the latter.
- *Ontology-based*: Ontologies are the core of the WSMO metamodel, allowing for enhanced information processing and automatic resolution of heterogeneity issues between resources. Ontologies are the data model throughout WSMO, such that all resource descriptions and data exchanged are ontologically described.
- *Ontological role separation*: The contexts within which requesters and providers of service functionality exist can be very different from one another. Thus, it is important that WSMO differentiates between the requirements that a given requester has and the functionality that service providers are willing to offer. This differentiation gives rise to two top-level elements of the WSMO metamodel, namely goals and Web Services.
- *Strict decoupling*: The Web is an open and distributed place, where resources are developed in isolation from one another. WSMO embraces this fact and states that resources should be strictly decoupled from one another. This means semantic descriptions are developed in isolation from one another without regard for their possible usage or interaction with other resources.
- *Centrality of mediation*: As resources are strictly decoupled from one another, there must exist some mechanism for resolving heterogeneity issues between resources. Mediation performs the role of resolving potential mismatches between resources that can occur at the data, protocol, or process levels. Mediation is a core concept of the WSMO metamodel and as such mediators are a top-level element of the WSMO metamodel.
- *Web compliance*: WSMO inherits the concept of Universal Resource Identifier (URI) from the Web as the mechanism for unique identification of resources. Providing this design principle within WSMO means that languages that formalize WSMO should use URIs for resource identification in order to be Web-compliant.
- *Execution semantics*: The formal execution semantics of reference implementations of WSMO, like the Web Service Execution Environment (WSMX) [95], provide a mechanism to verify the WSMO specification.

On the basis of these design principles the WSMO metamodel has four top-level elements, which can be seen in Fig. 3.1, namely, Ontologies, Web Services, Goals, and Mediators. To effectively describe Semantic Web Services we need to understand each of these four elements. WSMO makes use of the Meta-Object Facility (MOF) [160] specification to define its metamodel. The MOF provides a language and framework for specifying technology neutral metamodels. The benefit of using the MOF is that the model and the languages that are ultimately used to describe Semantic Web Services are separated from one another. This separation gives significantly more freedom than with competing approaches like OWL-S, which is described in

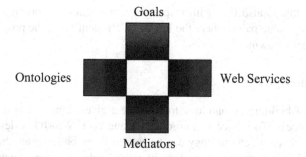

Figure 3.1. Web service Modeling Ontology top-level elements

more detail in Chap. 13. In the following sections we use the MOF specification to describe the four top-level elements of the WSMO metamodel and their child elements.

3.1.1 WSMO Ontologies

Ontologies in WSMO provide the terminology used across all other descriptions and are crucial to the success of Semantic Web Services, as they provide the means by which enhanced information processing becomes possible and complex interoperability problems can be solved. WSMO is an epistemological model in that it is general enough to intuitively capture existing languages used for describing ontologies. In Listing 3.1 a WSMO ontology is described using the MOF notation.

Listing 3.1. Ontology definition

```
Class ontology
    hasNonFunctionalProperty type nonFunctionalProperty
    importsOntology type ontology
    usesMediator type ooMediator
    hasConcept type concept
    hasRelation type relation
    hasFunction type function
    hasInstance type instance
    hasRelationInstance type relationInstance
    hasAxiom type axiom
```

Nonfunctional Properties

It is possible to add nonfunctional properties onto all WSMO elements. Nonfunctional properties are mainly used to describe nonfunctional aspects of a description, such as the creator and creation date, and to provide natural-language descriptions, etc. The elements defined by the Dublin Core Metadata Initiative [216] are taken as a starting point. Dublin Core is a set of attributes that define a standard for cross-domain information resource description. WSMO uses URIs for identification of elements and this is also true with respect to nonfunctional properties, which are specified as key value pairs, where the key is a URI identifying the property and the value is another element.

Imported Ontologies

The process of building an ontology to describe a given domain can be a complex and costly process. To reduce this complexity and cost, WSMO is designed to be modular such that a given ontology can be reused when building another ontology. This means when modeling a given domain, useful ontologies that contain concepts that are pertinent to this domain can be imported from existing ontologies. When an ontology is imported, all the statements from that imported ontology are added to this ontology. All top-level elements within the WSMO metamodel may use the *importsOntololgy* statement to import ontologies that contain the relevant concepts needed to build a description, for example, a WSMO Web service description will import those WSMO ontologies that contain concepts needed to describe the service in question.

Mediators for Importing Ontologies

Of course it may not always be possible to directly import a given ontology as mismatches between statements in the importing and imported ontology or between any two given imported ontologies may exist. In this case a mediator is required, such that the ontology is imported via this mediator. This mediator has the job of aligning, merging, or transforming the imported ontology so as to resolve any existing heterogeneity issues that may arise by importation. Like the *importsOntology* statement, the *usesMediator* statement may be used on all top-level elements within the WSMO metamodel.

Concepts

Concepts represent the basic agreed upon terminology for a given domain. From a high-level point of view a concept is made up of a set of attributes, where each attribute has a name and a type. Using the MOF notation, a concept is as shown in Listing 3.2.

Listing 3.2. Concept definition

```
Class concept
    hasNonFunctionalProperties type nonFunctionalProperties
    hasSuperConcept type concept
    hasAttribute type attribute
    hasDefinition type logicalExpression multiplicity = single-valued

Class attribute
    hasNonFunctionalProperties type nonFunctionalProperties
    hasRange type concept multiplicity = single-valued
```

A concept can also be a subconcept of one or more direct superconcepts using the *hasSuperConcept* statement. This statement allows the "is-a" relationship between concepts to be specified. One of the most important aspects of this relationship is that a subconcept inherits the signatures of all its superconcepts, for example, all attributes defined for a given concept will also be defined for any of its subconcepts.

Using the *hasAttribute* statement, one can specify a set of attributes on the concept. The MOF definition of an attribute is also specified in Listing 3.2. The range of an attribute can be constrained to a given concept, such that all instances of the concept that specify a value for this attribute must conform to this range restriction.

Furthermore a concept can be further refined by specifying a logical expression through the *hasDefinition* statement. This logical expression can be used to express additional constraints on the concept or relationships than cannot be captured through the *hasAttribute* or the *hasSuperConcept* statement.

Relations and Functions

When defining an ontology there is more to be done than just defining the terminology of the domain. Many relationships will exist between the defined terminology and in order to capture these relationships a WSMO relation can be used. The arity of a relation is not restricted; thus, a relation is able to model dependencies between two or more concepts. The MOF definition of a relation is presented in Listing 3.3.

Listing 3.3. Relation definition

```
Class relation
    hasNonFunctionalProperties type nonFunctionalProperties
    hasSuperRelation type relation
    hasParameter type parameter
    hasDefinition type logicalExpression multiplicity = single-valued

Class parameter
    hasNonFunctionalProperties type nonFunctionalProperties
    hasDomain type concept multiplicity = single-valued
```

Each relation can have zero or more superrelations. Being the subrelation of another relation means that the subrelation inherits the signature of the superrelation along with any associated constraints. Similarly to attributes for concepts, a relation can define a set of parameters, which may be a named set or an ordered unnamed set. It is possible to define the domain of each of the parameters, where this domain specifies the allowed values that can be placed in this slot of the relation when it is instantiated. WSMO ontologies can also have functions, specified with the *hasFunction* statement. Functions, as described in Listing 3.4, are special relations with a unary range, specified along with the parameters (the domain). Functions can

Listing 3.4. Function definition

```
Class function sub-Class relation
    hasRange type concept multiplicity = single-valued
```

be used to represent built in predicates of common data types. The semantics of a relation or function can be captured within a logical expression specified with the *hasDefinition* statement.

Instances of Concepts and Relations

As can be seen in Listing 3.5, it is possible to instantiate both concepts and relations defined within a WSMO ontology. When instantiating a concept or a relation, values are assigned to the attributes or parameters of the concept or relation being instantiated, where the type of the value being assigned conforms to the range of the attribute or the domain of the parameter. Instances may be defined explicitly within the ontology; however, in general a link to an external store of instances will be given when a large number of instances exist.

Listing 3.5. Instance definitions

```
Class instance
    hasNonFunctionalProperties type nonFunctionalProperties
    hasType type concept
    hasAttributeValues type attributeValue

Class relationInstance
    hasNonFunctionalProperties type nonFunctionalProperties
    hasType type relation
    hasParameterValue type parameterValue
```

Axioms

An axiom, as described in Listing 3.6, is a logical expression together with its nonfunctional properties. Axioms provide a mechanism for adding arbitrary logical expressions to an ontology, where these axioms can be used to refine concepts, relation, or function definitions in the ontology, to add arbitrary axiomatic domain knowledge, or to express constraints.

Listing 3.6. Axiom definition

```
Class axiom sub−Class wsmoElement
    hasDefinition type logicalExpression
```

3.1.2 WSMO Web Services

Web Services are computational entities that provide some functionality that has an associated value in a given domain. A WSMO Web service is a formal description of the Web Service's functionality, in terms of a capability, and the method to interact with it, in terms of an interface. A formal description of a WSMO Web service using the MOF notation is given in Listing 3.7.

Listing 3.7. Web service definition

```
Class service
    hasNonFunctionalProperty type nonFunctionalProperty
    importsOntology type ontology
    usesMediator type {ooMediator, wwMediator}
    hasCapability type capability  multiplicity = single-valued
    hasInterface type interface
```

Those ontologies that are required in order to define the service can be imported via the *importsOntology* or *usesMediator* statements. The *usesMediator* statement may also be used with a Web service to Web service mediator (wwMediator), in cases where process or protocol heterogeneity issues need to be resolved.

Nonfunctional Properties for Web Services

A service, like all other WSMO elements, can specify a set of nonfunctional properties. The nonfunctional properties of a service, besides those already presented, can include extra information about aspects of the service that are not directly related to the function of the service, for example, the reliability, performance, or scalability of the service.

Capabilities

The capability of the service describes the real value of the service and is described in MOF as shown in Listing 3.8.

Listing 3.8. Capability definition

```
Class capability
    hasNonFunctionalProperty type nonFunctionalProperty
    importsOntology type ontology
    usesMediator type ooMediator
    hasPrecondition type axiom
    hasAssumption type axiom
    hasPostcondition type axiom
    hasEffect type axiom
```

The capability of a service is made up of a set of axioms that describe the state of the world before the execution occurs and the state of the world afterwards. Using the *hasPrecondition* and *hasPostcondition* statements, one can make axiomatic statements about the expected inputs and outputs of the service, i.e., what information must be available for the service to be executed and what information will be available after the service has been executed. The *hasAssumption* and *hasEffect* statements can be used to state the assumed state of the world prior to execution and the guaranteed state of the world afterwards. The capability of a service can be used by a requester for discovery purposes, i.e., to determine if the functionality of the service meets the requester's functional needs.

Interfaces

While the capability of a service describes the function of a service, the interface describes how this function can be a achieved and is described in MOF as shown in Listing 3.9.

Listing 3.9. Interface definition

```
Class interface
    hasNonFunctionalProperty type nonFunctionalProperty
    importsOntology type ontology
    usesMediator type ooMediator
    hasChoreography type choreography
    hasOrchestration type orchestration
```

The interface of a service provides a dual view of the operational competence of the service. With use of the *hasChoreography* statement, a decomposition of the capability in terms of interaction with the service is provided, while with use of the *hasOrchestration* statement the capability can be decomposed in terms of the functionality required from other services in order to realize this service. The distinction between these two descriptions is the difference between communication and cooperation. The choreography provides a description of how to interact with a service, while the orchestration describes how the overall function of the service is realized through cooperation with other services. The interface of a service is presented in a machine-processable manner, allowing for software to determine the behavior of the service and to reason about it.

Both choreography and orchestration are defined using the same formalism, based on abstract state machines [93] (although the orchestration is still underdefined). The choreography of a service is defined in MOF as shown in Listing 3.10.

Listing 3.10. Choreography definition

```
Class choreography
    hasNonFunctionalProperties type nonFunctionalProperties
    hasStateSignature type stateSignature
    hasState type state
    hasTransitionRules type transitionRules
```

The most important parts of the definition are the state signature and the transition rules. The state signature defines the state ontology used by the service together with the definition of the types of modes the concepts and relations may have – which describes the service's and the requester's rights over the instances. The transition rules express changes of states by changing the set of instances [186].

Applying different transition rules, the choreography evolves from the initial state (which technically is the same as the state signature, if not otherwise specified) to the final state, going through several intermediate states; in the final state no further updates based on the transition rules can be applied.

The orchestration is envisioned to have a similar definition as the choreography, with the main difference being that the choreography considers two participants in a conversation, while the orchestration is a description of the cooperation of multiple participants.

3.1.3 WSMO Goals

Goals describe aspects related to the requirements of the end user. WSMO completely decouples the requester's desires from the Web Services that ultimately fulfill the desired functionality. With the MOF notation a WSMO goal is defined as shown in Listing 3.11.

Listing 3.11. Goal definition

```
Class goal
    hasNonFunctionalProperty type nonFunctionalProperty
    importsOntology type ontology
    usesMediator type {ooMediator, ggMediator}
    requestsCapability type capability  multiplicity = single-valued
    requestsInterface type interface
```

A WSMO goal can be seen as a description of services that would potentially satisfy the requester's desires. All of the elements that make up a goal have been previously described in this chapter. Specifically the capability of the goal can be seen in Listing 3.8 and the interface of the goal in Listing 3.9.

3.1.4 WSMO Mediators

Mediators describe elements that resolve interoperability problems between different elements, e.g., between two ontologies or two services. Mediators are a core element of WSMO and aim to resolve heterogeneity problems at the data, process, and protocol levels. The definition of a mediator using the MOF notation is as shown in Listing 3.12.

Listing 3.12. Mediator definition

```
Class mediator
    hasNonFunctionalProperty type nonFunctionalProperty
    importsOntology type ontology
    hasSource type {ontology, goal, Webservice, mediator}
    hasTarget type {ontology, goal, Webservice, mediator}
    hasMediationService type {Webservice, goal, wwMediator}
```

Like all WSMO elements a mediator can define a set of nonfunctional properties using the *hasNonFunctionalProperty* statement. Furthermore, the terminology needed from other ontologies to define this mediator can be imported using the *importsOntology* statement. The source component of a mediator defines the resources for which the heterogeneities are resolved, while the target component defines the resources that receive these mediated source components. A mediation service can be used to define the facility applied for performing the mediation using the *hasMediationService* statement. This service may explicitly link to a Web service description or may link to a goal describing the functionality needed, which can then be resolved to a Web service at run time using service discovery. There are four types of mediator within the WSMO metamodel:

1. *Ontology to ontology mediators.* Ontology to ontology mediators (ooMediators), as defined in Listing 3.13, provide a mechanism by which mismatches between two or more ontologies can be resolved. The source component of an ooMediator is an ontology or another ooMediator, and the source defines the resources for which mismatches will be resolved by the mediator. The target of an ooMediator can be an ontology, goal, Web service, or a mediator, and the target defines the target component which will receive the results of mediating the sources.

Listing 3.13. ooMediator definition

```
Class ooMediator sub-Class mediator
    hasSource type {ontology, ooMediator}
```

As described in Sect. 3.1.1, ooMediators are used across all WSMO top-level elements within the *usesMediator* statement in order to import terminology required by a resource description whenever there are mismatches between the ontologies to be used.

2. *Goal to goal mediators.* Goal to goal mediators (ggMediators), as defined in Listing 3.14, connect goals to one another and allow for relationships between different goals to be specified. A ggMediator can be used to specify that one goal is equivalent to another goal, or that the source goal is a refinement of the target.

Listing 3.14. ggMediator definition

```
Class ggMediator sub-Class mediator
    usesMediator type ooMediator
    hasSource type {goal, ggMediator}
    hasTarget type {goal, ggMediator}
```

The source of a ggMediator can be a goal or another ggMediator, which is also true for the target of a ggMediator. The ability to specify a ggMediator as source or target allows for mediators to be gained together.

3. *Web service to goal mediators.* Web service to goal mediators (wgMediators), defined in Listing 3.15, which could also be described as goal to Web service mediators, provide a mechanism for expressing relationships between Web Services and goals. Primarily wgMediators are used to prelink services to goals or to cache the results of previously performed discovery actions. For example, a wgMediator may be used to express that a given goal can be totally or partially fulfilled by a given Web service.

Listing 3.15. wgMediator definition

```
Class wgMediator sub-Class mediator
    usesMediator type ooMediator
    hasSource type {Webservice, goal, wgMediator, ggMediator}
    hasTarget type {Webservice, goal, ggMediator, wgMediator}
```

4. *Web service to Web service mediators.* Web service to Web service mediators (wwMediators), defined in Listing 3.16, provide a mechanism for expressing relationships between Web Services. These relationships could include stating that two Web Services provide equivalent functionality, a group of Web Services provide equivalent functionality to one Web service, or that one Web service is a refinement of another.

Listing 3.16. wwMediator definition

```
Class wwMediator sub−Class mediator
    usesMediator type ooMediator
    hasSource type {Webservice, wwMediator}
    hasTarget type {Webservice, wwMediator}
```

wwMediators can also be used to establish interoperability between Web Services in cases where they would otherwise be not interoperable, i.e., a wwMediator could be used to specify a mediation between the choreography of two Web Services, where mediation can involve the data, protocol, or process levels.

3.2 The Web Service Modeling Language

The Web service Modeling Language (WSML) [53] is a concrete formal language based on the conceptual model of WSMO [77], described in the previous section. As such, it provides a means for describing ontologies, goals, Web Services, and mediators in the way envisioned by WSMO. Besides providing a concrete language for WSMO, WSML presents a framework of different language variants, incorporating both description logics and logic programming, the latter extended with F-logic-based [121] metamodeling. Thereby, WSML aims to investigate the application and integration of description logics and logic programming for the Semantic Web and Semantic Web Services.

We see three main areas which benefit from the use of formal methods in Web service description: (1) ontology description, (2) declarative functional description of goals and Web Services, and (3) description of Web service dynamics, where the functional description corresponds to the Web service capability, and the dynamic description corresponds to the choreography and orchestration. WSML defines a syntax and semantics for ontology descriptions. The underlying formalisms which were mentioned earlier are used to give a formal meaning to ontology descriptions in WSML. For the functional description of goals and Web Services, WSML offers a syntactical framework, with Hoare-style semantics in mind. WSML does not commit one to a specific semantics of the functional descriptions of services; there are several proposals for such semantics, e.g., set-based [115, 138] and state-based [116] descriptions, where the latter are more expressive, but also more complex to write. The description of the dynamic behavior of Web Services (choreography and orchestration) in the context of WSML is currently under investigation, but has not been integrated in WSML at this point.

This section is further structured as follows. We present the design principles of WSML in Sect. 3.2.1. We proceed with a description of the WSML variants and their (intended) interrelationship in Sect. 3.2.2. We then introduce the WSML through its surface syntax in Sect. 3.2.3, and conclude with a description of possible ways of exchanging WSML using (Semantic) Web languages in Sect. 3.2.4.

3.2.1 Design Principles of WSML

In the first place, WSML is a concrete language for WSMO [77]. The main goal of WSML is to provide a syntax and semantics for WSMO. The design of WSML further follows three main principles:

1. *A language based on two useful well-known formalisms.* We conjecture that both description logics and logic programming are useful formal language paradigms for ontology description, and knowledge representation on the Semantic Web [120], and, consequently, for Semantic Web Services. The formal properties, as well as reasoning algorithms, for both paradigms have been thoroughly investigated in the respective research communities, and efficient reasoning implementations are available for both paradigms. WSML should leverage the research which has been done in both areas, and the implementations which are available, by catering for both language paradigms.

   The difference in the expressiveness and underlying assumptions of both paradigms should be overcome by defining means for interaction between descriptions in both paradigms. On the one hand, it is desirable to use a common subset of both paradigms for such interaction [88] so that it is not necessary to compromise on the computational properties and so that existing implementations for both paradigms can still be used. On the other hand, using a common subset requires compromising on expressiveness, which is not desirable in many situations; a common superset would include the expressiveness of both paradigms, but would require compromising on computational properties such as decidability [137].

2. *Web language.* WSML is meant to be a language for the Semantic Web; therefore, WSML needs to take into account and adopt the relevant (semantic) Web standards. We proceed to describe the Web standards which are relevant for WSML.

   The Web has a number of standards for object identification and the representation and manipulation of data which can be directly adopted by any Web language, including WSML. The Web architecture [110] prescribes the use of the standard URI [21], and its successor Internationalized Resource Identifier (IRI) [63], for the identification of objects on the Web. Therefore, such things as concepts, instances, relations, and axioms need to be identified using URIs. XML Schema [23] describes a number of data types (e.g. a string, integer, date); XQuery [142] describes a number of datatype functions and operators for manipulating and comparing data conforming to these types.

   A number of languages have been standardized for the exchange of information over the Semantic Web. The most basic of these languages is XML [28], which provides a structured format for exchange of data over the Web. In fact, XML is part of the foundation for the Semantic Web; XML is used, for example, for transmitting RDF data over the Web [15]. RDF [127] is the standard language for exchanging (semi-)structured data over the Semantic Web. RDF Schema [29] provides a lightweight ontology language for RDF which allows one to express classes, properties, and domain and range restrictions; furthermore, RDF Schema allows for metamodeling. OWL [58] is the standard ontology language for the Semantic Web, partially extending RDF Schema; the sublanguage OWL DL provides a means for exchanging description-logic-based ontologies over the Web. There is currently no standard rules language for the Semantic Web; however, such an effort has been started in the context of the Rule Interchange Format (RIF) Working Group.[1] One of the basic design principles for languages on the Semantic Web is to reuse existing (semantic) Web languages as much as possible. Therefore, WSML should use the mentioned languages as much as possible for the exchange of ontology (and Web service) descriptions.

We consider query languages such as SPARQL [179] beyond the scope of WSML. However, SPARQL may be used to query the RDF representation of WSML [52].

3. *User-friendly surface syntax.* It has been argued that tools hide language syntax from the user, and thus a user-friendly surface syntax is not necessary; however, as has been seen, for example, with the adoption of SQL, an expressive but understandable syntax is crucial for successful adoption of a language. Developers and early adopters of the language will have to deal with the concrete syntax of any new language; therefore, readability and understandability increase adoption of a language. This trend is also visible on the Semantic Web, with the development of surface syntaxes for RDF (e.g., N-Triples [87]) and OWL [103], which are easier to read and write for the human user than the standard exchange syntaxes [15, 58].

Different people may have different assumptions about the meaning of constraints [57]; for some, a constraint has an "inferring" meaning, whereas for others, a constraint has a "checking" meaning. Since WSML incorporates both paradigms, the surface syntax should make this distinction clear to the user.

A drawback of using a formal logical language is that the syntax of the language is often hard to understand and use by nonexpert users. Therefore, WSML should provide a means for hiding complex logical formulas from nonexpert users who are mainly interested in the conceptual modeling of ontologies, and not in complex logical axioms.

The following sections describe how these design principles are realized in WSML. Section 3.2.2 describes the framework of WSML variants, which correspond to the relevant well-known formalisms of the first design principle. Section 3.2.3 describes the different modeling constructs in WSML using the normative surface syntax, which is meant to be user-friendly, and in which URIs and XML datatypes

---

[1] http://www.w3.org/2005/rules/wg

play an important role; we also mention the mappings to XML, RDF (Schema), and OWL, enabling the exchange of WSML descriptions over the (semantic) Web using these languages.

3.2.2 The WSML Layering

Following the principle, detailed in the previous section, of the use of both the description logics and the logic programming paradigms, WSML incorporates a number of different language *variants*, corresponding to the description logics and the logic programming paradigms, and their possible (subset and superset) interaction. Figure 3.2(a) shows the WSML variants and their interrelationships. The variants differ in logical expressiveness and underlying language paradigms; they allow users to make a trade-off between the expressiveness of a variant and the complexity of reasoning, for ontology modeling on a per-application basis.

WSML-Core is based on an intersection of the description logic $\mathcal{SHIQ}$ and Horn logic, also known as description logic programs [88]. It has the least expressive power of the WSML variants, and functions as a common subset of the description-logic-based and logic-programming-based variants.

WSML-DL is the description logic variant of WSML, and captures the description logic $\mathcal{SHIQ}(\mathbf{D})$, which is a major part of (the description logic species of) OWL [58].

WSML-Flight is the least expressive of the two logic-programming-based variants of WSML; it is an extension of WSML-Core towards a powerful rule language. It adds features such as metamodeling, constraints, and nonmonotonic negation. WSML-Flight is based on a logic programming variant of F-logic [121] and is semantically equivalent to Datalog with inequality and (locally) stratified negation. WSML-Flight is a direct syntactic extension of WSML-Core and it is intended to be a semantic extension in the sense that every WSML-Core inference is also a WSML-Flight inference. Technical issues related to the layering between the (description-logic-based) WSML-Core and (F-logic-based) WSML-Flight are discussed in detail in [51].

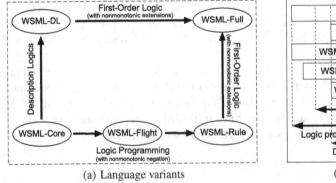

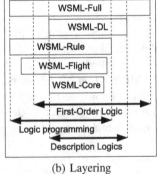

(a) Language variants   (b) Layering

Figure 3.2. Web Service Modeling Language (*WSML*) variants and layering

WSML-Rule extends WSML-Flight with further features from logic programming, namely, the use of function symbols, unsafe rules, and unstratified negation. There are two prominent semantics for logic programs with unstratified negation, namely, the stable model semantics [85] and the well-founded semantics [83]; with respect to the task of query answering, the latter can be seen as an approximation of the former. In version 0.21 of the WSML specification [53], the semantics of WSML-Rule was based on the well-founded semantics. However, since the stable model semantics is more general, we argue that WSML-Rule should adopt the stable model semantics, and that implementations may use the well-founded semantics as an approximation when considering query answering.

WSML-Full unifies WSML-DL and WSML-Rule under a first-order umbrella with extensions to support the nonmonotonic negation of WSML-Rule. A definition of the semantics for WSML-Full, generalizing WSML-DL and WSML-Rule, is proposed in [50, 51].

As shown in Figure 3.2(b), WSML has two alternative layerings, namely, WSML-Core $\Rightarrow$ WSML-DL $\Rightarrow$ WSML-Full and WSML-Core $\Rightarrow$ WSML-Flight $\Rightarrow$ WSML-Rule $\Rightarrow$ WSML-Full. For both layerings, WSML-Core and WSML-Full mark the least and most expressive layers. The two layerings are to a certain extent disjoint, namely, the interoperation between WSML-DL, on the one hand, and WSML-Flight and WSML-Rule, on the other, is only possible through a common subset (WSML-Core) or through a very expressive superset (WSML-Full). The precise properties of language layering are shown in [50, 51].

3.2.3 WSML Syntax

In this section we introduce the WSML syntax, following the design principles of "Web language" and "user-friendly surface syntax," described in Sect. 3.2.1. We introduce the surface syntax, and briefly mention the mappings of the surface syntax to XML, RDF, and OWL, for exchange of WSML descriptions over the (Semantic) Web. Since different WSML variants have different underlying language paradigms, there are differences in the language constructs which may be used in each of the variants.

Besides the mentioned mappings to XML, RDF, and OWL, which allow exchange over the Web, we address the "Web language" design principle through the use of IRIs [63] for the identification of objects and resources in WSML and we use XML Schema datatypes [23] for typing concrete data values, as described in the "Identifiers in WSML" section. The reuse of XQuery comparators and functions is addressed through the use of corresponding built-in predicates, as described in Appendix C.3 in [53].

The "user-friendly surface syntax" design principle is addressed through the definition of WSML in terms of a normative surface syntax with keywords based on WSMO. Furthermore, "inferring" and "checking" constraints on attributes are distinguished using the **impliesType** and **ofType** keywords. Finally, WSML makes a clear distinction between the modeling of the different conceptual elements, on the one hand, and the specification of complex logical definitions, on the other. To this end, the WSML syntax is split into two parts: the *conceptual syntax* and *logical expression syntax*. The conceptual syntax this based on the structure of the WSMO conceptual model, and is independent of the particular underlying logic; it shields the user from the peculiarities of the underlying formal language. The logical expression syntax provides access to the full expressive power of the language underlying the particular variant. The basic entry points for logical expressions in the conceptual syntax are the axioms in ontologies and assumptions, preconditions, postconditions, and effects in goal and Web service descriptions. We describe the conceptual syntax in the "Conceptual Syntax" section and the logical expression syntax in the "Logical Expression Syntax" section.

We conclude with a brief description of the mappings between WSML, XML, RDF, and OWL, and describe how these languages can be used for the exchange of WSML ontologies over the (Semantic) Web, in the "Logical Expression Syntax" section.

Identifiers in WSML

WSML has three kinds of identifiers, namely, IRIs, serialized qualified names (sQ-Names), which are abbreviated IRIs, and data values.

An IRI [63] uniquely identifies a resource in a Web-compliant way, following the Web architecture [110]. The IRI proposed standard is the successor of the popular URI standard and has already been adopted in various W3C activities such as SPARQL [179]. In the surface syntax, IRIs are delimited using an underscore and a double quote '_"' and a double quote '"', for example, _"http://www.wsmo.org/wsml/wsml-syntax#".

In order to enhance legibility, an IRI can be abbreviated to an sQName, and is of the form *prefix#localname* . The prefix and separator *prefix#* may be omitted, in which case the name falls in the default namespace. Our concept of an sQName corresponds with the use of QNames in RDF and is slightly different from qualified names (QNames) in XML, where a QName is not merely an abbreviation for an IRI, but is a tuple <namespaceURI, localname>. Since WSML is meant as a language for the Semantic Web, we follow the Semantic Web recommendation RDF in this respect.

Data values in WSML are strings, integers, decimals, or structured data values. WSML defines constructs which reflect the structure of data values. For example, the date "March 15, 2005" is represented as: _date(2005,3,15). Strings, integers, and decimals corresponds to the XML Schema datatypes [23] string, integer, and decimal. Furthermore, the datatypes recommended for use in WSML are the XML Schema datatypes (see Appendix C.1 in [53]); however, it is also possible to use datatypes beyond this set.

Conceptual Syntax

The WSML conceptual syntax allows for the modeling of ontologies, Web Services, goals, and mediators. It is shared between all variants, with the exception of some restrictions which apply on the modeling of ontologies in WSML-Core and WSML-DL.

Ontologies

An ontology in WSML consists of the elements **concept, relation, instance, relationInstance**, and **axiom**. Additionally, an ontology may have nonfunctional properties and may import other ontologies. We start the description of WSML ontologies with an example which demonstrates the elements of an ontology in Listing 3.17, and detail the elements below.

Concepts. The notion of concepts (sometimes also called "classes") plays a central role in ontologies. Concepts form the basic terminology of the domain of discourse. A concept may have instances and may have a number of attributes associated with it. The nonfunctional properties, as well as the attribute definitions, are grouped together in one frame, as can be seen from the example concept book in Listing 3.17.

Attribute definitions can take two forms, namely, *constraining* (using **ofType**) and *inferring* (using **impliesType**) attribute definitions.[2] Constraining attribute definitions define a typing constraint on the values for this attribute, similar to integrity constraints in databases; inferring attribute definitions imply that the type of the values for the attribute is inferred from the attribute definition, similar to range restrictions on properties in RDF Schema [29] and OWL [58]. Each attribute definition may have a number of features associated with it, namely, transitivity, symmetry, reflexivity, and the inverse of an attribute, as well as minimal and maximal cardinality constraints.

Constraining attribute definitions, as well as cardinality constraints, require closed-world reasoning and are thus not allowed in WSML-Core and WSML-DL. As opposed to features of roles in description logics, attribute features such as transitivity, symmetry, reflexivity, and inverse attributes are local to a concept in WSML. Thus, none of these features may be used in WSML-Core and WSML-DL. For a motivation on the use of constraining attributes, see [57].

Listing 3.17. An example Web Service Modeling Language (WSML) ontology

```
wsmlVariant _"http://www.wsmo.org/wsml/wsml-syntax/wsml-flight"
namespace {_"http://example.org/bookOntology#",
           dc _"http://purl.org/dc/elements/1.1/"}
ontology _"http://example.org/bookOntology"
  nonFunctionalProperties
    dc#title  hasValue "Example Book ontology"
    dc#description hasValue "Example ontology about books and shopping carts"
  endNonFunctionalProperties
  concept book
    title  ofType _string
    hasAuthor ofType author
  concept author subConceptOf person
    authorOf inverseOf(hasAuthor) ofType book
```

---

[2] The distinction between inferring and constraining attribute definitions is explained in more detail in Sect. 2 in [57].

```
concept cart
  nonFunctionalProperties
    dc#description hasValue "A shopping cart has exactly one id
      and zero or more items, which are books."
  endNonFunctionalProperties
    id ofType (1) _string
    items ofType book
instance crimeAndPunishment memberOf book
    title   hasValue "Crime and Punishment"
    hasAuthor hasValue dostoyevsky

relation authorship(impliesType author, impliesType document)
  nonFunctionalProperties
    dc#relation  hasValue authorshipFromAuthor
  endNonFunctionalProperties
  axiom authorshipFromAuthor
    definedBy
      authorship(?x,?y) :- ?x[authorOf hasValue ?y] memberOf author.
```

Relations. Relations in WSML can have an arbitrary arity, may be organized in a hierarchy using **subRelationOf**, and the parameters may be typed using parameter-type definitions of the form (**ofType** *type*) and (**impliesType** *type*), where *type* is a concept identifier. The usage of **ofType** and **impliesType** corresponds with the usage in attribute definitions. Namely, parameter definitions with the **ofType** keyword are used to check the type of parameter values, whereas parameter definitions with the **impliesType** keyword are used to infer concept membership of parameter values.

The allowed arity of the relation may be constrained by the underlying logic of the WSML variant. WSML-Core and WSML-DL allow only binary relations and, similar to attribute definitions, they allow only parameter typing using the keyword **impliesType**.

Instances. A concept may have a number of instances associated with it. Instances explicitly specified in an ontology are those which are shared as part of the ontology. However, most instance data exists outside the ontology in private databases. WSML does not prescribe how to connect such a database to an ontology, since different organizations will use the same ontology to query different databases and such corporate databases are typically not shared.

An instance may be member of zero or more concepts and may have a number of attribute values associated with it; see, for example, the instance crimeAndPunishment in Listing 3.17. Note that the specification of concept membership is optional and the attributes used in the instance specification do not necessarily have to occur in the associated concept definition. Consequently, WSML instances can be used to represent semistructured data, since without concept membership and constraints on the use of attributes, instances form a directed labeled graph. Because of this possibility to capture semistructured data, most RDF graphs can be represented as WSML instance data, and vice versa.

Axioms. Axioms provide a means to add arbitrary logical expressions to an ontology. Such logical expressions can be used to refine concept or relation definitions in the ontology, but also to add arbitrary axiomatic domain knowledge or express constraints. The axiom authorshipFromAuthor in Listing 3.17 states that the relation authorship exists between any author and any book of which he is an author; consequently, ⟨dostoyesksy, crimeAndPunishment⟩ is in the relation authorship. Logical expressions are explained in more detail in the "Logical Expression Syntax" section.

Web Services

A Web service has a capability and a number of interfaces. The capability describes the Web service functionality by expressing conditions over its prestates and poststates[3] using logical expressions; interfaces describe how to interact with the service. Additionally, WSML allows one to specify nonfunctional properties of a Web service. Listing 3.18 describes a simple Web service for adding items to a shopping cart.

Capabilities. Preconditions and assumptions describe the state before the execution of a Web service. While preconditions describe conditions over the information space, i.e., conditions over the input, assumptions describe conditions over the state of the world which cannot necessarily be directly checked. Postconditions describe the relation between the input and the output, e.g., a credit card limit with respect to its values before the service execution. In this sense, they describe the information state after execution of the service. Effects describe changes in the real world caused by the service, e.g., the physical shipment of some good. The **sharedVariables** construct is used to identify variables which are shared between the preconditions and postconditions and the assumptions and effects. Shared variables can be used to refer to the same input and output values in the conditions of the capability. Listing 3.18 describes a simple Web service for adding items to a shopping cart: given a shopping cart identifier and a number of items, the items are added to the shopping cart with this identifier.

Listing 3.18. A WSML Web service description

```
Webservice _"http://example.org/bookService"
  nonFunctionalProperties
    dc#title  hasValue "Example book buying service"
    dc#description hasValue "A simple example Web service for adding items to a shopping cart"
  endNonFunctionalProperties

  importsOntology _"http://example.org/bookOntology"
  capability
    sharedVariables {?cartId, ?item}
    precondition
      definedBy
        ?cartId memberOf _string and ?item memberOf book.
    postcondition
      definedBy
        forall ?cart (?cart[id hasValue ?cartId] memberOf cart implies
          ?cart[items hasValue ?item]).
```

---

[3] Prestate (poststate, respectively) refers to the state before (after, respectively) the execution of the Web service.

Interfaces. Interfaces describe how to interact with a service from the requester's point of view (**choreography**) and how the service interacts with other services and goals it needs to fulfill in order to fulfill its capability (**orchestration**), which is the provider's point of view. Choreography and orchestration descriptions are external to WSML; WSML allows one to reference any choreography or orchestration identified by an IRI.

Goals

Goals are symmetric to Web Services in the sense that goals describe desired functionality and Web Services describe offered functionality. Therefore, a goal description consists of the same modeling elements as a Web service description, namely, nonfunctional properties, a capability, and a number of interfaces.

Mediators

Mediators connect different goals, Web Services and ontologies, and enable interoperation by reconciling differences in representation formats, encoding styles, business protocols, etc. Connections between mediators and other WSML elements can be established in two different ways:

1. Each WSML element allows for the specification of a number of mediators through the **usesMediator** keyword.
2. Each mediator has (depending on the type of mediator) one or more sources and one target. Both source and target are optional in order to allow for generic mediators.

A mediator achieves its mediation functionality either through a Web service, which provides the mediation service, or a goal, which can be used to dynamically discover the appropriate (mediation) Web service.

Logical Expression Syntax

We will first explain the general logical expression syntax, which encompasses all WSML variants, and then describe the restrictions on this general syntax for each of the variants. The general logical expression syntax for WSML has a first-order logic style, in the sense that it has constants, function symbols, variables, predicates, and the usual logical connectives. Furthermore, WSML has F-logic [121] based extensions in order to model concepts, attributes, attribute definitions, and subconcept and concept membership relationships. Finally, WSML has a number of connectives to facilitate the logic programming based variants, namely, default negation (negation as failure), logic programming implication (which differs from classical implication) and database-style integrity constraints.

Variables in WSML start with a question mark, followed by an arbitrary number of alphanumeric characters, e.g., ?x, ?name, ?123. Free variables in WSML (i.e., variables which are not explicitly quantified) are implicitly universally quantified outside the formula (i.e., the logical expression in which the variable occurs is the scope of quantification), unless indicated otherwise, through the **sharedVariables** construct (see the previous section).

Terms are identifiers, variables, or constructed terms. An atom is, as usual, a predicate symbol with a number of terms as arguments. Besides the usual atoms, WSML has a special kind of atom, called *molecules*, which are used to capture information about concepts, instances, attributes, and attribute values. The are two types of molecules, analogous to F-logic:

1. An *isa* molecule is a concept membership molecule of the form *A* **memberOf** *B* or a subconcept molecule of the form *A* **subConceptOf** *B* with *A* and *B* arbitrary terms.
2. An *object* molecule is an attribute value expressions of the form *A*[*B* **hasValue** *C*], a constraining attribute signature expression of the form *A*[*B* **ofType** *C*], or an inferring attribute signature expression of the form *A*[*B* **ofType** *C*], with *A,B,C* arbitrary terms.

WSML has the usual first-order connectives: the unary negation operator **neg**, and the binary operators for conjunction **and**, disjunction **or**, right implication **implies**, left implication **impliedBy**, and dual implication **equivalent**. Variables may be universally quantified using **forall** or existentially quantified using **exists**. First Order formulae are obtained by combining atoms using the mentioned connectives in the usual way. The following are examples of First Order formulae in WSML:

```
// every person has a father
forall ?x (?x memberOf Person implies exists ?y (?x[father hasValue
?y])).
// john is member of a class which has some attribute called 'name'
exists ?x,?y (john memberOf ?x and ?x[name ofType ?y]).
```

Apart from First Order formulae, WSML allows the use of the negation-as-failure symbol **naf** on atoms, the special logic programming implication symbol **:-**, and the integrity constraint symbol **!-**. A logic programming rule consists of a *head* and a *body*, separated by the **:-** symbol. An integrity constraint consists of the symbol **!-** followed by a rule body. Negation-as-failure **naf** is only allowed to occur in the body of a logic programming rule or an integrity constraint. The further use of logical connectives in logic programming rules is restricted. The following logical connectives are allowed in the head of a rule: **and**, **implies**, **impliedBy**, and **equivalent**. The following connectives are allowed in the body of a rule (or constraint): **and**, **or**, and **naf**. The following are examples of logic programming rules and database constraints:

```
// every person has a father
?x[father hasValue f(?y)] :- ?x memberOf Person.
// Man and Woman are disjoint
!- ?x memberOf Man and ?x memberOf Woman.
// in case a person is not involved in a marriage, the person is a bachelor
?x memberOf Bachelor :- ?x memberOf Person and naf
Marriage(?x,?y,?z).
```

Table 3.1. Web service Modeling Language variants and feature matrix

Feature	Core	DL	Flight	Rule	Full
Classical negation (**neg**)	-	X	-	-	X
Existential quantification	-	X	-	-	X
(Head) disjunction	-	X	-	-	X
n-ary relations	-	-	X	X	X
Metamodeling	-	-	X	X	X
Default negation (**naf**)	-	-	X	X	X
Logic programming implication	-	-	X	X	X
Integrity constraints	-	-	X	X	X
Function symbols	-	-	-	X	X
Unsafe rules	-	-	-	X	X

Particularities of the WSML Variants

Each of the WSML variants defines a number of restrictions on the logical expression syntax. For example, logic programming rules and constraints are not allowed in WSML-Core and WSML-DL. Table 3.1 contains a number of language features and indicates in which variant the feature can occur, to give an idea of the differences between the logical expressions of each variant.

3.2.4 Exchanging WSML using Semantic Web Languages

In this section we give a brief overview of the mappings from the WSML surface syntax to XML, RDF, and OWL, along with pointers to the complete mapping(s).

WSML XML Syntax

The WSML XML syntax is essentially an XML version of the surface syntax, and is thus very similar, both in keywords and in structure. We have defined the XML syntax through a translation from the human-readable syntax [53] and have additionally specified an XML schema for WSML.[4] Note that all WSML elements fall in the WSML namespace http://www.wsmo.org/wsml/wsml-syntax#.

WSML RDF Syntax

WSML provides a serialization of all its conceptual modeling elements in RDF [52]. The WSML RDF syntax reuses the RDF and RDF Schema vocabulary to allow existing RDF(Schema)-based tools to achieve the highest possible degree of interoperation. As a result, WSML can be seen as an extension of RDF(Schema); it does not allow the use of language constructs in the language itself and does not allow full treatment of blank nodes, because this would require reasoning with existential information, which is not allowed in the rule-based WSML variants. WSML provides

---

[4] http://www.wsmo.org/TR/d16/d16.1/v0.21/xml-syntax/wsml-xml-syntax.xsd

a significant extension of RDF Schema through the possibility of specifying local attributes, range, and cardinality constraints for attributes and attribute features such as symmetry, transitivity, and reflexivity. Furthermore, WSML (in its rule-based variants) provides an expressive rule language which can be used for the manipulation of RDF data.

OWL

WSML-Core is, semantically speaking, a subset of OWL Lite. WSML-DL is semantically equivalent to OWL DL, with the caveat that WSML-DL does not allow nominals, which are allowed in OWL DL, and OWL DL does not allow qualified number restrictions, which are allowed in WSML-DL. There is a semantics-preserving mapping between the WSML surface syntax and the OWL abstract syntax. This mapping allows the import of all of OWL DLP[5] into WSML-Core (and thus also all other WSML variants), and the import of most of OWL DL into WSML-DL (and thus also WSML-Full). Additionally, this mapping allows the use of OWL as an exchange syntax for WSML-Core and WSML-DL ontologies. This mapping is described in detail in [53].

3.3 Summary

In this chapter we have provided an introduction to two key technologies needed for the successful realization of Semantic Web Services and semantically enabled service-oriented architectures, namely, WSMO and WSML. WSMO provides a conceptual model for Semantic Web Services which combines the design principles of the Web, the Semantic Web, and distributed service-oriented computing in order to provide a clear description of the elements needed to describe Web Services. WSML formalizes WSMO by providing a concrete formal language for describing Web Services semantically and a language framework of different language variants, incorporating both description logics and logic programming. This chapter is intended as a reference for the reader for WSMO and WSML providing the key foundational knowledge needed for the rest of the book.

---

[5] http://logic.aifb.uni-karlsruhe.de/wiki/DLP

Part II

SESA Environment

4

Introduction to Semantically Enabled Service-oriented Architectures

Computer science is on the edge of an important new period of abstraction. A generation ago we learned to abstract from hardware and currently we are learning to abstract from software in terms of Service-Oriented Architectures (SOA). A SOA is essentially a collection of services. It is the service that counts for a customer and not the specific software or hardware components that are used to implement this service. It is a common expectation that SOAs will quickly become the leading software paradigm. However, we believe that these SOAs will not scale without significant mechanization of service discovery, service adapation, service negotiation, service composition, service invocation, and service monitoring, as well as data, protocol, and process mediation. We envisage the future of applied computer science in terms of SOAs which are empowered by adding semantics as a means to deal with heterogeneity and mechanization of service usage. This approach is called Semantically Enabled Service-oriented Architectures or SESA for short.

4.1 SESA Background

In this section we provide an overview of the fundamental elements of the SESA architecture, one which enables the execution of Semantic Web Services and resolves the fundamental challenges related to the open SOA environment. We expect that in the near future a service-oriented world will consist of an "uncountable" number of services. Their computation will involve services searching for other services based on functional and nonfunctional requirements, and then resolving any interoperability conflicts from those services selected. However, services will not be able to interact automatically and existing SOA solutions will not scale without significant mechanization of the service provisioning process. Hence, machine processable semantics is essential for the next generation of Service-Oriented Computing (SOC) to reach its full potential. In this chapter we define methods, algorithms, and tools forming a skeleton of SESA, introducing automation to the service provisioning process, including service discovery, negotiation, adaptation, composition, invocation, and monitoring, as well as service interaction requiring data and process mediation.

SOA outside a tightly controlled environment cannot succeed until semantic issues are addressed and critical tasks within the service provisioning process are automated leaving humans to focus on higher-level problems. While this chapter describes how these building blocks are consolidated into a coherent software architecture, which can be used as a blueprint for implementation, following chapters present the basic conceptual and technical building blocks required to set up the SESA infrastructure.

SESA has evolved from the collaborative efforts of three research/standardization groups: OASIS Semantic Execution Environment Technical Committee (SEE TC), Web Service Modeling Execution Environment (WSMX) Working Group, and NESSI. The aim of the OASIS SEE TC is to provide guidelines, justifications, and implementation directions for an execution environment for Semantic Web Services. The resulting infrastructure incorporates the application of semantics to service-oriented systems and provides mechanisms for consuming Semantic Web Services. WSMX is the reference implementation of Web Service Modeling Ontology (WSMO) and SEE. It is an execution environment for business application integration where enhanced Web Services are integrated for various business applications. The aim is to increase business processes automation in a very flexible manner while providing scalable integration solutions. The WSMX Working Group builds a prototypical execution infrastructure for Semantic Web Services based on the SOA paradigm of loosely coupled components. Finally SESA also relates to the work carried out by the NESSI initiative addressing semantic aspects of the NESSI platform. NESSI semantic technologies provide the semantics-based solutions for search and integration, which aim to enable progressive development of SESA. The NESSI Semantic Technology Working Group aims to use SESA as its roadmap defining the development of its semantic technologies.

4.2 Service Orientation

The design of enterprise information systems has gone through several changes in recent years. In order to respond to the requirements of enterprises for flexibility and dynamism, the traditional monolithic applications have become substituted by smaller composable units of functionality known as services. Information systems must then be retailored to fit this paradigm, with new applications developed as services, and legacy systems to be updated in order to expose service interfaces. The drive is towards a design of information systems which adopt paradigms of SOC together with the SOA implementation architecture and relevant Web service technologies.

4.2.1 Service-Oriented Computing

SOC is a new computing paradigm that utilizes services as the fundamental elements for the development of rapid, low-cost, and easily integrable enterprise applications [171, 173]. One of the main goals of SOC is to enable the development of networks of integrated and collaborative applications, regardless of both the platform on which applications or services run (e.g., the operating system) and the programming languages used to develop them.

In this paradigm, services are autonomous, self-describing, and platform-independent computational entities, which provide a uniform and ubiquitous access to information for a wide range of computing devices (such as desktop computers, PDAs, cellular phones) and software programs across different platforms. Any piece of code and any application component deployed on a system can be reused and transformed into a network-available service. Service providers and service consumers remain loosely coupled as services, independent of the context in which they are used. Since these services are based on the service-orientation paradigm and distinguish characteristics of the service, they can be easily described, published, discovered, and dynamically assembled for developing distributed and interoperable systems.

The main goal of SOC is to facilitate the integration of newly built and legacy applications, which exist both within and across organizational boundaries. SOC must overcome and resolve heterogeneous conflicts due to different platforms, programming languages, security firewalls, etc. The basic idea behind this orientation is to allow applications which were developed independently (using different languages, technologies, or platforms) to be exposed as services and then interconnect them exploiting the Web infrastructure with respective standards such as HTTP, XML, SOAP, and WSDL and even some complex service orchestration standards like BPEL.

4.2.2 Service-Oriented Architecture

The service-oriented paradigm of computation can be abstractly implemented by the system architecture called SOA [24, 30]. The purpose of this architecture is to address the requirements of loosely coupled, standard-based, and protocol-independent distributed computing, mapping enterprise information systems isomorphically to the overall business process flow [174]. This attempt is considered to be the latest development of a long series of advancements in software engineering addressing the reuse of software components.

Historically, the first major step of this evolution was the development of the concept of *function*. Using functions, one decomposes a program into smaller subprograms and writing code is focused on the idea of the Application Programming interface (API). An API, practically, represents the contract to which a software component has to commit. The second major step was the development of the concept of *object*. An object is a basic building block which contains both data and functions within a single encapsulated unit. With the object-oriented paradigm, the notions of classes, inheritance, and polymorphism are introduced. In this way classes can be viewed as a lattice. The concept of *service* becomes the next evolutionary step introduced with the advent of SOC and its SOA implementation architecture.

Figure 4.1 shows the the *Web Services programming model*, which consists of three components: service consumers, service providers, and service registrars. Ignoring the detailed techniques for the connection of the three components, this model

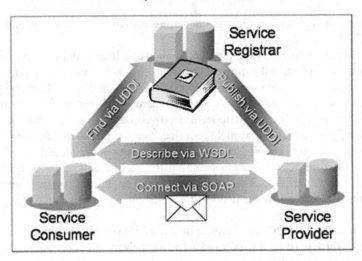

Figure 4.1. Web Services programming model

represents also the SOA basic model. A service registrar (also called service broker) acts as an intermediary between the provider and the consumer, so they are able to find each other. A service provider simply publishes the service. A service consumer tries to find services using the registrar; if it finds the desired service it can set up a contract with the provider in order to consume such a service and thus to do business.

The fundamental logic view of services in SOA is based on the division of service description (called usually interface) and service implementation [174]. Service interface defines the identity of a service and its invocation logistics. Service implementation implements the work that the service is designated to do. Based on this division, service providers and services consumers are loosely coupled. Furthermore, the services can be significantly reused and adapted according to certain requirements. Because service interfaces are platform-independent and implementation is transparent for the service consumers, a client from any communication device using any computational platform, operating system, and any programming language should be capable of using the service. The two facets of the service are distinct; they are designed and maintained as distinct items, though their existence is highly interrelated.

Based on the service autonomy and the clean separation of service interfaces from internal implementation, SOA provides a more flexible architecture that unifies business processes by modularizing large applications into services. Furthermore, enterprise-wide or even cross-enterprise applications can be realized by means of services development, integration, and adaptation. Some SOA distinguished requirements (or rather advantages) have been analyzed as follows [195]:

- **Loose coupling.** Interacting services are loosely coupled by nature. They run on different platforms, are implemented independently, and have different owners. The model has to consider the loose coupling of services with respect to one another.

- **Implementation neutrality.** The interface should only matter, not the implementation. Services are defined independently of their implementation and should behave neutrally with respect to it.
- **Flexible configuration.** Services are invoked dynamically after the discovery process through the service requester. That is, the binding of a service provider to the requester occurs at run time at the final phase.
- **Long lifetime.** Components/services should exist long enough to be discovered, to be relied upon, and to engender trust in their behavior.
- **Granularity.** The granularity of a service defines the complexity and number of functionalities defined by an individual service and is thus part of the service model. An appropriate balance between coarse-grained and fine-grained services depends on the way services are modeled. For too fine grained services, problems arise when there are frequent and rapid changes.
- **Teams.** Computation in open systems should be conceptualized as business partners working as a team. Therefore, a team of cooperating autonomous components/services is a better modeling unit, instead of framing computations centrally.

Besides the basic SOA model shown in Fig. 4.1, there are some extension works towards SOA which depict more concepts than service registration, discovery, and invocation. The extended SOA (xSOA) accounts for SOA deficiencies in such areas as management, security, service choreography and orchestration, and service transaction management and coordination [170]. The xSOA is an attempt to streamline, group together, and logically structure the functional requirements of complex applications that make use of the SOC paradigm.

4.2.3 SOA Implementations

Basically, Web Services seem to be becoming the preferred implementation technology for realizing the SOA promise of maximum service sharing, reuse, and interoperability. From Fig. 4.1, the Web service programming model is a typical SOA implementation. Defined by W3C, it is a software system identified by a URI, whose public interfaces and bindings are defined and described using XML. Its definition can be discovered by other software systems. These systems may then interact with the Web service in a manner prescribed by its definition, using XML-based messages conveyed by Internet protocols. Interactions between Web Services typically occur as Simple Object Access Protocol (SOAP) calls carrying XML data content. Interface descriptions of the Web Services are expressed using Web Services Definition Language (WSDL). The Universal Description, Discovery, and Integration (UDDI) standard defines a protocol for directory services that contain Web service descriptions. UDDI enables Web service clients to locate candidate services and discover their details. Service clients and service providers utilize these standards to perform SOA's basic operations. Service aggregators may use the Business Process Execution Language for Web Services (BPEL4WS) to create new Web Services by defining corresponding compositions of the interfaces and internal processes of existing services.

Web Services technology is simply a widespread accepted instantiation of SOC providing a platform on which it is possible to develop applications taking advantage of the already existing Internet infrastructure. This does not mean that the set of technologies we present here are the only ones which make it possible to realize SOC and implement SOA. Some other more conventional programming languages or middleware platforms may be adopted as well, such as, for instance, established middleware technologies like J2EE, CORBA, and IBM's WebSphere MQ, and can now also participate in a SOA, using new features that work with WSDL.

The broad use of Enterprise Application Integration (EAI) middleware supports a variety of hub-and-spoke integration patterns [172]. EAI comprises message acceptance, transformation, translation, routing, message delivery, and business process management. All of these can be used to develop services and then it also becomes service-orientated architecture. The Enterprise Service Bus (ESB) is an open, standards-based message bus designed to enable the implementation, deployment, and management of SOA-based solutions with a focus on assembling, deploying, and managing distributed SOAs. The ESB provides the distributed processing, standards-based integration, and enterprise-class backbone required by the extended enterprise [112].

4.3 Execution Environment for Semantic Web Services

With the underpinning computation approach SOC, SOA is one of the most promising software engineering trends for future distributed systems. Pushed by major industry players and supported by many standardization efforts, Web Services are a prominent implementation of the service-oriented paradigm. They promise to foster reuse and to ease the implementation of loosely coupled distributed applications.

Although the idea of SOA targets the need for integration that is more adaptive to changes in business requirements, existing SOA solutions will prove difficult to scale without a proper degree of automation. While today's service technologies around WSDL, SOAP, UDDI, and BPEL have certainly brought a new potential to SOA, they only provide a partial solution to interoperability, mainly by means of unified technological environments. Where content and process level interoperability is to be solved, ad hoc solutions are often hard-wired in manual configuration of services or workflows, while at the same time they are hindered by dependence on XML-only descriptions. Although flexible and extensible, XML can only define the structure and syntax of data. Without machine-understandable semantics, services must be located and bound to service requesters at design time, which in turn limits possibilities for automation. In order to address these drawbacks, the extension of SOA with semantics offers a scalable integration, more adaptive to changes that might occur over a software system's lifetime. Semantics for SOA allows the definition of semantically rich and formal service models where semantics can be used to describe both services offered and capabilities required by potential consumers of those services. Also the data to be exchanged between business partners can be semantically described in an unambiguous manner in terms of ontologies. By means of logical reasoning, semantic SOA thus promotes a total or partial automation of service discovery, mediation, composition, and invocation. Semantic SOA does not, however, mean replacing existing integration technologies. The goal is to build a new layer on the top of the existing service stack while at the same time adopting existing industry standards and technologies being used within existing enterprise infrastructures.

4.3.1 Challenges for the Semantic Web Service Execution Environment

Talking about technology challenges in the semantic domain, we consider semantics as an enabling technology to allow integration and interoperability of the heterogenous systems. What makes the integration based on semantics a challenge is twofold: first, the representation of information and the information itself used to be bound tightly together; and, second, that information frequently lacks any context. The programmer often thinks not of the data itself but rather of the structure of the data such as schemas, data types, relational database constructs, etc. These structures do not relate directly to the information, but rather to the assumption of what the data should look like. In tightly coupled architectures, data structures are absolutely necessary; since they provide for systems a way of coping with the information they are being fed. But this assumption does not hold for distributed systems, such as the SESA platform aimed to be.

In the upcoming years, semantics will be used more and more often as an enabling technology for new ways of assembling software on the fly in order to create ad hoc systems. Computer science is entering into a new phase, where semantics starts to play a major role. The previous generation of distributed systems was based on abstracting from hardware, but the emerging generation is already based on abstracting from software. In a world of distributed computing, it is the service that counts for a customer and not the software or hardware components that implement the service. However, current technological platforms are still restricted in their application context to in-house solutions.

Future enterprise systems will not scale without properly incorporating principles that made the Web scale to a worldwide communication infrastructure. There is a strong need for significant mechanization of service discovery, negotiation, adaptation, composition, invocation, and monitoring as well as service interaction requiring data, protocol, and process mediation; as well as a balanced integration of services provided by human and machines. All of these technologies can be only fully automated if the semantics is considered as the core enabling technology.

In a semantics-enabled world, the coordination between systems is executed through the use of well (semantically) described services, meaning discovered and selected on the basis of requirements, then orchestrated and adapted or integrated. Solving these problems is a major prerequisite to address technology challenges where the Web of services interconnects billions of entities without the need of using hard-coded adapters between these systems (as the current Web does for information sources) effectively that enable context awareness and discovery, advertising, personalization, and dynamic composition of services.

4.4 Governing Principles

We have identified a number of underlying principles which govern the design of the architecture, its middleware, as well as modeling of business services. These principles reflect fundamental aspects for a service-oriented and distributed environment which all promote intelligent and seamless integration and provisioning of business services. These principles include the following:

- **Service-oriented principle** represents a distinct approach for analysis, design, and implementation which further introduces particular principles that govern aspects of communication, architecture, and processing logic. This includes service reusability, loose coupling, abstraction, composability, autonomy, and discoverability.
- **Semantic principle** allows a rich and formal description of information and behavioral models enabling automation of certain tasks by means of logical reasoning. Combined with the service-oriented principle, semantics allows one to define scalable, semantically rich and formal service models and ontologies allowing one to promote total or partial automation of tasks such as service discovery, contracting, negotiation, mediation, composition, invocation, etc.
- **Problem-solving principle** reflects problem-solving methods as one of the fundamental concepts of artificial intelligence. It underpins the ultimate goal of the architecture which lies in so-called *goal-based discovery and invocation of services*. Users (service requesters) describe requests as goals semantically and independently of services, while architecture solves those goals by means of logical reasoning over descriptions of goals and services. Ultimately, users do not need to be aware of processing logic but only need to care about the result and its desired quality.
- **Distributed principle** allows one to aggregate the power of several computing entities to collaboratively run a task in a transparent and coherent way, so that from a service requester's perspective they can appear as a single and centralized system. This principle allows one to execute a process across a number of components/services over the network, which in turn can promote scalability and quality of the process.

4.5 SESA Vision – Global View

The global view of the architecture, depicted in Fig. 4.2, comprises several layers, namely, (1) stakeholders forming several groups of users of the architecture, (2) problem-solving layer building the environment for stakeholder access to the architecture, (3) service requesters as client systems of the architecture, (4) middleware providing the intelligence for the integration and interoperation of business services, and (5) service providers exposing the functionality of back-end systems as business services. In this section we describe these layers and define service types in the architecture and underlying concepts and technology we use for architecture implementation.

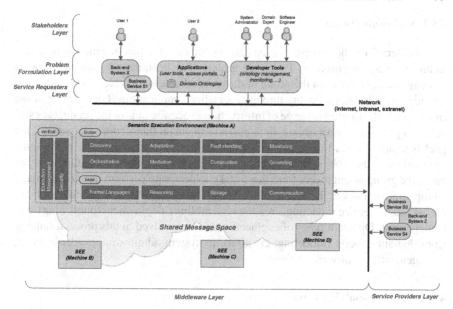

Figure 4.2. Global view of Semantically Enabled Service-oriented Architecture (SESA)

Realizing SESA principles and providing a platform incorporating them is the major necessity to implement the vision of Web Services. There are four types of business services of an infrastructure which are a must for Web Services to deliver their promises:

1. **The stakeholders layer**, which consists of ontologies, applications (e.g., e-tourism, e-government), and developer tools (GUI tools such as those for engineering ontology/Web service descriptions; generic developer tools such as language APIs, parsers/serializers, converters, etc.).

2. **The broker layer**, which consists of discovery, adaptation (including selection and negotiation), composition (Web service composition techniques such as planning), choreography, mediation (ontology mediation – techniques for combining ontologies and for overcoming differences between ontologies – and process mediation – overcoming differences in message ordering, etc.), grounding, fault handling (transactionality, compensation, etc.), and monitoring.

3. **The base layer**, which provides the exchange formalism used by the architecture, i.e., formal languages (static ontology and behavioral, i.e., capability/choreography/orchestration, languages, connection between higher-level descriptions, e.g., WSML), reasoning (techniques for reasoning over formal descriptions; logic programming, description logics, first-order logics, behavioral languages, etc.), and storage and communication.

4. **Vertical services** such as execution management and security (authentication/authorization, encryption, trust/certification).

4.5.1 Stakeholders Layer

Stakeholders form the group of various users which use the functionality of the architecture for various purposes. Two basic groups of stakeholders are identified: users and engineers. Users form the group of those stakeholders for which the architecture provides end-user functionality through specialized applications. For example, users can perform electronic exchange of information to acquire or provide products or services, to place or receive orders, or to perform financial transactions. In general, the goal is to allow users to interact with business processes on-line while at the same time reducing their physical interactions with back-office operations. On the other hand, the group of engineers form those stakeholders who perform development and administrative tasks in the architecture. These tasks support the whole SOA life cycle, including service modeling, creation (assembling), deployment (publishing), and management. Different types of engineers could be involved in this process, ranging from domain experts (modeling, creation), to system administrators (deployment, management), to software engineers.

4.5.2 Problem-Solving Layer

The problem-solving layer contains applications and tools which support stakeholders during formulation of problems/requests and generates descriptions of such requests in the form of user goals.Through the problem-solving layer, the user will be able to solve his/her problems, i.e., formulate a problem, interact with the architecture during processing, and get his/her desired results. This layer contains back-end systems which directly interface the middleware within business processes, specialized applications built for specific purpose in a particular domain, which also provide specific domain ontologies, and developer tools providing functionality for development and administrative tasks within the architecture. Developer tools provide a specific functionality for engineers, i.e., domain experts, system administrators, and software engineers. The functionality of developer tools covers the whole SOA life cycle, including service modeling, creation (assembling), deployment (publishing), and management. The vision is to have an integrated development environment (IDE) for management of the architecture. It should aid the developers through the development process, including engineering of semantic descriptions (services, goals, and ontologies), creation of mediation mappings, and interfacing with architecture middleware and external systems. By combining this functionality, a developer will be allowed to create and manage ontologies, Web Services, goals and mediators, create ontology-to-ontology mediation mappings, and deploy these mappings to the middleware. Applications provide a specialized functionality for architecture end-users. They provide specialized domain-specific ontologies, user interfaces, and application functionality through which stakeholders interact with the architecture and its processes. Through specialized applications in a particular application settings, the technology and its functionality are validated and evaluated.

4.5.3 Service Requesters Layer

Service requesters act as client systems in a client–server settings of the architecture. They are represented by goals created through problem/request formulation by which they describe requests as well as interfaces through which they wish to perform conversation with potential services. Service requesters are present for all applications and tools from the problem-solving layer and are bound to a specific service semantics specification.

4.5.4 Middleware Layer

Middleware is the core of the architecture providing the main intelligence for the integration and interoperation of business services. For purposes of the SESA, we call this middleware "semantic execution environment." The architecture defines the necessary conceptual functionality that is imposed on the architecture through the underlying principles defined in Sect. 4.2. Each such functionality could be realized (totally or partially) by a number of so-called middleware services (see Sect. 4.5.6) We further distinguish this functionality in the following layers: base layer, broker layer, and vertical layer.

The vertical layer defines the middleware framework functionality that is used across the broker and base Layers but which remains invisible to them. This technique is best understood through the so-called "Hollywood principle" that basically means "Don't call us, we'll call you." In this respect, framework functionality always consumes the functionality of broker and base layers, coordinating and managing overall execution processes in the middleware. For example, discovery or data mediation is not aware of the overall coordination and distributed mechanism of the execution management.

- **Execution management** defines the control of various execution scenarios (called execution semantics) and handles distributed execution of middleware services.
- **Security** defines a secure communication, i.e., authentication, authorization, confidentiality, data encryption, traceability, or nonrepudiation support applied within execution scenarios in the architecture.

The broker layer defines the functionality which is directly required for a goal-based invocation of Semantic Web Services. The broker layer includes:

- **Discovery**, which defines tasks for identifying and locating business services which can achieve a requester's goal.
- **Choreography**, which defines formal specifications of interactions and processes between the service providers and the client.
- **Monitoring**, which defines a monitoring of the execution of end-point services. This monitoring may be used for gathering information on invoked services, e.g., quality of service (QoS) related or for identifying faults during execution.
- **Fault handling**, which defines the handling of faults occurring within the execution of end-point Web Services.

- **Adaptation**, which defines an adaptation within a particular execution scenario according to the user's preferences (e.g., service selection, negotiation, contracting).
- **Mediation**, which defines interoperability at the functional, data, and process levels.
- **Composition**, which defines a composition of services into an executable workflow (business process). It also includes orchestration, which defines the execution of a composite process (business process) together with a conversation between a service requester and a service provider within that process.
- **Grounding**, which defines a link between a semantic level and a nonsemantic level (e.g., WSDL) used for service invocation.

The base layer defines functionality that is not directly required in a goal-based invocation of business services; however, they are required by the broker layer for successful operation. The base layer includes:

- **Formal languages**, which define syntactical operations (e.g., parsing), with semantic languages used for semantic description of services, goals, and ontologies.
- **Reasoning**, which defines reasoning functionality over semantic descriptions.
- **Storage and communication**, which defines persistence mechanism for various elements (e.g., services, ontologies) as well as inbound and outbound communication of the middleware.

The SESA middleware can operate in a distributed manner when a number of middleware systems connected using a shared message space operate within a network of middleware systems and empowering this way a scalability of integration processes. The SESA consists of several decoupled services allowing independent refinement of these services – each of them can have its own structure without hindering the overall SESA. Following the SOA design principles, the SESA separates concerns of individual middleware services, thereby separating service descriptions and their interfaces from the implementation. This adds flexibility and scalability for upgrading or replacing the implementation of middleware services which adhere to required interfaces.

4.5.5 Service Providers Layer

Service providers represent various back-end systems. Unlike back-end systems in the service requesters layer which act as clients in a client–server setting of the architecture, the back-end systems in the service providers layer act as servers which provide certain functionality for certain purposes exposed as a business service to the architecture. Depending on the particular architecture deployment and integration scenarios, the back-end systems could originate from one organization (one service provider) or multiple organizations (more service providers) interconnected over the network (Internet, intranet, or extranet). The architecture thus can serve various requirements for business-to-business (B2B) integration, EAI, or application-to-application (A2A) integration. In all cases, functionality of back-end systems is exposed as semantically described business services.

4.5.6 Services in SESA

While some of the SESA functionality is provided as services, the rest remain as the entities required to let the overall system function – they are not services in terms of a SOA. While the middleware and service requesters layers build SESA in terms of services (with some exceptions), the problem-solving layer adds the set of tools and entities which makes SESA a fully fledged semantic SOA.

The core aspect of SOA is the service. In this respect, we distinguish two types of services in SESA, namely, middleware services and business services:

1. **Middleware services** are necessary to enable particular functionality of the architecture – they are the main facilitators for integration, search, and mediation of business services.
2. **Business services** are exposed by service providers, their back-end systems which are external to SESA. Business services are subject of integration and interoperation within the architecture (facilitated by the middleware services) and usually provide a certain value for architecture stakeholders. Such services are in SESA semantically described conforming to a specific semantic service model.

In this respect, the SESA defines *the scope of particular middleware services* in terms of the functionality they should provide. In addition, the SESA defines a *semantic service model for the business services* on which the SESA operates. Particular business services are, however, subject to modeling in application-oriented scenarios. For this purpose, domain-specific ontologies can be designed as part of SESA application design or evaluation. With respect to the distinction between middleware services and business services , the SESA middleware is designed as the SOA on its own. However, it is designed as the facilitator for the integration of semantic business services and as such is not currently considered as semantically enabled but rather as semantically enabling. In order to illustrate the above, Fig. 4.3 depicts middleware and business services within the scope of SEE architecture and SESA, respectively.

4.5.7 Underlying Concepts and Technology

The SESA implementation will build on the underlying concepts and technology provided as the essential input for the work outlined by the roadmap. Development of these concepts and technology started before 2007. SESA builds on and further extends specifications around the conceptual model defined by WSMO, WSML, and reference implementation for the middleware called WSMX. WSMO provides a conceptual model describing all relevant aspects of Web Services in order to facilitate the total or partial automation of service discovery, composition, invocation, etc. The description of WSMO elements is represented using the WSML family of ontology

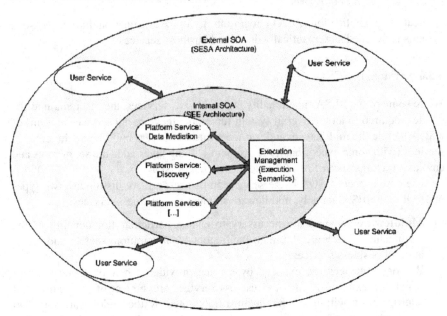

Figure 4.3. Middleware services and business services

languages which consists of a number of variants based on different logical formalisms and different levels of logical expressiveness. WSMO and WSML thus provide grounds for semantic modeling of services as well as for a middleware system
which specifically enacts semantic SOAs. Reference implementation of this middleware system is called WSMX. WSMO is the model being developed for purposes of
modeling of business services. WSMX is the reference implementation of the SESA
providing various functionalities in a form of middleware services which facilitates
integration of semantic business services. In addition, the Web Service Modeling
Toolkit (WSMT) provides an end-user IDE for modeling of business services and
run-time management of the middleware environment.

4.6 SESA Roadmap

With respect to the architecture vision described, we present the scope of the research
roadmap for the upcoming years. The research roadmap is defined in a number of
research areas, each having defined its goals for the period of the roadmap. Each
research goal usually combines major research challenges in Semantic Web Services
and SESA together with an implementation effort related to it. The research area
and its goals have a corresponding architecture component. Thus, on the basis of
the architecture vision and the global view, we identify the following research areas
as architectural components which are further distinguished in layers as depicted in
Fig. 4.4:

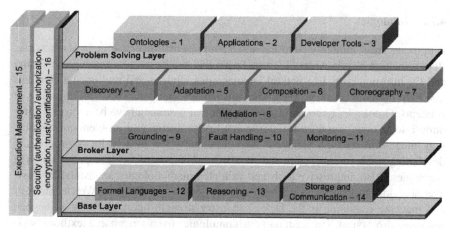

Figure 4.4. SESA components

- The problem-solving layer, which consists of ontologies, applications (e.g., e-tourism, e-business, e-government), and developer tools (GUI tools such as those for engineering ontology/Web service descriptions; generic developer tools such as language APIs, parsers/serializes, converters, etc.).
- The broker layer, which consists of discovery, adaptation (including selection and negotiation), composition (Web service composition techniques such as planning), choreography, mediation (ontology mediation – techniques for combining ontologies and for overcoming differences between ontologies – and process mediation – overcoming differences in message ordering, etc.), grounding, fault handling (compensation, etc.), and monitoring.
- The base layer, which provides the exchange formalism used by the architecture, i.e., formal languages (static ontology and behavioral, i.e., capability/choreography/orchestration, languages, connection between higher-level descriptions), reasoning (techniques for reasoning over formal descriptions; logic programming, description logic, first-order logic, behavioral languages, etc.), and storage and communication.
- Vertical services such as execution management and security (authentication/authorization, encryption, trust/certification).

Each of these components forms a research area for which further goals are identified in following sections.

4.7 SESA Research Areas and Goals

This section describes in more detail research areas which as a result build the functional components that play a role in the SESA. For each research area, the description of the area and the goals are described.

4.7.1 Ontologies

Ontologies are community contracts about a representation of a domain of discourse. Representation here includes (1) formal parts that can be used for machine reasoning and (2) informal parts like natural language descriptions and multimedia elements that help humans establish, maintain, and renew consensus about the meaning of concepts. Ontologies as formal representations of a domain have been proposed for quite a long time as a cure to interoperability problems and problems of application integration, and the Semantic Web community has made a lot of progress in developing stable infrastructure and standardized languages for the representation of ontologies. Also, impressive tools and validated methodologies are available. However, a major bottleneck towards business applications of Semantic Web technology and machine reasoning is the lack of industry-strength ontologies that go beyond academic prototypes. The design of such ontologies from scratch in a textbook-style ontology engineering process is in many cases unattractive, for it would require significant effort, and because the resulting ontologies could not build on top of existing community commitment. Also, real-world problems of data and systems interoperability can only be overcome using Semantic Web technology if ontologies exist that represent the very standards currently in use in systems and databases. Such standards, though mostly informal in nature, are likely the most valuable asset on the way to real business ontologies that can help solve real business interoperability problems, since they reflect some degree of community consensus and contain, readily available, a wealth of concept definitions. However, the transformation of such standards into useful ontologies is not as straightforward as it appears.

Goals and Tasks

- **Maturing Semantic Web foundations**, so that they become compatible with the real-world complexity and scale. In particular, the social interaction and economic dimension of ontologies must be defined.
  - *Ontology engineering.* Methodologies for and prototypes of industry-strength business ontologies, e.g. the gen/tax methodology for deriving ontologies from existing hierarchical standards and taxonomies (UNSPSC, eCl@ss, ...) and eClassOWL, the first serious attempt at building an ontology for e-business applications; and in general advancing the state of the art in e-business data and knowledge engineering, including metrics for content.
  - *Community-driven ontology building.* Methodologies and techniques for evolution of ontologies managed by the user community, including semi-automated approaches and OntoWiki – a Wiki-centric ontology building environment.
  - *Economic aspects of ontology building and usage.* Building ontologies consumes resources, and in an economic setting, these resources are justified and will be spent (by rational economic actors, at least) only if the effort needed to establish and keep alive a consensual representation of a domain of discourse is outweighed by the business gain, in terms of cost, added value, or

strategic dimensions, e.g., process agility. This research branch fuels the use of ontologies in business applications.

- **Building ontologies for core challenges of information systems** in order to realize and evaluate the business benefits and to identify the open research challenges.
  - *Application ontologies.* Ontologies developed for a particular domain such as in e-business, e-government, e-tourism, etc. This includes semantics-supported business process management for mechanization of business process management, ontology-supported electronic procurement, and analysis of the true complexity of business matchmaking, financial reporting, etc.

4.7.2 Applications

All the activities gathered around development of the SESA framework must be tightly coupled to the development and the implementations of the use cases proving the viability of the SESA framework. There are many technologies in the area of Semantic Web Services mainly presented in academic workshops and conferences where various use cases are being defined in alienation. In addition, there does not exist any unified methodology which could be used for comparing these technologies and more importantly, there is no way for industry to evaluate the robustness, applicability, and added values of these technologies. Therefore, progress in scientific development and in industrial adoption is thereby hindered.

Goals and Tasks

It is the goal of applications to analyze processes, infrastructures, and the results of existing real-world scenarios, and to develop a standard set of problems and a public repository for such problems. In addition, the goal is to develop and standardize a community-agreed evaluation methodology:

- **Define the set of standard problems and their levels.** Develop a methodology for evaluating the functionality (versus performance) of semantic service technologies. On the basis of our experience with a group working on the SWS Challenge initiative, applications aim to be involved in a larger community through the W3C Test-Bed Incubator Group.
- **Support of scalable public collaborative development of new problem scenarios and associated services.** In this development, the aim is to standardize the methodology and the infrastructure.
- **The standard methodology for peer review of solutions.** The applications should refrain from recommending technologies or from providing solutions to the Semantic Web Service problems. The focus should be on standardizing the evaluation methodology.

4.7.3 Developer Tools

An IDE is defined as a type of computer software that assists computer programmers to develop software and IDEs such as the Eclipse Java Development Toolkit (JDT) or the NetBeans IDE for developing software in the Java programming language have proven that the productivity of the Java developer can be improved by providing all the tools required by the developer side by side and integrated with one another. The breadth of the field of semantics means that one IDE for all the different languages and technologies is unlikely to happen; however, using technologies like the Eclipse platform will allow the developer to place individual tools or indeed individual IDEs together in order to build the IDE with the tools needed to perform the job at hand. A good example of where such a combination of IDEs would be useful is the Semantic Web Service field. The Eclipse Web Tool Platform (WTP) provides a collection of tools for simplifying the process of building Web service based applications, combining the WTP with an IDE for describing Web Services semantically. With semantics becoming more centric to modern computer science, many different combinations of tools that at this stage cannot even be contemplated will be required. The flexibility of platforms like Eclipse gives a form of future-proofing and puts the design and scale of the resulting IDE into the hands of the user. When describing tools for semantic technologies it is very easy to become focused primarily on ontologies and to forget that there are many different technologies that require tool support. Research topics like Semantic Web Services and semantic business processes are producing many forms of semantic description that must be created by some developer in order to deploy such technologies. Only now are developers of semantic descriptions receiving limited tool support that allows them to focus on the problem at hand and stop grappling with low-level problems like syntax, testing, and deployment of their descriptions. Within the scope of this roadmap the aim is to provide guidelines for the types of tools that should exist within an IDE for a given semantic technology.

Goals and Tasks

- **Creation and maintenance.** Tool support must be available for creating the actual descriptions themselves. It is important that users of different skill levels are supported within the IDE; thus, editing support at different levels of abstraction should be provided. Some users may be very comfortable dealing with textual semantic descriptions, while others may require more visual paradigms for creating descriptions. These different levels of abstraction can also benefit the skilled engineer. Considering ontologies, it may be more convenient for the engineer to create an ontology using a textual representation within a text editor and then to use a graph-based ontology engineering solution to learn more about the ontology and tweak the model that has been created.
- **Validation.** The most common problem that occurs when creating semantic descriptions is incorrect modeling. It can be very easy for an engineer to make a mistake without any tool support. Validation of semantic descriptions is a nontrivial task and validation at both the syntactic and the semantic level can vastly reduce the time developers spend debugging their descriptions. By syntactic validation we mean checking that the actual syntactic structure of the semantic description is correct and by semantic validation we refer to checking that syntactically correct descriptions are semantically valid.

- **Testing.** Once valid semantic descriptions exist the engineer needs to ensure that they behave in the expected manner in their intended environment prior to deploying them. Having testing integrated into the development environment reduces the overhead of the user performing a lengthy, iterative, deploy-test scenario. The engineer will more than likely perform a deploy-test scenario anyway, but having an initial cycle within the development environment can significantly reduce the length of this cycle and the time taken to perform it.
- **Deployment.** Ultimately the descriptions created within the development environment must be used in some run-time system. Deploying descriptions can also be a huge overhead for the engineer and having tool support in an IDE can prevent mistakes occurring at this crucial stage of the process.

4.7.4 Discovery

Within a SOA the discovery of services is the essential building block for creating and utilizing dynamically created applications. However, current technologies only provide a means to describe service interfaces on a syntactical level, providing only limited automation support. Existing solutions for service discovery include UDDI, a standard that allows programmatically publishing and retrieving a set of structured information belonging to a Web service; however, it allows one to retrieve services by predefined categories and keywords, not by their actual semantic properties. There is a lack of means that allow the description of functional and nonfunctional properties of a service on a semantic level. Only with such descriptions is a precise discovery possible.

Given a description of a service, the problem of discovering a desired service can be seen as an information-retrieval problem, which uses keywords to express the desire and uses a document index to match them. However, for mechanizing the discovery task a more fine-grained approach to discovery is required, e.g., to restrict the search space along specific parameters, like location, provider, price, etc. It can be seen as a search for a semistructured entity. Here approaches developed in the context of the Semantic Web, in particular the use of ontologies are a promising approach.

Goals and Tasks

- **Service and domain ontologies.** In order to provide a semantic discovery service both service requests and offers need to be described on a semantic level. While there exist some proposals for upper-level ontologies like WSMO and OWL-S, we need to refine them and provide guidelines for their usage and accompanying domain ontologies.
- **Language and reasoning integration.** Potentially many different logical formalisms can be used to annotate services. Each comes with a specific trade-off between expressivity and computational complexity. It has to be investigated for which use cases a particular formalism is suitable. In addition the reasoning engine for a particular formalism needs to be integrated into the discovery context, such that its usage becomes transparent to the user of a discovery engine.

- **Nonfunctional properties.** Research around service discovery has so far paid much attention to the specification of the functional properties of a service; however, only little effort has been spent on the investigation of the usage of nonfunctional properties within the discovery process. Specific ontologies and matchmaking techniques have to be developed in order to allow a semantic retrieval on nonfunctional properties.
- **Field deployment and verification of existing discovery strategies.** While many concrete formalisms have been proposed, only a few case studies have been performed to validate the appropriateness of a particular approach. Further real-world use cases are required in order to adopt the existing semantic discovery approaches for practical needs.

4.7.5 Adaptation

After discovering a set of potentially useful Web Services, a semantic user agent needs to find out the concrete offers available at the Web Services and that are relevant to the user's goal, generally by communicating with the Web service or with its provider. This process filters out the discovered Web Services that cannot fulfill the goal. This step is required as it is not feasible for a Web service to provide an exhaustive semantic description of all its potential offers. The process of checking whether and under what conditions a service can fulfill a concrete goal is called negotiation in SESA. The results of negotiation are filtered using the functionality of the discovery component to consider only the services that have the appropriate functionality and also nonfunctional properties acceptable to the user. Filtering is followed by building a ranking/order relation based on nonfunctional property criteria like price, availability, etc. Once a list of Web Services than can fulfill the user's concrete goal has been prepared, a SESA must then choose one of the services to invoke. It is important that this selection is tailored to the user's needs, as, for example, while one user may require high quality, another may prefer low price. This process is called selection. Negotiation, ranking, and selection are tasks of the Adaptation Working Group.

Goals and Tasks

- **Semantic and multicriteria based ranking and selection.** Ranking and selection of services could be done along more than one dimension. For example, users might be interested in the cheapest and fastest service providing a certain functionality. A ranking and selection solution which uses semantic descriptions of multiple nonfunctional properties and ranks the services on the basis of their attached logical expressions' nonfunctional properties representations should be developed. This involves development of semantic and multicriteria ranking algorithms and design and implementation of a semantic and multicriteria ranking component.
- **Context-based ranking and selection.** Service ranking and selection must consider contextual information in order to provide relevant results. The goal is to

develop models and algorithms for context-aware ranking and selection. This involves development of context-ranking algorithms.

- **Social-based ranking and selection.** Service ranking and selection remains an open and controversial problem in terms of both social and technical aspects. From a social point of view an honest and fair mechanism is required. An aspect which might be useful especially for ranking services is the "social" aspect of consuming services. Previous customers who have used a service could provide feedback about the service. Furthermore not only users but also groups of users, communities, can be used to "compute" the ranking values of services.
- **Negotiation algorithms.** Negotiation support with use of communication to establish details of Web service offers relevant to user's needs.

4.7.6 Composition

Composition involves methods for Web service composition (WSC), starting from Web service descriptions at various levels of abstraction, specifically, the functional level and the process level. The WSC area is stillat a very early stage of its development. Several techniques have been proposed, mostly based on AI planning or on logical deduction, but all of those still have severe shortcomings. The existing techniques (1) largely or even completely ignore the constraints given in the background ontology in which the Web Services are specified, or (2) largely or even completely ignore the complex inner behavior and interfaces of Web Services, or (3) have severe scalability problems, solving only toy problems with few services, or they suffer from several of these deficiencies.

Goals and Tasks

- **Development of a scalable tool for WSC with powerful background ontologies and partial matches.** The goal is to overcome the lack of a technique that combines adequate treatment of background ontologies (deficiency 1 described above) with scalability (deficiency 3 described above). This will be achieved by building on logics-based search space representations and heuristic functions originating in the area of AI planning.
- **Development of a scalable tool for WSC with plug-in matches, dealing with business policies.** The goal is to overcome the lack of a combination of deficiencies 1 and 3 described above through a particular focus on business process management scenarios. In those, scalability is particularly urgent, since enterprises deal with thousands of services from which the composed service should be combined. Further, business policies – rules governing how services can be executed within or between enterprises – are of paramount importance. Scalability, even in the presence of business policies, will be achieved by exploiting plug-in matches rather than partial matches, and by exploiting the typical forms of ontologies occurring in practice.
- **Integration of techniques for functional-level and process-level WSC.** The goal is to overcome the lack of a combination of deficiencies 2 and 3 described

above, and potentially to build technology that overcomes all three deficiencies (1–3). The idea is to combine techniques from functional-level and process-level WSC, first by establishing ways for their interplay, and later by integrating their underlying core principles. Regarding their interplay, functional-level and process-level WSC essentially provide different trade-offs between accuracy and computational cost; they can be combined to mutually profit from each other's benefits. Regarding the underlying principles, the most effective process-level composition methods today are based on binary decision diagrams; this will be replaced with the logics-based search space representation underlying advanced functional-level composition. This approach allows for more flexibility and can be used to model and take into account also the background ontology, while at the same time reducing computational costs through consequent exploitation of problem structure.

4.7.7 Choreography

Techniques for service choreography play a key role in creation of new opportunities for collaborations between service requesters and providers, and thus for creation of new services. The choreography part of SESA defines formal specifications of inter-actions and processes between the service providers and clients. Current approaches to service choreography languages have been criticized for being too procedurally oriented. With the move towards service orientation, where entities are autonomous and need to agree on the collaborations between them, where no central point of control might exist, a more declarative modeling style for interactions is required (i.e., "what" without having to state the "how"). Moreover, reasoning techniques for such a language that would enable a flexible and dynamic integration of service requesters and providers in a collaborative environment are currently missing.

Goals and Tasks

- **Declarative choreography language.** The goal here is to develop a declarative process language which should allow for formal specifications of interactions and processes between the service providers and clients, Such a declarative language would enable non-IT experts to easily represent service behaviors and interactions, enabling a more flexible way of engaging in new collaborations.
- **Reasoning tasks for choreography.** The goal here is to define reasoning tasks that should be performed using the declarative language. Verification techniques such as contracting or enactments are examples of reasoning tasks. Such techniques will enable an automated, flexible, and dynamic integration of service requesters and providers in a collaborative environment.
- **Tool support for choreography.** The goal here is to implement an engine to support the execution of interactions, as well as to support reasoning in the proposed declarative language.

4.7.8 Mediation

Heterogeneity problems and mediators have been intensively investigated in the last decade but the key solution that would enable the decisive leap towards automation is yet to be found. Semantics is changing the problem specifications and service-orientation paradigms offer new ways of designing, deploying, and using mediators while at the same time posing new challenges and setting new requirements. That is, data and processes can be formally and unambiguously described, while services and SOAs allow the development of decoupled, transparent, and flexible software components, including mediators.

Goals and Tasks

- **Advanced support for data mediation.** Semiautomatic design-time tools should be developed in order to allow domain experts to identify and capture the heterogeneity problems between different models of overlapping domains. Special attention will be given to user profiles and expertise levels in order to separate the tools for trained domain experts and the tools designated for casual users of ontologies. Furthermore, at this level, alignments between various models will be part of a community validation process where users can add and remove links between the models in order to achieve and maintain agreed-upon interlinked models.
- **Advanced support for process mediation.** Heterogeneity appears on the process level as well no matter whether these processes are enterprise internal processes or public processes used in describing the visible behavior of particular services. Such heterogeneous processes need to be part of collaborative scenarios that can range from simple peer-to-peer interaction to complex compositions. Semiautomatic tool support allowing the tailoring of such processes in order to overcome the heterogeneity problems should be provided. Further, more such tools should support annotation of existing process representation standards with semantics based on ontological domain models.
- **Service mediation by mediation services.** Mediator systems able to resolve specific types of heterogeneity problems should be encapsulated and deployed as mediation services. Such services should be developed for well-defined mediation scenarios while preserving the generality of their offered functionality.
- **Semantic descriptions for the mediation services and mediation libraries.** Mediation services should be semantically described as any other resources. In this way their functionality can be properly advertised and their intended usage explicitly stated. Furthermore, they can become part of an intelligent mechanism for service discovery, composition, and invocation. Additionally, such semantically described mediation services will be organized in semantic mediation patterns that can be directly applied in complex heterogeneity scenarios. In addition, such services should be organized in libraries supporting intelligent mediation service retrieval (by providing customizable mediators classifications), patterns construction (based on the semantic descriptions of the mediation service and on the mediation goal to be achieved), and governance mechanisms (by exploring service and patterns dependencies and impact analysis).

4.7.9 Grounding

Legacy systems represent valuable assets for most of their owners and usually completely replacing them is not an option. As such, methodologies that will allow the integration of these systems with the new emerging paradigms and technologies have to be developed. For example, XML schemas and XML data have to be lifted to ontological level in order to allow semantic-aware systems to act on this data. In addition, since all tasks related to discovery, selection, composition, etc. operate in SESA on semantic descriptions, the link between a semantic service and the underlying technology for communication (e.g., HTTP, SOAP, etc.) needs to be defined. The basis for grounding has been established within the W3C Semantic Annotations for WSDL Working Group (SAWSDL WG), allowing hooking semantic descriptions with WSDL elements.

Goals and Tasks

- **Semiautomatic tools allowing the creation of transformation between syntax-based and semantic models.** Specifying the transformations between Web service XML messages and the semantic data currently requires deep knowledge both of the structure of the XML message and of the ontology. Methods for semiautomated creation of grounding should be created.
- **Grounding to other specifications.** Grounding definitions to specifications other than WSDL should be defined. It should be possible to use, e.g., REST services with semantic descriptions, etc.

4.7.10 Fault Handling

Fault handling defines the handling of faults or errors occurring within the execution of end-point Web Services. Fault handling is important in SESA as the effect of a Web service failure will reach beyond the scope of the individual service if it is part of a composition. The aim of fault handling is to ensure that the failure of the service has a minimal impact, and that the most appropriate action is taken to deal with it. This may be simply returning an error message to the user and terminating any further actions. It may involve more complex tasks such as replacement of a failed service with a substitute service, or rolling back actions previously carried out by other services in a composition .Currently the BPEL specification has some provision for fault handling via the catches and some support for rollback. The WS-Transaction family of specifications from OASIS also has provision for basic fault handling, including distinguishing application faults from communication faults.

Goals and Tasks

- **Increased automation of fault handling.** Semantic descriptions of services in SESA will enable an increased level of automation in fault handling. Current fault handling techniques allow either a very generic level of fault handling (e.g., gracefully exit and report errors) for all services, or require specific actions to be hard-coded for each service. The aim will be able to make full use of the semantic descriptions and reasoning to make intelligent decisions about fault handling automatically (e.g., in this context a particular error can be ignored).

- **More complex fault handling tasks.** Tasks such as automatic service substitution are rarely carried out in current SOA-based systems, as there is not sufficient semantic information about services to allow an equivalent service to be identified and substituted. The aim will be to increase the use of more complex fault handling tasks in SESA with the aid of semantic descriptions and reasoning.

4.7.11 Monitoring

Monitoring is concerned with checking the progress of service execution and advising the user/agent of abnormal events. Within SESA, monitoring of services is essential as the behavior of individual services has an effect on successful completion of a composition. Detecting failure or abnormalities will require some action to be taken (e.g., rollback previous actions, or substitute failed service).

Currently the most popular methods for Web service monitoring are based around the Management Using Web Services (MUWS) OASIS specification, which defines a flexible, expandable approach to monitor manageable resources. Specifically Web service monitoring is handled under a subspecification called Management of Web Services (MOWS).

MUWS defines how the ability to manage, or, how the manageability of, an arbitrary resource can be made accessible via Web Services. Manageable resources can be accessed with a Web service end point. The manageability consumer exchanges messages with the end point in order to subscribe to events, get events, and request. The type of information available is things such as number of requests, number of failed requests, number of successful requests, service time, maximum response time, and last response time.

Goals and Tasks

- **Monitoring framework based on ontologies.** Currently MUWS defines parameters for monitoring based on a rigid XML schema. A move to a more flexible ontology-based definition would give more expressivity and allow monitoring to be tailored to a specific context.
- **Increased automation of monitoring and link to fault handling.** In a more automated SESA-based system, the system should be able to proactively monitor the execution of services, identify when a particular abnormality has occurred, and take the best action at the time to deal with it. For example, if a service failed the system should detect it and replace it with another service that performs the same task. Current methods of monitoring will identify problems with Web Services but there is no automatic next step to fault handing and recovery. This should be included in the scope of SESA.

4.7.12 Formal Languages

Descriptions in SESA need different formal languages for the specification of different aspects of knowledge and services. These descriptions can be decomposed into four dimensions: static knowledge (ontologies), functional description (capabilities), behavioral description, and nonfunctional properties. There are several knowledge-representation formalisms used for formal languages, including description logic and logic programming, datalog subset of F-logic, Horn subset of F-logic with negation under the well-founded semantics, description logic SHIQ, first-order language with nonmonotinic extensions, etc.

Goals and Tasks

The major objective is to integrate first order logic based and nonmonotonic logic programming based languages, the explicitization of context for use with scoped negation, and the development of rules for the Semantic Web (through the W3C RIF working group). Furthermore, requirements for the functional descriptions of services and as well as semantics for Web service functionality need to be devised. Requirements need to be gathered for the description of a choreography and an orchestration and a semantics needs to be devised. Finally, the purpose and usage of nonfunctional requirements need to be investigated. In particular, the goals will be:

- **Integrating knowledge based on classical first-order logic and nonmonotonic logic programming.** Important issues are the representational adequacy of the integration, as well as decidable subsets and a proof theory, so that reasoning becomes possible; scoped default negation; rules for the Semantic Web – RIF Working Group; connection between Semantic Web languages RDF, OWL.
- **Functional specification of services and a semantics needs to be devised** which can be combined with the language for the description of ontologies, in order to enable the use of ontologies for the description of Web service functionality. An important use case for the functional description of services is discovery. Therefore, it is expected that many requirements for the functional description of services will come from the discovery research goal.
- **Advanced behavioral description.** There exist several formal languages which are suitable for behavioral description. Examples are transaction logic, situation calculus, and action languages. Requirements need to be gathered for the description of choreography and an orchestration and semantics needs to be devised. A key challenge is the combination of this language with ontology languages in order to enable the reuse of ontology vocabulary in the choreography and orchestration descriptions. Finally, this language needs to be connected to the language for capability description in order to prove certain correspondences between the functional and behavioral descriptions of services.
- **Nonfunctional properties.** Nonfunctional properties can at least be divided into two categories: (1) metadata, e.g., author, description, etc., of the WSML statements in a description and (2) actual nonfunctional properties, i.e., actual properties of services (e.g., pricing, QoS, transactions). Nonfunctional properties require a deeper investigation into their purpose and their usage.

4.7.13 Reasoning

The SESA necessitates effective reasoning for different tasks such as service discovery, process and data mediation, and integration. To enable processing of these tasks in an automated manner, the SESA utilizes machine reasoning over formally represented service specifications. We are developing an Integrated Rule Inference System (IRIS) which is a scalable and extensible reasoner tool for WSML. The system implements different deductive database algorithms and novel optimization techniques.

Goals and Tasks

- **Reasoning techniques with large data sets.** In the context of the Semantic Web, applications might require vast volumes of data to be processed in a short time. Current reasoning algorithms are developed rather for small, closed, trustworthy, consistent, and static domains. Therefore, these algorithms need to be extended and adapted in order to be applied to large and dynamically changing knowledge bases. One challenging approach to achieve a scalable reasoning is to combine existing deductive and database techniques with methods for searching the Web (utilizing semantic annotations). This line of research considers reasoning in distributed environments as well.
- **New techniques for description logics reasoning.** Description logics are a family of knowledge-representation formalisms characterized by sound, complete, and (empirically) tractable reasoning. However, applications in areas such as e-science and the Semantic Web are already stretching the capabilities of existing description logics systems. Key issues here are the provision of efficient algorithms that allow (advanced) applications (1) to scale up to knowledge bases of practical relevance and (2) to leverage expressive languages for capturing domain knowledge.
- **Reasoning with integrating frameworks based on classical first-order logic and nonmonotonic logic programming.** Two lines of research will be explored:
  - Reasoning with decidable fragments of such integrating frameworks.
  - Reasoning with undecidable fragments using proof-theoretic techniques.

4.7.14 Storage and Communication

Storage and communication form the underlying mechanisms of the SESA needed for coordination of the execution of middleware services within the platform. The novel communication and coordination paradigm is called triple-space computing (TSC). TSC is recently receiving attention in open distributed systems like the World Wide Web and pervasive computing environments. TSC supports the Web's dissemination idea of persistently publishing and reading. Furthermore, it is based on the convergence of tuple-space technology (originating from Linda) and Semantic Web (service) technology where RDF triples provide the natural link from tuple spaces to triple spaces. Having machine-understandable semantics integrated in the middleware makes this approach particularly useful for SESAs. TSC can be used for dynamic management of middleware services, coordination of middleware services, resource management and external communication with SESA.

Goals and Tasks

- **TSC establishment.** Interaction interfaces, specification of security and trust support, ontology-driven space management for the development of self-adaptive, and reflective triple-space kernels for the integration of scalable semantic clustering and distributed querying.
- **Dynamic management of middleware services.** Asynchronous coordination of middleware services through local triple spaces, running middleware processes over triple spaces.
- **Resource management.** A unified storage infrastructure with standardized access policies and interfaces replacing dedicated repositories and hiding the complexity of different types of resources. Thus, interfacing of triple-space kernels with the resource management, installing RDF-based access to resources, and management of distributed resources need to be developed.
- **External communication with SESA based on TSC.** SOAP-enabled Web service execution over triple spaces, grounding of SOAP messages to TSC, lifting of RDF-based messages to SOAP.

4.7.15 Execution Management

Execution management as the kernel of the SESA is responsible for the coordination of middleware services. It realizes the overall operational semantics of the middleware which lets the system achieve the functional semantics of its client-side interface. It orchestrates the functionality of the middleware services into a coherent process in an orderly and consistent fashion. This process is defined by so -alled execution semantics which defines how particular middleware services need to interact so that SESA can provide particular functionality to its users. The research focuses on the functional as well as the operational combination of the individuals services of the middleware.

Goals and Tasks

- **Definition and refinement of execution semantics.** Definition of various execution semantics for particular execution scenarios.
- **TSC Integration.** Interkernel communication and coordination, distributed execution of tasks;. The communication between execution management and middleware services through publishing and subscribing to the data as sets of triples over triple space. Other than the benefits of asynchronous communication, it will achieve decoupling of individual middleware services.

4.7.16 Security

In the context of SESA, security will cover many areas, including authenticating access to services, preventing misuse of services, encryption, and data privacy. Security will be an important concern to ensure that services are accessed correctly, by the authorized people, and that confidential or sensitive data is securely stored and transmitted. There are currently many Web Services standards relating to security, the most prominent being the recently completed WS-Security 1.1 specification from OASIS.

4.8 Summary

This chapter outlined a comprehensive framework that integrates two complimentary and revolutionary technical advances, SOAs and the Semantic Web, into a single computing architecture that we call SESA. We presented an emerging SOC paradigm and the implemental architecture SOA as the starting point. After analyzing the advantages and shortcomings of SOA, we provided the Semantic Web Services execution environment challenges and requirements, all of which are involved with the semantics extension on SOA. Based on those prerequisites, SESA is proposed as a Semantic Web Services execution environment. While SOA is widely acknowledged for its potential to revolutionize the world of computing, this success is dependent on resolving two fundamental challenges that SOA does not address, namely, integration, and search or mediation. In a service-oriented world, millions of services must be discovered and selected on the basis of requirements, then orchestrated and adapted or integrated. SOA depends on but does not address either search or integration. Basically, we provide SESA grounding principles and global views with various layers. More detailed component description and technical building blocks are provided in the following chapters.

5

SESA Middleware

This chapter provides a technical description for the middleware layer of the semantically enabled service-oriented architecture (SESA), introduced in the last chapter, following the view-centric guidelines of the IEEE Recommended Practice for Architectural Descriptions of Software-Intensive Systems (IEEE 1471). We look in more detail at the functionality required of each of the middleware services and suggest technology-neutral interfaces for them. The chapter also includes a description of the technology used to design and implement an open-source prototype for the SESA middleware and provides the middle chapter of three describing the overall SESA environment. The last chapter provided a high-level view of what is meant by SESA. This chapter extends the technical description by providing a view of the processes supported by SESA and how they are defined.

IEEE 1471 [89] recommends that software architecture descriptions be organized into one or more constituents called architectural views. Each view is used to represent the concerns of a particular viewpoint of one or more stakeholders in the architecture. In this context, stakeholders have an interest in, or concerns relative to, the system. Concerns include system considerations such as performance, reliability, scalability, security, etc.

A system stakeholder is defined as "an individual, team or organization (or classes thereof) with interests in or concerns relative to a system." The purpose of describing a system architecture is to record the architecture in such a way that it addresses the concerns and interest of these various perspectives. Identifying architecture stakeholders enables multiple different, sometimes overlapping, perspectives to be taken into account. We identify the following stakeholders:

- System designers (may wish to incorporate aspects of SESA into a system).
- A designer of a Semantic Web Services execution environment (like WSMX [95] or IRS [153]).
- A developer of any of the services defined for the Semantic Execution Environment (SEE) middleware that enables SESA applications.
- Information modelers, including those responsible for WSMO descriptions of goals, Web Services, ontologies, and/or mediators.

- Clients of SESA-based systems, e.g., a client who has a goal that needs to be fulfilled on the basis of a SESA.

Each set of stakeholders has various concerns with respect to the architecture from their particular perspective, including:

- What is the functionality of a SESA system?
- What are the architectural properties associated with SESA? For example, extensability, evolvability, degree of coupling, provability of goal–Web service matching, etc.
- How do I interact with the system?
- Are there any constraints on how individual services should be designed and implemented?
- What kind of technology can be used to build a SESA?
- What processes does SESA support and can these be configured?

This is just a sample of possible concerns and is by no means exhaustive. Each view of the architecture is associated with at least one stakeholder and must reflect the concerns of the stakeholder. IEEE 1471 defines views as "a representation of a whole system from the perspective of a related set of concerns." Viewpoints then are described as a "pattern or template from which to develop individual views by establishing the purposes and audience for a view and the techniques for its creation and analysis." In the previous chapter, we focused on a global view of what is meant by SESA. This chapter looks at two additional views:

1. Services view: Functional descriptions and interfaces of the middleware and base services.
2. Technology view: A look at the technology used in the design and implementation of the WSMX prototype for SESA.

The following chapter describes a view on the execution semantics for SESA, which is the mechanism by which the processes SESA supports are described.

5.1 Services Viewpoint

Services are the basic building blocks of the SESA, meaning SESA itself uses a Service-Oriented Architecture to provide the middleware for flexible service-oriented applications. This leads to a somewhat fractal structure as SESA, with its Service-Oriented Architecture, facilitates the construction of service-oriented applications. It means that the middleware services provided by SESA can themselves be used by SESA to allow for changing data models, process strategies, implementations, or policy. Three logical layers within the SESA middleware services were identified in Figure 4.2:

1. **Broker services** that directly enable a service requester to discover a provider and mediate between potentially heterogeneous models.

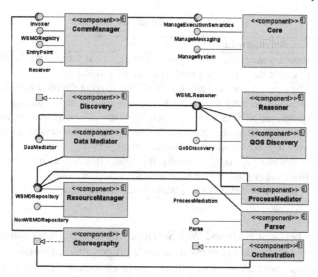

Figure 5.1. UML component diagram for middleware services

2. **Base services** used by the broker services for logical inferencing and reasoning support, support for declarative ontological languages, and persistent storage.
3. **Vertical services** required across the board by the SESA middleware, including security and trust.

Figure 5.1 illustrates a UML component model showing the interfaces that are provided and required by the services in the broker and base layers. Interfaces are represented as lines terminated with a circle (sometime referred to as lollypop sticks). Where one service requires an interface provided by another, a line with a cup at the end is drawn from the dependent service to the desired interface. An example is that the data mediator service requires the reasoner interface.

In the following subsections we describe the three middleware service layers, with one exception. Security is a major topic in its own right and we make the assumption that SESA adopts the security mechanisms of the underlying technologies on which it builds (Web service and message-based systems). We are most interested in the broker and base services as they provide the novel aspects of the middleware.

5.1.1 Broker Services

Service Discovery

The discovery service is concerned with finding Web service descriptions that match the goal specified by the service requester. A service requester provides the WSMO description of a goal to be achieved (described in terms of a desired capability with preconditions, assumptions, effects, and postconditions). This is matched against WSMO descriptions of Web Services available to the discovery service. As the level

Table 5.1. Discovery service interface

Aspect	Detailed information
Description	Provides access to the Semantic Web Service discovery mechanism of SESA based on the conceptual model provided by WSMO.
Provided to	The core service has responsibility for managing the life cycle of instances of execution semantics and it therefore may need to invoke the discovery service (processes on SESA are executed as instances of execution semantics as described in Chap. 6). Additionally, the orchestration engine service may also need to make invocations to the discovery service.
Inputs	A WSMO goal and, optionally, input data specified as instances of concepts from one or more WSMO ontologies.
Outputs	A list of unordered WSMO Web service descriptions.

of description between goals and Web Services will naturally vary and because it is impractical for service descriptions to include all possible information on the service they provide, we define service discovery to contain three distinct phases. Our approach builds on that put forward in [114, 202]. Both suggest a two-phase discovery approach, to which we add an additional phase, called data-fetch [213], where information unavailable in the static service description may be *fetched* from the candidate services at discovery time. The interface provided by the discovery service is described in Table 5.1.

Semantic Web Services discovery may be enriched through the addition of ontologically defined quality-of-service (QoS) attributes as described in [215]. The focus here is on providing upper-level ontologies for describing various domains for QoS attributes that may be relevant to service descriptions. Nonfunctional properties are introduced to the Semantic Web Service descriptions whose values are defined in these QoS ontologies. A suitable reasoner is able to compare required versus offered QoS characteristics and return a list of matching services, ordered by criteria specified by the service requester. For example, an ontological definition for response times may be shared by both the goal and the service descriptions and a goal may be specified to include a requirement on response times along with a request to return any matching service descriptions in descending order of how quickly they promise to respond. The corresponding interface, *QoSDiscovery*, is described in Table 5.2.

Data Mediation

Every time data is exchanged as messages between services, the owners of each service must be confident that they will be able to correctly interpret the data types used in the messages and that all parties to the message exchange share a common understanding of the meaning of those data types. This often turns out to be nontrivial owing to the independent nature of service evolution even within a single organization.

In the SESA, the data mediation service has the role of reconciling the data heterogeneity problems that can appear during discovery, composition, selection, or

Table 5.2. Quality-of-service discovery service interface

Aspect	Detailed information
Description	Provides access to the discovery mechanism extended to take account of quality-of-service attributes and their respective values.
Provided to	As with the discovery interface in Table 5.1, QoSDiscovery may be called by the core service as part of the execution of an instance of an execution semantics.
Inputs	A WSMO goal including quality-of-service attributes, optional input data specified as instances of one or more WSMO ontologies, and a WSMO defining a model for ranking the list of discovered services.
Outputs	A list of ordered WSMO Web service descriptions, ordered in the terms specified by the input ranking ontology.

Table 5.3. Data mediation interface

Aspect	Detailed information
Description	Applies mapping rules between ontologes on instances of the source ontology to create corresponding instances of the target ontology.
Provided to	Data mediation may be required during service discovery, orchestration, and as an essential part of process mediation.
Inputs	IRIs identifying the source and target ontologies and a set of instances of concepts from the source ontology.
Outputs	A set of instances of concepts from the target ontology corresponding to the input source ontology instances. The relationship between the input and output instances is exactly defined by the mapping rules.

invocation of Web Services. We propose that that this service use the interontology mappings described in a declarative mapping language, such as that defined in [149]. This allows for scaling, as a single logical service can provide all data mediation requirements, independent of the number of ontologies that must be supported. Naturally, the run-time aspect of this service depends on the availability of the mappings. We hold that the creation of these mappings requires the involvement of domain experts but their job is significantly aided by the availability of mapping tools such as that provided in the Web Services Modeling Toolkit (WSMT).[1]

Two aspects of these mappings need to be taken into account in the design of the data mediation service. The first is that the mappings need to be stored, implying the data mediation service has a requirement for access to a persistent mappings repository. The second is that the mappings are not tied to a formal language and require grounding to such a language before they can be used. Once grounded, the mappings can be used by a reasoner to provide instances of a target ontology on provision of instances of the source ontology. This implies a dependency of the data mediation service on the logical reasoner service. There is a single interface for the data mediation service and this is shown in Table 5.3.

---

[1] http://sourceforge.net/projects/wsmt/

Choreography Engine

In WSMO, choreography interface descriptions define both the messages that an
entity expects to send and receive, and the control flow between those messages.
Choreography interfaces belonging to Web Services are related to how the overall
capability of the service can be achieved, while those belonging to goals are related to
how the supplier of the goal wishes to get the capability being sought. For example,
a Web service selling IBM notebook computers may use the RosettaNet PIP3A4[2]
protocol to specify that it expects to send and receive the following messages in this
order:

- Receive a purchase order message.
- Send a purchase order acknowledgement message.
- Send a purchase order conformation message.
- Receive a purchase order conformation acknowledgement message.

This message exchange can be considered as a definition of a business process
to achieve a given capability. It does not care whether a service with that capability
is designed to implement all its functionality by itself or if it uses other services for
some of the steps. What the choreography interface is explicitly stating is that the
only way to obtain the service functionality is through the exchange of the specified
messages in the specified order. WSMO choreography interfaces are defined using
ontologized abstract state machines. In essence, each time a goal and a Web service
are determined to match each other an instance of each of their choreographies must
be created and the flow of messages through those choreography interfaces handled.
The choreography engine is responsible for this task.

As abstract machines state machines, choreography interfaces consist of a universe (the kinds of data available to the choreography) and a set of rules (conditional,
update, block-parallel) that operate on instances of data from the universe. The choreography engine service for SESA has to be able to handle these descriptions where
the universe is represented by the *state signature*, in terms of WSMO ontologies,
and the rules are specified using logical expressions written in terms of the WSML
variant being used (WSML-Rule [54] is used for all the examples in this thesis).

The engine works as follows. Choreography interface instances for the goal and
Web service are created. Each has an associated knowledge base to which instances
of ontological concepts can be added. After each change to either knowledge base,
the conditions in the headers of the respective sets of rules are examined to see if any
of the rules *fire*. The firing of a rule may result in data being either sent to or from
the goal or Web service owning that choreography interface. The interface for the
choreography engine is described in Table 5.4.

Orchestration Engine

The WSMO model for Web Services recognizes that each Web service may achieve
its functionality through a composition of other Web Services. This is described as

---

[2] http://www.rosettanet.org/

Table 5.4. Choreography engine interface

Aspect	Detailed information
Description	Allows registration and state-update operations. Registration involves telling the engine to create an instance of a choreography interface (and associated knowledge base) in its internal memory. This may be a new or a preexsiting choreography interface. The latter is the case for long-running interactions whose state should be stored in persistent storage and reloaded when new messages for that choreography instance arrive. Updating the state means providing the instance of the choreography interface with data needed by the control flow it specifies. Rules are run over the data provided and may result in the invocation of a service.
Provided to	The choreography engine can be invoked directly after discovery if no data or process mediation is required. Otherwise, it is expected that the mrocess Mediation service creates the messages that this service receives.
Inputs	A set of ontological instances corresponding to a subset of the concepts defined in the state signature of the choreography.
Outputs	No value is returned.

the *orchestration* of the Web service and resembles a process definition. Each step in the orchestration can be represented as a WSMO goal or Web service description. Describing a process in terms of goals to be achieved at each step adds great flexibility as the binding of goals to services can be deferred to execution time and handled by the execution environment.

Although it may seem counterintuitive to provide internal details of how a service is composed in the service description itself, this can prove to be very useful in environments where dynamic service composition is a requirement or where the software process is stable but the providers of steps in the process may change. For example, a Web portal for a telecoms broker may allow a customer to create a request for a product bundle including broadband, landline, and provisioning for a Web site. The broker has access to multiple service providers for each product and wants to defer choosing the best set of providers for each bundle request until run time. The customer request is written as a goal and matched against a Web service with an orchestration having three steps (one for each product being ordered) each represented by a WSMO goal. Using goals means that the broker retains the flexibility of allowing each goal to be bound to the most suitable service at run time when the service is needed. This is in contrast to hard-wiring a business process to specific services when the process is designed.

As with any other form of integration, each goal in a composition described by an orchestration may have its own information model. This mirrors a common situation in workflows where the data flow aspect can only be defined across heterogeneous data models through the use of data transformations. These data transformations are often designed to work on the structure rather than the semantics of the data. We have already described how the data mediation service enables data heterogeneity to be overcome through mappings between ontological concepts. This more generic and flexible approach can be applied to data flow between steps in a service orchestration.

Table 5.5. Orchestration engine interface

Aspect	Detailed information
Description	An instance of an orchestration must be registered to the engine before it can be used. The registration operation creates an orchestration instance and its associated knowledge base. The ontologies used by the orchestration may be imported to the knowledge base at this point or later, e.g., when the first message for the orchestration arrives. A second operation of the interface called updateState is required to allow new data be made available to the orchestration instance so that its state can be updated.
Provided to	The orchestration engine is accessed by the core of SESA which executes the abstract descriptions of the various supported execution semantics. We describe the core in Sect. 5.1.2.
Inputs	The initialization of the orchestration requires the identifier (IRI) of the Web service description containing the orchestration.
Outputs	The registration returns an identifier to the instance of the orchestration. The updateState operation does not return any value.

Data mediation in this context can be explicitly or implicitly declared. Implicit means that when the orchestration description is created, specific data mediation steps are introduced into the orchestration description. Explicit means that the engine executing the orchestration description has sufficient information available to it, at run time, to determine (1) if mediation is required and (2) if a mapping between the source and target ontologies is available to be executed.

Assuming that suitable mappings exist between the two ontologies, it is possible for the orchestration engine to find these mappings and apply them on-the-fly at run time. This is because an orchestration is essentially a composition of choreographies, where the output of the choreography of a goal (or service) at one step provides input for the choreography of another step. Where a data mismatch occurs, the orchestration engine can examine respective choreographies to determine the ontologies used. It can then identify if a set of conceptual mappings exist (see the "Data Mediation" section) and apply the mappings to the instance of the concept to be transformed.

In practice, it may prove more effective for this work to be carried out when the orchestration is being composed. That way, explicit calls to the data mediation service can be incorporated into the orchestration description as required. Table 5.5 describes the required interface for the orcestration engine.

5.1.2 Base Services

The base services represent functional services fundamental to the infrastructure of the SESA system. They are described in the following sections in terms of their functionality and interfaces.

Core

The SESA essentially supports distribution as each part of its functionality is provided as a service that can be designed and implemented as part of a distributed system.

However, the architecture is not designed as a pure peer-to-peer (P2P) network. There is a need for a coordinating service (the core) that takes responsibility for providing a messaging infrastructure and for managing administrative tasks such as the loading of services and fault monitoring. Service loading can occur either through a defined list when the core is started (bootstrapping) or on-the-fly (hot-deployment). It is important to note that the only functional restriction on the location of services with respect to the core is that they be uniquely identified using Web identifiers and reachable through the chosen messaging implementation. For example, a shared tuple space would mean that services could be located on any physical machine or network that has access to that shared space.

The messaging infrastructure must be transparent to the other services in the architecture. This maintains the property of strong decoupling of services from each other and avoids restrictions on the designers of the implementation for the various services. To achieve this transparency, the loading and hot-deployment of services must take care of adding whatever deployment code is necessary to services. One possible technique for this is the use of deployment configuration files and wrappers. The core is responsible for handling three main functional requirements:

1. A framework for the management, including monitoring and starting and stopping the system.
2. Facilitating the communication between services. Messages must be accepted and routed to a suitable target service, enabling the communication between as well as the coordination of services.
3. Support for the life cycle of execution semantics. Execution semantics specify the process types that are available to run on the SESA. They enable the separation of the definition of what the architecture does from how it achieves it. Multiple definitions of execution semantics are supported and multiple instances of each execution semantics may run concurrently.

There are three interfaces for the core. These are ManageSystem, Messaging, and ExecutionSemantics, shown in Tables 5.6, 5.7, and 5.8, respectively.

External Communications Manager

While the core provides the infrastructure for messaging between the various services that make up the SESA middleware, there is also a need to interact with services and entities that are external to SESA. This is the role of the external communications manager (ECM) service. The service should be open to supporting as many transport and messaging protocols as possible and this support should be transparent to SESA.

The link between the semantic description of a service and the concrete specification of the service's end points and operations (e.g., provided by WSDL) is defined by the grounding. When a service is to be invoked, the ECM service must be able to manage any transformations necessary in terms of data representation and/or communication protocols. For example, typically Web Services expect to receive SOAP messages over HTTP with the SOAP payload represented in XML conforming to a specified XML Schema definition. As the internal representation of data within

Table 5.6. Core: ManageSystem interface

Aspect	Detailed information
Description	In this design, the Core provides the microkernel for the SESA system. It must be explicitly started and stopped, it must be possible to add and remove services while the system is running, and it should be possible to extract information on the health of the system as a whole.
Provided to	The operations provided by this interface are aimed at system administrators and would most likely be best presented through a graphical user interface dashboard type of application.
Inputs	Starting takes no input. Stopping takes an identifier of the system. Monitoring requires the system identifier and identifiers of one or more monitor types on which information should be gathered.
Outputs	Starting returns an identifier for the started system. Stopping and service management have no explict functional return information aside from possible confirmation messages. Monitoring returns information such as the health and throughput of services and the system as a whole.

Table 5.7. Core: Messaging interface

Aspect	Detailed information
Description	The core provides the functionality of a message bus accepting messages represented as events and routing each of them to a target service that has subscribed to that event. The routing takes place in the context of a particular instance of an execution semantics.
Provided to	All services in the architecture participate in the messaging mechanism but this should be transparent to them. The transparency should be made possible by the addition of whatever additional code is necessary at the time the service is deployed to the SESA system, using a service deployment descriptor (typically an XML file). It is this additional code that interacts with the messaging system, isolating it from the service. The service should only be invoked by its defined interface.
Inputs	Subscription requires the specification of an event type for the message and an identifier for the service instance. Sending a message must specify the message type and the instance of the execution semantics to which it belongs. Receiving a message means that the core must be able to *push* a message to services that have subscribed to that particular message type. (Another possibility that does not require subscription is to use a *pull* method where services check the core at regular intervals to see if any message of a suitable type is available.) Either way, the target service must receive the message and the instance of the execution semantics specifing the context in which it was sent.
Outputs	In terms of the logical functionality, there is no explicit output.

SESA is in terms of WSMO, this must be *lowered* from a rich semantic language to the structure syntax of XML.

Communication must naturally also be supported in the opposite direction, i.e., from a service requester to SESA. Continuing the last example of a Web service using SOAP over HTTP with XML content, messages must be *lifted* to WSML before

Table 5.8. Core: Execution Semantics interface

Aspect	Detailed information
Description	Execution semantics is the name given to the process definitions that the SESA can support. It separates the description of the process from its implementation.
Provided to	SESA provides an external interface that allows for a service requester to request that a goal be achieved or that a specific service be invoked. This interface is attached to the communication manager service. Each such user request results in the creation of an instance of a suitable execution semantics to deal with the request. Once an instance of an execution semantics exists, it is driven by the receipt of events representing messages from specific services. For example in the execution semantics description for the AchieveGoal process, once the execution semantics receives an event indicating that the discovery service has been completed successfully, it will raise an event for process mediation to take place.
Inputs	Creation of an instance of execution semantics requires the identifier of the corresponding type. Updating an instance of an execution semantics requires its identifier and an event indicating the outcome of some services functionality.
Outputs	Starting an execution semantics returns an identifier. Receiving an event requires the event identifier and the identifier for the instance of the execution semantics (assuming that these identifiers point to the complete data in persistent storage).

they can be further processed by the services making up SESA. Although, currently very popular, the combination of SOAP, HTTP, and XML is not guaranteed to be the only message, transport and data specifications used by external services. Many other valid combinations are possible and where practical should be supported by the ECM. There are two interfaces defined for the ECM service: Invoker, described in Table 5.9, and Receiver, described in Table 5.10.

Parser

The information model for the content of all messages passed between the internal services is defined by the WSMO metamodel. Consequently, the language used to represent the content and define the semantics of these messages is WSML. However, WSML in its native state is not easily consumable by the implementation of the individual services. It is useful to be able to parse WSML into a form that is more suitable for application programming. Such a form is provided by WSMO4J [2], an API and reference implementation for WSMO using Java.

WSMO4J is a convenient programming abstraction for WSMO semantic descriptions. However, it is not a prerequisite. Likewise the parser functionality is only required if the SESA design cannot natively work with WSML at the interfaces of each component. For descriptive purposes and convenience, we make the assumption that WSMO4J is used in SESA for the remainder of this chapter.

When and where parsing takes place is a design and implementation issue. In designs where the services are implemented in Java and hosted on a common Java virtual machine (JVM), or on multiple JVMs that can exchange objects, it may make

Table 5.9. External communications manager (*ECM*): Invoker interface

Aspect	Detailed information
Description	The ECM Invoker handles all invocations from the SESA to external services. It is responsible to carry out any necessary transformations and if security or encryption is required, it should coordinate any associated tasks.
Provided to	The choreography engine service is responsible for raising events that lead to the Invoker interface being called.
Inputs	The identifier of the service being invoked, the list of WSML instances to be sent, and the identifier of the grounding that identifies exactly which operation and end point for the invocation.
Outputs	The invocation of a service is treated as asynchronous from the perspective of the choreography engine raising the invocation event. In actual fact the *wrapper* attached to the ECM at deployment times shields the choreography engine from needing to know about this. If the Web service invocation is synchronous, then the wrapper should use an individual thread to wait until the Web service response is returned and then raise a suitable event to be passed to the messaging mechanism of the core. Where the Web service invocation is synchronous, there is no return data immediately associated with the invocation. Rather the service must make a subsequent callback to an end point on the SESA if it has data to return.

Table 5.10. ECM: Receiver interface

Aspect	Detailed information
Description	The ECM Receiver handles all incoming messages from external entities. There are two categories of messages. The first are from SESA users who wish to run one of the processes defined by the definitions of execution semantics provided for SESA. These include service discovery, goal achievement, and specific Web service invocation. We will look at these in Chap. 6. The second category is for messages that are sent to SESA from a service as part of an already ongoing conversation, e.g., the asynchronous response to a Web service operation mentioned in the description of the Invoker interface.
Provided to	External entities using SESA for particular tasks.
Inputs	When achieving a goal, the goal description or an IRI that resolves to the goal description along with WSML instance data to act as input must be provided. The inputs for executing a Web service are almost the same, with Web service description required in place of the goal description. For discovery, the goal identifier is needed along with optional ontological instance to restrict the set of valid discovered services.
Outputs	Achieving a goal may result in output WSML data being returned to the external requester. Likewise, the execution of a specific service. For discovery, a possibly empty set of Web service descriptions is returned.

sense to parse WSML messages as soon as they arrive at the Receiver interface and then use the internal WSMO4J model as the internal SESA representation. Where services are designed as standalone Web Services, it may makes sense to exchange messages between SESA services in WSML and allow each service to carry out WSML parsing as they require. Table 5.11 describes the Parser interface.

Table 5.11. Parser interface

Aspect	Detailed information
Description	The Parser transforms WSML descriptions into the Java object model provided by WSMO4J.
Provided to	Accessible by any of the SESA services that wish to use WSMO4J as their internal object model.
Inputs	A WSML document.
Outputs	A set of WSMO4J objects.

Table 5.12. Reasoner interface

Aspect	Detailed information
Description	The Reasoner enables queries that may require logical inferencing to be made over a knowledge base defined by ontologies using a defined formal logic model, e.g., description logic.
Provided to	Accessible by any of the SESA services but is required by discovery, data and process mediation. It is also required by the algorithms defined in this chapter for the choreography and orchestration engines.
Inputs	One or more ontologies must be available to the reasoning engine to establish its knowledge base. Queries to the engine take the form of logical expressions.
Outputs	A possibly empty set of identifiers that provide an answer to each query put to the Reasoner.

Reasoner

At the heart of the motivation for the SESA architecture is the flexibility enabled by providing rich semantic descriptions of the entities involved in the use of Web Services as a technology for application and system integration. To realize this flexibility requires an engine that can understand the semantic descriptions, including the axioms and relations defined for them, and be able to answer questions on the knowledge those descriptions represent. This is the role of the reasoner service.

In particular, the discovery, data mediation and process mediation services rely on the logical reasoning. For service discovery, the reasoner must determine if the capability of a goal, expressed in terms of logical expressions, can be matched by the capability of one or more Web Services, also expressed as logical expressions. This requires a reasoning engine that answers queries on the basis of the underlying formal logic model used by the semantic language. It is desirable that the reasoning engine interface be provided either through Java, supporting WSMO4J, or as a Web service that accepts and returns WSML expressions. The interface for the Reasoner is described in Table 5.12.

Resource Manager

The resource manager service provides access to persistent storage for the SESA. Persistence at the system level is required for all WSMO entities used during operation of the WSMX system as well as the non-WSMO entities, e.g., those representing

Table 5.13. WSMO Repository interface

Aspect	Detailed information
Description	This provides retrieval, add, update, and remove (and possibly archive) operations on a repository of WSMO descriptions for Web Services, goals, ontologies, and mediators.
Provided to	Accessible by any of the SESA services.
Inputs	When adding or updating a WSMO element, a valid WSML description or corresponding set of WSMO4J Java objects is required. When removing a WSMO element, the identifier(s) for the element(s) to be removed must be provided. Individual WSMO elements can be retrieved by specifying their unique identifier, while it should be possible to retrieve all WSMO descriptions of a particular type, i.e., Web service or goal or mediator or ontology.
Outputs:	When adding, updating, or removing a WSMO element there is no specific output beyond possible confirmation messages. When retrieving a WSMO element a WSML document containing all the requested elements or a corresponding set of WSMO4J objects should be returned.

Table 5.14. NonWSMO Repository interface

Aspect	Detailed information
Description	There are many aspects of the operation of the SESA that require persistent storage. One example is that instances the choreography engine service should remain stateless, storing and retrieving instances of choreographies as required based on unique identifiers for those instances. Another example is that the architecture should keep track of the life cycle of events, representing messages between services in the context of an instance of an execution semantics. This is important for monitoring the health of the system and for maintaining historical information for performance monitoring over time.
Provided to	Accessible by any of the SESA services. Ideally, this service takes advantage of an object-relational mapping framework like Hibernate that abstracts the details of the persistence from the application developer.
Inputs	Depends on the SESA service.
Outputs	Also depends on the SESA service.

messages and their states used during the execution of processes provided by the architecture (through execution semantics). Individual services are responsible for any additional specific persistence required by their own design. There are two interfaces defined for the resource manager: WSMO Repository (Table 5.13) and Non-WSMO Repository (Table 5.14).

5.2 Technology Viewpoint

In this section, we provide some details on the technology used in the design of the core component of the Web Services Execution Environment[3] (WSMX), an

---

[3] http://sourceforge.net/projects/wsmx

open-source prototype of the SESA. The purpose is to provide some insight into the challenges of creating a software design that realizes the SESA.

5.2.1 Core Design

The core component takes the role of component coordinator for the architecture. It manages the interaction between the other components through the exchange of messages containing instances of WSMO concepts expressed in WSML and provides the microkernel and messaging infrastructure for the architecture. The component is responsible for handling the three main functional requirements:

1. A framework for the management and monitoring to start and stop the system and allow its health to be monitored.
2. The core facilitates the communication between the components, it accepts messages and routes them to a suitable target component, enabling the communication between as well as the coordination of components.
3. Support for the life cycle of execution semantics (declarative definitions of the allowed operational behavior of the architecture). Multiple definitions of execution semantics are supported and multiple instances of each execution semantics may run concurrently.

The WSMX prototype for the core is realized as a microkernel utilizing Java Management Extensions (JMX) and is described in detail in [98].

Management

In common with middleware and distributed computing systems, management of components involved in the system becomes a critical issue. In the architecture we make a clear separation between operational logic and management logic, treating them as orthogonal concepts. Without the separation of these two aspects, it is increasingly difficult to maintain the system and keep it flexible. The very process of making management explicit captures an invariant that helps to leverage the support for dynamic change of the rest of the system. Figure 5.2 presents an overview of the infrastructure provides by the core to the components, which allows the management and monitoring of the system.

The core is a management agent that offers several dedicated services, the most essential of which is perhaps the *bootstrap service*, responsible for loading and configuring the application components. The necessary information is obtained by a combination of reflection and supplied information in the form of a distributed configuration. The agent plays the role of a driver, in other words, it is built into the application, as opposed to a daemon approach.

The core also employs *self-management* techniques such as scheduled operations, and allows *administration* through a representation-independent management and monitoring interface that allows for a number of different management consoles, serving different purposes. Text-terminal-, Web-browser-, and Eclipse-framework-based consoles have been implemented.

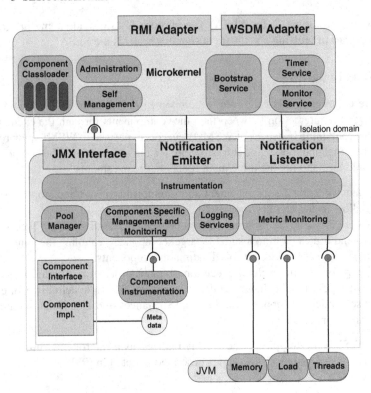

Figure 5.2. Component management in the architecture core

As is common with middleware and application servers, the core hosts a number of subsystems that provide services to components and enable intercomponent communication. Besides systems that are responsible for communication matters, *pool management* takes care of handling several component instances, along with a number of the abovementioned subsystems. The core is in the unique position of offering services to the individual components, such as logging services, transport services, and life-cycle services. Presenting a coherent view of all management aspects of components and, at the same time, not getting lost in complexity are two conflicting goals and are subject to compromise.

One of the principles underlying the architecture design is support for distribution. The design of the core allows for transparent distribution of middleware services in two ways. Firstly, the use of a shared virtual message space allows services to be physically located on different servers. Secondly, it is possible for multiple WSMX implementations to be configured as a federation of agents, where each agent is represented as a WSMX implementation. Where a middleware service is not available at one site, the core at that location can send a message to another WSMX requesting the middleware service at that remote site.

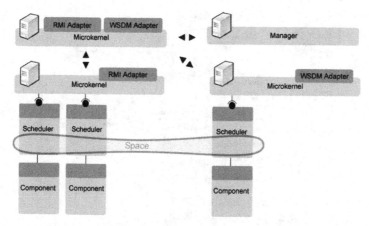

Figure 5.3. Communication and coordination in the architecture core

Communication and Coordination

The architecture avoids hard-wired bindings between components – communication is based on events. Whenever a middleware service is required an event representing a request for that service is created and published. Any services subscribed to the event type can fetch and process the event. The event-based approach naturally allows asynchronous communication. As illustrated in Fig. 5.3 event exchange is conducted using a shared tuple space (originally demonstrated in Linda [84]), which provides persistent shared space enabling interaction between parties without direct event exchange between them.

The tuple space enables communication between distributed units running on remote machines or on the local machine. It should be emphasized that the functional components themselves (discovery, mediation, etc.) are completely unaware of this distribution. That is, an additional layer provides them with a mechanism of communication with other components that shields them from the actual mechanism of transport which can be local or remote.

Through the infrastructure provided by the core, component implementations are separated from communication issues. This infrastructure is made available to each component implementation during instantiation of the component carried out by the core during a *bootstrap* process. This is the process that occurs when a component is identified and loaded by the WSMX prototype. Through the use of JMX and reflection technology, this can occur both at start-up as well as after the system is up and running. In particular, the communication infrastructure carries the responsibility to interact with the transport layer (a tuple space instance).

To enable one middleware service to request functionality of another, a proxy mechanism is utilized. The calling service asks the WSMX core for a proxy to the other middleware service it wishes to invoke. Once it has been provided, the proxy can be used as if it were a direct interface to the required service. In fact, the proxy

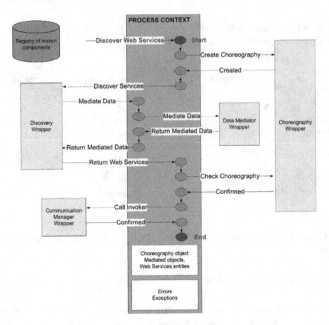

Figure 5.4. Process, its wrappers, and context

is implemented to publish an event with a type targeted at the required service and returns any results to the calling service.

Each middleware service has associated configuration metadata which allows the core to pick up that service and generate wrappers for it as it is deployed. Figure 5.4 shows a process represented by an execution semantics including the middleware services and associated wrappers. The wrappers are generated and managed by the core to separate middleware services from the transport layer for events. One wrapper raises an event with some message content and another wrapper can at some point in time consume this event and react to it.

Wrappers are generic software units that separate the implementation of WSMX components from the communication mechanism. They provide methods to components enabling communication with other components. Wrappers are automatically generated and attached to each component during instantiation (this is carried out by the WSMX kernel). There are two major parts:

1. **Reviver**. Its responsibility is to interact with the transport layer (i.e., the tuple space). Through the transport layer, Reviver subscribes to a proper event-type template. Similarly, Reviver publishes result events in the tuple space. This level of abstraction reduces the changes required to code if the transport layer changes.
2. **Proxy**. To enable one component to request another's functionality, a proxy is utilized. The calling component specifies the required component's name, the method to be invoked, and the required parameters. The proxy creates the proper event for this data and publishes it in the tuple space. A unique identifier is

assigned to the outgoing event and is preserved in the response event. Proxies subscribe to the response event by specifying a unique identifier in the event template. It guaranties that only the proxy that published this event will receive the result event.

Space-based messaging enables communication between distributed units running on remote machines. We emphasize that components themselves are completely unaware of any distribution. The additional layer of wrappers provides them with a mechanism to communicate with other components.

5.3 Summary

In this chapter we described the architecture for the SESA middleware. Two key sets of middleware services were identified. Broker services provide functionality for discovering, mediating, and invoking Semantic Web Services. Base services provide infrastructural functionality that is used by the broker services.

In the second part of the chapter we looked in some detail at the technological design for SESA that enables the various services to be managed and to evolve independently of each other. We described an overview of the management of services and the communication between them, including introducing the notions of proxies and wrappers as used in the WSMX design of a SESA system.

6

SESA Execution Semantics

The advent of service-orientated architecture (SOA) makes it more practical to separate the definition of how a system operates from the implementation of the system itself. We define execution semantics as formal descriptions of the operational behavior of the system (analogous to business process descriptions in BPEL, but at the system level). By separating the description of the system behavior from the system's implementation, we can achieve greater flexibility in how the implementations of the Semantically Enabled Service-Oriented Architectures can be used and avoid the necessity to rebuild the system in the event of a new or changed requirement for how the system should operate. In terms of the behavior of the architecture, we differentiate two types of services: middleware services and business services. Middleware services provide the functional services required by SESA to operate. Business services are exposed by information systems external to the SESA and the role of the SESA platform is to coordinate interoperation between them. The execution semantics is defined in terms of the middleware services describing in a formal, unambiguous way how the system built of loosely coupled middleware services operates.

This chapter describes mandatory execution semantics which should be supported by SESA. We identify three fundamental scenarios that should be supported and present them graphically using Unified Modeling Language (UML) activity diagrams to allow their essence to be easily grasped. We do not constrain execution semantics only to these mandatory scenarios provided in the subsequent sections. On the contrary, we envision new, dynamically created execution semantics reflecting changing business needs where middleware services can be composed in the flexible way according to the principles of SOA. We provide an example which shows how execution semantics operating on middleware services can be used to solve existing problems. We also look at the execution semantics from a WSMX technical perspective.

6.1 Motivation

Specification of system behavior can be viewed as control and data flow between system components (services in SOA), where the actual actions take place. System designers tend to create architectures for specific, current needs, which often results in rigid system behavior difficult to adapt to the changing requirements. The SESA takes a quite different approach, where the middleware services that makes up the system building blocks are well defined and ready to be utilized in various scenarios (all of which may not be known at design time). For instance, one execution semantics may specify goal-based discovery of Semantic Web Services, while another may define Semantic Web Service invocation. Both execution semantics are defined explicitly using the same middleware services but with different data flows and controls. Middleware services cooperate with each other on the interface level but they do not refer to each other's implementation directly.

A software design process should result in a design that is both an adequate response to the user's requirements and an unambiguous model for the developers who will build the actual software. A design therefore serves two purposes: both to guide the builder in the work of building the system and to certify that what will be built will satisfy the user's requirements. We define execution semantics, or operational semantics, as the formal definition of system behavior in terms of computational steps. As such, it describes in a formal, unambiguous language how the system operates. Since in a concurrent and distributed environment the meaning of the system, to the outside world, consists of its interactive behavior, this formal definition is called execution semantics.

The major advantages of specifying system behavior by execution semantics over informal methods are the following:

- **Foundations for model testing.** It is highly desirable to perform simulation of the model before the actual system is created and enacted. It allows one to detect anomalies like deadlock, livelock, or tasks that are never reached. However, as pointed out by Dijkstra [60], model simulation allows pointing out the presence of errors, but not the lack of them. Nevertheless, it is paramount to detect at least some system malfunctions during the design time instead of during the run time. Therefore, the semantics of utilized notations has to be perfectly sound in order to create tools enabling simulation of created models. Only formal, mathematical foundations can meet these requirements.
- **Executable representation.** Similarly like in the case of model testing, using formal methods provides a sound foundation to build an engine able to execute created models. Such an engine would not necessarily need to be able to detect livelock or other model faults. This distinguishes this advantage from the previous one.
- **Improved model understanding among humans.** Soundness of the utilized method significantly improves or even rules out ambiguities in model understanding by humans.

Several methods exist to model software behavior. Some of them model system behavior in a general way like UML diagrams; others impose more formal requirements on the model, for instance, Petri net-based methods, process algebra, modal and temporal logics, and type theory. These methods have different characteristics: some are more expressive than others; some are more suited for a certain problem domain than others. Some methods provide graphical notation like UML or Petri nets; some are based on syntactic terms like process calculi and logics; some methods have tool support for modeling, verification, simulation, or automatic code generation and others do not.

We impose two major requirements on the methodology utilized for modeling most fundamental SESA behavior. Firstly, it has to use understandable and straightforward graphical notation; secondly, it has to be unambiguous. These two requirements are met by UML activity diagrams, which are familiar to the engineering community and whose execution semantics can be disambiguated, for instance, in the semantics specified by Eshuis [66].

6.2 Proposed Description Formalism

UML 2.0 is a widely accepted and applied graphical notation in software modeling. It comprises of a set of diagrams for system design capturing two major aspects, namely, static and dynamic system properties. Static aspects specify system structure, its entities (objects or components), and dependencies between them. These structural and relational aspects are modeled by diagrams like class diagrams, component diagrams, and deployment diagrams. Dynamic aspects of the system are constituted by control and data flow within the entities, specified as sequence diagrams, state machine diagrams, and activity diagrams. Originally UML was created for modeling aspects of object-oriented programming (OOP). However, it has to be emphasized that UML is not only restricted to usage in the OOP area, but is also applied in other fields like, for instance, business process modeling.

The primary goal of UML diagrams is to enable common comprehension of the structure and behavior of modeled software among the involved parties (e.g., designers, developers, other stakeholders). To the detriment of UML notation, this information is conveyed in an informal way that may lead to ambiguities in certain cases as pointed out in [96]. Since we want to model the behavior of SESA in a widely used and understood manner, UML is a natural choice.

UML activity diagrams depict a coordinated set of activities that capture the behavior of a modeled system. They are used to specify control and data flow between the entities providing language constructs that enable one to model elaborate cases like parallel execution of entities or flow synchronization. For the SESA, they are used to identify the middleware services used in each specific execution semantics along with the control and data flow between them.

In each of the activity diagrams provided in this chapter, the actions that provide steps in the execution semantics are identified inside a dashed-line box. The middleware services, for discovery, mediation, selection, etc., are drawn as UML activities with interfaces that accept inputs and provide output as data objects. These interfaces are consistent with the defined SESA middleware services. In each of the activity diagrams provided, rounded rectangles with small square input pins denote actions. The pins represent input and output data ports. Rounded rectangles with large rectangular boxes at their boundaries (e.g., communication manager in Fig. 6.1) indicate activities that correspond to SESA middleware services. The rectangular boxes at the boundaries represent parameters that the activity accepts as input or provides as output. Data flow directional arrows can be identified as those beginning or ending at a data pin or a parameter box. The actions inside the dashed-line boundary are the responsibility of the execution semantics. Control flow directional arrows have no associated data and go from action to action inside the execution semantics. Finally, the vertical thick black bars are data-flow branches. Data flowing into a branch is made available at all outgoing flows. Where multiple input pins are available on an action, the action does not commence until data has arrived at each of those pins. Data becomes available on all outgoing pins of an action, as soon as that action is completed.

Owing to the wide proliferation of UML notation, several efforts were carried out to make concrete its semantics, especially regarding the dynamic aspects of UML notation. The semantics for UML activity diagrams, in the context of work-flow modeling, was specified in [66]. UML activity diagrams fulfill our requirements; therefore, they are used as the graphical notation in this chapter, consistently with the semantics given by Eshuis, to specify the operational behavior of SESA.

6.3 Mandatory Execution Semantics

We define three fundamental execution semantics identified for the SESA and describe the details of each in the following subsections. The SESA defines a set of middleware services that are required to achieve the functionality of a Semantic Web Services execution environment. Interfaces are defined for each middleware service, defined in terms of the conceptual model provided by WSMO. The combination of all interfaces provides the basis for the SESA application programming interface (API). Section 6.3.1 describes the scenario where goal-based service discovery without service invocation is desired. Section 6.3.2 is an extension of the scenario described in Sect. 6.3.1 – both service discovery and service invocation are required. The client's goal and all data instances the client wishes to send to the potential provided service are specified together as input. In Sect. 6.3.3, the situation described relates to where a client already knows the service that is to be invoked and the data required for this invocation is available.

In each of the subsequent sections, the execution semantics are linked to defined entry points to the SESA. Entry points can be considered as input ports, to which messages can be sent, for initiating specific execution semantics. The following notation is used (similar to the convention used by the JavaDoc documentation system), where execSemName stands for the name of the entry point to the system for the execution semantics, input data types are the types of the input parameters required to start the execution semantics, and return data type is the data type returned if the execution semantics completes successfully:

execSemName (Input data types): Return data type

We do not show the Parser component in the following sections since we treat it as a transformation component whose only role is to perform the transformation and validation from the textual form of WSML to object-oriented representation which can be more easily utilized by other SESA components.

6.3.1 Goal-Based Web Service Discovery

The following entry point initiates this system behavior:

getWebServices(WSMLDocument): Web Services

A service requester wishing to discover a list of Semantic Web Services fulfilling its requirements provides its requirements as a goal description using WSML. A set of WSML Web service descriptions whose capability matches the goal is returned.

Figure 6.1 shows the activity diagram. A message containing a WSML goal is received and passed to the communication manager, which takes care of whatever message persistence may be required. The goal is sent to the discovery activity, which looks for WSMO Web service descriptions with capabilities that match that of the goal. The discovery activity may need data mediation as part of its internal design but this internal aspect of that activity is not modeled as part of this execution semantics. Discovery continues until a set of matching Web Services is compiled. Assuming this

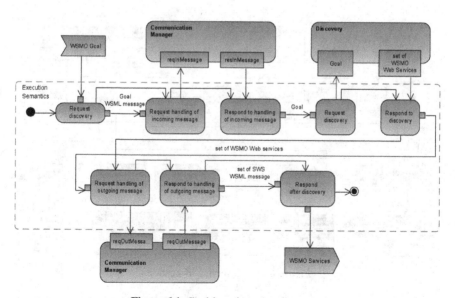

Figure 6.1. Goal-based service discovery

set is nonempty, the selection activity determines which of the discovered services to return to the service requester. The WSMO description of the selected service must be transformed to WSML and packaged into a message that can be sent back to the requester. The communication manager takes care of this activity, ending the execution semantics for goal-based discovery.

6.3.2 Web Service Invocation

The following entry point initiates this system behavior:

invokeWebService(WSMLDocument, Context): Context

Where the service requester already knows which Semantic Web Service is required to be invoked, the execution semantics illustrated in Fig. 6.2 is used. The first input signal provides the WSML content, while the second provides a conversation context. If this is the first message being sent to the Web service, there will be no existing conversation and this context signal will be empty. As in the other two scenarios, the WSML input message is unpacked by the communication manager activity. In this case, however, the WSML input contains both the target Web service description and the input instance data.

After the WSML input has been received, the WSMO Web service description and the instance data are passed to the data mediation activity to handle any data mapping that may be required (may require a WSML reasoner to be invoked internally).

After that, process mediation has all input data at its input pins and can commence. We do not describe the internal design of the process mediation activity here but we do note that it is responsible for matching the message exchange patterns

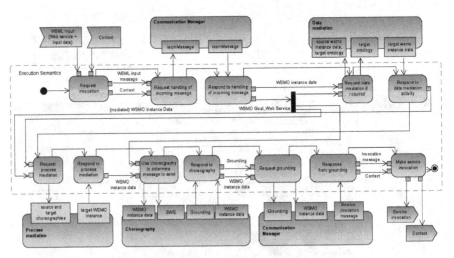

Figure 6.2. Web service invocation

required by the goal and offered by the Semantic Web Service description. This matching includes both the message patterns and the data types used by the respective messages. Process mediation determines how the input data instances need to be organized so that they can be understood by the Web service choreography description. The output of process mediation is WSMO data instances organized in this manner.

Once output from process mediation is available, the choreography activity has all required input and (most likely using a reasoning engine as part of its internal design) determines which messages need to be sent out on the basis of the choreography description (an abstract state machine) of the Web service. This WSMO data must be transformed into a format defined by the Web service grounding information (taken from the WSDL service binding) and sent to the Web service end point. This activity is carried out by the communication manager.

6.3.3 Goal-Based Service Execution

The following entry point initiates this system behavior:

achieveGoal(WSMLDocument): Context

A service requester wishing to use SESA for all aspects of goal-based service invocation (discovery, mediation, invocation) provides both the goal and the input data descriptions in a single WSML document. A unique identifier for the conversation initiated by the receipt of the goal is returned by the execution semantics to the service requester. In parallel the goal and the WSML instance input data are processed by the execution semantics to discover and invoke a service whose capability matches that described by the goal description.

This scenario illustrated in the UML activity diagram in Fig. 6.3 is based on the assumption that the service requestor is able to provide, up-front, all input data required by the discovered Web service.

The execution semantics is initiated by the receipt of the goal and input data messages. As in Fig. 6.1, the communication manager activity is used to unpack the WSML content of the messages. Then the discovery execution semantics commences as described in Sect. 6.3.1, after which the selection takes place, and the resulting Semantic Web Service is sent to the Web service invocation execution semantics activity as presented in Sect. 6.3.2.

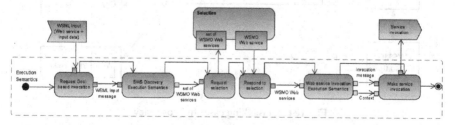

Figure 6.3. Goal-based service execution

Note that this execution semantics, without the discovery and selection activities, could be used to handle messages returned from the Web service to be sent back to the service requester, assuming that the service requester provided an invocable end point at which it could receive such messages.

6.4 Case Study Example of SESA Execution Semantics

In this section we provide an example case study which shows how SESA and its execution semantics can be utilized to solve existing problems. We present here a case study from the DIP EU Integrated Research Project[1] on Semantic Web Services. Figure 6.4 shows a simplified architecture for an eBanking prototype for a stockbroking application. To remain competitive in their markets, banks require the means to be adaptive to the changing needs of their clients. The hard-wired nature of many distributed computing systems makes it difficult to provide this flexibility at the business-to-customer (B2C) interface of the bank. The stockbroking scenario allows bank clients to specify their request, in their own language, at the bank's Web portal. This request is analyzed by the WSML goal adapter, which attempts to match it with a WSML goal from a predefined goal repository. The goal is dispatched to the SESA middleware, which carries out reasoner-based discovery, quality of service based selection, mediation, choreography, (possibly orchestration, if the goal consists of multiple subgoals), and invocation. Assuming a suitable service is identified, it is invoked and the result returned via the SESA middleware and transformed into a presentation format using the WSML adapter.

Figure 6.5 shows a UML sequence diagram of calls to SESA components used by the eBanking prototype for the scenario of buying stock when a certain recommendation is received. The business rules to buy stock (or not) are implemented by the WSML adapter. In this sequence diagram, the eBanking adapter has responsibility

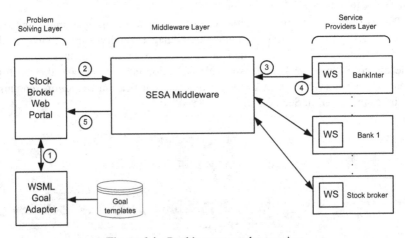

Figure 6.4. eBanking case study overview

---

[1] http://dip.semanticweb.org/

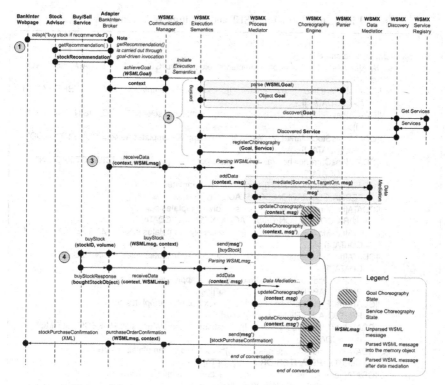

Figure 6.5. Sequence diagram for eBanking case study scenario

for managing part of the business process in addition to transformation to and from WSML. This is a specific implementation required for this case study containing additional business logic that organizationally is separate to the adapter functionality but is included in the implementation for practical reasons.

6.4.1 1 – Sending Request

A Web page front end allows bank clients to enter that they wish to purchase a certain stock if the expert recommendation is "buy." The adapter transforms the natural language request into a WSML goal using the repository of predefined goals as a guide. The inputs for the goal are provided by the client's inputs on the Web page and the information gathered from a call to a stock adviser, which returns a *stockRecommendation*. For space reasons, we do not show the calls to get the recommendation but assume that this is achieved through goal-based invocation. The inputs, for buying stock, are lifted to WSML by the adapter using XSLT, a fragment of which is shown in Listing 6.1 With the WSML goal available, the adapter invokes the achieveGoal() entry point of the SESA using the SOAP document-style message protocol. In return, a *context* is received containing the identification of the *conversation* as well as an identification of the *role* of the sender (i.e., *requester* or *provider*). This information is used in subsequent asynchronous calls from the requester.

Listing 6.1. Lifting in XSLT and resulting WSML message

```
1    /* Lifting rules from XML message to WSML */
2    <xsl:template match="STOCK" >
3        <![CDATA[instance ]]><xsl:apply-templates select="CODIGO_ISIN"/><![CDATA[ memberOf
             sm#Stock]]>
4            <![CDATA[isPartOfcompany hasValue "]]><xsl:apply-templates select="NOMBRE_VALOR"
                 /><![CDATA["]]>
5            <![CDATA[hasISIN hasValue "]]><xsl:apply-templates select="CODIGO_ISIN" /><![CDATA
                 ["]]>
6            <![CDATA[hasStockMarket hasValue "]]><xsl:apply-templates select="COD_MERCADO"
                 /><![CDATA["]]>
7            <![CDATA[hasCurrency hasValue "]]><xsl:apply-templates select="DIV_COTIZACION"
                 /><![CDATA["]]>
8            <![CDATA[hasDate hasValue "]]><xsl:apply-templates select="
                 FECHA_COTIZACION_COMP_ACCIONES" /><![CDATA["]]>
9            <![CDATA[hasTime hasValue "]]><xsl:apply-templates select="
                 HORA_COTIZACION_COMP_ACCIONES"/><![CDATA["]]>
10           <![CDATA[hasMaximum hasValue "]]><xsl:apply-templates select="MAX_SESION" /><![
                 CDATA["]]>
11           <![CDATA[hasMinimum hasValue "]]><xsl:apply-templates select="MIN_SESION" /><![
                 CDATA["]]>
12           <![CDATA[hasOpeningPrice hasValue "]]><xsl:apply-templates select="
                 PRECIO_APERTURA"/><![CDATA["]]>
13           <![CDATA[hasPreviousPrice hasValue "]]><xsl:apply-templates select="
                 PRECIO_ANTERIOR"/><![CDATA["]]>
14           <![CDATA[hasLastPrice hasValue "]]><xsl:apply-templates select="PRECIO_ULTIMO"
                 /><![CDATA["]]>
15           <![CDATA[hasValueChange hasValue "]]><xsl:apply-templates select="
                 DIF_CIERRE_ANTERIOR"/><![CDATA["]]>
16           <![CDATA[hasVariation hasValue "]]><xsl:apply-templates select="
                 TPC_CIERRE_ANTERIOR"/><![CDATA["]]>
17           <![CDATA[hasVolume hasValue "]]><xsl:apply-templates select="VOLUMEN" /><![CDATA
                 ["]]>
18   </xsl:template>
19
20   <xsl:template match="NOMBRE_VALOR" >
21       <xsl:variable name="buffer" select="." />
22       <xsl:value-of select ="normalize-space($buffer)" />
23   </xsl:template>
24
25   /* message in WSML after transformation */
26   instance ES0113679338 memberOf Stock
27               isPartOfcompany hasValue "BANKINTER"
28               hasISIN hasValue "ES0113679338"
29               hasStockMarket hasValue "055"
30               hasCurrency hasValue "EUR"
31               hasDate hasValue ""
32               hasTime hasValue ""
33               hasMaximum hasValue "53.3"
34               hasMinimum hasValue "53.1"
35               hasOpeningPrice hasValue "53.3"
36               hasPreviousPrice hasValue "53.4"
37               hasLastPrice hasValue "53.2"
38               hasValueChange hasValue "-0.2"
39               hasVariation hasValue ""
40               hasVolume hasValue "114618"
```

6.4.2 2 – Discovery and Conversation Setup

The *achieveGoal* entry point is implemented by the communication manager – the middleware service, which facilitates the inbound and outbound communication with the SESA middleware. After receipt of the goal, the communication manager initiates the *execution semantics* which manages the whole integration process. The communication manager sends the WSML goal to the instance of the execution semantics, which in turn invokes the parser, returning the goal parsed into an internal system object.

The next step is to invoke the discovery middleware service in order to match the requested capability of the goal with the capabilities of services registered in the repository. Services matching the requested capability are returned to the execution semantics. For space reasons, we show a simplified discovery without selection. For the purposes of the diagram, we assume that exactly one service is discovered that matches the goal capability.

Once a service is discovered, the execution semantics registers both the requester's as well as the provider's choreography with the choreography engine (these choreographies are part of the goal and service descriptions, respectively). Both choreographies are set to a state where they wait for incoming messages that could fire a transition rule. This completes the conversation setup.

6.4.3 3 – Conversation with Requester

The instance data for the goal is sent from the BankInter adapter to WSMX asynchronously by invoking the *receiveData* entry point. Along with the instance data, the context is also sent to WSMX in order to identify the sender and the conversation (the context has been previously obtained as a result of invocation of the *achieveGoal* entry point).

The data in WSML (WSMLmsg) is passed through the communication manager to the execution semantics, which again first parses the data into internal system objects using the parser. In general, multiple independent conversations can be running inside WSMX; thus, information carried by the context is used to identify the specific conversation to which the message belongs. The execution semantics then passes the data obtained to the process mediator.

The first task of the process mediator is to decide which data will be added to which choreography, i.e., requester's or provider's choreography.[2] This decision is based on analysis of both choreographies and concepts used by these choreographies and is described in detail in [45]. In our scenario, the process mediator first updates the memory of the requester's choreography with the information that the

---

[2] Note that the choreographies of WSMO services are modeled as abstract state machines [186] and are processed following the semantics of abstract state machines. Each choreography has its own *memory* containing instance data of ontological concepts. A choreography rule (ASM rule) whose antecedent matches available data in the memory is selected from the rule base and by execution of the rule's consequent, the memory is modified (data in the memory is updated, deleted, or removed).

purchase order request has been sent. The process mediator then evaluates how that data should be added to the memory of the provider's choreography. In the use case, data mediation must be first performed to the ontology used by the provider (service ontology). For this purpose, the source ontology of the requester, the target ontology of the provider, and the instance data are passed to the data mediator. Data mediation is performed by execution of mapping rules between both ontologies (these mapping rules are stored within WSMX and have been created and registered during the integration setup phase). More information on the design and implementation of the data mediator can be found in [25]. Once mediation is complete, the mediated data is added to the provider's choreography.

6.4.4 4 – Conversation with Provider (Buying Stock)

Once the requester's and provider's choreographies have been updated, the choreography engine processes each to evaluate if any transition rules have been fired. In our scenario, the requester's choreography remains in the waiting state as no rule can be evaluated at this stage.

For the provider's choreography, the choreography engine finds the rule shown in Listing 6.2 (lines 14–21). Here, the choreography engine matches the data in the memory with the the antecedent of the rule and performs the action of the rule's consequent (i.e., update/delete of the memory). The rule says that the message *buy-Stock* with data, *stockId, volume*, should be sent to the service provider (this data had been previously added to the choreography memory after the mediation. The choreography engine then waits for the *buyStockResponse* message to be sent as a response from the provider. Sending the message to the service provider is carried out by choreography engine passing the message to the communication manager, which, according to the grounding defined in the choreography, further passes the message to the *purchaseOrderConfirmation* entry point of the BankInter adapter.

Listing 6.2 shows the fragment of the provider's choreography and the selected rule described above. The choreography is described from the service point of view; thus, the rule says that the service expects to receive the *buyStock* message and send the reply *buyStockResponse* message. In the *StateSignature* section (lines 3–11), concepts for the *input, output*, and *controlled* vocabulary are defined. Input concepts correspond to messages sent to the service, the output concept corresponds to messages sent out of the service, and controlled concepts are used for controlling the states, and the transition between states during processing of the choreography. Each concept used is prefixed with the namespace definition (e.g., bank, oasm) corresponding to the imported ontologies (lines 4, 5). The choreography is part of the service definition, which in addition also contains definition of *nonfunctional properties* and *capability*. For brevity, these elements are not included in the listing.

In the adapter, lowering the WSML message to XML is performed using transformation rules from the BankInter ontology to the corresponding XML schema used by the Web front end.

Listing 6.2. Provider's service choreography

```
1     ...
2     choreography BuyStockChoreography
3        stateSignature _"http ://www.example.org/ontologies/BuyStockWS#statesignature"
4           importsOntology { _"http://www.example.org/ontologies/DIP/Bank",
5                            _"http ://www.example.org/ontologies/choreographyOnto" }
6
7        in bank#buyStock withGrounding { _"https://www.theBank.com/wsBrokerService/
                             Service1.asmx?WSDL#wsdl.interfaceMessageReference(BrokerServiceSoap/
                             performBuySell/in0"}
8           ...
9        out bank#buyStockResponse
10          ...
11       controlled ControlState
12
13    transitionRules _"http ://www.example.org/ontologies/buyStock#transitionRules"
14          forall {?controlstate, ?request} with (
15                        ?controlstate [oasm#value hasValue oasm#InitialState] memberOf
                              oasm#ControlState and
16                        ?request memberOf bank#buyStockRequest
17             ) do
18                        add(?controlstate[oasm#value hasValue oasm#BuyingStock])
19                        delete(?controlstate [oasm#value hasValue oasm#InitialState])
20                        add(_# memberOf bank#buyStockResponse)
21          endForall
22          ...
```

After that, the actual service for buying the stock is invoked, passing the parameters of the *stockID* and *volume*. The service executes and sends its results in XML to the adapter. As before, the XML data is lifted to the bank ontology, passed to the WSMX, parsed by the parser, and after the evaluation of the process mediator, the data is added to the provider's and requester's choreography memory, respectively. Once the choreographies have been updated, the reasoning engine is used to check if any transition rules can fire as a consequence of the new information. In this case, there is only one further message to be sent. This is a confirmation message for the service requester that the stock purchase has been completed.

After the message has been sent, no additional rules can be evaluated from the requester's choreography; thus, the choreography gets to the end of conversation state. Since both the requester's and the provider's choreography are in the state of end of conversation, the choreography engine notifies the execution semantics and the conversation is closed.

6.5 Technical Perspective on Execution Semantics

In this section, we provide some details on the technology used for enabling execution semantics operating on the middleware services (components) in WSMX, which is a reference implementation of SESA. The purpose is to show how execution semantics can be run on such a system and to give an insight into existing challenges.

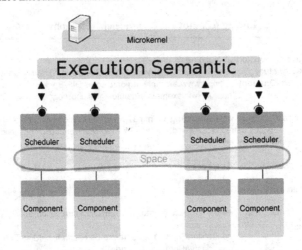

Figure 6.6. Execution semantics in the architecture core

Execution semantics are declarative descriptions of the processes that make up the allowed operation of the SESA system. Figure 6.6 indicates that the definition provided by the execution semantics is used by the WSMX core microkernel to drive the scheduling and sequencing of calls to the middleware services. The core infrastructure provides the engine that enforces the general computation strategy by running the execution semantics, operating with both the transport mechanism and the middleware service interfaces. It keeps track of the current state of execution and may preserve data obtained during execution for use at a later stage.

Execution semantics enables the composition of loosely coupled WSMX middleware services and provides a necessary execution logic (e.g., conditional branching, fault handling). As depicted in Fig. 6.7 an instance of execution semantics is part of each event published in a tuple space (publish/subscribe transport mechanism used by WSMX). Execution semantics has a state that changes over time while traveling and executing across distributed component locations. Additional data obtained during execution can be preserved in the instance of execution semantics.

There are two approaches to an execution semantics representation in WSMX, namely, expressing execution semantics as a Java code and as a workflow model. Execution semantics specified in Java can be carried out in the current version of WSMX. The latter approach represents the future vision of WSMX execution semantics embedded in a distributed workflow model.

Java-based execution semantics is represented by a state-aware piece of code that is executed while being fetched by a *Wrapper*. The execution path is represented similarly as in abstract state machines and the current state is encoded in an execution instance. When execution semantics is executed, component implementation represented by *Wrapper* is exploited and additional steps can be conducted. According to the result returned from the component, the next step can be taken. The next event type is passed on to *Wrapper* and the state of the execution semantics instance is changed. Additionally, some data can be stored for further processing

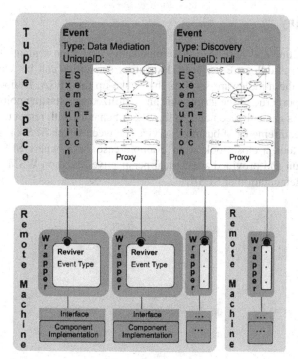

Figure 6.7. Distributed execution semantics in WSMX

in an instance of execution semantics. Finally the updated event is published in a tuple space. Although the different parts of the execution semantics are executed on different distributed components, the execution semantics can be specified centrally.

Workflow-based execution semantics is envisioned as a next step in developing WSMX component composition and coordination. The general rules are similar to thh case of Java code representation. The workflow approach possesses certain advantages over Java representation, but there also are some challenges. Among the advantages of the workflow approach is its graphic representation, capability to perform prior model correctness checking, flexible response to changes, and on-the-fly execution of the created model. Models created for of WSMX components should not be affected by the WSMX tuple space communication paradigm and the capability to use all available expressions (patterns) for the chosen workflow language should be preserved. A crucial aspect is to provide an instance synchronization mechanism for executed models. It is especially relevant in cases of parallel execution where a race condition might occur; thus, it is necessary to ensure the validity of the context when executing tasks in a component. Before a task is finalized one needs to check whether context relevant for the task has changed. If the context has changed (i.e., input data and variables required for task execution), tasks must be executed again. It needs to be stressed that all aspects related to distributed workflow execution have to be considered in this case.

6.6 Summary

We have identified and described three mandatory execution semantics for loosely coupled SESA middleware services. Execution semantics can be seen as an orchestration of the middleware services that make up the SESA. Defined execution semantics support crucial scenarios and can be utilized as a starting point for the further refinements and enhancements of the SESA behavior with respect to the changing business requirements of business services between which SESA is applied. Additionally we took a close look at an example case study where SESA execution semantics is run and provided a technical perspective based on WSMX, which is a reference implementation of SESA.

Part III

SESA Services

7

Reasoning

This chapter tackles the often abused and underdefined term "reasoning." Since reasoning is so frequently ambiguously referred to, at least within the semantic technologies community, there are several sections in this chapter that cover the topic from different perspectives. First, from a conceptual perspective, highlighting the fact that reasoning lies at the heart of Semantically Enabled Service-oriented Architectures (SESAs), and proving the necessity of an efficient reasoner within SESA in the abstract examination of what must be present in order to draw conclusions of any sort, i.e., a knowledge base (e.g., the Web), and a way to form judgments or draw conclusions based on some sort of logical process (e.g., a reasoner) (Sect. 7.1). Section 7.2 provides a brief background on two well-known logical formalisms, namely, description logics and logic programming. Subsequently we focus on current reasoning tasks in these two formalisms, as well as their benefits and drawbacks. Moreover Sect. 7.3 highlights the WSML variants and their specific requirements for reasoning engines. Section 7.4 focuses on reasoning within SESA by outlining which components require which reasoning functionalities. A generic framework for reasoning with WSML, namely, WSML2Reasoner, is introduced in Sect. 7.5. Section 7.6 focuses on an additional layer to the standard reasoner architecture, a Rule Interchange Format (RIF) layer, which aims to specify a common format for rules in order to allow rule interchange between diverse rule systems. The development of this format (or language), which shares a common agenda with the W3C RIF Working Group, will conclusively provide an interlingua into which rule languages can be mapped, allowing rules written in different languages to be executed in the same reasoner engine. Finally Sect. 7.7 discusses future research and concludes by returning to the conceptual perspective and highlighting the importance of reasoning within SESAs.

7.1 Reasoning Requirements

The SESAs necessitate effective reasoning for the successful completion of different tasks, such as discovery, choreography, or mediation. The reasoning functionality itself is not used directly in a goal-based invocation of services, but is part of the underlying base layer in the global view of SESA, as described in Chap. 4.

Deductive reasoning describes the task of deriving new knowledge from a given set of statements or a knowledge base. It exploits the information about the world, or some part of the world (the so-called domain of discourse), which is captured by the knowledge base in order to infer properties of entities in the domain that are not explicitly specified in the knowledge base.

A classic and comprehensive example from deductive reasoning is the famous syllogism originating from Greek philosophers:

- All humans are mortal (premise 1).
- Socrates is a human (premise 2).
- Socrates is mortal (conclusion).

This syllogism is a valid inference in traditional logic in which one proposition (the conclusion) follows out of two others (the premises). Whether this is a valid inference does not depend though on the truth of the premises or the conclusion, but only on the form of the inference. If the two premises are true, then the conclusion must be true too. But it is also a valid inference if a premise and the conclusion are false (e.g., by replacing "mortal" in the above example by "immortal").

Clearly, reasoning depends on the concrete language that is used in order to describe and formalize the domain of discourse. By providing a fixed set of modeling primitives, the chosen formal language especially has a huge impact on how the domain of discourse can be described and what details can be captured (expressiveness) as well as how difficult it is to derive new knowledge from the knowledge base (in other words to find proofs for statements in the language, or the computational complexity of the reasoning tasks). We will briefly introduce two common logical formalisms in Sect. 7.2, namely, description logics and logic programming.

Reasoning with Semantic Web Services

The goal of Semantic Web Services is the fruitful combination of Semantic Web technology and Web Services. By using ontologies as the semantic data model for Web service technologies, Web Services have machine-processable annotations just as static data on the Web. But all efforts in semantic annotation (specification or description) of Web Services are far from being actually effective as long as there is no way for *computerized* agents (instead of human beings) to *actually process* this kind of information about the services. Only then, the dynamic composition of software systems could be achieved. Thus, the development of high-quality techniques for automated discovery, composition, and execution of services, i.e., processing, empowered by logical inference, of semantically enhanced information is crucial for the success of Semantic Web Services.

In this context, "processing" means to apply the formalized knowledge *intelligently* to solve a given problem, i.e., to actually exploit the semantics of the given description. In one way or the other, this boils down to performing simple inference steps over existing knowledge until enough knowledge has been generated to solve the task.

Thus, agents need support for *reasoning about Semantic Web Service descriptions* in order to effectively utilize semantic annotations. Efficient reasoning about Semantic Web Services will significantly simplify time-consuming and tedious tasks for humans in the context of Semantic Web Services and the dynamic construction of Web-service-based systems.

Ontologies and Semantic Web Service Descriptions

As we mentioned above, reasoning exploits the information about a specific domain of discourse. In the scope of Semantic Web Services, this domains of discourse are Web Services as well as the world they are embedded and used in, e.g., business interactions between customers and providers and the respective business area, like the tourism domain. We are, e.g., interested in a property that states that the functionality provided by a specific service can help to achieve a particular well-defined client goal, like the booking of tickets for a specific game during the soccer world championship in a specific year.

Domains of discourse are generally formalized by means of ontologies. Ontologies are a popular knowledge representation formalism in computer science and became one of the main fundamental building blocks of the Semantic Web and Semantic Web applications. Following the interpretation of ontologies among philosophers, in computer science an ontology is understood as a "formal, explicit specification of a shared conceptualization of a problem domain" [90]. It provides a formal vocabulary for denoting the elements of interest in the problem domain at hand, e.g., in the area of tourism these could be the elements *person, smoker, non-smoker, accomodation, hotel, pension, youth hostel, transportation means, flight, train*, etc., as well as their characteristic properties, e.g., attributes like *age, name*, and *ranking*, as well as relations between these elements, e.g., *is accomodated in* between *person* and *accomodation*. Whereas concepts denote sets of objects in a problem domain (which are somehow similar), it is often very useful to collect known instances of such concepts (or classes) in an ontology as well. Hence, one can additionally describe a set of instances for concepts that are known or existing in the problem domain along with their properties. Finally, one might want to reflect certain constraints or laws that hold between the described elements from the ontology within the problem domain. Such constraints are captured by so-called axioms, i.e., logical statements that restrict the interpretation of the various elements in the ontology in the intended way. An example of such an axiom could be that there is no object which simultaneously belongs to the concepts *male* and *female*.

As such, ontologies can be seen as problem-oriented knowledge bases that have a close relation to databases: in general, one can distinguish between an instance (or data) level and a schema level in an ontology. The vocabulary of the ontology (concepts, relations, attributes) and the axioms represent the schema of the problem domain, whereas the instances constitute data which populates the schema. Hence, ontologies can be seen as rich, semantic data models.

Thus, queries against ontologies (meaning the respective knowledge bases) to find individuals with specific properties are very relevant for Semantic Web applications. Hence, query answering is a very important reasoning task here (for more details on query answering please refer to Sect. 7.3).

Independent of the concrete formalism used for the specification of a Semantic Web Service, such descriptions necessarily need to be based on shared conceptual model of a problem domain, since otherwise providers and requesters of Web Services will not be able to understand each other. Ontologies perfectly fulfill this need and provide a shared and explicit conceptualization of a problem domain along with the (shared) vocabulary which allows one to talk about the problem domain. Because of this intimate relation of Semantic Web Service descriptions to ontologies, query answering over ontologies is an essential reasoning task in the context of Semantic Web Services and their descriptions as well.

Web Service Modeling Language

WSML is a family of formal languages that allows one to capture various aspects of Web Services. Fundamentally, WSML provides a particular ontology language. All other descriptions, such as Web service functionalities, are based on ontologies as an underlying conceptual and formal data model. In the context of WSML, ontology reasoning is thus the most fundamental form of reasoning that is required to realize higher-level tasks such as Web service discovery or composition of Web Services. In particular, the provision of a variety of different service modeling languages with different expressivity and computational properties is an appealing property which actually makes WSML suitable for all practical applications.

7.2 Logical Background

Logics, which can be traced back to the ancient Greeks, are the foundation of knowledge representation. Thus, they serve as a natural starting point in the design of knowledge-based systems: A logic defines a formal language for expressing knowledge about some domain and statements to be derived from this knowledge (and thus fixes the set of modeling primitives that can be used in describing the world), it precisely defines the formal semantics of each statement in the corresponding language, and, last but not least, it is equipped with a calculus, i.e., a formal (computable) procedure for proving new facts (described in the corresponding language) from a given set of statements in the language.

We will concentrate in the rest of this chapter on two well-known logical formalisms which were identified in Chap. 3 as those formalisms on which WSML is based, namely, description logics and logic programming. They can both be used for ontology descriptions, knowledge representations, and Semantic Web Service descriptions; they have been thoroughly investigated and provide efficient reasoning implementations.

7.2.1 Description Logics

Description logics are a subset of first-order logic and constitute a family of logic-based knowledge representation formalisms. They evolved from semantic networks and frame systems, which were nonlogical approaches, based on the use of graphical interfaces, also called network-based structures. Description logics differ from those systems in that they provide a precise semantic characterization of the modeling language.

Description logics have become a cornerstone of the Semantic Web for its use in the design of ontologies. They are based on concepts (classes) and roles. Concepts are designated by unary predicate symbols and represent classes of objects sharing some common characteristics. Roles are designated by binary predicate symbols and are interpreted as relations between objects. The latter can also be defined as attributes attached to objects. The language is compositional, i.e., concept descriptions are built by combining different subexpressions using constructors.

The Description Logics Family

Description logics form a family of different logics, distinguished by the set of constructors they provide. Usually each constructor is associated with a different capital letter. For example, $\mathcal{SHOIQ}$ describes the basic description logic (enabling the use of the conjunction $\sqcap$, the disjunction $\sqcup$, the negation $\neg$, the existential quantifier $\exists$, and the universal quantifier $\forall$) extended with transitive roles ($\mathcal{S}$), inverse roles ($\mathcal{I}$), role hierarchies ($\mathcal{H}$), nominals ($\mathcal{O}$), and qualified number restrictions ($\mathcal{Q}$). Detailed information about description logics in general, and about the most known extensions, can be found in [10].

Description Logics Knowledge Base

Within a knowledge base, there is a clear distinction between intensional knowledge (general knowledge about the problem domain) and extensional knowledge (specific to a particular problem). Analogously, the description logics knowledge base is separated into two components, a TBox and an ABox.

TBox

A TBox contains the terminological knowledge of a knowledge base. The basic form of declarations in a TBox are concept definitions, where new concepts are defined in terms of previously defined concepts. Such a concept definition describes general properties of a concept.

Two sorts of axioms describe the structure of a domain in a TBox:

1. **Definition axioms** introduce macros/names for concepts. The left-hand side of a definition can only be an atomic concept name. Example: *Woman* $\equiv$ *Human* $\sqcap$ *Female*, denoting that a woman is equivalent to the intersection of human and female.

2. **(General) inclusion axioms** (general concept inclusion, GCI) assert subsumption relations. Both sides of the definition can be complex concept expressions. An example is $\exists hasChild.Female \sqsubseteq \exists hasChild.Human$, denoting that the concept of having at least one female child is a subconcept of having at least one human child.

Most of the early description logics systems did not allow TBoxes to contain terminological cycles. But as recursive definitions are very common in modeling application domains, modern systems all provide unrestricted support for cyclic concept definitions.

The basic task in constructing a terminology is classification, which amounts to placing a new concept expression in the proper place in a taxonomic hierarchy of concepts (see Sect. 7.3.1).

ABox

The ABox contains assertional knowledge (knowledge about the individuals of a domain). Individuals are introduced and the ABox asserts their properties using concept definitions.

Two sorts of axioms describe concrete situations in an ABox:

1. **Concept assertions.** For example, $Mary : (Woman \sqcap \exists hasChild.Female)$, denoting that Mary is a woman and has at least one female child.
2. **Role assertions.** For example, $< Mary, Jack > : hasChild$, denoting that Jack is the child of Mary.

When the description logic used is extended with nominals, ABox assertions can also be described as TBox concept subsumptions: $a : C$ is equivalent to $\{a\} \sqsubseteq C$.

Unique Name Assumption

Description logics often adopt the *unique name assumption*, which means that different names always denote different individuals.

Open World Assumption

Description logics knowledge bases adopt an *open world* semantics. The *open world assumption* entails that the given information can be incomplete. Thus, what we cannot prove must not necessarily be false. Analogously a *closed world assumption* would entrain that the information from a knowledge base is regarded as complete. This means that everything that cannot be proven from the available information is regarded as false.

For example, given a knowledge base that contains the axioms $Jack : Man$, $Bob : Man$, and $< Jack, Bob > : hasChild$, the query "Are all of Jack's children male?" results in "yes," if the knowledge base adopts a closed world semantics, and results in "unknown" under an open world semantics, as there is no information available that tells us if Bob is the only child of Jack. So we do not know whether there is some more information missing about Jack and possible other children.

7.2.2 Logic Programming

Logic Programming is a declarative programming paradigm that is based on the Horn subset of first-order logic. A logic program consists of simple "if ... then ..." rules, which form a simple way of knowledge representation. A rule is formed from a *head* and a *body*:

$$H :- B_1, ..., B_n.$$

The *head* of the rule consists of one positive literal (e.g., H), whereas the *body* of the rule consists of a number of literals (e.g., $B_1, ..., B_n$). There exist two different notations for such rules, both being semantically equal: $H :- B_1, ..., B_n$ is sometimes written as $H \leftarrow _1 \wedge ... \wedge B_n$. Such a rule can be read as *if < body > then < head >*. Literals are atoms and can be either positive, as, e.g., $p(x)$, or negative, as, e.g., *not* $p(x)$. An atom without variables is a *ground* atom. Such a ground atom, i.e., a rule without a body, as, e.g., $p(a_1, ..., a_n)$, is called a *fact*. A rule without a head is a query: $?- B_1, ..., B_n$.

Examples are:
    Rule: $hasDaughter(x, y) :- hasChild(x, y), female(y)$.
    Rule: $hasGrandfather(x, z) :- hasParent(x, y), hasFather(y, z)$.
    Rule: $female(x) :- not\ male(x)$.
    Fact: $person(jack)$.
    Fact: $female(mary)$.
    Query: $?- hasGrandfather(jack, x)$.
    Query: $?- hasDaughter(jack, mary)$.

Negation-as-Failure

The use of *negation-as-failure* in logic programming is an extension of Horn logic and allows one to derive *not p* from the failure to derive *p*: Whenever a fact is not entailed by the knowledge base, its negation is entailed. Negation-as-failure is closely related to the closed world assumption that concludes that what is not known to be true is false.

For example, given a logic program that contains the fact $hasChild(Jack, Bob)$, the query "Is Peter a child of Jack?" results in "no," if a knowledge base adopts a closed world semantics, i.e., we can conclude *not* $hasChild(Jack, Peter)$, as the fact $hasChild(Jack, Peter)$ is not entailed by the logic program. Under an open world assumption it would result in "unknown," as there is no information available that tells us if Bob is the only child of Jack. The rule $female(x) :- not\ male(x)$, e.g., that uses negation-as-failure, states that a given x that is not known to be male is female.

Through the use of negation-as-failure, logic programs become *nonmonotonic*. Most classical logics are monotonic, i.e., adding rules or facts to a knowledge base only allows us to derive new knowledge from them; no derivations done earlier are lost. But adding rules or facts to a nonmonotonic program may result in a reduction of known derivations. Staying with the example above, this means that we may need to retract the conclusion *not hasChild(Jack, Peter)*, as soon as the fact *hasChild(Jack, Peter)* is added to the logic program.

Prolog

Prolog (programming in logic) is a logical programming language based on first-order predicate calculus, originally restricted to only allow Horn clauses (i.e., a disjunction of literals with the property that at most one literal is positive). It was, however, extended to include negation-as-failure. As described for logic programming in general above, a Prolog program is built of rules and facts.

The execution of a Prolog program is an application of theorem proving by first-order resolution. It is initiated by the posting of a query, as, e.g., ?- *hasChild*(x, y), which would result in an enumeration of all possible answers. Prolog is not declarative in the sense that the order of rules in the program matters for the program evaluation.

Datalog

Datalog is a subset of Prolog, which in contrast to the latter does not allow function symbols and unsafe rules (i.e., variables in Datalog are limited in that each variable that occurs in a rule must occur in a positive body literal which does not correspond to a built-in predicate). Furthermore Datalog programs must be stratified with regard to the use of negation and recursion. In contrast to Prolog, the ordering of clauses is usually irrelevant in Prolog.

According to [53], WSML-Core is based on plain (function- and negation-free) Datalog, WSML-Flight is semantically equivalent to Datalog extended with inequality and (locally) stratified negation, and WSML-Rule is defined through a mapping to full logic programming (i.e., with function symbols and unsafe rules) with inequality and unstratified negation.

7.3 Reasoning Tasks

Traditionally, reasoning refers to inferring new statements (so-called conclusions) from a set of given ones (the assumptions) which have the property that they are true (or they hold) whenever the assumptions are true. Formally, reasoning refers to checking a specific semantic relationship between statements in a formal logic: the logical entailment relation. Logics usually are equipped with a system of (computable) rules which allow one to derive conclusions from a set of assumptions. Such a system is called a proof calculus. In general, when designing a proof calculus for a specific logic, one is interested in a system which faithfully captures the semantic relationship *logical entailment*, i.e., the system should be sound and complete. Depending on the expressivity of the language for defining statements about a problem domain, this system can be infeasible or even untractable. The latter can very easily be the case. Checking logical entailment for first-order logic, for instance, is a problem which is undecidable.

However (and despite the fact that it is considered as standard reasoning task), checking for logical entailment is not the only reasoning task of interest for applications. More generally, one might be interested in deriving all conclusions of a given set of statements in an effective way.

Similarly, one might be interested in efficiently finding all objects known in the domain model which have specific properties, for instance, all adults who have an ancestor who smoked and died of lung cancer. This task is usually called query answering and is very important in the area of information and database systems as well as for Semantic Web applications in general.

In the case of description logics – less expressive but usually tractable knowledge representation systems – the most common reasoning tasks to be supported are subsumption checking and satisfiability checking. The first task is concerned with formally proving that a given concept description is more specific than a given other one and can be seen as a special form of logical entailment check. The second task is concerned with determining whether a given knowledge base is satisfiable, i.e., does not contain any contradictive statements. Often reasoning tasks can be reduced to other reasoning tasks, for instance, logical entailment in many logics can be expressed in terms of satisfiability checking. However, the possibility of doing such translations does not necessarily lead to systems that efficiently deal with certain reasoning tasks. Sometimes, very different techniques are needed and used to efficiently address different reasoning tasks.

In summary, a reasoning system in general is built to support a specific reasoning task in an efficient way. The applications that need reasoning support essentially define the kind of reasoning tasks that the reasoner needs to deal with. If different reasoning tasks need to be supported, a reasoning infrastructure needs to implement different reasoners. Finally, the language used to model a problem domain constrains and determines the techniques which can be used for implementing a reasoning task.

7.3.1 Description Logics

In description logics, there are different basic reasoning tasks for reasoning with TBoxes or ABoxes. As described in [10], the main inference procedures with TBoxes are concept subsumption and concept satisfiability. With ABoxes, the main reasoning tasks are ABox consistency and instance checking. These different reasoning tasks are not independent; often one of them can be reduced to another.

The OWL community focuses on entailment and query answering as the key inference services. Entailment can be reduced to satisfiability, while query answering amounts to computing the result of a query over a database or an ABox, respectively. This is based on working with a database-style conjunctive query language.

For the main description logics reasoning tasks mentioned above, there often exist both sound and complete algorithms given a knowledge base. A sound proof procedure for entailment proves only entailed sentences, whereas a complete proof procedure for entailment can prove every entailed sentence. In the usage of knowledge-based systems, it is often necessary to have a guarantee that the inferencing algorithms are sound and complete. Most state-of-the-art reasoners today are based on tableaux-calculi techniques.

Reasoning algorithms are not only evaluated by their effectiveness but also by their complexity. Baader et al. [10] talk about the tradeoff between the expressiveness of a representation language and the computational complexity. The more expressive the language is, the harder the reasoning over it is.

More detailed information about reasoning tasks and algorithms in expressive description logics and about the reasoning complexity can be found in [10].

The following sections deal with the main reasoning tasks, as described above, and offer a quick overview of some of the main nonstandard inference problems.

Knowledge Base Consistency

Checking knowledge base consistency is about ensuring that an ontology does not contain any contradictory facts. It is checked if a given ABox $\mathcal{A}$ and TBox $\mathcal{T}$ have a common nonempty model.

Concept Subsumption

Subsumption is usually written as $C \sqsubseteq D$. Determining subsumption is about checking whether the subsumer concept D is more general than the subsumee concept C. This means that C must denote a subset of the set denoted by D.

Example: *Mother* $\sqsubseteq$ *Woman*.

Two other relationships between concepts are equivalence and disjointness. Both of them can be reduced to subsumption:

- *C and D are equivalent* $\Leftrightarrow$ *C is subsumed by D and D is subsumed by C.*
- *C and D are disjoint* $\Leftrightarrow$ $C \sqcap D$ *is subsumed by* $\bot$.

Subsumption is also used to compute a subsumption hierarchy (taxonomy) of all named concepts. This helps for classification, which means to place a new concept expression in the proper place in a taxonomic hierarchy of concepts. Classification is a basic task in constructing a terminology.

Concept Satisfiability

Concept satisfiability is the problem of checking whether there exists a model of the knowledge base in which C is interpreted as nonempty (has an individual).

Description logics semantics are defined by an interpretation $\mathcal{I} = (\Delta^{\mathcal{I}}, \cdot^{\mathcal{I}})$. $\Delta^{\mathcal{I}}$ is the domain of the interpretation (a nonempty set) and $\cdot^{\mathcal{I}}$ is the interpretation function. The latter assigns meaning to nonlogical symbols: it maps concept names into subsets of the domain, role names into subsets of the Cartesian product of the domain, and individual names into elements of the domain.

So a concept C is satisfiable if and only if there exists an interpretation $\mathcal{I}$ such that $C^{\mathcal{I}} \neq \emptyset$. $\mathcal{I}$ is then called a model of C.

Satisfiability can be reduced to subsumption: C is unsatisfiable $\Leftrightarrow$ C is subsumed by $\perp$. In the case of description logics with negation support, subsumption can be reduced to satisfiability by C is subsumed by $D \Leftrightarrow C \sqcap \neg D$ is unsatisfiable.

For example, $Mother \sqsubseteq Woman \Leftrightarrow Mother \sqcap \neg Woman$ is unsatisfiable.

ABox Consistency

ABox consistency is the problem of checking whether there is a nonempty model for $\mathcal{A}$. In general, it is checked with respect to a TBox (see the "Knowledge Base Consistency" section above)

Instance Checking

Instance checking verifies whether a given individual is an instance of a specified concept. Other reasoning services can be defined in terms of instance checking, e.g., knowledge base consistency (see the "Knowledge Base Consistency" section above), realization (see the "Most Specific Concept and Realization" section later), and retrieval (see the "Retrieval" section later). They are described in the following section about nonstandard inference problems.

Instance checking itself can be reduced to ABox consistency.

Nonstandard Inference Problems

All description logics systems provide the standard inference services described above. According to [10], it has turned out, however, that these services are not sufficient for optimally building and maintaining large description logics knowledge bases.

Nonstandard reasoning tasks can support the building and maintenance of knowledge bases, as well as the retrieval of information about the knowledge in them. Hereafter some more prominent nonstandard inference problems are briefly described.

Least Common Subsumer

The least common subsumer (LCS) of two concepts C and D is the minimal concept that subsumes both of them and is thus a concept describing the commonalities of C and D.

E is the LCS of C and D if:

1. $C \sqsubseteq E$ and $D \sqsubseteq E$.
2. For every F with $C \sqsubseteq F$ and $D \sqsubseteq F$, we have $E \sqsubseteq F$.

Most Specific Concept and Realization

The most specific concept (MSC) is the least concept description that an individual is an instance of, given the assertions in the knowledge base. The problem of determining the MSC of a given individual is called realization.

C is the MSC of an individual a in an ABox A if:

1. $A \models a : C$.
2. For each D with $A \models a : D$, we have $C \sqsubseteq D$.

Retrieval

Retrieval is about retrieving all instances of a given concept.

Unification of Concept Terms

Unification of concept terms extends, according to [12], the equivalence problem by allowing one to replace certain concept names by concept terms before testing for equivalence. This is necessary, because often testing for equivalence is not sufficient to find out whether, for a given concept term, there already exists another concept term in the knowledge base describing the same notion.

Although the following concept terms are not equivalent, they represent the same concept:

- *Woman* $\sqcap \forall child. Woman.$
- *Female* $\sqcap$ *Human* $\sqcap \forall child.(Female \sqcap Human).$

The two terms can be made equivalent by replacing the atomic concept $Woman$ by the concept term $Female \sqcap Human$. So those two terms obviously unify.

Matching of Concepts

Matching of concepts with variables is a special case of unification. It was initially meant to help to discard unimportant aspects of large concepts in knowledge bases.

Given a concept description D, containing variables, and a concept description C, without variables, the matching problem asks for a substitution σ (of the variables by concept descriptions) such that $C \sqsubseteq \sigma(D)$. More detailed information about the concept matching problem can be found in [9].

Concept Rewriting

The idea of rewriting is, given a concept expression, to find a concept which is related to the given concept according to equivalence, subsumption, or some other relation. This can be used to reformulate concepts during maintenance of a knowledge base or to translate concepts from one knowledge base to another.

According to [11], the problem of rewriting a concept can be described as follows: Given a set of concept definitions (TBox) $\mathcal{T}$ and a concept description C that does not contain concept names defined in $\mathcal{T}$, can this description be rewritten into a related description E by using some of the names defined in $\mathcal{T}$?

Absorption

Absorption is a rewriting optimization that tries to eliminate GCI axioms (see the "Description Logics Knowledge Base" section above) [208].

Explanation

We use explanations all the time in our daily life to justify our opinions and decisions. Depending on the context in which they are used, those explanations can have many different forms.

While a description logics reasoner can be used to derive inferences from or detect contradictions in an ontology, most users have difficulties in understanding inferences and/or fixing errors in an ontology. This is because most reasoners only report inferences (or errors) in the ontology without explaining how or why they are derived.

So an approach to explanation in knowledge-based systems is the following: The user asks why a conclusion has been reached and gets presented with the reasoning trace of the system [200]. This helps the user in understanding how the system works, to be confident in the system's output, and to eventually debug an ontology.

7.3.2 Logic Programming

As already stated in Sect. 7.2.2, logic programming is a declarative programming paradigm. It is the appropriate calculus to execute query answering, as there are well-known techniques for query answering in the area of logic programming and deductive databases [209]. Datalog programs can be evaluated by techniques such as, e.g., naïve evaluation, seminaïve evaluation, seminaïve evaluation with magic sets, query–subquery evaluation [4], or dynamic filtering [122].

Query Answering

The main reasoning task in logic programming is query answering, i.e., the computation of all ground substitutions of free variables in a query such that the ground version of the query under any of these substitutions is logically entailed by an ontology (or more generally a knowledge base). Posing a query to a Prolog or a Datalog program yields a set of tuples that instantiate the vector of variables in the query.

Examples:

Ground query "Is Jack the father of Peter?": ?- $father(jack, peter)$.
Nonground query "Who are the siblings of Bob?": ?- $sibling(bob, x)$.

Nonground queries can be reduced to ground queries, by replacing the variables with possible instatiations. For example, ?- $sibling(bob, x)$. can be replaced by ?- $sibling(bob, peter)$., etc.. Thus, query answering can be reduced to checking entailment of ground facts and therefore also to satisfiability checking.

Ground Entailment

Entailment means, given some formula A, to check if no constraint in an ontology O is violated and if in all models I of the constraint-free projection of O (i.e., the ontology which can be derived from O by removing all constraining description elements, such as attribute type constraints, cardinality constraints, integrity constraints, etc.) it holds that all ground instances of A in O are satisfied.

Such entailment of ground facts is equivalent to answering ground queries.

Ontology Consistency

Consistency checking means checking whether an ontology O is satisfiable. More precisely, it is about checking if no constraint in O is violated and if the constraint-free projection of O has a model I.

The task is executed by querying for the empty clause. If the resulting set is empty, the empty clause could not be derived from the logic program and the ontology is satisfiable, otherwise it is not.

Instance Retrieval

When the task of instance retrieval is executed on a given ontology O and with a query with free variables, we expect a resulting set that contains all tuples for which an instantiation of the query expression is entailed by O.

As for ground entailment, the instance retrieval task can be performed by posing ground queries to the Datalog program (as nonground queries can be reduced to ground queries).

Query Containment

Query containment is about checking whether the results of one query are contained in the results of another query [136]. Query containment can be tested by different approaches, such as, e.g., containment mapping or the "frozen facts" algorithm, presented in [180].

7.3.3 Benefits and Drawbacks

Both approaches, description logics reasoning and logic programming reasoning, have benefits and drawbacks, owing to the characteristics of the underlying logical paradigm.

Description Logic Reasoning

Description logics are logics which have been specifically designed for describing terminologies and relations between the elements of the terminology like concepts and relations. Thus, an important application domain of description logics is the formalization and reasoning over ontologies. Particular emphasis is usually put on decidability of common reasoning tasks like subsumption checking between concepts/relations or satisfiability checking of concepts. Thus, they have very limited expressive power and in particular are not able to describe general properties involving variables since there is no such modeling primitive available in description logics.

Furthermore, it is well known that reasoning over (large) sets of instances (the so-called ABox) cannot be done efficiently by pure description logics systems. But description logics reasoning over individuals is an important aspect of the vision behind the Semantic Web and it is crucial in applications of ontologies in areas such as, e.g., Web service discovery. This also poses new challenges for ontological reasoning. Firstly, applications might now require vast volumes of individuals exceeding the capabilities of existing reasoners. Secondly, while one can assume that changes in the terminological part of an ontology are relatively infrequent, various scenarios, such as Web service discovery, postulate dynamic, frequent, and, possibly, concurrent modification of the information related to the individuals in ontologies.

In order to overcome the problem of efficient ABox reasoning for description logic reasoners a well-known idea in knowledge representation, namely, supporting reasoning by means of databases, can be applied. Assertions over individuals are stored in a database, together with information inferred using a description logic reasoner over the position in the ontological taxonomy of their corresponding descriptions. This allows one to reduce the amount of reasoning to pure terminological reasoning.

Concluding, reasoning on Web service descriptions that is purely based on description logic reasoning ensures the scalability of the approach and of available reasoning systems, owing to the guarantee of the computational tractability of description logics. But, on the other hand, the restricted expressiveness of description logics constrains modeling and comprehension of service descriptions: the description-logic-based service description languages and reasoning systems a priori have strictly limited capabilities. In principle, this is one possible approach but it is widely recognized as insufficient for many real-world applications, among which in our specific domain are semantic descriptions of Web Services.

Logic Programming Reasoning

Logic programming allows the specification of constraints and rules and is in that more expressive than description logics. This enables the creation of and reasoning over more complex and expressive real-world applications, such as, e.g., Semantic Web Service descriptions.

Logic programming query engines provide efficient query answering, and this also over large datasets, i.e., including large sets of instances. As already mentioned, this is crucial for applications of ontologies in areas such as the Semantic Web or Web service discovery.

Logic programming reasoners are not meant to be used as subsumption reasoners. Still, as shown in [88], subsumption reasoning can be reduced to query answering for the subset of description logics that intersects logic programming, named description logic programs (DLP).

As for description logic reasoners, reasoning with logic programming engines can be optimized by the use of a database for the storage of facts, or even for query evaluation.

7.3.4 Reasoning Tasks and WSML Variants

In this section we provide a short description of each of the WSML variants (except for WSML-Full, as the semantics of WSML-Full is at this point in time still an open research issue), as well as the specific requirements that each variant has on a reasoner.

WSML-Core

WSML-Core is based on the well-known description Horn logic (DHL) fragment [55, 88], which is that subset of the description logic $\mathcal{SHIQ}(\mathbf{D})$ (close to the language underlying OWL [104]) that falls inside the Horn logic fragment of first-order logic without equality and without existential quantification.

Two different types of reasoning can be done with WSML-Core, namely, (1) subsumption reasoning and (2) query answering. Subsumption reasoning is equivalent to checking entailment of nonground formulae and can thus be reduced to checking satisfiability using a first-order style or a description logic style calculus. Query answering is equivalent to checking entailment of ground facts. Thus, query answering can also be reduced to satisfiability checking. However, using a first-order or description logic calculus for query answering is not very efficient [55, 107]. Fortunately, there are well-known techniques for query answering in the area of logic programming and deductive databases [209].

For subsumption reasoning, the following are the requirements for a reasoner for WSML-Core:

- Subsumption reasoning for WSML-Core can be done through unsatisfiability with tableaux reasoning, theorem proving, or any other technique for checking satisfiability of first-order theories or query containment.[1]
- In order to handle datatypes in WSML-Core, a datatype oracle is required which has a sound and complete procedure for deciding satisfiability of conjunctions of datatype predicates. Such requirements are described in [166].

---

[1] While query containment for logic programs is in general undecidable, some restricted forms of logic programs containment can be decided. The simplest form, checking containment of conjunctive queries, is well known to be NP-complete [43]. In [37, 38] several more expressive query classes and methods to decide query containment for these are discussed.

For query answering, the following are the requirements for a reasoner for WSML-Core:

- A Datalog engine which can handle integrity constraints (for checking datatypes).
- Built-in predicates for handling strings and integers. For integers, basic arithmetic functions ($+$, $-$, $/$, $\times$) should be provided, as well as basic comparison operators ($=$, $\neq$, $>$, $<$). For strings, at least the (in)equality predicates should be built in.
- The symbols *true* and *false*. The former represents universal truth; the latter represents falsehood. If *false* is derived form the program, the program is inconsistent. These symbols can be eliminated through simple preprocessing steps [56].

WSML-Flight

WSML-Flight extends WSML-Core with the full expressive power of Datalog rules, default negation, the full-blown use of integrity constraints (note that constraints are already in WSML-Core; however, they are only used for datatype predicates), (in)equality for abstract individuals, and metamodeling.

The semantics of WSML-Flight is grounded in logic programming. Since there exists no efficient implementation of query containment and since this problem is undecidable in general, the only reasoning task we envision for WSML-Flight is query answering (i.e., entailment of ground facts). Notice that subsumption reasoning can always be done for the WSML-Core subset of an ontology.

The additional requirements for a WSML-Flight reasoner over the requirements for a WSML-Core reasoner are:

- Full Datalog support.
- Support for (stratified) default negation.
- A built-in equality predicate (in the body of the rule).

Equality could also be axiomatized in the program; however, this would seriously degrade the performance of query answering. Therefore, we state this as a formal requirement.

The other features added in WSML-Flight compared with WSML-Core can be eliminated in a preprocessing step. However, it would be favorable to have also the following feature in the reasoner:

- *Metamodeling* (treating classes as instances, etc.) can be translated to plain Datalog [55, 74, 107]. However, if metamodeling were built into the reasoner, less effort would be required in the preprocessing step. Also, query answers might have to be rewritten in order to deal with metamodeling [74].

WSML-Rule

WSML-Rule extends WSML-Flight with function symbols and additionally allows unsafe rules. We furthermore expect an extension of WSML-Rule with unstratified negation under the well-founded semantics [82].

WSML-DL

WSML-DL is an extension of WSML-Core to a full-fledged description logic with an expressiveness similar to OWL DL, namely, $\mathcal{SHIQ}(\mathbf{D})$. Both query answering and subsumption can be done by similar techniques as developed and implemented in any of the currently popular description logic reasoners, such as FaCT++, Pellet, and RACER.

Both WSML-Core and WSML-DL are based on the $\mathcal{SHIQ}(\mathbf{D})$ description logic. However, WSML-Core correspondsto a restricted subset of $\mathcal{SHIQ}(\mathbf{D})$ which falls in the Horn fragment. Thus, WSML-DL adds the following features to WSML-Core: disjunction, (classical) negation, and existential quantification. In terms of complexity, we know that the upper bound for the combined complexity for WSML-Core (not taking into account the datatypes) is in ExpTime [48], because WSML-Core is a subset of Datalog.

Summary

The major reasoning modes with WSML are the following:

- *Query answering*, which is the computation of all ground substitutions of free variables in a query such that the ground version of the query under any of these substitutions is logically entailed by an ontology (or more generally a knowledge base).
- *Logical entailment*, which is given a set of statements (called assumptions) and a (in general nonground) query, check whether the query can be inferred from the assumptions.

Clearly, both reasoning modes are somehow related: For decidable languages,[2] query answering can be reduced to logical entailment. Therefore, the system takes all permutations of known terms as answers and checks which of these are entailed in a given knowledge base. In the case of languages with an undecidable logical entailment relation, this reduction can only be applied when one does not insist on completeness of query answering.

Checking logical entailment of ground formulae can be solved by means of query answering and in this respect usually with more efficient techniques than the general problem of logical entailment of nonground formulae.

However, reductions from query answering to logical entailment (or the other way around) often result in very inefficient algorithms for query answering (or logical entailment), such that very different techniques have been developed to solve both tasks. Nevertheless this is not always the case. There are hybrid reasoning engines that do such reductions in a rather efficient way. The KAON2[3] reasoning engine,

---

[2] More precisely, we mean languages for which the logical entailment relation $\models$ is decidable.

[3] http://kaon2.semanticweb.org/

for example, uses algorithms which reduce description logic knowledge bases to disjunctive Datalog programs. It thus uses queries to solve logical entailment in description logic reasoning.

7.4 Reasoning Within SESA

Different components within SESA necessitate efficient reasoning functionality. In the following we briefly outline these components and their reasoning requirements.

7.4.1 Discovery

Services can be described in various ways, as Chap. 8 will point out. In the simplest case, a Web service can be considered and modeled as a set of objects. Taking a more fine-grained perspective, Web Services could as well be considered as state transitions on an abstract state space. The formal relation between the states of a transition (called prestate and poststate) is captured by so-called preconditions and postconditions.

Whereas in the former case, a simple ontological reasoning can be sufficient and query answering can be applied, in the latter case, logical entailment between preconditions and postconditions of Semantic Web Service descriptions and the client's goals will need to be checked in general. To support this fine-grained Web service perspective, a reasoner needs thus to provide the reasoning task of checking (general) logical entailment.

Thus, the discovery component can use both a description-logic-based and a logic-programming-based reasoning engine, depending on the requested reasoning task.

7.4.2 Selection

In Chap. 9, the problem of ranking services on the basis of their nonfunctional properties will be described as an integrated part of the service selection. The ranking process generates an ordered list of services out of candidate service sets.

During the ranking process, reasoning is used for evaluating the logical rules that are used to model the nonfunctional properties of services. The nonfunctional property values obtained by the evaluation are sorted and used to build an ordered list of services.

As the selection component only reasons over rules, it is an optimal user of a logic-programming-based reasoning engine.

7.4.3 Mediation

Data Mediation

In most data mediation scenarios in a semantic environment, the data to be mediated is represented by ontology instances. As will be pointed out in Chap. 10, the automatic mediation task relies on a semiautomatic approach (i.e., with user interaction) of ontology mapping during design time.

A common mediation scenario is then *instance transformation*, which corresponds to the task of mediating data between different actors. The instance transformation task is part of a run-time process and needs to be executed completely automatically, based on already existing mappings created on the schema level during the design-time phase. The mapping rules, the source instances, and, if necessary, source and target schema information are loaded into the reasoning space. The last of these is queried for instances of target concepts, and if semantically related source instances exist, the rules produce as a result the target instances.

The logical mapping rules can be represented in several languages, depending on the available reasoning support.

Process Mediation

The process mediation addresses the behavioral mediation problem in the context of Semantic Web Services, i.e., it is responsible for resolving mismatches between the service requester's and the service provider's choreographies. Chapter 10 describes an example scenario in which problems occur when two actors are communicating, and where mismatches between their communication patterns can be found. The process mediation uses reasoning to check whether messages (containing instances of concepts, in terms of the sender's/targeted partner's ontology) are expected at a certain phase of the communication. This is done by evaluating transition rules.

7.5 A Generic Framework for Reasoning with WSML

The WSML2Reasoner[4] framework (Fig. 7.1) is a generic, flexible architecture for reasoning with the different variants of the WSML family. During the design phase, great importance was attached to system modularity, reuse of existing technologies, and flexibility in configuration and customization of a reasoning system for specific reasoning tasks. The fact that WSML is based on (theoretically and practically) well-studied knowledge representation paradigms, for which various systems have already been implemented and tested, supported this design decision. The WSML2Reasoner framework allows the easy integration of such external reasoning components.

Consequently instead of implementing new reasoners, one can use existing reasoner implementations for WSML through a wrapper that maps WSML expressions first into common (shared) knowledge representation formats (different ones for the rule-based or description-logic-based WSML variants), and then via specific adapters into the appropriate syntaxes of concrete reasoning engines. The wrapper thus contains various validation, normalization, and transformation functionalities that are reusable across different WSML variants.

This generic approach allows people to use their specific existing reasoner of choice (which is independent of WSML) in the WSML context, and it provides people with the possibility to exploit systems that have already been developed already and that are therefore well tuned with respect to performance and stability.

---

[4] http://tools.deri.org/wsml2reasoner/index.html

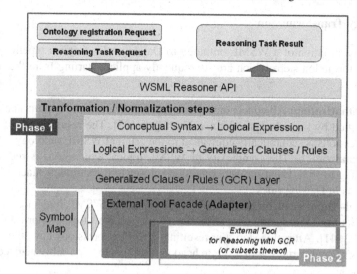

Figure 7.1. High-level architecture of the reasoning system and development phases

7.5.1 Reasoning with Rule-Based WSML

We present a framework for reasoning with rule-based WSML variants (with focus on WSML-Core, WSML-Flight, and WSML-Rule) that builds on existing infrastructure for inferencing in rule-based formalisms.The framework is based on a semantics-preserving syntactic transformation of WSML ontologies to Datalog programs [47] with (in)equality and integrity constraints, as described in the WSML specification [53]. To make use of existing rule engines, the reasoning framework performs various syntactical transformations to convert an original ontology in WSML syntax into a semantically equivalent Datalog program. The WSML reasoning tasks of checking knowledge base satisfiability and of instance retrieval are then realized by means of Datalog querying via calls to an underlying Datalog inference engine that is fed with the rules contained in this program.

Besides these standard reasoning tasks, the framework provides debugging features that support an ontology engineer in the task of ontology development: violated constraints are pointed out together with some details on the ontological entities that cause the violation. Such a feature helps to improve the error reporting in situations of erroneous modeling.

Instead of directly mapping WSML entities, i.e., concepts, instances, and attributes, to Datalog predicates and constants, we use special metalevel predicates and axioms which form a vocabulary on reified entities for reproducing the WSML constructs in Datalog. This way of using Datalog as an underlying formalism facilitates the metamodeling features of WSML.

Ontology Transformation

The transformation of a WSML ontology to Datalog rules forms a pipeline of single transformation steps which are subsequently applied, starting from the original ontology:

- **Axiomatization:** All conceptual elements are converted into appropriate axioms specified by logical expressions, according to [53]. The resulting set of logical expressions is semantically equivalent to the original WSML ontology.
- **Normalization:** The complexity of WSML logical expressions is reduced according to [53], bringing the expressions closer to the simple syntactic form of literals in Datalog rules.
- **Lloyd–Topor transformation:** The (still) complex WSML logical expressions are flattened, producing simple rules according to the Lloyd–Topor transformations [141]. After this step, the resulting WSML expressions have the form of proper Datalog rules with a single head and conjunctive (possibly negated) body literals.
- **Datalog rule generation:** In a final step all WSML logical expressions are transformed to a Datalog program with generic Datalog rules that represent the content of the original WSML ontology.
  The resulting Datalog rules are of the form

$$H : -B_1 \wedge \cdots \wedge B_n,$$

where H and B_i are literals for the head and the body of the rule, respectively.

Architecture and Internal Layering

Figure 7.2 shows the internal architecture of the WSML2Reasoner framework that is related to the rule-based variants of WSML, as well as the data flow during a prototypical usage scenario. The outer box outlines a WSML reasoner component that allows a user to register WSML-Core, WSML-Flight, or WSML-Rule ontologies and to pose queries on them. The inner box illustrates the transformation pipeline introduced earlier and shows its subsequent steps in a layering scheme.

Registered ontologies go through all the transformation steps, whereas user queries are injected at a later stage, skipping the nonapplicable axiomatization and constraint replacement steps. Here, the internal layering scheme allows for an easy reorganization and reuse of the transformation steps on demand, ensuring high flexibility and modularity.

The core component of the framework is an exchangeable Datalog inference engine wrapped by a reasoner facade which embeds it in the framework infrastructure. This facade mediates between the generic Datalog program produced in the transformations and the tool-specific Datalog implementation and built-in predicates used by the external inference engine.

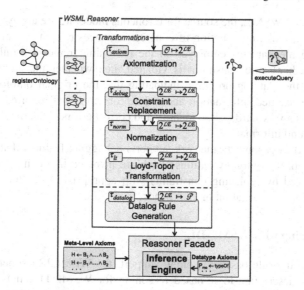

Figure 7.2. WSML2Reasoner – rule-based internal framework architecture

Supported Reasoning Tasks

The following reasoning tasks are realized by performing Datalog queries on a Datalog program. As result, a query yields a set of tuples that instantiate the variables in the query.

- **Query answering:** The task of computing all ground substitutions of free variables in a query such that the ground version of the query under any of these substitutions is logically entailed by an ontology.
- **Ontology consistency:** This task of checking a WSML ontology for consistency is done by querying for the empty clause. If the resulting set is empty, then the empty clause could not be derived from the program and the original ontology is satisfiable, otherwise it is not.
- **Entailment:** The reasoning task of entailment of ground facts by a WSML ontology can be done by using queries that contain no variables.
- **Retrieval:** Instance retrieval can be performed by posing queries that contain variables to the Datalog program. The resulting set contains all tuples for which an instantiation of the query expression is entailed by the original ontology.

Debugging Support

During the process of ontology development, an ontology engineer can easily construct an erroneous model containing contradictory information. In order to produce consistent ontologies, inconsistencies should be reported to engineers with some details about the ontological elements that cause the inconsistency.

In rule-based WSML, the source for erroneous modeling are always constraints, together with a violating situation of concrete instances related via attributes. The plain Datalog mechanisms employed in the reasoning framework only allow for checking whether some constraint is violated, i.e., whether the empty clause is derived from the Datalog program, indicating that the original ontology contains errors – more detailed information about the problem is not reported. Experience shows that it is a very hard task to identify and correct errors in the ontology without such background information.

The WSML2Reasoner framework supports debugging features that provide information about the ontology entities which are involved in a constraint violation. This is achieved by replacing constraints with appropriate rules that contain the needed additional information in their heads.

7.5.2 Reasoning with WSML-DL

In addition to the rule-based reasoning support, the WSML2Reasoner framework also supports description-logic-based reasoning for WSML-DL. It is based on a semantics-preserving syntactic transformation of WSML-DL ontologies to OWL DL ontologies, as described in [113]. The WSML reasoning tasks of checking ontology consistency, entailment, and instance retrieval can then be performed by means of OWL DL reasoning applied on a transformed ontology. Thus, the framework directly builds on top of existing OWL DL or description logic reasoning engines.

Besides the reasoning tasks, the framework provides validation of WSML-DL ontologies, as well as the serialization of the latter to OWL DL. However the serialization to OWL DL is not complete, and details of the restrictions are given in the following section on ontology transformation.

Ontology Transformation

The transformation of a WSML-DL ontology to an OWL DL ontology is done in a line of single transformation steps that are applied subsequently.

- **Relations to attributes:** Replace relations, subrelations, and relation instances by attributes and axioms, according to the preprocessing steps described in [113].
- **Axiomatization:** All conceptual elements are converted into appropriate axioms specified by logical expressions, according to [53]. The resulting set of logical expressions is semantically equivalent to the original WSML ontology.
- **Implication reduction rules:** Replace equivalences and right implications in logical expressions by left implications.
- **Inverse implication reduction rules:** Replace conjunctions on the left side and disjunctions on the right side of an inverse implication by left implications.
- **Molecule decomposition rules:** Replace complex molecules inside a logical expression by conjunctions of simple ones.

- **OWL API transformation:** All logical expressions that result from the transformation and normalization steps described above are processed one by one. Each logical expression is translated into the corresponding OWL description, according to the mapping described in [113].

The transformation from WSML-DL to OWL DL is not complete. The restrictions are mainly due to the differences in the description logics underlying WSML-DL ($\mathcal{SHIQ}(D)$) and OWL DL ($\mathcal{SHOIN}(D)$). OWL DL does not support the following WSML-DL features:

- **Datatype predicates:** Datatype predicates are lost during the transformation.
- **Qualified number restrictions:** Qualified number restrictions (QNRs) are lost during the transformation. In [113] a possible workaround is mentioned, as well as a nonendorsed OWL extension; both would allow one to translate QNRs into OWL DL (only approximated with the workaround).

Architecture and Internal Layering

Figure 7.3 shows the internal architecture of the WSML2Reasoner framework that is related to WSML-DL, as well as the data flow during a prototypical usage scenario. The outer box outlines a WSML reasoner component that allows a user to register WSML-DL ontologies and to reason over them. The inner box illustrates the transformation pipeline introduced earlier and shows its subsequent steps in a layering scheme.

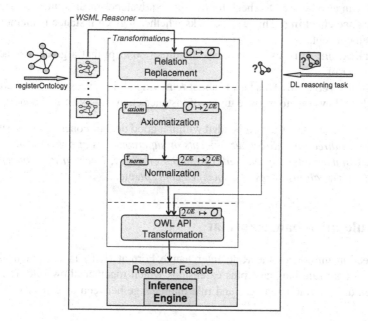

Figure 7.3. WSML2Reasoner – description-logic-based internal framework architecture

Registered ontologies go through all the transformation steps, whereas the user reasoning tasks are injected at a later stage, skipping the nonapplicable axiomatization and normalization steps. Here, the internal layering scheme allows for an easy reorganization and reuse of the transformation steps on demand, ensuring high flexibility and modularity.

The core component of the framework is an exchangeable description logic or OWL DL inference engine wrapped by a reasoner facade which embeds it in the framework infrastructure. This facade mediates between the OWL DL ontology produced in the transformations and the tool-specific implementation used by the external inference engine.

Supported Reasoning Tasks

The following reasoning tasks are supported by the WSML-DL reasoner within the WSML2Reasoner framework:

- **Knowledge base consistency:** This task of checking a WSML-DL ontology for consistency ensures that the ontology does not contain any contradictory facts. It checks whether the TBox and the ABox of the knowledge base do have a common, nonempty, model.
- **Concept satisfiability:** This task checks whether there exists a model of the knowledge base in which a given concept is interpreted as nonempty.
- **Concept subsumption:** This tasks checks whether a concept A is more general than a concept B, i.e., whether B denotes a subset of the set denoted by A. This task can also be used to check for concept equivalence or disjointness.
- **Instance checking:** This tasks checks whether a given instance is member of a given concept.
- **Realization:** This task determines the direct concept that a given instance is a member of.
- **Instance retrieval:** This task is about retrieving all instances of a given concept. It also allows one to retrieve tuples of instances that satisfy certain conditions.

The reasoning tasks are embedded within a good deal of concrete tasks, such as, e.g., *Get all direct or indirect subconcepts or superconcepts of a given concept*, *Get all constraint or inferring attributes from the ontology*, *Check if two concepts are equivalent*, *Get all instances of a specified concept*, etc.

7.6 Rule Interchange Format

This section introduces the Rule Interchange Format (RIF) layer, which aims to specify a core rule language plus extensions which together allow rule translation between diverse rule languages and rule interchange between diverse rule systems, including publishing, sharing, and reusing of existing rules. The work on RIF is led by the W3C RIF Working Group[5] and can be seen as an advancement of existing logic programming.

Although rule-based systems and rule languages have already played an important role in the history of computer science, they seem to have had a new life since the continuous growth of the Semantic Web. So far there is no standard for rule-based technologies; the establishment of such standards is the goal of the RIF Working Group. The standards shall be characterized by their easy extensibility, which will allow them to deal with the further evolution of rule-based technologies.

There is a large interest in RIF on the part of both industry and different user communities, such as, e.g., business rules and Semantic Web users. Their specific needs are expressed within a set of use case scenarios that are representative for the types of application scenarios that the RIF is intended to support.[6] They can then be taken into account for the eventual specification of extensions.

7.6.1 Architecture

The RIF Working Group is first developing a Core Condition Language that will be a shared part of all RIF dialects. The RIF has been designed as a "layered architecture organized around the notion of a dialect."[7] A dialect is a rule language with a well-defined syntax and semantics, whereas the latter must be model-theoretic, proof-theoretic, or operational. Targeted logical paradigms for RIF dialects are, e.g., production rules, logic programming, first-order-logic-based rules, reactive rules, and normative rules (integrity constraints); all dialects need to extend the RIF Core dialect.

7.6.2 Syntax and Semantics

According to the RIF Core Design Working Draft,[8] RIF Core corresponds to the language of definite Horn rules with equality (and with a standard first-order semantics). The semantics of RIF seem hence to be similar to the semantics of WSML, as described in Chap. 3.

Syntactically RIF has been designed as a Web language, supporting, e.g., URIs as identifiers and XML Schema datatypes. Nevertheless, this does not prevent RIF interoperability with rule languages in general, independent of, or not limited to, the Web. To be precise, three different syntaxes are meant to be developed for RIF: (1) a human-readable syntax, (2) an abstract syntax, and (3) an exchange syntax (e.g., XML or RDF). The concrete human-readable syntax is still open, i.e., work in progress.

---

[5] http://www.w3.org/2005/rules/wg.html

[6] http://www.w3.org/TR/rif-ucr/

[7] http://www.w3.org/TR/rif-core/

[8] http://www.w3.org/TR/rif-core/

7.7 Conclusion

In the following we will provide a conclusion concerning the path we went through the domain of reasoning, and will outline some future research possibilities.

7.7.1 Conclusion

In this chapter we have defined what we understand by the often used and abused term "reasoning," i.e., the task of inferring new (i.e., not explicitly stated) knowledge from a given set of statements (or a knowledge base). We have shown the major reasoning requirements, with focus on Semantic Web Services. Next we briefly introduced the two well-known logical formalisms that have served as a basis for WSML, namely, description logics and logic programming. We have explained concepts such as "unique name assumption" and "open/closed world assumption," which are important in the design of ontologies using the two logical formalisms. Related to the Semantic Web, to ontologies, and depending on the underlying logical formalism, we have shown some major reasoning tasks, such as, e.g., checking ontology/knowledge base consistency, query answering, concept subsumption, and instance retrieval.

As the main application domain of description logics we have shown the design of ontologies, i.e., describing terminologies and relations between the elements of the terminologies. Reasoning tasks such as subsumption checking or satisfiability checking are executed efficiently by description logic reasoning engines. However, we have also identified two major drawbacks of description logics, i.e., they have only limited expressivity owing to a lack of available modeling primitives and they cannot efficiently handle reasoning over large sets of instances.

The main application domain of logic programming lies in the specification of rules and constraints, which allows more complex descriptions for, e.g., Semantic Web Services. Logic programming reasoners deal very well with query answering, but they are not meant to be used as subsumption reasoners.

We have defined the reasoning requirements of the different WSML variants, and have outlined the need for reasoning of the SESA components discovery, selection, and mediation. Then we introduced WSML2Reasoner, a generic framework for reasoning with WSML, and showed in more detail the functioning of reasoning with rule-based WSML and with WSML-DL. Their syntaxes are transformed from WSML to Datalog or OWL DL, respectively, and then the framework enables the use of existing Datalog, or OWL DL, reasoning engines.

Furthermore we briefly introduced the RIF, which aims to become an interlingua into which rule languages can be mapped, even allowing the interchange of rule reasoning engines.

Throughout the chapter we have focused on the importance of reasoning for the success of the Semantic Web and Semantic Web Services. We have shown that reasoning systems are the crucial infrastructure which is needed for exploiting the semantics of service descriptions in any form, e.g., in service discovery. Thus, without reasoning, semantic information cannot be efficiently used.

7.7.2 Future Research

The following outlines some topics in the reasoning area that are still the subject of research, as well as possible future reseach topics:

- Reasoning in distributed environments.
- Reasoning with heterogeneous and conflicting information.
- Reasoning over (very) large data (instances) sets.
- Reasoning about nonfunctional aspects of Web Services.
- Reasoning about Web service interface descriptions, i.e., choreographies and orchestrations.
- reasoning with integrating frameworks based on classical first-order logic and nonmonotonic logic programming.
- New techniques for description logic reasoning.
- Hybrid reasoning based on description logics and logic programming.

8

Discovery

Realizing the vision of the Semantically Enabled Service-oriented Architecture (SESA) involves a number of tasks. Within this chapter we will focus on the discovery task, the annotations necessary to automate it, and the tools to process them (discovery engine).

WSMO provides a conceptual framework for semantically describing Web Services and their specific properties. We discuss how WSMO can be used for service discovery and provide a proper conceptual grounding. We will discuss how different mechanisms can be used to discover Web Services and especially what consequences those mechanisms have on the complexity of the required annotations as well as on the quality of the results. It is important to understand the conceptual model and the particular assumptions underlying a discovery solution in order to utilize their results properly.

8.1 A Conceptual Model for Discovery

A workable approach to automating service discovery must define precisely its conceptual model and its assumptions. A logical formalism alone without a proper conceptualization cannot solve the underlying problem. To describe such an approach, we start by aiming to provide a common understanding of what a service is and the levels of abstraction in its description, on the basis of [178], and we also state our assumptions about the elements involved in the process of locating suitable services for service requesters.

First, let us clarify the terms "service" and "Web service" themselves. The English word "service" is overloaded in its meaning. In the business world, a "service" normally denotes the provision of a general business activity which provides a certain value to the customer [14]. In computer science, in contrast, the term "service" is often used synonymously with "Web service", i.e., a software component accessible over the Internet via a standardized interface. Preist [178] defines these terms as follows:

- *Service.* A service is defined as the provision of a concrete product or abstract value in some domain. As an example, let us consider a user who wants to book a flight from Innsbruck to Frankfurt. Following our definition of a service, we mean the actual transport, fulfilling user constraints such as a certain date. The provision of the service as such, and the contractual issues around this service provision, are independent of how the supplier and the provider interact. It is irrelevant whether the requester goes to an airline ticket office or uses the airline's Web site to book the flight. We understand the term "service" in this sense, that is, as a provision of value.
- *Web service.* Web Services are defined as computational entities accessible over the Internet (using Web service standards and protocols) via platform- and programming-language-independent interfaces. Returning to our previous example, an airline might provide a software component accessible via Web service standards, i.e., a Web service to request the booking of a flight; the Web service is an electronic means to request a service, but is not the service itself. We understand the term "Web service" as a means to request a service over standard protocols, described using widely accepted standards. Thus, a Web service is a means to consume an actual service, or to place a contract for an actual service.

In order to deliver a service, a service provider usually needs certain information from the requester. For instance, booking a flight requires the name of the person flying, the itinerary, and a valid credit card number as input information. This input data will determine what has to be provided. In the real world, we have a further complication in regard to discovery and Web service description. In general, a service offered by a provider does not stay the same, but changes over time. For example, the availability of seats in an airplane changes over time.

This also has implications on how Web Services are described. Clearly it is not feasible to describe the availability of an entire fleet of airplanes within the semantic annotation of the Web service interface. In fact (1) this would partially duplicate the functionality of the actual service and (2) such a description would be quickly outdated. In general, our assumption is that for discovery it is not required to describe each single possible service that can be provided (e.g., a particular ticket for a specific date), but that the overall capability of the service is of interest, i.e., that the service sells flight tickets for charter flights to popular holiday destinations within Europe.

In the following we discuss in a more concrete way what such descriptions can look like in various levels of abstraction and how these can be expressed using the WSMO framework.

8.2 Web Services at Various Levels of Abstraction

We now discuss in more detail how Web service discovery is addressed within the WSMO framework. We outline several different levels that require different efforts for annotation and description of both goals and services and deliver results of different accuracy. Each approach addresses a different level of abstraction in Web service descriptions. The various techniques taken together help to create a workable solution to the problem of Web service discovery which addresses practical requirements and is based on realistic assumptions.

The descriptions of Web Services, as published by service providers, and the goals of service requesters need to be compared with one another during the discovery process in order to identify matching Web Services and goals. In essence, matching in the discovery process is about finding common elements in these descriptions. Depending on the level of detail in which we consider these entities, we end up with models of Web Services at varying levels of abstraction.

At the most fine-grained level, we can consider services as concrete state transitions from a prestate to a poststate. These states determine precisely how the world is before and after the service has been provided. On a more abstract level, we can ignore the detailed structure of services (i.e., the respective states), understand them purely as abstract objects, and characterize their specific properties. In terms of ontologies, we would then consider services as instances and Web Services as concepts. At the most abstract level, we can abstract even further in the description of abstract services by ignoring the description of the possible elements of the set. At this level, we would simply use a term or keyword for describing the abstract service and neglect any information about the fine-grained structure. Essentially, we are considering keyword-based descriptions here.

Each of these levels of abstraction implies a different description of Web Services, ranging from detailed characterizations of possible state transitions, less detailed descriptions using (complex) concepts in an ontology, to simple unstructured keywords. Consequently, the achievable accuracy of a result in the discovery process varies significantly, since more or less structure is reflected in the descriptions. On the other hand, the ease of providing the descriptions varies drastically between these levels as well. Whereas simple keywords are easy to provide, the description of concepts already requires more effort. Detailed state-based descriptions can only be created by specially trained experts. The more fine-grained a Web service description is, not only the effort of creating it increases, but also the algorithms that deal with these descriptions become more complex.

Therefore, there is an interesting trade-off between the possible achievable accuracy, the ease of creating the descriptions, and the degree of computational efficiency of the discovery process.

8.3 Keyword-Based Discovery

Keyword-based discovery is a basic ingredient in a complete framework for Semantic Web Service discovery. By performing a keyword-based search, one can filter or rank the huge number of available services rather quickly.

In a typical keyword-based scenario, a keyword-based query engine is used to discover services. A query, which is basically a set of keywords, is provided as input to a query engine. The query engine matches the keywords in the user's input against the keywords used to describe the service. A query with the same meaning can be formulated by using a dictionary of synonyms, such as WordNet [71]. The semantics of the query remains the same but, because of the different keywords used (synonyms of previous ones), more services than possibly fulfill the user's request are found. Moreover, by using dictionaries such as WordNet, as well as natural-language processing techniques, one can, in principle, achieve an increase in the semantic relevance of the search results (with regard to the search request) [182]. Nonetheless, such techniques are inherently restricted by the ambiguities of natural language and the lack of semantic understanding of natural-language descriptions by algorithmic systems.

The two major advantages of using keyword-based discovery are that the annotations required are already present if WSDL-based Web Services are used and that keyword-matching engines already have a high maturity and can scale up easily with a high number of services. However, up to now only little work has been done to optimize existing indexing and retrieval systems for the Web service domain. The service description in the form of a WSDL document is a well-structured XML document; terms used in different contexts (interface, operation, input/output) have a substantially different meaning. In the case of Web documents major search engines already use the context of the term to influence the ranking, such that a term appearing in the URL or title is considered more important than others.

In the following we give a brief overview of existing approaches that rely on keyword-based matching. We also give some quantitive data of the currently publicly accessible Web Services. As mentioned earlier, different discovery scenarios have different requirements with respect to the precision of annotation and quality of discovery results. Clearly when looking at publicly available services the amount of control over the publishers is minimal and thus the quality of annotations is rather on the lower bound of the spectrum.

8.3.1 Existing Approaches for Keyword-Based Discovery

As we cannot make any statements about private, or intranet, usage of Web Services by its definition, all empirical results presented are based on publicly available Web Services. On the basis of previous work [13, 62, 68, 123] and our own observation, we have identified three major approaches for discovering publicly available Web Services:

1. Universal Description, Discovery, and Integration (UDDI) [16] is a standard for centralized repositories. The first UDDI business registry (UBR) nodes were run by IBM, Microsoft, SAP, and NTT Com.
2. Service directories (or portals) which gather services using focused crawlers or manual registration and offer a search functionality via a HTML interface.
3. Standard Web search engines which are able to restrict the search in some way to retrieve WSDL descriptions. Although this is no guarantee of finding services, this possibility provides the biggest coverage.

When looking at these approaches, we focus on two aspects: (1) the number of services; (2) the quality and quantity of information that is associated with them. For example, how many aspects of a service are described and how accurate those descriptions are.

Number of Services

As the first step we have investigated in more detail the number of services that can be found using the various means. In the case of UDDI we had to realize that the public repositories were shut down at the beginning of 2006,[1] so we could not do an analysis ourselves. However earlier work from 2004 [123] reported that only one third of the 1,200 registered services contained references to valid WSDL files. To examine the number of services available in the various Web portals (see Table 8.1 for a complete list) we extracted the number of unique WSDL files referenced from each site and subsequently verified whether the documents were still accessible. To determine the number of services available via search engines like Google[2] or Yahoo![3] we encountered two problems. First, there are no means to retrieve all results.[4] The second major problem is that there are no means to formulate a query that only returns Web service descriptions. The numbers are obtained by querying for all resources having the keyword "wsdl" in the URL. Of course there is no guarantee that the document retrieved from those URLs will includes a WSDL document; however, we could only verify this for the results we obtained from the Alexa[5] search engine, where about 12% of the URLs did resolve to WSDL documents.

Table 8.1. Survey results

Repository	No. of services claimed	No. of WSDL documents retrieved	Liveliness	Categorization
UBR	1,200	300	No	Yes
RemoteMethods	319	205	No	Yes
StrikeIron	638	508	Yes	Yes
Woogle	751	312	Yes	Yes
XMethods	505	460	No	No
ProgrammableWeb	80	77	Yes	No
Google	262,000	NA	No	No
Yahoo!	61,800	NA	No	No
Alexa	30,846	3,630	No	No

NA not available

---

[1] http://www.uddi.org/find.html
[2] http://google.com
[3] http://yahoo.com
[4] Both Google and Yahoo! show only the first 1,000 results per query
[5] http://alexa.com

Available Information

As we did not have access to the UDDI repositories, we could not evaluate the quality of information. However very low quality with respect to the data was reported in [123], i.e., many service descriptions that are pure tests or references to nonexisting WSDL files. Search engines like Google do not collect specific service-related information: the ranking is based on the number of incoming links and the matching is done on a keyword level without considering the WSDL structure: moreover no availability or other service-related information is given. The Web service directories provide more information. This includes pricing data, scoring and review systems, provider information, textual descriptions, and links to online documentation. Only Woogle [62] operates solely on the information given with the WSDL document. ProgrammableWeb,[6] as one of the portals considered, has the most information fields (30); however, many services only have filled out a small subset of those. Moreover it is a generic repository for Web APIs and not only for Web Services that use the WSDL technology; in fact only 20% of the 400 registered services use WSDL.

Table 8.1 summarizes our observations. The first column gives the number of services that are reported by the respective means of discovery, the second column gives the number of WSDL documents we could retrieve, and the third and fourth columns indicate if particular information is available.

Summary

One has to conclude that for publicly available Web Services the UDDI-based approach has failed and has been discontinued. Using normal search engines, one can achieve the broadest coverage; however, one has to spend considerable time in browsing through results, since one cannot efficiently filter those for Web Services. The various dedicated portal pages are at present the most convenient way to find Web Services. Except for Woogle, they rely on manually maintained repositories and have only a limited number of services. We also included ProgrammableWeb as a repository; however, only a small portion of the APIs registered use WSDL technology.

8.3.2 A Keyword-Based Service Search Engine

On the basis of the empirical studies described in the previous section, we have developed a Web service search engine. We start off by crawling the Web for WSDL files. Although a WSDL document is only a technical interface specification it is the basis for our analysis aiming to extract high-level functional description. From our experience more than 40% of all the WSDL files include textual documentation. And even if a WSDL file has no textual documentation it still contains very valuable information, e.g., method names such as "SendSMSToIndia" with inputs like "FromEmailAddress," and "MobileNumber." However, one needs to consider

---

[6] http://www.programmableweb.com/

the particularities of a WSDL document. The meaning of a keyword can have a different impact on the overall functionality depending on its position: if "fax" is part of the service name (or port type), it has a different relevance than if it occurs only somewhere within the XML schema as part of the input information.

Implementation

We have implemented the method described above. Our prototype is available at http://seekda.com. In the analysis step we removed duplicates and WSDL files that did not include any valid end point definition. Within out experiments we could gather about 10,000 different services. For filtering duplicates, we used the interface identifier (porttype) together with the specific end-point URL as criteria.

For allowing keyword-based search, we implemented a tokenizer and lexical analyzer on top of the tsearch2 library.[7] For example we added specific routines to the tokenizer for taking care of the CamelCasing[8] often used by developers (such as "WeatherForecastService"). These tokens are then reduced to lexemes by their respective dictionaries. That is, e.g., the term "messages" is reduced to its linguistic stem, i.e., "message." In order to provide ranked results for a particular keyword we assigned to each keyword one of four different weights depending on its position within the document.

Regarding the technical properties we have so far monitored the response time, and if a particular end point does adhere to the protocols it claims to support. Moreover we have included the results of an IP to geographic database mapping. A further ranking criteria that we have included is the number of known Web pages that point to a service description. While this characteristic has, in our opinion, not the same relevance as for static content, it still provides a reasonable indicator for relevance. Figure 8.1 shows a screen shot of the search engine prototype.

8.3.3 Summary and Conclusion

The standard model of syntactic search engines like Google alone is not well suited for Web service discovery. Neither the identification of potential services through keyword extraction nor the relevance ranking based on hyperlinks provides much use in a Web service scenario. At the same time, approaches that have aimed at a complete automation or focused only on a machine-to-machine interface such as UDDI or several works in the area of Semantic Web Services are also not suitable for a heterogenous and open Web environment.

Thus, in an environment where only little control can be put on the publishers of services, keyword-based retrieval provides a reasonable compromise between accuracy in retrieval and the effort required to produce usable descriptions. The recently founded company Seekda[9] has developed a keyword search engine for this purpose.

---

[7] http://www.sai.msu.su/ megera/postgres/gist/tsearch/V2/

[8] CamelCasing is a convention to avoid spaces by concatenating two words while making the first letter always uppercase

[9] http://seekda.com

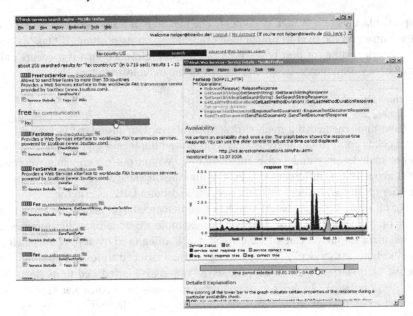

Figure 8.1. A keyword-based service search engine

Its approach is to postprocess interface description and to leverage as much structural information to weight terms as possible. Although we are at the beginning of our work our prototype shows that existing solutions cannot meet the already achieved combination of broad coverage together with relative accuracy in the retrieval.

8.4 Discovery Based on Simple Semantic Descriptions

Keyword-based search is a widely used technique for information retrieval; however, it does not use explicit, well-defined semantics. The keywords used to retrieve relevant information do not have an explicit formalization and, therefore, do not allow inferencing to improve the search results.

We consider the use of controlled vocabularies with explicit, formal semantics. Ontologies are excellent and prominent conceptual means for this purpose. They provide an explicit and shared terminology, explicate interdependencies between single concepts, and thus are well suited for the description of Web Services and requester goals. Moreover, ontologies can be formalized in logics which enables the use of inference services for exploiting knowledge about the problem domain during discovery.

In this section we present a formal modeling approach for Web Services and goals which is based on set theory and exploits ontologies as a formal, machine-processable representation of domain knowledge. We discuss Web service discovery based on this approach for simple semantic descriptions and describe how we implemented the set-based model in the formal framework of logic.

8.4.1 The Model

One main characteristic of object-oriented approaches is that the problem domain is understood as a set of objects and single objects can be grouped together into sets or classes. Each class captures common (syntactic and semantic) features of its elements. Features can be inherited between classes by defining class hierarchies. This way, a problem domain can be structured as classes of objects and is basically understood as a collection of classes (or sets of things). In particular, ontologies are a popular knowledge-representation technique which usually exploits the very same modeling paradigm.

In such modeling approaches the main semantic properties that one is interested in are certain relationships between such sets or objects of the universe. Establishing and checking such relationships is the main reasoning task which allows agents to exploit knowledge formalized in the domain model (or ontology).

8.4.2 Describing Web Services and Goals

A Web service provides some value to its invoker and can be invoked by a client. The invocation itself is based on Web service technologies like SOAP and WSDL; however, these technical details of invocation are not necessarily relevant for discovery based on functional specifications. Only if one considers discovery together with the adaptation/invocation of the service one needs to cater for the particularities of the invocation mechanism. To judge if the functionality offered by a Web service matches the one requested it is not necessary to also check the compatibility on the interface level, since it might be possible to bypass mismatches by mediators. The execution of the Web service with particular input values generates certain information as an output and achieves certain changes of the state of the world. An output as well as an effect can be considered as objects which can be embedded in some domain ontology, which means a formal conceptualization of the problem domain under consideration.

Goals specify the desire of a client that he wants to have resolved after invoking a Web service, which means they describe the information the client wants to receive as the output of the Web service execution as well as the effects on the state of the world that the client intends to achieve by invoking the Web service. This desire can be represented as sets of elements which are relevant to the client as the outputs and the effects of a service execution. Thus, goals refer to the state of the world which is desired by executing some Web service.

Web Services and goals are represented as sets of objects in the approach described here. The single descriptions of these sets refer to ontologies that capture general knowledge about the problem domains under consideration. Hence, the objects described in some Web service description and the objects used in some goal description can or might be interrelated in some way by ontologies. Eventually, such an interrelation is needed to establish a match between goals and services. We define domain-independent notions of match in Sect. 8.4.3.

An important observation in the approach is that the description of a set of objects for representing a goal or a Web service actually can be interpreted in different ways and thus the description by means of a set is not semantically unique: A modeler basically might want to express that either *all* of the elements that are contained in the set are requested (in case of a goal description) or can be delivered (in case of a Web service description), or that only *some* of these elements are requested (or can be delivered).

Clearly, a modeler has some specific intuition in mind when specifying such a set of relevant objects for a goal or Web service description and this intention essentially determines whether we consider two descriptions to match or not. Thus, these intuitions should be stated explicitly in the descriptions of service requests or service advertisements.

For the sake of simplicity, we will consider in the following only outputs of a service and do not treat effects explicitly. The separation of effects and outputs in WSMO is a conceptual one and effects can basically be dealt with in the very same way as postconditions. Nonetheless, it is useful to distinguish both since they are conceptually different and we believe that it is beneficial for users to have the ability to apply *different criteria for matching* to outputs as well as effects in a service discovery request. To augment the model discussed here accordingly is a straightforward endeavor.

Given our previous considerations we can model goals and Web Services as follows: A goal (G) as well as a Web service (W) is represented by a description as a set of objects from a common universe $(\{G, W\} \in U)$ which represents the set of *relevant objects* for the description, as well as an explicit specification about the corresponding intention $I \in \{\forall, \exists\}$ of the set.

8.4.3 Matching Web Services and Goals

In order to consider whether a goal G and a Web service W match on a semantic level, the sets G and W describing these elements have to be interrelated somehow; precisely speaking, we expect that some set-theoretic relationship between G and W has to exist. The most basic set-theoretic relationships that one might consider are the following:

$G = W$: Set equality
$G \subseteq W$: Goal description subset of Web service description
$W \subseteq G$: Web service description subset of goal description
$G \cap W \neq \emptyset$: Common element of goal and Web service description
$G \cap W = \emptyset$: No common element of goal and Web service description

These set-theoretic relationships basically provide the basic means for formalizing our intuitive understanding of a match between goals and Web Services in the real world. In this scope, they have been considered to some extent already in the literature, for instance, in [138, 168] in the context of service matchmaking based on description logics. The terminology for matching notions in these papers was inspired by work done in the context of component matching based on component specifications [219].

On the other hand, we have to keep in mind that in our model these sets actually only capture one part of the semantics of goals and Web service descriptions, namely, the relevant objects for the service requester or service provider. The intentions of these sets in the semantic description of the goal or Web service are not considered but clearly affect whether a certain existing set-theoretic relationship between G and W is considered to actually correspond to (or formalize) a match in the intuitive sense. Hence, we have to consider the intentions of the respective sets as well. In the following we will discuss the set-theoretic relationship for one example in detail and summarize all theoretical combinations in a corresponding matrix.

Example: Intersection Match

We provide a detailed discussion for the case where there exist common elements in goal and Web service description. For reasons of available space, the remaining cases are only summarized in Fig. 8.2. In this case the set of relevant objects that are advertised by the service provider and the set of relevant objects for the requester have a nonempty intersection, i.e., there is an object which is relevant for both parties. In a sense, this criterion can be seen as the weakest possible criterion for semantic matching in this set-based modeling approach.

- $I_G = \forall$, $I_W = \forall$: The service requester wants to get all of the objects and the service provider claims that the Web service is able to deliver all the objects specified. In this case, the requester's needs cannot be fully satisfied by the service. However, the service can contribute to resolve the desire of the client. Thus, we consider this case as a partial match.
- $I_G = \exists$, $I_W = \forall$: The service requester wants to get some of the objects, whereas the service provider claims that the Web service is able to deliver all the objects specified. In this case, the requester's needs are fully covered by the Web service. The requester might also receive objects which are not relevant for him.
- $I_G = \forall$, $I_W = \exists$: The service requester wants to get all of the objects, whereas the service provider claims that the Web service is able to deliver only some of the objects specified. In this case, the requester's needs are not fully covered. We are not even able to determine whether the Web service can actually deliver any of the objects desired by the requester and hence we consider this match as a possible partial match.

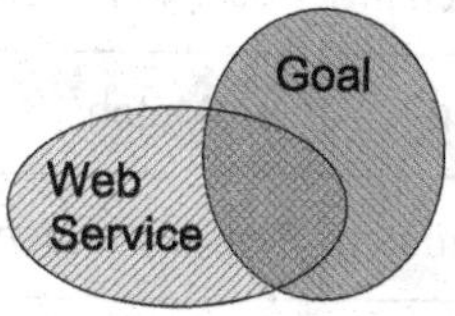

$G \cap W \neq \emptyset$	$I_W = \forall$	$I_W = \exists$
$I_G = \forall$	Partial match	Possible partial match
$I_G = \exists$	Match	Possible match

Figure 8.2. Common elements in goal and Web service description

- $I_G = \exists$, $I_W = \exists$: The service requester wants to get some of the objects and the service provider claims that the Web service is able to deliver some of the objects specified. In this case we have a possible match.

In [138] the situation where $G \cap W \neq \emptyset$ can be established is called *intersection match*. However, in our model we do not necessarily consider the goal and the Web service only as partially matching, as we have a match in the case where the goal has an existential and the Web service a universal intention.

For a complete discussion of all possible matches we refer the reader to [115]. However, given the discussion for the case of an intersection match, it is straightforward to apply it to the remaining cases. In the next subsection we give a brief summary of all possible combinations.

Summary of Understanding of Matching

Given some goal G and some Web service W, Table 8.2 summarizes the discussion and shows under which circumstances the presence of which set-theoretic relationship between G and W is considered as a match, a partial match, a possible match, a possible partial match, or a nonmatch.

In existing approaches to service discovery like those in [138, 168] the notion of "intention" has at present not been reflected explicitly. As we have shown above, intentions capture an important aspect of goal and Web service descriptions and affect essentially the situations in which certain set-theoretic criteria represent our intuitive understanding of matches properly.

The existing approaches so far basically can be understood as covering only the second column of the table, namely, the situation where a goal has an existential intention and a Web service has universal intention ($I_G = \exists$, $I_W = \forall$).

We believe that certain pairs of intentions will occur more often in practice than others: Web service providers, for example, have a strong interest in their Web Services being discovered. If we compare the number of possible matches with a given

Table 8.2. Interaction between set-theoretic criteria, intentions, and our intuitive understanding of matching

	$I_W = \forall$ $I_G = \forall$	$I_W = \forall$ $I_G = \exists$	$I_W = \exists$ $I_G = \forall$	$I_W = \exists$ $I_G = \exists$
$G = W$	Match	Match	Partial match	Match
$G \subseteq W$	Match	Match	Possible match	Possible match
$G \supseteq W$	Partial match	Match	Partial match	Match
$G \cap W \neq \emptyset$	Partial match	Match	Possible partial match	Possible match
$G \cap W = \emptyset$	Nonmatch	Nonmatch	Nonmatch	Nonmatch

goal under existential and universal intentions, it seems most likely that providers tend to use universal intentions, even if the description does not necessarily model the real-world capability of the service accurately and promises too much. However, if a service provider wants to be more accurate with his Web service description, then in many situations he would have to use the existential intention.

For service requesters (in particular in an e-Business setting) we expect that the existential intention will suffice in many situations; however, the requester has the freedom to properly express stronger requests than existential goals (using universal intention) if he needs to and thus get more accurate results in these situations.

8.4.4 Consistency of Descriptions

What we have not considered so far is the possibility of inconsistent descriptions for goals and Web Services. We consider an empty set as an inconsistent description. Obviously, such descriptions do not make any sense: A requester who is asking for nothing as well as Web Services that do not deliver anything are simply superfluous and undesired. Nonetheless, they might occur in cases where the descriptions are quite complex or refer to several complex ontologies which are not themselves designed by the modeler.

Additionally, when just being ignored they can have an undesired impact on matching and thus discovery: Consider, for example, an inconsistent goal description, i.e., $G = \emptyset$. If we check G for matching Web Services using the Plugin criterion, i.e., $G \subseteq W$, then obviously every Web service matches. For a user (who is not aware that his description is inconsistent, since otherwise he would usually not pose the query) the result would seem rather strange and even incorrect because all checked services actually will be matched. From a logical perspective this is indeed not wrong, on the other hand it does not seem to be the best way to deal with the situation, since the user gets neither a hint that his goal description is inconsistent nor does he get (from his perspective) reasonable results.

Ignoring the possibility of inconsistent descriptions seems to be a bad idea, since it will lead to nonintuitive results (garbage in–garbage out principle). However, to check for inconsistent goal and Web service descriptions is not a task that is only applicable at the design time. It should be good practice to forbid the creation of a description which denotes an empty set, but the consistency does not depend exclusively on the description itself, it also depends on all ontologies that the description refers to. Hence, changes to such ontologies potentially can lead to inconsistent descriptions. Moreover, since Web service and goals description may refer to different ontologies, the combination of them (during matchmaking) may make a previously satisfiable goal description unsatisfiable. Thus, before checking for a match, one must check for the satisfiability of each description involved.

8.4.5 Ranking Matches

As shown in Fig. 8.2, we basically have for each pair of intentions for a goal and a Web service several formal criteria that capture actual matches, partial matches, possible matches, as well as nonmatches. According to elementary set theory the single criteria are not completely separated, but the following interdependencies hold (note that for some conclusions we require a description to be nonempty as discussed before):

$$
\begin{aligned}
G = W &\Rightarrow G \subseteq W, \\
G = W &\Rightarrow G \supseteq W, \\
G \subseteq W, G \neq \emptyset &\Rightarrow G \cap W \neq \emptyset, \\
G \supseteq W, W \neq \emptyset &\Rightarrow G \cap W \neq \emptyset.
\end{aligned} \tag{8.1}
$$

That means that certain formal set-theoretic criteria that we consider here are logically stronger notions than others: if the stronger relationship holds then the weaker relationship must hold as well. Using these properties, we can partially order the set-theoretic criteria: $C_1 \preceq C_2$ iff C_2 is logically weaker (or equivalent) than C_1, i.e.,

$$
(G = W) \quad \preceq \quad (G \subseteq W), (G \supseteq W) \quad \preceq \quad (G \cap W \neq \emptyset). \tag{8.2}
$$

Given a goal and a Web service description let "subsumes match" be the criterion that captures the actual match. When a "subsumes match" holds, then a logically weaker criterion, such as "intersection match," also holds. However, one has to note that the logically stronger criterion provides additional knowledge about the relationship between the goal and the Web service. In this particular example "subsumes match" also guarantees that no additional objects are delivered besides the one requested. Since this property might be important for a requester, it does make sense to allow the use of a particular criterion for the matching between goal and Web service descriptions by the requester. A service requester basically can exploit this property during a discovery process in order to ensure certain convenient properties from the discovered Web Services.

To sum up, we have seen that there are cases where a client could benefit from exploiting the additional semantics captured by matching criteria that are stronger (i.e., $\preceq$-smaller) than the weakest (i.e., $\preceq$-maximal) criterion which represents an actual match. Hence, it makes sense to not only allow the use of the weakest (i.e., $\preceq$-maximal) criterion that actually denotes a match to be applied for matching but to allow the user to manually raise the semantic requirements that are captured by the criterion to apply and thus to reflect his interest faithfully. In particular this makes sense for the case that a client does not want to accept that a Web service that potentially delivers objects that have not been explicitly requested (in this case a subsumes or an exact match has to be requested).

We have seen as well that in our general framework there is only one such additional property that actually can be considered as useful, namely, the property of a Web service to not deliver objects that are irrelevant to the user. This leads us to allow the client to specify what particular kind of match he is accepting, by specifying the two following dimensions:

1. Match, partial match, possible partial match, possible match.
2. Within each match it can be additionally specified if a service is allowed to deliver objects that are not requested.

Table 8.3. Formal criteria for checking different degrees of matching

	$I_W = \forall$		$I_W = \exists$	
	Additional objects OK	No additional objects allowed	Additional objects OK	No additional objects allowed
$I_G = \forall$ match	$G \subseteq W$	$G = W$	–	–
$I_G = \exists$ match	$G \cap W \neq \emptyset$	$G \supseteq W$	$G \supseteq W$	$G \supseteq W$
$I_G = \forall$ partial match	$G \cap W \neq \emptyset$	$G \supseteq W$	$G \supseteq W$	$G \supseteq W$
$I_G = \exists$ partial match	$G \cap W \neq \emptyset$	$G \supseteq W$	$G \supseteq W$	$G \supseteq W$
$I_G = \forall$ possible match	$G \subseteq W$	$G = W$	$G \subseteq W$	–
$I_G = \exists$ possible match	$G \cap W \neq \emptyset$	$G \supseteq W$	$G \cap W \neq \emptyset$	$G \supseteq W$
$I_G = \forall$ possible partial match	$G \cap W \neq \emptyset$	$G \supseteq W$	$G \cap W \neq \emptyset$	$G \supseteq W$
$I_G = \exists$ possible partial match	$G \cap W \neq \emptyset$	$G \supseteq W$	$G \cap W \neq \emptyset$	$G \supseteq W$

Partial Order on "Match"

Similar to the partial order that is defined for the basic set-theoretic matching criterion, we can also define a logical order on our intuitive understanding of the matching notion with respect to the real world.

$$\text{Match} \preceq \text{partial match} , \text{possible match} \preceq \text{possible partial match} \qquad (8.3)$$

The partial ordering can be exploited during matchmaking: in order to ensure that a property is satisfied when matching (e.g., $I_G = \exists, I_W = \forall$, additional objects might be delivered), the discovery component has to apply only the weakest criterion still fulfilling the request and not all. In the given example it is only required to check for an intersection match ($G \cap W \neq \emptyset$) and not for all set-theoretic relations separately. Table 8.3 represents the result of this discussion for all possible combinations. Matching criteria that are colored gray in Table 8.3 indicate that the criterion does in fact not check the intuitive matching criteria specified (e.g., partial match or match), but one which also satisfies the requested criteria owing to the partial order on the intuitive matching notions.

8.4.6 Summary

It should be clear that a detected match in this framework for Web service discovery is based on simple semantic annotation only and thus cannot provide very strong guarantees for the actual accuracy of the results in each case. A detected match between a goal and a Web service actually does not ensure that the Web service can really be used for resolving the goal in the real world, since important information that affects this possibility is not specified in the descriptions: Is the requester actually able to satisfy the requirements of the Web service when invoking and interacting with the service, namely, the preconditions and choreography?

Nevertheless, the approach is based on a formal semantic model and uses formal domain knowledge to detect matches. Thus, the achievable accuracy of the approach (although being inherently limited) in general will be a lot higher than with keyword-based approaches.

In this respect, it still can be considered as a semantic-driven heuristic for locating Web Services which can resolve the goal of a service requester. We briefly summarize the main advantages and drawbacks of the modeling approach discussed.

The main advantages are:

- This modeling approach is based on a very simple and intuitive perspective of the world where everything is considered in terms of sets (or concepts).
- In contrast to other approaches, we start from building a model and analyzing the intuitive understanding of a match and then try to capture the intuitive semantics of the match. This results in giving the modeler more freedom to express his/her desire, e.g., through the use of intentions.
- The approach represents a general framework which does not fix the language to be used for describing goals and Web Services. It allows descriptions which cannot be expressed using description logics and thus provides increased expressiveness.
- Because of the same conceptual modeling style, this approach potentially allows a seamless integration of descriptions formalized in different languages, such as present in the WSML family of languages.

The main drawback is that this approach does not capture the actual relation between service input and the corresponding outputs. Thus, the semantics of a Web service is only described in a conceptual manner. In fact, this can be too coarse-grained for enabling the automation of the discovery and later execution of a service.

8.5 Discovery Based on Rich Semantic Descriptions

This section presents a model which allows for a precise definition of the notion Web service. The model is not based on any specific logical formalism and thus can be formally represented in various logics of sufficient expressivity to enable reasoning with semantic descriptions of Web service capabilities. We will illustrate the model in an intuitive fashion; for the formal definitions we refer the reader to [116].

8.5.1 A Changing World

We consider the world as an entity that changes over time. Entities that act in the world – which can be anything from a human user to some computer program – can affect how the world is perceived by themselves or other entities at some specific moment in time. At each point in time, the world is in one particular state that determines how the world is perceived by the entities acting therein. We need to consider some language for describing the properties of the world in a state. In the following we assume an *arbitrary* (but fixed) signature Σ that usually is based on domain ontologies, and some language $\mathcal{L}(\Sigma)$.

We use classical first-order logic for illustration purposes as this can easily be applied to other languages such as WSML or OWL. Consider a signature $\Sigma \supseteq \{isAccount(\cdot), balance(\cdot), \geq, 0, 1, 2, \ldots\}$ that denotes bank accounts and their balance. It allows comparison of the respective values in $\mathcal{L}(\Sigma)$, for instance, containing expressions like $\forall ?x.(isAccount(?x) \rightarrow balance(?x) \geq 0)$ stating that the balance of any account needs to be nonnegative. In the context of the dynamics and properties of the world that can change, it is useful to distinguish between symbols in Σ that are supposed to have always the same, fixed meaning (e.g., $\geq$, 0) and thus cannot be affected by any entity that acts in the world, and symbols that can be affected and thus can change their meaning during the execution a Web service (e.g., $isAccount(\cdot)$, $balance(\cdot)$). We refer to the former class of symbols by *static symbols* (denoted by Σ_S) and the latter by *dynamic symbols* (denoted by Σ_D).

Abstract State Spaces

We consider an abstract state space $\mathcal{S}$ to represent all possible states s of the world. Each state $s \in \mathcal{S}$ completely determines how the world is perceived by each entity acting in $\mathcal{S}$. Each statement $\phi \in \mathcal{L}(\Sigma)$ of an entity about the (current state of) the world is either true or false.[10]. Thus, a state $s \in \mathcal{S}$ in fact *defines* an interpretation $\mathcal{I}$ (of some signature Σ). However, not all Σ-interpretations $\mathcal{I}$ represent senseful observations since $\mathcal{I}$ might not respect some "laws" that the world $\mathcal{S}$ underlies, e.g., that the balance of any bank account is not allowed to be negative. In the following, we assume that these laws are captured by a background ontology $\Omega \subseteq \mathcal{L}(\Sigma)$ and denote the set of Σ-interpretations that respect Ω by $Mod_\Sigma(\Omega)$. Considering our example signature from above, the following interpretations denote states $s \in \mathcal{S}$:

$$s_0 : balance(acc_1) = 10 \land balance(acc_2) = 100,$$
$$s_n : balance(acc_1) = 30 \land balance(acc_2) = 80.$$

Changing the World

By means of well-defined change operations, entities can affect the world that denote state transitions in $\mathcal{S}$. In our setting, these change operations are single concrete *executions* of Web Services W. Following [114, 115], a change operation is represented by a *service* S that is accessed via a Web service W. S is achieved by executing W with some given input data $i_1, \ldots, i_n$ that specify *what* kind of particular *service* S accessible via W is requested by the client, i.e., $S \approx W(i_1, \ldots, i_n)$.

---

[10] We consider classical logic (and thus only *true* and *false* as truth values) here. However, the model presented can be used as it is in the context of nonclassical logics by just considering a different class of interpretations $\mathcal{I}$, e.g., in the case of multivalued logics, we can use multivalued interpretations.

Given input data $i_1, \ldots, i_n$, the execution of a Web service W essentially causes a state transition τ in $\mathcal{S}$, transforming the current state of the world $s \in \mathcal{S}$ into a new state $s' \in \mathcal{S}$. However, a transition τ will in general not be an *atomic transition* $\tau = (s, s') \in \mathcal{S} \times \mathcal{S}$ but a sequence $\tau = (s_0, \ldots, s_n) \in \mathcal{S}^+$, where $s_0 = s$, $s_n = s'$ and $n \geq 1$. In every intermediate state s_i in τ some effect can already be perceived by an entity. This is especially relevant for Web Services that allow accessing long-lasting activities that involve multiple conversation steps between the requester and the Web service W. Note, that $\tau = (s_0, \ldots, s_n) \in \mathcal{S}^+$ implies that we assume Web service executions *terminate*. We consider this assumption as a useful one that should be met in all practical application scenarios.

Let us consider an international bank transfer having as concrete input data the information to transfer \$20 from acc_1 to acc_2. The model of the world might have between s_0 and s_n the following intermediate state:

$$s_1 : balance(acc_1) = 10 \wedge balance(acc_2) = 80.$$

Outputs as Changes of an Information Space

During the execution $W(i_1, \ldots, i_n)$ of a Web service W, W can send some information as output to the requester. We consider these outputs as updates of the so-called *information space* of the requester of a service S. More precisely, we consider the *information space* of some service requester as a set $IS \subseteq U$ of objects from some universe U. Every object $o \in IS$ has been received by the requester from W during the execution $W(i_1, \ldots, i_n)$. During the execution the information space itself evolves: Starting with the empty set when the Web service is invoked, the execution leads to a monotonic sequence of information spaces $\emptyset = IS_0 \subseteq IS_1 \subseteq \ldots \subseteq IS_k$. Monotonicity of the sequence models that information that has been received by the user will not be forgotten until service execution completion.

Within our bank transfer example, during some transaction we might receive first a message acknowledgment, and then a confirmation that the transaction has been approved and initialized.

$$IS \models ack(20051202, msgid23)$$
$$confirm(acc_1, acc_2, 20)$$

Observations in Abstract States

Our aim is to describe *all* the effects of Web service executions for a requester. Obviously, a requester can observe in every state $s \in \mathcal{S}$ world-related properties represented by statements ϕ in $\mathcal{L}(\Sigma)$ that hold in s. Additionally, he can perceive the information space $IS \subseteq U$ described above. Thus, the abstract state space $\mathcal{S}$ in a sense "corresponds" to the observations that can be made in s, namely, all pairs of Σ-interpretations $\mathcal{I} \in Mod_\Sigma(\Omega)$ and (possible) information spaces $IS \subseteq U$. Consequently, we represent the observations related to a state s by an observation function $\omega : \mathcal{S} \rightarrow Mod_\Sigma(\Omega) \times \mathcal{P}(U)$ that assigns to every state $s \in \mathcal{S}$ a pair

$(\mathcal{I}, IS)$ of a Σ-interpretation $\mathcal{I}$ (respecting the domain laws Ω) and an information space IS. We denote the first component of $\omega(s)$ by $\omega_{rw}(s)$ (*real-world properties*: how an entity perceives the world) and the second component by $\omega_{is}(s)$ (*information space*: how the invoker perceives the information space). However, we require the observation function ω to be a (fixed) total function as it *cannot* be arbitrary. This means that the observations $\omega(s)$ of any entity are well defined in *every* abstract state s. Moreover, any perception representable in terms of $\mathcal{L}(\Sigma)$ and U that is consistent with the domain model Ω should actually correspond to some abstract state $s \in S$ by means of ω, so that ω is surjective. However, since we assume a fixed signature Σ and thus a limited language for describing observations about the world, we do not assume that ω is injective, i.e., there could be distinct states s, s' of the world which *cannot* be distinguished by the (limited) language $\mathcal{L}(\Sigma)$, i.e., $\omega_{rw}(s) = \omega_{rw}(s')$.

The former means that a state $s_i : balance(acc123) = -10$ is not a model since it is inconsistent with the domain ontology (we previously required the balance to be positive). The latter determines that there is always a corresponding abstract state to a set of sentences. However, not all states in $\mathcal{A}$ can be distinguished. For example. if we model the transfer of money between two accounts and do not include details of the transaction system, we cannot express the states between the initialization of the transaction and its commit states. However, there are intermediate states, and only by the limitations of $\mathcal{L}(\Sigma)$ we cannot distinguish them.

Web Service Executions

Given some input $i_1, \ldots, i_n$, the Web service execution $W(i_1, \ldots, i_n) = (s_0, \ldots, s_m)$ starting in state s_0 induces a sequence of observations $(\omega(s_0), \ldots, \omega(s_m))$ which can be made by the service requester during the execution. However, not all such sequences τ of abstract states actually represent a meaningful state transition caused by an execution of W. For τ to faithfully represent some $W(i_1, ..., i_n)$ we need to require at least that for any two adjacent states s, s' in $W(i_1, \ldots, i_n)$ some change can be observed by the invoker, and that objects which are in the information space (i.e., have been received by the invoker) at some point in time during the execution cannot disappear until the execution is completed. As discussed later, in general we need to require some further constraints on a sequence τ such that we can interpret τ as a possible run $W(i_1, \ldots, i_n)$ of a Web service W. We call s_0 the prestate of the execution, s_m the poststate of the execution, and all other states in $W(i_1, ..., i_n)$ intermediate states.

$$s_0 : balance(acc_1) = 10 \wedge balance(acc_2) = 100$$
$$s_1 : balance(acc_1) = 10 \wedge balance(acc_2) = 80$$
$$s_n : balance(acc_1) = 30 \wedge balance(acc_2) = 80$$

In the case of the transaction example s_0 is the prestate with the initial balances. In the intermediate state s_1 the balance of acc_2 has already been reduced by \$20, but acc_1 has not yet been increased. s_n is the poststate of the transaction where the money transfer has succeeded.

Web Services

A Web service W then can be seen as a set of executions $W(i_1, \ldots, i_n)$ that can be delivered by the Web service in any given state of the world to a requester when equipped with any kind of valid input data $i_1, \ldots, i_n$. However, in order to keep track of the input data that caused a specific execution, we need to represent a Web service in terms of a slightly richer structure than a set, namely, a mapping between the provided input values $i_1, \ldots, i_n$ and the resulting execution[11] $W(i_1, \ldots, i_n)$.

In our running example the Web service of a bank accepting two account numbers (i_1, i_2) and some amount (i_3) can yield an example. For all valid accounts (given a sufficient initial balance) it will transfer the amount (i_3) from i_1 to i_2. And thus the actual Web Services corresponds to a set of state transitions (and not only one), where each transition is determined by the concrete input values supplied.

Figure 8.3 illustrates the model presented. The Web service W provides four different concrete services $(S_1 \ldots S_4)$. Each single state is determined by the two components of ω – the information space and the real world. The Web service is a set of possible transitions that is denoted by a dark area inside the abstract state space.

The model presented gives a thorough mathematical model. For the formal definitions of this model we refer the reader to [116]. For the purpose of this book the previous intuitive description should suffice. It is important to understand that this model is defined in order to allow an unambiguous interpretation of Web service and goal descriptions, i.e., that it provides a semantic to the syntactical description within a capability. In the following we outline some basic semantic analyses that can be performed on top of this model.

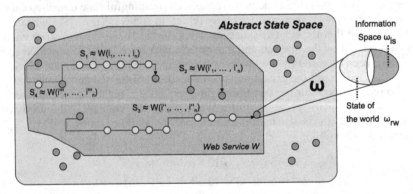

Figure 8.3. An abstract model of the world and the Web Services therein

---

[11] This implies that we use a *deterministic* model for Web Services here. An extension to a nondeterministic perspective is straightforward.

8.5.2 Applying the Formal Model for Semantic Analysis

To demonstrate the suitability of the proposed model, this section shows its beneficial application for semantic analysis of functional descriptions. Based on our model-theoretic framework, we can carry over several semantic standard notions from mathematical logic [65, 79] that refer to formal descriptions and are based on the *model* notion to our particular context in a meaningful way.

Realizability

We can now define *realizability* of a description as the corresponding notion to satisfiability in a logic. In logic a set of formulae is satisfiable if it has a model, i.e., if there exists an interpretation of the formulae that is true. The very same notion can be applied to Web Services. Consider the following functional description $\mathcal{D} = (\phi^{pre}, \phi^{post}, IF_{\mathcal{D}})$ describing Web Services for account withdraws: $IF_{\mathcal{D}} = \{?acc, ?amt\}$.

$$\phi^{pre} : ?amt \geq 0 \qquad \phi^{post} : balance(?acc) = balance_{pre}(?acc) - ?amt$$

At a first glance, the description given seems to be implementable within some Web service W that satisfies $\mathcal{D}$. However, on taking a closer look at the respective domain ontology it becomes obvious that this actually is not the case. The ontology defines that a balance might not be negative, but the precondition does not prevent the balance being less than the withdrawal. Let us assume that there is a Web service W realizing $\mathcal{D}$. When considering an input binding β with $\beta(?amt) > balance_{pre}(?acc)$, the precondition is satisfied and thus the postcondition should hold in the final state of the respective execution, i.e., $\omega_{rw}(s_m), \beta \models \forall?acc.balance(?acc) < 0$. However, this is inconsistent with the domain ontology since $\Omega \models balance(?acc) \geq 0$ and thus s_m cannot exist in $\mathcal{A}$. This is a contradiction and shows that no Web service W with $W \models_{\mathcal{F}} \mathcal{D}$ can exist. To fix the description such that it becomes realizable, we need to extend the precondition to $\phi^{pre} : 0 \leq ?amt \wedge ?amt \leq balance(?acc)$.

The example illustrates the usefulness of the notion of realizability. It provides a tool for detecting functional descriptions that contain flaws that might not be obvious to the modelers. Moreover as we will see soon, we can often rephrase the problem of realizability of a description $\mathcal{D} \in \mathcal{F}$ to a well-understood problem in $\mathcal{L}$ for which algorithms already exist. We first turn to important other notion, of which realizability turns out to be a special case (in conformance as with the original notions in mathematical logic).

Functional Refinement

Similar to the notion of satisfiability, we can look at the notion of logical entailment, which is usually defined as follows: A formula ϕ logically entails a formula ψ iff every interpretation $\mathcal{I}$ which is a model of ϕ (i.e., $\mathcal{I} \models_{\mathcal{L}} \phi$) is also a model of ψ. Substituting interpretations by Web Services, formulae by functional descriptions, and the satisfaction $\models_{\mathcal{L}}$ by capability satisfaction $\models_{\mathcal{F}}$. In a similar way we can define the notion of functional refinement that corresponds to the notion of logical entailment: We use $\mathcal{D}_1 \sqsubseteq \mathcal{D}_2$ to denote that description $\mathcal{D}_1$ is a functional refinement of description $\mathcal{D}_2$ in $\mathcal{A}$.

Intuitively speaking, $\mathcal{D}_1 \sqsubseteq \mathcal{D}_2$ means that $\mathcal{D}_1$ is more specific than $\mathcal{D}_2$: Every Web service (no matter which one) that provides $\mathcal{D}_1$ can also provide $\mathcal{D}_2$. In other words, $\mathcal{D}_1$ must describe some piece of functionality that always fits the requirements $\mathcal{D}_2$ as well. However, Web Services that provide $\mathcal{D}_2$ do not have to satisfy $\mathcal{D}_1$ and, therefore, a Web service that provides $\mathcal{D}_1$ can do something more specific than required by $\mathcal{D}_2$.

For illustration, consider some Web service description $\mathcal{D}_1 = (\phi_1^{pre}, \phi_1^{post}, IF_1)$ with $IF_1 = \{?prs, ?acc\}$ that advertises the ability to provide access credentials for a particular Web site ($http://theSolution.com$). A domain ontology specifies that if some Web site has some content and someone can access the Web site, then he (is able to) know about the content. Furthermore, $http://theSolution.com$ is a Web site providing the ultimate answer to life (the universe and everything) and some constant $accessFee$ has a value less then 42.[12]

$$\phi_1^{pre} : account(?prs, ?acc) \wedge balance(?acc) \geq accessFee$$

$$\phi_1^{post} : balance(?acc) = balance_{pre}(?acc) - accessFee$$

$$\wedge \, \mathbf{out}(password(?prs, http://theSolution.com))$$

$$\wedge \, isValid(password(?prs, http://theSolution.com))$$

$$\Omega \models \forall?ws, ?co, ?prs. \, content(?ws, ?co) \wedge access(?prs, ?ws) \rightarrow knows(?prs, ?co)$$

$$content(http://theSolution.com, answer2Life), accessFee \leq 42$$

$$\forall?prs, ?ws. \, isValid(password(?prs, ?ws)) \rightarrow access(?prs, ?ws))$$

Using our formal definition we now can examine another definition $\mathcal{D}_2 = (\phi_2^{pre}, \phi_2^{post}, IF_2)$ with $IF_2 = \{?prs, ?acc\}$ and check if it is a functional refinement of the previous description.

$$\phi_2^{pre} : account(?prs, ?acc) \wedge balance(?acc) \geq 100 \quad \phi_2^{post} : knows(?prs, answer2Life)$$

This notion can beneficially be applied within functionality-based matchmaking. For instance, let us assume that a person me is seeking for the ultimate answer to life ($knows(me, answer2Life)$); me has an account $acc123$ with a current balance of \$174. Given this information (and our domain ontology Ω) and considering the specific input binding $\beta(?prs) = me, \beta(?acc) = acc123$, we can infer that any Web service W that is advertised to provide capability $\mathcal{D}_2$ can serve for me's purpose as the precondition ϕ_2^{pre} is satisfied for the input β. In consequence, for the specific input β the service delivers what is described by the postcondition ϕ_2^{post}; therefrom, we can infer $knows(me, answer2Life)$. However, since $\mathcal{D}_1 \sqsubseteq \mathcal{D}_2$ we know as well, that any Web service W' that is advertised to provide capability $\mathcal{D}_1$ is perfectly suitable for me and his endeavor as well. The notion of functional refinement can

---

[12] Note that we do not expect such knowledge in one central domain ontology, but in a number of knowledge bases (generic, provider-, and requester-specific). For simplicity we assume Ω has already been aggregated.

then be used to preindex some set of Web service descriptions, such that for a given request it is not necessary to consider all available descriptions but only a subset identified by the preindexing.

Reasoning over Functional Descriptions

We now have defined two basic forms of semantic analysis in our descriptions. They allow us to make use of the descriptions during the Web service life cycle. E.g. Functional refinement can be used to automate Web service discovery. Since we closely base our model on classical logic we are able to reuse existing inference engines. In [116] we showed in more detail the relation between the definitions in our formal model for Web Services and the underlying logic language used. This gives us the following: If there is an algorithm or an implemented system that allows us to determine logical entailment in $\mathcal{L}$, then we can use the very same system or algorithm to determine functional refinement.

8.5.3 Complete and Incomplete Descriptions

A common problem in the specification of functionality of computational entities that can alter the state of the world is the so-called *frame problem*: Descriptions usually describe positive information about what changes happen, however, to keep descriptions simple and manageable, they do not explicitly state what does not happen.[13] Incomplete descriptions can pose difficulties when processing such descriptions for some higher-level task such as Web service discovery, since they are weaker (i.e., contain less information) as complete descriptions.

Complete descriptions can be achieved by adding supplementary descriptions about all things that stay the same during the execution. Given a fixed model of the world, such a completion process can be automated by adding so-called frame axioms to the existing (incomplete) description. However, the manual addition of such axioms is a tedious task for humans and should be avoided.

There are two options that one can take to resolve this problem. First, one can decide to interpret all functional descriptions as being complete, and generate the frame axioms automatically. This relieves the modeler from writing larger specifications, but has the drawback that it is no longer possible to write down incomplete descriptions on purpose (for instance, to express vague knowledge or minimal guarantees about the behavior of some computational entity). Second, one can allow the modeler to express *explicitly* as part of the description whether the description is complete or not by means of a keyword. This way, we avoid the drawback of the first approach, while keeping simplicity of descriptions for modelers.

Functional descriptions consist of various independent elements, which are descriptions (of states) themselves. Again, we have some freedom in our approach, which we need to decide upon. First, we can mark a capability description as a whole

---

[13] In particular, one can expect that there are substantially many more things that *do not happen* during the execution of a Web service than things that actually occur and can be observed.

as being complete or incomplete. Second, we can mark the single elements individually as being complete or incomplete. We will take the second approach, since it is more fine-grained. As we will see in the next paragraph, for the basic language $\mathcal{F}$ indeed both alternatives are the same.

As we explained above, completeness and incompleteness are relevant for all descriptions that are related to *what* happens (or alternatively, what does not). This is the case for postconditions (as well as executional invariants in the case of $\mathcal{F}_{inv}$). However, these properties are *not* relevant to description elements that specify *when* (more precisely, under what circumstances) something happens, i.e. ,preconditions.

8.5.4 Summary

The model outlined provides a very fine grained model to describe Web Services and goals. It requires significant skills to write those descriptions, but allows one to capture a great deal of the behavior of a real world Web service. Still the model has some limitations regarding what can be expressed or captured:

- **Only finite processes can be described.** A specific (inherent) limitation of precondition and postcondition style descriptions is that they are based on the assumption that there will be a final state of a computation, i.e., the computation terminates. Although, this might be a valid assumption for a wide variety of Web Services, it does not allow the specification of nonterminating components which deliver senseful functionality though. An example in a technical system would be the operating system of a computer which does not terminate or a Web service that implements a clock and periodically sends the current time to a subscribed client.
- **Statements about intermediate states.** Like in common specification frameworks, our model for the semantics of Web Services considers a Web service as a set of *atomic* state changes, i.e., possible intermediate states during an execution of a service are invisible for an external observer and cannot be referred to in a formal specification. For planning purposes it might be relevant or useful to allow services to be described in a more detailed way, for instance, as a constraint on possible execution paths.

  For the same reason, it is not possible to express properties which do hold during the whole execution of the service,[14] which have been studied in dynamic logics in the context of *throughout* modalities. As an example think about the property of an account balance which must not be negative. Note that the formal model presented can be adapted to this setting as well; this can essentially be achieved by replacing pairs (s, s') of states by sequences $(s_0, \ldots, s_n)$ of states in our model and the formal definitions. An assertion language $\mathcal{L}$ (used for expressing

---

[14] Such properties P are different from invariants, since they are guarantees local to a service rather than global properties of a system; Furthermore, they are different from strengthening preconditions and postconditions by P since throughout properties apply as well to any intermediate state of an execution.

preconditions and postconditions) which provides syntactic means to refer to intermediate states of a service execution can exploit these richer semantic structures.

8.6 Summary

In this chapter we have defined what we understand about service discovery, i.e., to find similarities between the semantic description of a user's desire (goal) and a service offer (Web service). We also made clear that service descriptions will inherently be incomplete, since otherwise they would duplicate the actual service functionality. With this knowledge we have discussed various levels of abstraction that can be used to describe Web Services:

- Keyword-based
- Simple semantic descriptions (a service as a set of objects)
- Rich semantic descriptions (a serv as a state transition)

Obviously each level requires a different effort to model the actual descriptions. While keyword-based discovery can often be employed on existing descriptions, a rich description of a service requires a trained expert. On the other hand, a match that has been detected by a keyword-based discovery engine provides only very little potential for automation. In the end it depends on the concrete scenario that determines which level of description is suitable. For example, in order to find publicly available Web Services, currently a keyword-based approach is still adequate, since there is so little control over the publishers of the respective descriptions. On the other hand, with the continuous increase of popularity for ontology languages on the Web it might soon be reasonable to extend this approach with a classification system based on lightweight ontologies. On the other hand, use cases in several research projects have shown that richer descriptions of goals and services allow a complete automation of discovery (within a restricted domain).

9

Selection

This chapter discusses one important Semantic Web Service related task, namely, *selection*. Selection is the process where one service which best satisfies the user preferences is selected from the candidate services returned from the service discovery stage. Before describing the service selection process itself, the first part of this chapter will present our solution for modeling nonfunctional properties of services. These descriptions are vital for selection, since scenarios such as "I want the cheapest and fastest service," involving price and execution time nonfunctional properties, are very common. The last part of this chapter focuses on the service selection process describing our approach with a strong emphasis on a core subprocess, namely, service ranking.

9.1 Introduction

Service-Oriented Architecture (SOA) is becoming a widespread solution for realizing distributed applications. Empowered by semantic technologies, this solution is evolving into what is known as semantically enabled SOA (SESA), bringing more automatization and accuracy to various service-related tasks, such as discovery, composition, and *selection*. Among these tasks discovery and selection are the building blocks of SESA search solution. As with most of the search products available on the market, it is not only important to determine the relevant results given a user request, but it is also extremely important to provide the results in a relevant order and furthermore to select the ones which best fit the requirements. This is exactly the purpose of the service selection process, which complements the discovery process.

While problems such as discovery [6, 138, 168, 205, 212] and composition [41, 176, 220] for Semantic Web Services have been intensively studied, the service selection and ranking problem has not attracted so much attention. However, we argue that selection and ranking are important tasks in the overall service usage process and thus they need to be treated accordantly. Any solution for these tasks is directly influenced by how services are described. Three different aspects must be considered when describing a service: (1) *functional*, (2) *behavior*, and (3) *nonfunctional*. The *functional* description contains the formal specification of what exactly the service can do. The *behavior* description contains the formal specification of how the functionality of the service can be achieved. Finally, the *nonfunctional description* captures constraints on the previous two [44]. Among these aspects, nonfunctional properties need to be addressed given the high dynamism of any SOA- and SESA-based system. Furthermore, these descriptions are highly relevant for many of the service-related tasks. For *selection* especially, nonfunctional properties are fundamental input data that need to be considered when building sorted sets of services and selecting the most relevant ones. Our solution for modeling nonfunctional properties of services is an integrated part of the Web Service Modeling Ontology (WSMO) [185] conceptual model and its associated language Web Service Modeling Language (WSML) [53]. The same representation formalism (WSMO/WSML) is used in our service selection solution, but the solution itself is independent of the formalism used.

In this context, this chapter gives an overview of our service selection approach. We start by describing in Sect. 9.2 our approach for modeling and attaching nonfunctional properties descriptions to services. As mentioned already nonfunctional properties are input data to be processed by the service selector. In Sect. 9.3 a detailed description of the service selection is provided, with a focus on service ranking as the core process in the overall selection process. Related work is discussed in Sect. 9.4. Finally, Sect. 9.5 concludes this chapter and points out perspectives for future research in the area of service selection.

9.2 Nonfunctional Properties

This section describes our solution for how to semantically describe nonfunctional properties of services in WSMO/WSML. In our approach for service selection, nonfunctional properties are fundamental means to describe selection criteria. Therefore, providing an appropriate support for modeling these properties and attaching them to services and goals is essential. The rest of this section is organized as follows. First, Sect. 9.2.1 talks about the types of nonfunctional properties. The modeling of these properties in WSMO/WSML is discussed afterwards in Sect. 9.2.2. Finally, Sect. 9.2.3 proposes our solution for how to attach nonfunctional properties descriptions to services, goals, and other elements in WSMO/WSML.

9.2.1 Nonfunctional Properties Types

In this section we discuss what are the types of nonfunctional properties. More precisely (1) we distinguish between two types of nonfunctional properties and (2) we investigate what are the properties that belong to each of these two categories.

A closer look at nonfunctional properties shows that there are two categories into which these properties can be divided: (1) *annotations* – which provide metadata about any type of element description (service, goal, ontology, etc.) – and (2) *nonfunctional properties/quality of service* – which are properties that strictly belong to a service, properties other than functional and behavioral.

Annotations, the first category of nonfunctional properties, are properties which can apply to all element descriptions, e.g., services, goals, mediators, and ontologies. They simply provide a way to annotate, to provide metadata about any type of element description.

In this category we can include the following properties: *contributor, coverage, creator, date, format, identifier, language, owner, publisher, rights, source,* and *version*.

Properties like *subject, title, type,* and *description* can be used to add extra information about the service description and the service itself. Additionally they can contain information about the functionality of the service (e.g., service category).

The second category of nonfunctional properties are those properties which strictly belong to a service and which are not functional and behavioral. We call these properties *nonfunctional properties/quality of service*.

This category includes properties that describe the following aspects of a service: *locative, temporal, availability, obligation, price, payment, discounts, rights, trust, quality of service, security, intellectual property, rewards, provider, reliability, robustness, scalability, performance,* and *transactional*.

It is important to mention that the set of nonfunctional properties from both categories is extensible. Service providers and requesters might add other properties to annotations or nonfunctional properties/quality of service categories except the ones mentioned above.

The properties from the last category, nonfunctional properties/quality of service, are the properties most relevant for service selection and ranking tasks. In the rest of this chapter we use the term "nonfunctional properties" to refer to the last category of properties, namely, nonfunctional properties/quality of service.

9.2.2 Nonfunctional Properties Ontologies

An important challenge towards supporting nonfunctional properties of services is the modeling of these properties. The approach we adopt is based on Semantic Web technologies. More precisely we have defined *a set of ontologies which provide nonfunctional properties terminology*. These ontologies are used afterwards when the nonfunctional properties of services are specified. Ontologies which describe the nonfunctional properties domain can be imported and concepts referring to nonfunctional properties can be instantiated and used in the service descriptions. We have defined a set of nonfunctional properties ontologies[1] in WSML based on the models provided in [164]. These ontologies provide formal conceptualization for Web service nonfunctional properties like availability, security, etc.

The set of nonfunctional properties includes models for locative, temporal, availability, obligation, price, payment, discounts, rights, trust, quality of service, security, intellectual property, rewards, provider, measures, and currency aspects. In the rest of the section we briefly describe each ontology in terms of purpose and important concepts:

---

[1] http://www.wsmo.org/ontologies/nfp/

1. **Locative ontology.** The locative ontology provides the locative concepts that are needed for locative descriptions of a service. Using the terminology provided in this ontology, one can model aspects such where a service can be requested from and where it can be provided. The main concepts include *LocativeEntity*, *GeoLocation*, *Address*, *RouteSpecification*, etc.

2. **Temporal ontology.** The temporal ontology provides the temporal concepts that are needed for time-related descriptions of a service. Different temporal granularities are considered. Using the terminology provided in this ontology, one can express restrictions such as when the service can be requested, provided, or queried for further information. The main concepts include *TemporalEntity*, *TimeInterval*, *TimePoint*, *TimeZone*, *TemporalDate*, etc.

3. **Availability ontology.** The availability ontology provides the terminology needed to specify when, where, and to whom a service is available. Concepts included are *Availability* and *RequestAvailability*.

4. **Obligation ontology.** The obligation ontology provides the terminology needed to describe various obligations which may be connected to service request and provision. This includes, for example, pricing and payment obligations. Pricing obligations are related to service providers and include information regarding refund procedures, negotiability, etc. Payment obligations are related to service requesters, who have the obligation to pay for the service and include information such as payment discounts, charge, etc. The main concepts include *Payment-Obligation*, *PricingObligation*, etc.

5. **Price ontology.** The price ontology provides the terminology needed to describe properties of a service related to price. Different types of prices are modeled. The main concepts include *Price*, *AbsoutePrice*, *ProportionalPrice*, *RangedPrice*, *MechanismAuction*, etc.

6. **Payment ontology.** The payment ontology provides the terminology needed to describe how service requesters can fulfill their payment obligations. Payment and price ontology contain two views of the same thing but from different perspectives. The main concepts include *PaymentInstrument*, *PaymentScheme*, *CashInstrument*, *ElectronicCashType*, etc.

7. **Discounts ontology.** The discounts ontology provides the terminology needed to describe various types of discounts. Discounts are dependent on how a requester pays (e.g., early payment, type of payment instrument, etc.) and who the requester is (e.g., age group, student, membership, etc.). The main concepts include *Discount*, *PayeeDiscount*, *StudentDiscount*, *MembershipDiscount*, etc.

8. **Rights ontology.** The rights ontology provides the terminology needed to describe rights granted to service providers or service requesters. The main concepts include *Right*, *RightOfWarranty*, *RightOfAccess*, etc.

9. **Trust ontology.** The trust ontology provides the terminology needed to describe the trust aspect of a service. This model is directly influenced by other models such as *endorsement*. The main concepts include *Endorsement*, *InternallyManagedEndorsement*, and *ExternallyManagedEndorsement*.

10. **Quality of service ontology.** The quality of service ontology provides terminology relative to a standard, an industrial benchmark, and/or a ranking schema. The main concepts include *Standard*, *Rating*, *Rated*, *Ranking*, etc.

11. **Security ontology.** The security ontology contains concepts such as *IdentificationRequirement, Confidentiality, EncryptionTechnique, IdentificationType*, etc. Two aspects are modeled: identification and confidentiality.
12. **Intellectual property ontology.** The intellectual property ontology provides the concepts that are needed to describe intellectual property aspects. The main concepts include *IPRight, Trademark, Patent, Design*, etc.
13. **Rewards ontology.** The rewards ontology includes concepts such as *AccumulatedReward, AccumulatedPriceReward, RedeemableReward*, etc.
14. **Provider ontology.** The provider ontology provides the basic terminology that is required when talking about service providers. The main concepts include *Provider, ProviderMembership, Compliance, PartnerType*, etc.
15. **Measures ontology.** The measures ontology provides a general measures terminology. The main concepts include *UnitOfMeasure, MeasurableQuantity, Distance*, etc.
16. **Currency ontology.** The currency ontology is a simple ontology that contains the most used currencies.

9.2.3 Attaching Nonfunctional Properties to WSMO Elements

Once a model for nonfunctional properties is available, a second challenge that has to be addressed is how to attach nonfunctional properties descriptions to WSMO services and goals. This section provides our solution to this problem.

Nonfunctional Property Syntax

Nonfunctional properties of services or goals are modeled in a way similar to that in which capabilities are currently modeled in WSMO/WSML [185]. A service is an entity which provides a functionality (e.g., given a date, a start location, a destination, and information about a client, a service can book a ticket for the desired trip), but at the same time a service can be seen as an entity which provides one or more nonfunctional properties (e.g., given a particular type of client, a service charges a particular price, etc.). A simplified model of a WSMO service following this approach is as follows:

```
Webservice
    capability idCapability
        precondition definedBy axiom1
        postcondition definedBy axiom2
        assumption definedBy axiom3
        effect definedBy axiom4
    nonFunctionalProperty idNFP
        definition definedBy axiom5
```

Nonfunctional property blocks are delimited with the keywords `nonFunctionalProperties` and `endNonFunctionalProperties` or short forms `nfp` and `endNfp`. Following the keyword is a list of attribute values, which consists of the attribute identifier, the keyword `hasValue`, and the value for the attribute, which may be an identifier or a variable symbol (or a set of such symbols). This is followed by an optional annotations block, an optional `importsOntology` block, and an optional `usesMediator` block.

In case the value of the attribute in the name–value pair is an identifier, this value may be an IRI, a data value, an anonymous identifier, or a comma-separated list of the former, delimited with curly brackets. In case it is a variable symbol, a axiom definition block should follow, in which the variable symbol is used. If the axiom definition block is missing or the variable symbol is not used in it, then implementations should issue a warning to the user. The axiom definition block starts with the `definedBy` keyword followed by one or more logical expressions. The language allowed for the logical expression differs per WSML variant. The logical expressions are restricted to rule bodies for the Core, Flight, and Rule variants, and to descriptions (i.e., tree-shaped formulas) for the DL variant.

Nonfunctional properties are defined using logical expressions in the same way as preconditions/postconditions, assumptions, and effects are defined in a capability. The terminology needed to construct the logical expressions is provided by nonfunctional properties ontologies [207].

Nonfunctional Property Semantics

The central notion for nonfunctional properties is the *value* of the property. The nonfunctional properties semantics described in this section defines the values of a specific nonfunctional property.

Given a logical expression logExp, a variable substitution θ is a mapping from free variables in logExp, denoted $var(\text{logExp})$, to identifiers: $\theta : var(\text{logExp}) \to$ **Id**. With logExpθ we denote the application of θ to logExp, i.e., the replacement of every free variable x in logExp with $\theta(x)$.

Let $\langle \ldots, \textbf{ontID}, \ldots, \{\ldots, nfp, \ldots\}, \ldots \rangle_x$ be a WSML Web service, goal, capability, interface, or mediator, where **ontID** is the set of imported ontologies and $nfp = \langle \text{name, value}, \textbf{logExp} \rangle_{nfp}$ is a nonfunctional property, let $\mathfrak{O}$ be an ontology map such that $dom(\mathfrak{O}) = \textbf{ontID}$, and let Θ be the set of variable substitutions such that for every $\theta \in \Theta$ it holds that for all logExp $\in$ **logExp**, $\mathfrak{O} \models$ logExpθ. Then, an identifier $i \in$ **Id** is a *value* of name if there is a $\theta \in \Theta$ such that $i = \theta(\text{value})$.

Observe that if value is an identifier, the logical expressions function as a filter: if all of the logical expressions are entailed by the ontologies, value is a value of the property.

So, the logical expressions of the nonfunctional property can be seen as queries over the ontologies, and the query answers are projected onto value.

9.2.4 Modeling Examples

For exemplification purposes we use services and goals from the SWS Challenge[2] Shipment Discovery scenario. We have extended the initial scenario by defining challenges that address discovery, selection, and ranking of services on the basis of

---

[2] http://sws-challenge.org/

nonfunctional properties descriptions. In the extended scenario,[3] the set of shipping services descriptions (i.e., Mueller, Racer, Runner, Walker, and Weasel) are augmented by describing nonfunctional properties aspects such as discounts and obligations. The shipping services allow requesters to order a shipment by specifying the sender's address, the receiver's address, package information, and a collection interval during which the shipper will come to collect the package.

Listing 9.1 displays a concrete example of how to describe one nonfunctional property of a service (i.e., Runner), namely, obligations. Owing to space limitations the listing contains only the specification of obligations aspects without any functional, behavioral, or any other nonfunctional descriptions of the service. In an informal manner, the service obligations can be summarized as follows: (1) in case the package is lost or damaged, Runners liability is the declared value of the package but no more than $150 and (2) packages containing glassware, antiques, or jewelry are limited to a maximum declared value of $100.

Listing 9.1. Runner's obligations

```
namespace { _"WSRunner.wsml#",
    runner _"WSRunner.wsml#",
    so _"Shipment.wsml#",
    dc _"http :// purl.org/dc/elements/1.1#",
    pay _"http :// www.wsmo.org/ontologies/nfp/paymentNFPOntology#",
    wsml _"http :// www.wsmo.org/wsml/wsml−syntax/",
    obl _"http :// www.wsmo.org/ontologies/nfp/obligationsNFPOntology.wsml,
    up _"UpperOnto.wsml#"}

Webservice runnerService
    nonFunctionalProperties
    obl#Obligation hasValue ?o
        definedBy
            // in case the package is lost or damaged Runners liability is
            // the declared value of the package but no more than 150 USD
            hasPackageLiability(?package, 150):−
                ?package[so\#packageStatus hasValue ?status] and
                (?status = so\#packageDamaged or ?status = so\#packageLost) and
                packageDeclaredValue(?package, ?value) and ?value>150.

            hasPackageLiability(?package, ?value):−
                ?package[so\#packageStatus hasValue ?status] and
                (?status = so\#packageDamaged or ?status = so\#packageLost) and
                packageDeclaredValue(?package, ?value) and
                ?value =< 150.

            // in case the package is not lost or damaged Runners liability is 0
            hasPackageLiability(?package, 0):−
                ?package[so\#packageStatus hasValue ?status] and
                ?status != so\#packageDamaged and ?status != so\#packageLost.

            // packages containing glassware, antiques or jewelry
            // are limited to a maximum declared value of 100 USD
            packageDeclaredValue(?package, 100):−
                ?package[so\#containesItemsOfType hasValue ?type, so\#declaredValue hasValue
                    ?value] and
                (?type = so\#Antiques or ?type = so\#Glassware or ?type = so\#Jewelry) and
                    ?value>100.
```

---

[3] http://wiki.wsmx.org/index.php?title=Discovery:NFPUseCase

```
packageDeclaredValue(?package, ?value):−
  ?package[so\#containsItemsOfType hasValue ?type, so\#declaredValue hasValue
    ?value] and
  ((?type != so\#Antiques and ?type != so\#Glassware and ?type != so\#Jewelry) or
    ?value<100).

capability  runnerOrderSystemCapability
interface  runnerOrderSystemInterface
```

According to the model defined in Sect. 9.2.3, Runner's obligations are expressed
as logical expressions, more precisely as logical rules in WSML. In a similar way
other nonfunctional properties can be described for any of the services in the scenario. Further on, consider the concrete goal of shipping one package (GumblePack-
age) to a specified address (GumbleAddress) of a specific receiver (Gumble). A goal
in WSMO is described in a similar manner to a Web service. Our concrete goal is
specified in Listing 9.2.

Listing 9.2. Goal description

```
namespace {_"Goal.wsml#",
  so _"Shipment.wsml#",
  dc _"http :// purl .org/dc/elements/1.1#",
  wsml _"http :// www.wsmo.org/wsml/wsml−syntax/",
  obl _"http :// www.wsmo.org/ontologies/nfp/obligationsNFPOntology.wsml,
  up _"UpperOnto.wsml#",
  pref _"Preferences.wsml#"}

goal Goal1
  annotations
    up#order hasValue pref#ascending
    up#nfp hasValue obl#Obligation
    up#top hasValue "1"
  endAnnotations

  capability  requestedCapability
  postcondition
    definedBy
      ?order[
        so#to hasValue Gumble,
        so#packages hasValue GumblePackage
      ] memberOf so#ShipmentOrder
      and
          Gumble[
            so#firstName hasValue "Barney",
            so#lastName hasValue "Gumble",
            so#address hasValue GumbleAddress
          ] memberOf so#ContactInfo
          and
          GumbleAddress[
            so#streetAddress hasValue "320 East 79th Street",
            so#city hasValue so#NY,
            so#country hasValue so#US
          ] memberOf so#Address
          and
          GumblePackage[
            so#length hasValue 10
            so#width hasValue 10
            so#height hasValue 10
```

```
        so#weight hasValue 10
        so#declaredValue hasValue 150
        so#containesItemsOfType hasValue so#Glassware
] memberOf so#Package.
```

User preferences are part of the goal. For example, the user can specify which nonfunctional property will be used as a ordering dimension during the selection and ranking process. In this case the ordering dimension is the obligations nonfunctional property (up#nfp hasValue obl#Obligation). Furthermore, the user can specify how the results should be ordered (i.e., ascending or descending), in this case ascending (up#order hasValue pref#ascending), the importance of the nonfunctional properties, e.g., for a user the price is less important than the execution time, and the number of best services to be selected (up#top hasValue "1"). The background knowledge used during the selection and ranking process is usually extracted from the capability section of the goal.

9.3 Selecting Services

As mentioned before, selection is the process where one or more services which best satisfy the user preferences are selected from the candidate services returned from the service discovery stage. As selection criteria, specified by the user, various nonfunctional properties such as service level agreements, quality of services, etc. can be obtained from the goal description. On the service side the requested nonfunctional properties values are either directly specified in the service description or are provided (computed or collected) by a monitoring tool. Nonfunctional properties specified in goal and service descriptions are expressed in a semantic language (i.e., WSML), by means of logical rules using terms from nonfunctional properties ontologies, as exemplified in Sect. 9.2.4.

In this section we describe our solution for service selector. We see selection as a two-step process. First the list of services identified as fulfilling a user's request during the discovery process are order according to specified preferences. This step, called "ranking," is discussed in Sect. 9.3.1. The second and last step, much simpler than the first one, is simply about selecting the top k candidates from the ordered list of services built in the previous step. This step is briefly described in Sect. 9.3.2.

9.3.1 Ranking

An integrated part of the selection is the ranking process, which generates an order list of services out of the candidate services set. This section provides some background notions and defines what we understand by ranking in, discusses several types of ranking, and describes our ranking solution.

Background

The problem of ranking services on the basis of their nonfunctional properties can be seen as a particular implementation of a much more general problem investigated in mathematics. Research around this problem gave birth to a special branch of mathematics called *order theory* [86]. Order theory is a branch of mathematics which studies various kinds of relations that capture the intuitive notion of mathematical ordering. We introduce a set of definitions from order theory which are afterwards used to formally describe the problem of ordering in general, and thus the problem of ranking services on the basis of their nonfunctional properties in particular.

In order theory the notion of *order* is very much related to the notion of *relation*. More precisely orders are a special type of relation: *binary relations*.

Definition 9.1 (partial order). *A partial order $\leq_P$ on a set P is a binary relation on P having the following properties: (1) $\leq_P$ is reflexive: $a \leq_P a$, $\forall a \in P$; (2) $\leq_P$ is antisymmetric: if $a \leq_P b$ and $b \leq_P a$ then $a = b$, $\forall a, b \in P$; and (3) $\leq_P$ is transitive: if $a \leq_P b$; and $b \leq_P c$ then $a \leq_P c$, $\forall a, b, c \in P$.*

A set on which a partial order is defined is called a partial order set, or poset.

Definition 9.2 (total order). *A partial order $\leq_P$ on a set P is a total order if $\forall a, b \in P$ and $a \neq b$ the following holds: $a \leq_P b$ or $b \leq_P a$.*

Given the above definitions the problem of ranking could be defined in a formal way as a function as shown below:

Definition 9.3 (ranking). *Given a set P of objects and an partial order relation $\leq_P$ on this set, a ranking function f can be defined as follows: $f(P, \leq_P) = R$, where R is the set of objects containing the same elements as P ($R = P$) and $\exists s$ a sequence $s(1, 2, ..., |R|) \rightarrow R$ such that $\forall i, j \in \{1, 2, ..., |R|\}$, with $i <= j \Rightarrow s(i) \leq_P s(j)$.*

One may have noticed that defining an order relation over a set of elements is fundamental when describing the ranking task. This implies that the elements of the set need to be quantifiable and comparable.

Service Ranking Types

Service ranking remains an open and controversial problem in terms of both social and technical aspects. From a social point of view an honest and fair mechanism is required. Intuitively, a self-ranking mechanism is unreliable since service providers tend to overadvertise their services. A third-party ranking mechanism seams a better solution when considering reliability aspects. Most of the existing solutions follow this approach. However, a single point of failure might affect such solutions. A distributed solution which integrates feedback from users is therefore required. Involving the human users in the ranking process, by means of social networking approaches such as tagging, could improve the accuracy of the ranking result. Furthermore, principles extracted from social models could be applied when defining solutions for service ranking. We call the ranking process which considers all the abovementioned types of information *social ranking*.

From a technical point most of the current approaches [140, 181] consider only numerical or keyword values associated with the entities to be ranked. Such approaches are less flexible and often less accurate since an ontological representation of nonfunctional properties aspects used along with logical expressions attached to goals and Web Services descriptions will allow a semantic ranking mechanism to provide more accurate results.

Additionally an appropriate *multicriteria ranking* mechanism which considers multiple nonfunctional properties dimensions is required. In the case of multiple-criteria ranking, the most used approach is to use a matrix-based solution and to compute afterwards a weighted average over the nonfunctional properties of each service [221]. However, other solutions for multicriteria ranking which provide better results in terms of precision and recall could be developed. Since users usually express their preferences in terms of multiple nonfunctional properties, we plan to investigate the multicriteria ranking problem in order to provide more accurate solutions. Additionally, ranking with missing or incomplete specified nonfunctional properties needs to be addressed.

Finally, specification and reasoning with context and preferences is required when ranking services in a given situation, *context-based ranking*. To our knowledge most of the service ranking approaches do not consider context information. The need for such a support is illustrated by the following situation. Let us consider that a requester wants to receive the list of services fulfilling the goal ordered by price. She/he is looking for the cheapest one. Even when the ranking system is precise in building the ranking list according to the price dimension, this list could be, however, wrong if the context information is not considered. It might be the case that services that are ranked higher in the list are not available for invocation at that moment in time (context) and thus keeping them in the in the ranked list would make no sense. Therefore, context and relations between nonfunctional properties must be considered during ranking. Models that capture relations between nonfunctional properties and models for context are also required to fill the gap.

Ranking Solution

In [81] a categorization of ranking approaches is provided based on two dimensions: (1) *local* or *global*, depending on whether local or global knowledge is needed, and (2) *absolute* or *relative*, depending on whether the measurements is of absolute scope or refers to a particular client request. Considering these dimensions a set of four types of ranking can be defined: (1) *local and absolute*, (2) *local and relative*, (3) *global and absolute*, and (4) *global and relative*. The popular PageRank ranking approach of Google belongs to the global and absolute category. It is *absolute* because ranking of the entire collection is not done on the basis of each client request and it is *global* because the knowledge required for ranking is distributed in the entire collection. On the other hand, ranking based on nonfunctional properties is seen as being local and relative since the ranking is done according to the user query (*relative*) and local knowledge is sufficient to perform the ranking (*local*). Our ranking mechanism for services based on their nonfunctional properties will be developed in the same context:local and relative. This fits well with the SEE/WSMX environment [95] in which the ranking mechanism will be integrated.

The approach we take to solve the problem of ranking services on the basis of their nonfunctional properties is to develop ranking algorithms along two dimensions: (1) the *level of abstraction*, i.e., keywords, semantic descriptions, and

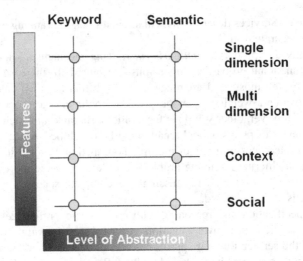

Figure 9.1. Ranking engine space

(2) *features derived from the problems addressed*, i.e., singe-criteria ranking, multicriteria ranking, and social ranking. Figure 9.1 presents the ranking engines/algo-
rithms which we identified as part of our ranking solution.

Once algorithms that cover the ranking engine space in Fig. 9.1 are available,
they need to be integrated such that given a user preference the most appropriate engine or combination of engines is used. The approach we take here is to develop a
ranking framework similar to the one developed in [115] for service discovery. This
framework will handle incoming requests from the user considering the nonfunctional requirements specifications and will manage the internal workflow between
the ranking engines. A simple workflow could be, for example, to use the ranking
based on specified values of nonfunctional properties first and afterwards to perform
the semantic ranking. Similar or more complicated workflows that include one or
more ranking engines will be handled by the framework. Additionally the framework
will provide input/output data for the ranking engines taking care that nonfunctional
properties values are normalized and compared on the same scale.

Since the ranking operation is usually time-consuming, an appropriate support
for reducing the processing time is required. A feasible approach is to develop indexing and caching mechanisms. Note that such an index mechanism is built over the
values of nonfunctional properties described in the service descriptions or collected
by a monitoring system. By maintaining index structures on nonfunctional properties, the time to retrieve and rank services on these properties will decrease. An efficient mechanism in terms of time and resource consumption is even more required
in the context of semantic ranking. Therefore, precomputing semantic matching between nonfunctional properties specifications of registered services and possible
nonfunctional requirements of the user is needed. In the same context a caching
mechanism could speed up the ranking process by caching ranking results after a
request has been processed. Later on, the cached results could be considered when a
request similar to a previously answered request is received.

As part of our solution we have addressed so far only two aspects of ranking services as discussed in the "Service Ranking Types" section, namely, semantic ranking and multicriteria ranking. Nonfunctional properties of services and goals used in the prototype are semantically described as presented in Sect. 9.2.4. The logical rules used to model nonfunctional properties of services are evaluated, during the ranking process, by a reasoning engine. Additional data is required during the rules evaluation process. This data represents mainly user preferences and includes (1) which nonfunctional properties the user is interested in, (2) the level of importance of each of these nonfunctional properties, (3) how the list of services should be ordered, i.e., ascending or descending, as well as (4) concrete instances data extracted from the goal description. The nonfunctional properties values obtained by evaluating the logical rules are sorted and the order list of services is built.

The algorithm for multicriteria ranking based on nonfunctional properties is presented in Algorithm 1. First, a set of tuples containing nonfunctional properties and their associated importance is extracted out of the goal description (line 3). Considering the goal example provided in Listing 9.2, the list contains only one nonfunctional property, namely, *obligations*. If no importance is specified, the default value is considered to be 0.5, which specifies a moderate interest in the nonfunctional property. The importance is a numeric value ranging from 0 to 1, where 1 encodes the fact that the user is extremely interested in the nonfunctional property and 0 encodes the fact that the nonfunctional property is not of interest for the user. Further on, instance data from the goal is extracted (line 4) and a knowledge base is created. In our example the extracted instance data contains information about the receiver, the package, and the destination address. The last step in extracting relevant information for the ranking process is to identify how the results should be ordered, i.e., ascending or descending (line 5).

Once the preprocessing steps have been done, each service is checked to determine if the requested nonfunctional properties specified in the goal are available in the service description. In the case of a positive answer the corresponding logic rules are extracted (line 11) and evaluated (line 12) using a reasoning engine which supports WSML rules (e.g., MINS[4], KAON2[5], or IRIS[6]). A quadruple structure is built (lines 13 and 16) containing for each service and nonfunctional property the computed value and its importance. An aggregated score is computed for each service by summing the normalized values (line 24) of the nonfunctional properties weighted by importance values (line 25). The results are collected in a set of tuples, where each tuple contain the service ID and the computed score (line 27). Finally the scores values are sorted according to the ordering sense extracted from the goal and the final list of services is returned (line 29).

[4] http://tools.deri.org/mins/
[5] http://kaon2.semanticweb.org/
[6] http://sourceforge.net/projects/iris-reasoner/

Data: Set of services S_{Ser}, Goal G.
Result: Order list of services L_{Ser}.

```
1  begin
2      Ω ⟵ ∅, where Ω is a set of tuples [service,score];
3      λ = extractNFPs(G), where λ is a set of tuples [nfp, importance];
4      G_Know = extractInstancesKnowledge(G);
5      d = extractOrderingSense(G);
6      β ⟵ ∅, is a set of quadruples [service,nfp,nfpvalue,importance];
7      for s ∈ S_Ser do
8          for nfp ∈ λ do
9              imp = lambda.getImportance(nfp);
10             if nfp ∈ s.nfps then
11                 rule = extract(nfp, s);
12                 nfpvalue = evaluateRule(rule, G_Know);
13                 β = β ∪ [s, nfp, nfpvalue, imp];
14             end
15             else
16                 β = β ∪ [s, nfp, 0, 0];
17             end
18         end
19     end
20     for s ∈ β do
21         score_s = 0;
22         for nfp ∈ β do
23             nfpvalue = β.getNFPValue(s, nfp);
24             nfpvalue_max = max(β.npf);
25             score_s = score_s + imp * (nfpvalue / nfpvalue_max);
26         end
27         Ω = Ω ∪ [s, score_s];
28     end
29     L_Ser ⟵ sort(Ω, d);
30 end
```

Algorithm 1: Multicriteria ranking

9.3.2 Selection

Once the ranking process has been completed, as a final step of the selection process the best candidate service or best candidate services are selected. This process is much simpler than the previous process, service ranking. It simply selects the top k services from the order list returned in the previous step. The k value is specified by the user in the goal description by means of an annotation. Considering the goal example provided in Listing 9.2, the k value is 1 (up#top hasValue "1"). In case no such value is provided in the goal description, the default value is 1, meaning that the first service in the list is selected.

9.4 Related Work

The terms "selection" and "ranking" are used in many areas of computer science, including information retrieval [187] and areas connected to it such as classical search engines, and additionally in may new emerging areas such as Web Services, Semantic Web, and Semantic Web Services. In this section we briefly point out some relevant approaches for service selection and ranking from these research areas.

In information retrieval [187] the problem of ranking documents given a query is classically addressed using statistical models. The query and the documents that need to be ranked are basically lists of terms that are represented as vectors in a vector space model [133]. Statistical information such as terms frequency, document length, etc. is used to compute the similarity degree of the document and the query, and is implicit the document's rank. As a similarity function, cosine similarity is the most used. Other models for representing documents and queries can be used as well, e.g., latent semantic indexing [64] model and probabilistic models [143].

One approach which bases its tremendous success on a ranking algorithm is that of Google.[7] Within the past few years, Google has become probably the most utilized search engine worldwide. A decisive factor in Google's success, besides the high performance and ease to use and simple interface, is the superior quality of the search results compared with those of other search engines, which stems from an interesting ranking algorithm called PageRank [165].

PageRank is an algorithm for computing a Web page score on the basis of the graph inferred from the link structure of the Web. The basic idea behind PageRank is that the number of inbound links for a document measures its general importance. Hence, a Web page is generally more important, if many other Web pages link to it. However, not only their number counts, but also their importance. This model applies globally and the rank of a Web page is always determined recursively by the PageRank value of other Web pages. Given a Web page p, its PageRank value is computed as follows:

$$\mathbf{PR(p_i)} = \frac{(1-d)}{N} + d \sum_{p_j \in M(p_i)} \frac{PR(p_j)}{L(p_j)}$$

In the above formula d is a dumping factor which is usually set to 0.85. It basically represents the probability that a random user will get bored and select a different page. $p_j, j = 1...N$ are the pages under consideration, $M(p_i)$ is the set of pages that link to p_i, $L(p_j)$ is the number of links coming from page p_j, and N is the total number of pages.

One can see PageRank as a specific type of ranking based on nonfunctional properties, in this case the nonfunctional property being the importance, or the reputation, of the Web page being ranked.

---

[7] http://www.google.com

Although [221] does not focus directly on the problem of selection and ranking of services on the basis of their nonfunctional properties/quality of service values, this approach is interesting since it uses a multicriteria computation model to determine the importance of a service, which is afterwards used in the selection process. This is just one of the steps of a composition mechanism. At the execution time for each particular task of the composite service, the system collects the quality of service values of the services that can fulfill the task (*candidate services*). Out of these quality of service values *quality vectors* are built. By merging the quality vectors of the candidate services, one creates a quality matrix, in which each row corresponds to a service and each column corresponds to a quality of service criterion. The simple additive weighting method, introduced in the context of multi multiple criteria decision making [108] research, is used to select the optimal Web service. Using this method, one computes a set of scores for each service, on the basis of which the services can be ranked afterwards.

In [214] a quality of service based Web service selection and ranking mechanism with trust and reputation management support is presented. The solution is developed under two basic assumptions: (1) users and services have a probabilistic behavior, which means there is a difference between the quality of service values they obtain and the quality of service values they report, which follows a probabilistic distribution, and (2) there exit a few trusted third parties, which are usually well-known agents that provide trusted measurements of quality of service parameters. The quality of service values are collected from four sources: user feedback, service descriptions, trusted agents, and predictions.

9.5 Summary

In this chapter we discussed one core task for any service-oriented system, namely, service selection. First we described our solution to a directly connected problem, namely, the modeling and attaching of nonfunctional properties descriptions to services and goals. A set of ontologies [207] in WSML based on the models provided in [164] were created to provide formal conceptualization for services' nonfunctional properties such as obligations, availability, security, etc. Furthermore, we distinguished between two categories of nonfunctional properties and we provided the means to attach nonfunctional properties descriptions to services and goals as logical rules. In the second part of the chapter we detailed the service selection solution with a special focus on service ranking as a core process. The ranking mechanism uses logical rules describing nonfunctional properties of services and evaluates them using a reasoning engine. As a last step it builds an ordered order list of services on the basis of values computed during the evaluation step.

As future work we plan to refine the set of existing nonfunctional properties ontologies to capture aspects such as relations between nonfunctional properties. Also left as future work is the full specification and implementation of a ranking framework which integrates various types of ranking, i.e., single-criteria ranking, multi-criteria ranking, context-aware ranking, and social ranking. Further on, a set of open issues and improvements need to be addressed and integrated with the current selection solution. These include, but are not limited to, how to integrate nonfunctional properties values called by monitoring tools with the service selector, how to predict nonfunctional values of services, which are the best solutions to collect and incorporate user feedback, and last but not least to consider trust and reputation issues.

10

Mediation

An intense research activity regarding the Semantic Web, Web Services, and their combination, Semantic Web Services, has been going on during the last few years. But only the semantic descriptions attached to data or to the Web Services deployed using today's technologies do not solve the heterogeneity problem that may occur owing to the distributed nature of the Web itself. As such, the heterogeneity existing in representing data, in the multitude of choices in representing the requested and the provided functionalities, and in the differences in the communication patterns (public processes) are problems that have to be solved before we are able to fully benefit from the semantically enabled Web and Web Services. Considering that these problems cannot be avoided, dynamic mediation solutions that fully exploit the semantic descriptions of data and services are required.

This chapter is formed of two main parts: the first describes the main techniques for data mediation in a semantic environment, while the second focuses on behavior mismatches and process mediation.

The data mediation scenario to be analyzed in this chapter is the automatic transformation of the data part of heterogeneous messages exchanged in peer-to-peer (P2P) communications. One of the main assumptions in a semantic environment is that all manipulated data is described in terms of ontologies. As such, data to be mediated represents in fact ontology instances and the automatic mediation task relies on ontology mappings created during design time.

While data mediation solutions are mandatory in heterogeneous contexts, they are not enough to enable communication when mismatches at the behavioral level are also present. Solutions towards behavior mediation, where behavior is represented as processes, are discussed and a classification of solvable/unsolvable mismatches is provided.

10.1 Preliminaries

Data heterogeneity remains a problem even in the context of Semantic Web and Semantic Web Services. That is, different conceptualizations of the same domain (i.e., ontologies) might be used in describing the data used by various parties, making the interchange of such data impossible. The major advantage compared with previous attempts in solving data mismatches [139, 147, 162] is that ontologies better describe the data to be mediated [161]. As such, they offer the means to solve the heterogeneity problems at the schema level and to apply the findings to the actual data during run-time processes. The schema mapping process can fully benefit from the semantic descriptions present in the ontologies, changing from a manual and error-prone task to a semiautomatic one (machine assisted) or even an automatic one.

Semantic Web Services rely on ontologies to semantically describe their interfaces and capabilities. As a consequence the heterogeneity problems introduced by different ontologies modeling the same domain are inherited in this context as well. In order to enable service interaction, communication, and interoperation, ontology-based data mediation is a prerequisite of any framework dealing with Semantic Web Services. Mappings created between ontologies have to be exploited during the actual invocation of the Web Services and applied to specific data that has to be interchanged.

As mentioned already, heterogeneity problems occur both at the data level as well as at the behavioral level of business logics, message-exchange protocol, and Web service invocation. Process mediation is one of the crucial points on the road towards establishing new, ad hoc cooperation on the Web between various business partners. If semantically enhanced data enables dynamic solutions for coping with data heterogeneity, semantically enhanced Web Services can do the same for behavioral heterogeneity. Such a mediator acts on the public processes of the parties involved in a communication and adjusts the bidirectional flow of messages to suit the requested/expected behavior of each party.

10.1.1 Layers of Mediation

Mediation can be approached on two different layers: the *implementation layer* and the *specification layer*. The first one offers concrete solutions for a given heterogeneity problem, providing the actual component able to solve that problem. The specification layer covers the semantic descriptions of mediators. Semantic techniques need to be employed to create high-level descriptions, called *semantic mediation patterns*, which rely on the functionality offered by the *mediation services*. A semantic mediation pattern prescribes a way of using several mediation services, no matter if they are concerned with data mediation or process mediation. As a consequence, a mediation service can be associated with multiple semantic mediation patterns and a semantic mediation pattern will point to at least one mediation service. As ontologies are used to semantically describe the emantic mediation patterns, extra semantic information can be provided by semantically describing the mediation services as well (i.e., they become in this way *semantic mediators*; Fig. 10.1). These semantic mediators are nothing other than ontological entities, which can be described in a similar manner as prescribed by the Web Service Modeling Ontology (WSMO), presented in Chap. 3.

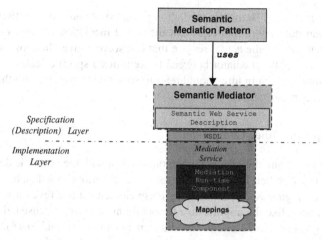

Figure 10.1. The layering of semantic mediation patterns, semantic mediators, and mediation services

As such, the specification layer can be seen as being composed of two sublayers: the *semantic mediation patterns layer* and the *semantic mediators (description) layer*.

This chapter will mainly focus on the actual mediation services for data and process mediation, as further described in Sects. 10.2 and 10.3. The other two levels have already been covered in Chap. 3, as the WSMO mediators are nothing other than semantic mediator patterns, while any mediator described on the basis of these WSMO mediators is a semantic mediator (for example, a specific ooMediator between two given ontologies O1 and O2).

10.1.2 Mediation's Role in Semantically Enabled Service-Oriented Architecture

This section explains in more detail why mediation and the mediation tool are an important part in the semantically enabled service-oriented architecture (SESA). For this, we will analyze the problem from two perspectives: the definition of the elements used in SESA and the actual implementation.

Elements' Definitions

As previously specified in this book, every element considered by SESA has to have a semantic description. Three of the four main components (*ontologies*, *goals*, and *Web Services*) have in their definition the `usesMediator` attribute, whose range is defined by the fourth main modeling element, the *mediators*. As described in Chap. 3, there are four types of mediators to be considered, depending on the type of elements they link or bridge, namely, ontology to ontology mediators, goal to goal mediators, Web service to Web service mediators, and Web service to goal mediators.

But all these mediators (semantic mediation patterns) are only descriptions of what a mediator can do; they do not represent the actual mediation description between two given elements, or the actual service that can solve a given heterogeneity problem. For describing the mediator between two entities a specific semantic mediator has to be defined, which in turn should refer to specific components, by the attribute hasMediationService.

Relationship with Other Component

Both the discovery and the selection components deal with the semantic descriptions of the goals and Web Services, performing several operations based on these description. If the ontologies used for specifying these elements differ (even if we consider minor differences, like the minimal age for obtaining a driving license being considered in one greater than 17 and in the other greater than or equal to 18), those two components need the services of data mediators in order to fulfill their functionalities.

Service Invocation

SESA is meant to provide automatic support for every phase of service invocation, from the moment a requester publishes a certain goal until that goal is fulfilled. One important aspect is the communication between the service requester and the service provider. For having a truly automatic communication, with no human intervention, tool support for solving any behavioral heterogeneity problems between the requester and the provider of a service need to be available.

10.2 Ontology-Based Data Mediation

Ontologies can offer substantial support towards the automation of data mediation. Even if there will always be a trade-off between the degree of automation and the level of accuracy of the data mediation process, semantics can help combine semiautomatic methods with automatic techniques in order to obtain flexible and robust solutions.

Ontologies semantically describe the data to be mediated, representing in fact a schema for this data. As a consequence, it is possible to distinguish between a design-time and a run-time phase, where the first represents the support (a prerequisite) for the second. At design time the mappings between ontologies have to be established (i.e., between the source and the target ontologies), while at the run-time phase these mappings are applied in concrete scenarios.

In the design-time phase semiautomatic techniques are used, that is, the human domain expert is required to perform a set of validations and choices based on machine findings, in order to ensure that the mappings between the source and the target ontologies are correct. It is important to note that since these mappings are created on the ontology level (i.e., schema level), they are created only once and they can be used multiple times with no other updates (as long as the ontologies do not evolve). The mappings are applied during run time on concrete data multiple times without any human intervention, in an automatic manner.

This chapter provides a description of various ontology mapping techniques that can be used as semiautomatic approaches for creation of mappings. It also defines mechanisms that can be used in applying these mappings in the instance transformation scenario. We use the approach presented in [150] to exemplify the most common strategies and the methodologies behind ontology mapping and a data mediation run-time engine. While some of the methods presented in the rest of this chapter are specific to this particular work, most of them can be found in several forms in other approaches as well.

10.2.1 Data Mediation Scope and Scenario

The scope of the ontology mapping approach (design-time phase) in the SESA context can be defined in terms of the evaluation criteria proposed in [159]. These criteria are:

- *Input requirements*: What are the elements of interest from the source ontologies, which of them are required, what knowledge representation paradigm is supported.
- *Level of user interaction*: How are the results presented to the user.
- *Type of output*: What is the output of the mapping process.
- *Content of output*: Which elements of the input ontologies are correlated in the output.

They form a set of *pragmatic criteria* which help in identifying a set of requirements for ontology mapping from the user's perspective. In this respect, the SESA reference implementation for ontology mapping [150] is characterized by the following features:

Input requirements: There are two ontologies used as inputs for the mapping process: the source and the target ontology. The ontologies can be expressed using Web Service Modeling Language[1] (WSML), and the focus is on concepts, attributes, and instances. The mappings are created on the schema level, so the concepts, the attributes, and their types are required for the mapping process, while the instances are optional, mainly used in adding conditions on the mappings.

Level of user interaction: In the context of Web Services the correctness of mappings is vital. As a consequence, a semiautomatic approach with 100% accuracy is preferred to an automatic approach where the accuracy can vary. This semiautomatic approach offers support to the human user during the process in the form of suggestions and guidance. The user validation and the tool support are part of

---

[1] Even if the targeted ontology language is WSML, ontologies expressed in some other languages could be potentially used if appropriate wrappers are provided.

an iterative and interactive process where decisions are taken on the basis of the tool support and the tool support improves on the basis of the user's decisions.

Type of output: WSMO and Semantic Web Services are based on a set of principles that includes strict decoupling and centrality of mediations [184]. Considering this, neither the input ontologies are altered in any way, nor is a merged ontology created. In both cases, the parties involved in the interaction would have to adjust their information systems or even the business logics to support the new version of their ontology. As these types of solutions are not feasible (because of, e.g., high costs and latency) in a dynamic environment such as the Web, an alignment between the two ontologies is created, in such a way that both the source and the target ontologies remain unchanged. This alignment can consist of mappings either expressed in a specialized mapping language (such as the Abstract Mapping Language described in [188]) or expressed directly in the ontologies' representation language.

Content of output: The alignment that is generated between the two source ontologies contains a set of mappings that capture the semantic relationships between the two ontologies. If the mappings are expressed in an abstract language, an extra step is needed to associate a formal semantics to these mappings, in respect to the mediation scenario they are used in.

In the SESA reference implementation it has been decided that the created alignment should consist of abstract mappings and not of rules created in a particular ontology representation language. There are several reasons behind this decision:

Reusability: The same set of mappings can be used in various mediation scenarios. A grounding mechanism can be later applied and a formal semantics can be associated with these mappings in order to suit the targeted scenario.

Manageability: If the ontologies are evolving, the set of mappings existing between them has to be updated as well. If mappings are represented as rules in a particular ontology language, the special features and peculiarities of this language are reflected in the rules as well. By this, the management of the mappings becomes extremely difficult because there are two types of correspondences that have to be maintained at all time:

1. The correspondences between those entities in the ontologies that have changed and the mapping rules
2. The correspondences between these entities and the semantics of the rules themselves

Since in the reference approach presented in this chapter, the formal semantics is associated later with the mappings, the one in charge of updates has to handle only the first type of correspondence. The second type of correspondence is automatically enforced when the grounding is applied to the already updated abstract mappings.

In the SESA context we choose to exemplify the usage of design-time-created mappings in one of the most common mediation scenarios, namely, *instance transformation*. The instance transformation scenario can be summarized as follows. Different business actors use ontologies to describe their internal business logic, and

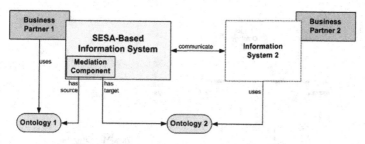

Figure 10.2. Instance transformation scenario

more important for us in this case, their data. Each of these actors uses its own information system (e.g., a SESA-based information system) and tries to interact with
other actors of other (probably more complex) business processes (Fig. 10.2). There
is need for a specialized service able to transform the data expressed in terms of
a given ontology (the source ontology) into the terms of another ontology (target
ontology), allowing the two actors to continue using their own data representation
formats.

Being part of a run-time process, the instance transformation has to be performed
completely automatically on the basis of the already existing mappings created on
the schema level during the design-time phase.

10.2.2 Ontology Mapping

The process of creating mappings represents one of the most important phases in
a mediator system. It is a design-time process and as mentioned before in order
to obtain high accuracy of the mappings the human user has to be present in this
process. By offering a set of strategies and methods for creating these mappings, one
can reduce this usually error-prone and laborious process from a manual task to a
truly semiautomatic one.

The mapping process (i.e., the design-time phase of the mediation process) basically requires three types of actions from the domain expert [148]:

1. **Browse the ontologies**: The domain expert has to discover the ontology elements
   he/she is interested in. This step involves different views of the input ontologies,
   and strategies for reducing the amount of information to be processed by the human user (e.g., context-based browsing).
2. **Identify the similarities**: This step involves the identification of semantic relationships between the entities that are of interest in the two ontologies. For doing
   this the human user can make use of the suggestions offered by a set of lexical
   and structural algorithms for determining the semantic relationships.
3. **Create the mappings**: This last step involves the capturing of the semantic relationships by mappings. This means that the domain expert has to take the proper
   actions in order to capture the semantic relationships in the mapping language
   statements or maybe in predefined mapping patterns [49].

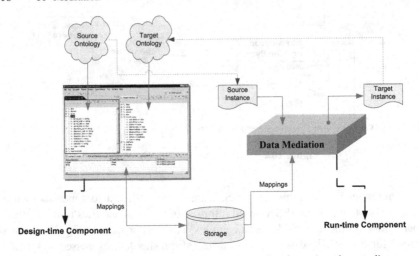

Figure 10.3. Overview of the ontology mapping tool and run-time data mediator

The ontology mapping tool used to illustrate the design-time mediation process in this chapter is implemented as an Eclipse plug-in, part of the Web Service Modeling Toolkit[2] (WSMT) [117], an integrated environment for ontology creation, visualization, and mapping (see Fig. 10.3). It is currently compatible with WSMO ontologies (but if appropriate wrappers are provided, different ontology languages could be supported). It offers different ways of browsing the ontologies using views (or perspectives) and allows the domain expert to create mappings between two ontologies (source and target) and to store them in a persistent mapping storage [150].

10.2.3 Perspectives

As described in [148], the graphical point of view adopted to visualize the source and the target ontologies makes it easier to identify certain types of mappings. These viewpoints are called perspectives and by switching between combinations of these perspectives on the source and the target ontologies, one can create certain types of mappings using only one simple operation, map, combined with mechanisms for ontology traversal and contextualized visualization strategies. Figure 10.4 shows how the perspectives are represented in the ontology mapping tool.

A perspective contains a subset of the ontology entities (e.g., concepts, attributes, relations, and instances) and the relationships existing between them. Usually the perspective used for browsing the source ontology (source perspective) and the perspective used for browsing the target ontology (target perspective) are of the same type, but there could be cases when different view types are used for source and target. In each of the perspectives there are a predefined number of *roles* which the ontology entities can have. In general, particular roles are fulfilled by different

---

[2] Open-source project available at http://sourceforge.net/projects/wsmt

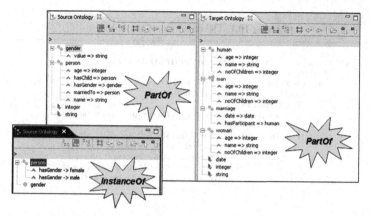

Figure 10.4. Perspectives in the ontology mapping tool

ontology entities in different perspectives and the algorithms (such as the one described in Sect. 10.2.4) refer to roles rather than to ontology entities. The roles that can be identified in a perspective are *compound item*, *primitive item*, and *description item*. A compound item has at least one description associated with it, while a primitive item does not have any description associated. A description item offers more information about the compound item it describes and usually links it with other compound or primitive items. By this the *successor* of a description item is defined as the compound or primitive item it links to.

Not all of the information modeled in the ontology is useful in all stages of the mapping process. As such, a *context* is a subset of a perspective that contains only those ontological entities, from that perspective, relevant to a concrete operation.

A notion tightly related with contexts is the *decomposition*. A context can be created from another context (this operation is called context update) by applying decomposition on an item from a perspective or a context. Decomposition allows navigating between contexts and links consecutive nested levels; the way the contexts are navigated when creating mappings influences the creation types of mappings that are created.

10.2.4 Decomposition Algorithm

The decomposition algorithm is used to offer guidance to the domain expert in the mapping process and to compute the structural factor as part of the suggestion algorithms (described later in this chapter). By decomposition the descriptions of a compound item are exposed and made available to the mapping process. The decomposition algorithm can be applied to description items and returns the description items (if any) for the successors of those particular description items. An overview of this algorithm is presented in Listing 10.1

Listing 10.1. The decomposition algorithm

```
void decompose(Collection collectionOfItems){
    Collection result;
    for each item in collectionOfItems do{
        result = result + [item];
        if isCompound(item){
            result = result + getDescriptions(item);
        }
        if isDescriptionItem(item){
            Item successorItem = getSuccessor(item);
            if (not createsLoop(succesorItem)){
                result = result + [successorItem];
                result = result + getDescriptions(item);
            }
        }
    }
    return result;
}
```

The implementation of *isCompound, isDescriptionItem, getDescriptions, getSuccessor*, and *createsLoop* differs from one view to another – for example, the cases when loops are encountered (i.e., the algorithm will not terminate) have to be addressed for each view in particular.

10.2.5 Suggestion Algorithms

In order to deliver a truly semiautomatic mapping tool, suggestion algorithms are a necessity. The suggestion algorithms are used to help the domain expert to make decisions during the mapping process, regarding the possible semantic relationships between the source and the target items in the current mapping context. A combination of two types of such algorithms is used: the first being a lexical algorithm and the second being the structural algorithms that consider the description items in their computations. Brief descriptions of the functionality that could be provided by such algorithms are provided below.

For each pair of items the suggestion algorithms compute an *eligibility factor*, indicating the degree of similarity between the two items: the smallest value (0) means that the two items are completely different, while the greatest value (1) indicates that the two items may be similar. For dealing with the values between 0 and 1 a threshold value is used: values lower than this value indicate different items and values greater than this value indicate similar items. Setting a lower threshold ensures a greater number of suggestions, while a higher value for the threshold restricts the number of suggestions to a smaller subset.

The eligibility factor is computed as a weighted average between a *structural factor*, referring to the structural properties, and a *lexical factor*, referring to the lexical relationships determined for a given pair of items. The weights can be chosen on the basis of the characteristics of the ontologies to be mapped. For example, when mapping between ontologies developed in dissimilar spoken languages, the weight of the lexical factor should be close to 0, in contrast with the case when mapping between ontologies developed in the same working groups or institutions (the usage of similar names for related terms is more likely to happen).

Even if the structural factor is computed using the decomposition algorithm, the actual heuristics used are dependent on the specific perspectives where it is applied. In a similar manner the current perspectives determine the weight for the structural and lexical factors as well as the exact features of the items to be used in computations.

The lexical factor is computed on the basis of the syntactic similarities between the names of a given pair of items. There are two main aspects used in these computations: first, the lexical relationships between the terms as given by WordNet[3] and, second, the results returned by string analysis algorithms. WordNet is an on-line lexical reference, inspired by current psycholinguistic theories of human lexical memory [146].

The structural factor is computed on the basis of the structural similarities between the two terms. It is directly dependent on the the number of mappings between *description items* that can be found by decomposition (see Listing 10.1) starting from the given source and target items.

The eligibility factor might seem very expensive to compute between a selected source item and all the items from the target, especially when mapping large ontologies. The performance is drastically improved by the use of contexts since the set of item pairs for which the eligibility factor has to be computed is significantly cut down.

The algorithms briefly mentioned in this section assist the user in finding correspondence between ontological entities. They provide suggestions based on simple measures. Research on schema matching is, however, a dynamic area. Various algorithms are continuously being developed and more and more meaningful and complex mappings are successfully being discovered using these algorithms. To achieve improved results they exploit additional information, like the structure of the ontology, external resources like the Web or a corpus, and the available instance data. The alignment format described in [67] provides an output format to represent mappings for such algorithms.[4] Used as an exchange format, it allows our tool to use suggestions made by these algorithms.

10.2.6 Bottom-Up Versus Top-Down Approach

Considering the algorithms and methods described above, two possible approaches during the ontology mapping can be followed: bottom-up and top-down approaches.

The *bottom-up approach* means that the mapping process starts with the mappings of the primitive items (if possible) and then continues with items having more

---

[3] More details are available at http://www.cogsci.princeton.edu/wn/

[4] The Ontology Alignment Evaluation Initiative evaluates the performance of matching algorithms (http://oaei.ontologymatching.org/). It uses this alignment format as the exchange format to compare generated mappings.

complex descriptions. By this, the pairs of primitive items act like a minimal, agreed-upon set of mappings between the two ontologies, and starting from this minimal set, one could gradually discover more complex relationships. This approach is useful when a complete alignment of the two ontologies is desired.

The *top-down approach* means that the mapping process starts with mapping compound items and it is usually adopted when a concrete heterogeneity problem has to be resolved. This is done when the domain expert is interested only in resolving a particular item's mismatches and not in fully aligning the input ontologies. The decomposition algorithm and the mapping contexts it updates will help the expert to identify all the relationships that can be captured by using a specific type of view and which are relevant to the problems to be solved.

In the same way as for the other algorithms, the applicability and advantages/disadvantages of each of these approaches depends on the type of view used.

10.2.7 Instance Transformation

A *run-time engine* plays the role of the data mediation service in SESA. It uses the abstract mappings created during design time, grounds them to WSML, and uses a reasoner to evaluate them against the incoming source instances. The mapping rules, the source instances, and, if necessary, source and target schema information are loaded into the reasoning space in what could be seen as a "pseudo-merged" ontology (i.e., the entities from the source and the target and the rules are strictly separated by namespaces). By querying the reasoning space for instances of target concepts, if semantically related source instances exist, the rules fire and produce as results the target instances.

The storage used could be a relational data base as well as a simple file-system-based repository for mapping documents. Figure 10.5 gives a more detailed overview

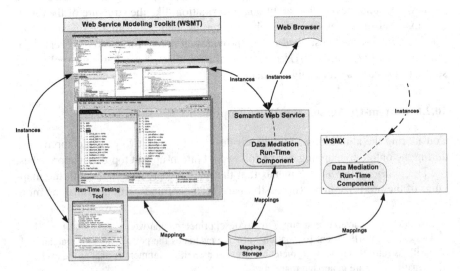

Figure 10.5. Run-time data mediator usage scenarios

of the mediation support tools and their relationships for the reference implementation, together with the several possible usage scenarios identified for the run-time data mediator engine.

It is important to note that the mappings grounding module is considered as being part of the run-time engine (in the case when the ontology alignment is expressed by using an abstract mapping language). In this way, the same set of mappings (i.e., abstract, ontology language independent mappings) can be grounded to different languages depending on the scenario the run-time mediator is used in. A second reason is that by grounding, a formal semantics is associated with the mappings, meaning that only at this stage it is stated what exactly it means to have two items mapped to each other. These formal semantics differ from one mediation scenario to another, i.e., different grounding has to be applied when using the abstract mappings in instance transformation than when using them in query rewriting. The third reason is an easier management of mappings that form the ontology alignment. If ontologies evolve, the mappings have to be updated accordingly and it becomes more efficient to perform these updates free of any language-related peculiarities.

In the context of this discussion the main scope of the run-time data mediator engine is to serve as a data mediator service in the SESA environment. Additionally it can be made available as a Web service (i.e., a Semantic Web Service) that can be invoked directly via SOAP from specialized tools or through a Web interface using a Web browser. And finally, the run-time data mediation engine can be offered as a standalone application that helps in testing and evaluating the mappings during the mapping process at design time. For more convenience, the standalone version can be integrated and delivered together with the ontology mapping environment as a helper tool for the ontology mapping.

10.3 Behavioral Mediation

We address the behavioral mediation problem in the context of Semantic Web Services. In this scenario, the problems may occur only when two partners are communicating, and there are mismatches between their communication patterns. This type of mediation can also be considered protocol mediation (as communication can also refer to the communication protocol), but in the semantic community these communication patterns are usually referred to as public processes [31, 33, 76] and the communication protocol used by the two partners is not important in this context.

10.3.1 Behavioral Mediation Scenario

We will refer further to behavior mediation as process mediation since in the case of Semantic Web Services the behavior is modeled as public processes. For addressing the problem of process mediation we have to define first what a process means. We adopt the standard definition of a process: collection of activities designed to produce a specific output for a particular customer, based on specific inputs [1], an activity being a function, or a task that occurs over time and has recognizable results.

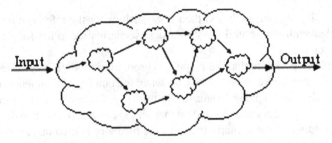

Figure 10.6. Process consisting of multiple processes

Depending on the level of granularity considered, each process can be seen as being composed of different, multiple processes. The smallest process possible consists of only one activity. Figure 10.6 illustrates a process obtained by combining multiple processes. The output of one process (or more processes) is considered the input of one or many other processes.

One can distinguish between two type of processes: *private processes*, which are carried out internally by an organization, and usually are not visible to any other entity, and *public processes*, which define the behavior of the organization in collaboration with other entities [75]. From the process mediation point of view we are interested only in the public processes; the private process not being visible to the exterior cannot be the object of process mediation in the Semantic Web Services' context, where mediation is intended to facilitate the services' discovery, invocation, and composition. For example, if a client of a bank wants to find his account balance using a Semantic Web Service, he only needs to know that by providing his account number, and maybe some security-related data, the service will return the balance. But he does not need to know, and probably he is not interested in knowing, what kind of computations are performed internally to produce this result.

10.3.2 Process Compatibility

In this context, we understand process compatibility to mean full matching of the communication patterns between the source and the target of the communication; that is, when one of them sends a message, the other one is able to receive it.

Since a business communication usually consists of more than one exchange message, finding equivalences in the message exchange patterns of the two (or more) parties is not at all a trivial task. Intuitively, the easiest way of doing this is to first determine the mismatches, and then search for a way to eliminate them. In [75], the three possible cases of communication mismatches which may appear during message exchange are identified:

1. **Precise match**: The two partners have exactly the same pattern in realizing the business process, which means that each of them sends the messages in exactly the order that the other one requests them. In this ideal case the communication can take place without using a process mediator. However, this does not mean that the services of a data ,ediator may not be required.

2. **Solvable message mismatch**: Here, the two partners use different exchange patterns, and several transformations have to be performed in order to overcome the mismatches (for example, when one partner sends more than one concept in a single message, but the other one expects them separately; in this case the mediator can "break" the initial message and send the concepts one by one).
3. **Unsolvable message mismatch**: One of the partners expects a message that the other one does not intend to send. Unless the mediator can provide this message, the communication reaches a dead end.

In order to communicate, two end points have to define compatible processes, or use an external mediation system as part of the communication process. The role of the mediator system will be to transform the client's messages and/or the Web Service's messages, in order to obtain a sequence of equivalent processes. This should be done only by operating on the messages sent by the two partners, as no modifications are allowed at the interface level (i.e., both the service and the requester have well-defined interfaces, and assume the other partner is conforming to these interfaces).

The process mediation work is concerned with determining patterns of solvable and unsolvable mismatches, and with providing support for overcoming the problems raised by the solvable mismatches. For this, a set of minimal solvable mismatches needs to be determined; this set should be further used in decomposing more complex mismatches, and addressing those simply by splitting a big and complex communication problem into smaller, easier-to-solve ones.

10.3.3 Mismatches: Solvable or Unsolvable?

In this section, we will analyze the two situations relevant for the process mediation: solvable and unsolvable mismatches. For illustrating the mismatches, this section also introduces a simple example of behavioral heterogeneity.

Behavioral Heterogeneity Example

The example introduced in this section refers to the simple scenario of booking a plane ticket between two given locations. The requester and the provider of the service have well-defined choreographies that can be modeled using the WSMO choreography definition, or any other process representation formalism. From the mediation perspective, the useful information is the message exchange patterns of the two participants in the conversation, which is graphically represented in Fig. 10.7.

In this example we assume there are no data heterogeneity problems, that is, the same underlying ontologies are used by the requester and the provider of the service. The only existing problem is that each of them has a different message exchange pattern, and the messages sent by one of them are not expected in exactly the same format or order by the other one. In this situation, even if all the information is available, and the communication can theoretically take place, the services of a process mediator are needed during the interaction.

Figure 10.7. An example of heterogeneous behaviors

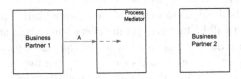

Figure 10.8. Stopping an unexpected message

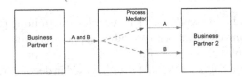

Figure 10.9. Splitting a message

Solvable Mismatches

In order to be able to solve process mediation mismatches, we have to first determine what these mismatches are, and in what conditions they may appear. We identify a set of basic mismatches, which can be addressed with the help of a process mediator. By combining these mismatches, we can obtain some other solvable mismatches. This basic mismatches are further described in this section:

- **Case A: stopping an unexpected message**. This is the simplest mismatch from the set we identified: one of the partners sends a message that the other one does not want to receive (Fig. 10.8).

  In the previously described example, the instance of `flight_availablity` concept is sent by the service, but is not expected by the client; in this case, the instance is simply stopped by the process mediator.

- **Case B: splitting a message**. In this case one of the partners sends in a single message multiple information that the other partner expects in different messages (Fig. 10.9). There may be two different situations: (1) the message consists of two or more instances that should be split in multiple messages or (2) the message consists of an instance that can only be represented in the targeted partner's ontology as multiple instances.

In the example previously presented the instance of the `route` concept needs to be split into an instance of `to` and an instance of `from`; these two instances are further sent separately to the service

- **Case C: combining multiple messages**. This is the opposite case of the one previously presented: two or more messages should be combined in a single message (Fig. 10.10).

  In the example presented the instance of `person_name` and the instance of `miles_more_account` should be combined by the process mediator in a single message.

- **Case D: inverting the order of messages**. This mismatch occurs when one of the partners sends the information in an order different from that in the other one wants to receive it (Fig. 10.11).

  In the previously presented example the message containing the instance of the `travel_dates` concept is sent after the `person_name` and `miles_more_account` instances are sent; however, the service expects to receive this instance first.

- **Case E: sending a dummy acknowledgement**. Sending a dummy acknowledgement is needed in case one of the partners is blocked expecting an acknowledgement for a message previously sent. In case the targeted partner received the message, but conforming to its choreography it is not going to send an acknowledgement for receiving this message, the process mediator should generate a dummy one (Fig. 10.12).

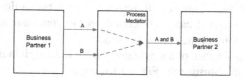

Figure 10.10. Combining multiple messages

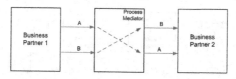

Figure 10.11. Inverting the order of messages

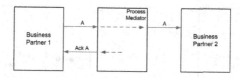

Figure 10.12. Sending a dummy acknowledgement

In the example presented at the beginning of this section the process mediator should generate a dummy acknowledgement for the message containing the instance of `miles_more_account`.

Unsolvable Mismatches

The types of mismatches that we consider unsolvable can be generated by one of the following situations (see Fig. 10.13):

- One of the partners expects information that the other one is not going to send during the conversation.
- Both partners are blocked waiting for messages that are going to be sent further in the communication.

Combinations of Mismatches

By combining the basic mismatches, one can obtain more complex mismatches. Any combination of solvable mismatches will lead to more complex, but still solvable mismatches. Figure 10.14 presents an example of such a combination, including cases A, B, C, and D.

In this example, the process mediator first has to split the first message sent by business partner 1 and to combine part of it with the second message sent. The other part of the first message has to be retained for further use. The second message sent by business partner 2 also has to be split in two, but in this case some of the information contained in it can be discarded, as the communication partner is not expecting it at any point of the communication.

However, the occurrence of a single unsolvable mismatch in the communication leads to an unsolvable mismatch (Fig. 10.15). In the previous example, simply inverting the order of sending C and receiving E for business partner 1 leads to the

Figure 10.13. Unsolvable mismatches

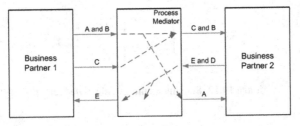

Figure 10.14. Mismatch consisting of a combination of solvable mismatches

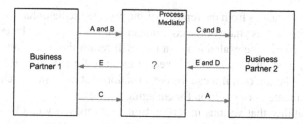

Figure 10.15. Mismatch containing an unsolvable mismatch

situation where both partners are blocked waiting for messages that are going to be sent further in the conversation (that is, business partner 2 will not send E until C has been received, while business partner 1 will not send C before receiving E).

As a consequence, a simple compatibility check before the actual invocation will have to determine if one unsolvable atomic mismatch is present in the interaction. If it is, then the communication is not possible. However, the fact that two behaviors are compatible does not guarantee a successful communication, as during the communication any of the partners can send a message that violates an internal rule for the other partner.

10.3.4 Process Mediator Prototype

A process mediator able to solve the types of mismatches previously described has already been developed. This section presents the algorithm implemented by this process mediator.

The process mediator is triggered when it receives a message and a conversation ID. The message contains instances of concepts, in terms of the sender's ontology. The conversation ID is needed as we assume that the same process mediator can be simultaneously used for multiple conversations and it uniquely identifies the instances of the choreographies involved in the communication.

After being invoked, the process mediator performs the following steps:

1. It loads the two choreographies from the repository – as the process mediator cannot influence the transformations done by the conversation partners it has to maintain copies of the choreographies, called `choreography instances`.
2. It adds the instances contained in the message to the corresponding choreography instance (the sender's choreography instance); this step is needed considering that the choreography instances contain the information prior to the transmission of the current message.
3. It mediates the incoming instances in terms of the targeted partner ontology, and checks if the targeted partner is expecting them, at any phase of the communication process. This is done by checking the `in` and `shared` lists; if the owner of a certain instance (the concept that was instantiated) is part of any of these two lists. The instances that are expected by the targeted partner are stored in an internal repository.

4. For all the instances from the repository, the process mediator has to check if they are expected at this phase of the communication, which is done by evaluating the transition rules. The evaluation of a rule will return the first condition that can not be fulfilled, that is, the next expected instance for that rule. This means that an instance is expected if it can trigger an action (not necessary to change a state, but to eliminate one condition for changing a state).

   The possibility that various instances from this repository can be combined in order to obtain a single instance expected by the targeted business partner is also considered.

5. Each time the process mediator determines that one instance is expected, it sends it, deletes it from the repository, updates the targeted partner's choreography instance, and restarts the evaluation process (step 4). When a transition rule can be executed, it is marked as such and is not reevaluated at further iterations.

   The process mediator only checks if a transition rule can be executed, and does not execute it, since it cannot update any of the two choreography instances without receiving input from one of the communication partners. By evaluating a rule, the process mediator determines that one of the business partners can execute it, without expecting any other inputs.

   This process stops when, after performing these checks for all the instances from the repository, no new message is generated.

6. For each instance forwarded to the targeted partner, the process mediator has to check if the sender is expecting an acknowledgement. If the sender expects an acknowledgement, but the targeted partner does not intend to send it, the process mediator generates a dummy acknowledgement and sends it. Simultaneously, it updates the sender's choreography instance.

7. The process mediator checks all the sender's rules and marks the ones that can be executed.

8. The process mediator checks the requester's rules to see if all of them are marked; when all are marked, the communication is over and process mediator deletes all the data regarding this conversation, from both its internal repository and the WSMX repository.

This algorithm is implemented by the process mediator in order to solve the communication heterogeneity problem.

10.3.5 How To Solve the Unsolvable

The process mediator previously described deals with overcoming a set of heterogeneity problems, called solvable mismatches in the previous subsections. But this kind of automatic mediation cannot solve any heterogeneity problem, as it does not consider the possibility of changing the message exchange pattern of the participants in the conversation (as both of them are supposed to have previously well defined interfaces).

   For changing the public processes of the business partners involved in a conversation, one requires the input of a domain expert. That is, a new component, a design-time process mediation, which provides the necessary interface for process mediation is needed. Such a component should be able to display in a certain process representation formalism the two public processes ,and should guide the domain expert in changing the order of messages (sent or received) for any of the processes involved in the interaction. There is no such tool currently available, but the semantic community is more and more interested in this approach. One such tool should result from the research activities carried out in one of the ongoing European projects, SUPER.[5]

10.4 Summary

This chapter has presented several aspects regarding one of the most challenging problems in SESA, the mediation. The chapter began with a brief overview of the mediation role in SESA, underlying why mediators are important from the very definition of Semantic Web Services until the actual invocation. The diversity in mediation usage leads to the definition of several mediation layers, presented at the beginning of the chapter: semantic mediators, semantic mediation patterns, and mediation services.

Further on, the chapter focused on two mediation services, for providing data and process mediation. For both of these services, the description began with the conceptual consideration, the ideas and approaches taken in solving different heterogeneity problems, and continued with a presentation of the actual implementation.

It is important to note that the two approaches and the solutions for data and behavior mediation described in this chapter are not unique. A multitude of other techniques could be employed to achieve the same results, each of them with its advantages and disadvantages in handling the peculiarities of a particular heterogeneity problem. Along this line of thought, it is easy to realize the advantages offered by the SESA infrastructure, which allows the seamless integration and usage of specialized components that can perform more efficiently in certain contexts.

---

[5] http://www.ip-super.org/

Storage and Internal Communication

This chapter describes the functionality and working of storage and internal component communication of Semantically Enabled Service-oriented Architectures (SESA). The storage component is responsible for providing a means to persistently store the Semantic Web Services elements (e.g., Web service descriptions, mediators, goals, and ontologies) as well as intermediate workflow and event data and execution semantics. Moreover, it further investigates the use of the triple space computing paradigm [73] for communication and coordination of the individual components of SESA, based on the principle of publishing and reading the semantic data. It further details how internal communication using triple space computing can help in decoupling the individual components and their effective communication [129] within the SESA framework.

The storage and internal communication service in SESA is required to provide support in two major aspects. Firstly, for storing information in distributed and scalable storage repositories and, secondly, using the persistent publication to carry out the communication based on the publication and reading of data in order to make it compatible with the principle of the Web.

The storage space is based on the Web and semantics, i.e., it can be accessed over the Web and has Resource Description Framework (RDF) triples as the fundamental storage element. It supports storing information both at run time and at design time. It allows storage of formal descriptions of ontologies, Semantic Web Service descriptions, mediation mappings, user goals along with any contextual information about their use, and any intermediary data during interplatform services communication. The storage space can be composed on a single repository or widely distributed on multiple Web-accessible storage repositories and is visible as single virtual storage.

The storage service in SESA is not only about semantic data storage but also about scalable communication and coordination of Semantic Web Services based on emerging triple space computing [193]. It has been achieved by extending tuple space computing to support RDF and carding out communication and coordination based on persistent publication and reading to enable decoupling based on time, reference, and location [129]. It supports the communication between components within SESA; hence, it enables the decoupling of the platform services of

Kappa Service-Oriented Architecture (SOA). It also supports communication between different SEE systems to form a SEE cluster; hence it enables the decoupling of different Semantic Web Services based on SESA.

A resource manager is used in SESA to provide a homogenous interface to the underline storage services. The resource manager is responsible for the management of the repositories that store definitions of any semantic descriptions of services, i.e., Web service descriptions, goals, ontologies, mediators, and any other nonsemantic data in SESA. Depending on the scope of data stored in the underlying registries, SESA distinguishes registries as being local or global. Data stored in a local registry is relevant for the operation of SESA in a particular context. In some cases individual functional components may also require local storage. On the other hand, a global registry can be shared across several domains (e.g., registries of semantic descriptions of services). While both stored data and accessibility to this data might differ considerably between registries, the resource manager remains the only entry point for them, which means it is not possible to access any of the registries directly, but only through the resource manager (in this way the burden of accessing any of the repositories is delegated to the resource manager). A component that needs to retrieve, modify, or add any data in one of the repositories has to invoke the resource manager. The operations that need to be performed to retrieve the data and the repository that stores the data remain transparent.

The rest of the chapter has been structured as follows. It gives an introduction to the triple space computing concept and provides the internal design details of triple space computing kernel architecture. It explains the role of triple space computing in SESA in different aspects. It further provide details of some evaluation strategies that are to be analyzed to determine the benefits obtained from using triple space computing in SESA, followed by a summary.

11.1 Introduction to Triple Space Computing

Aiming at enhancing the facilities for automated information processing on the Internet, Tim Berners-Lee (the inventor of the World Wide Web and Director of the W3C) introduced the the vision of the Semantic Web. Since existing Web technologies around URI, HTTP, and HTML do not support automated processing of Web content, the aim is to develop technologies that allow the description of Web content in a structured manner; furthermore, semantically defined metadata shall help to overcome the problem of heterogeneity within the Internet as an open and distributed system. Ontologies have been identified as the basic building block for the Semantic Web, as they provide machine-processable, semantic terminology definitions.

In conjunction with the idea of the Semantic Web, Web Services are proposed as the technology for automated information processing, thus combining the benefits of the Web with the strength of component-oriented computation. In fact, Web Services promise to allow automated interaction and seamless integration of several entities of the Web; thus, they are considered as the technology for next-generation information systems with special regard to enterprise application integration, buisiness-to-business (B2B) technologies, and e-commerce. As initial Web service technologies around Simple Object Access Protocol (SOAP), Web Services Description Language (WSDL), and UDDI failed to realize the promise of seamless interoperability, the concept of Semantic Web Services has been conceived. Through the addition of semantics to Web service descriptions, intelligent inference-based mechanisms shall allow automated discovery, composition, and execution of Web Services.

Space-based computing has its roots in parallel processing. Linda was developed by David Gelernter in the mid-1980s at Yale University. Initially presented as a partial language design, it was then recognized as a novel communication model on its own and is now referred to as a coordination language for parallel and distributed programming. Coordination provides the infrastructure for establishing communication and synchronization between activities and for spawning new activities. There are many instantiations or implementations of the Linda model, embedding Linda in a concrete host language. Examples include C-Linda, Fortran-Linda and Shared-Prolog. Linda allows one to define executions of activities or processes orthogonal to the computation language, i.e., Linda does not care about how processes do the computation, but only how these processes are created. The Linda model is a memory model. The Linda memory is called tuple space and consists of logical tuples. There are two kinds of tuples. Data tuples are passive and contain static data; process tuples, or "live tuples," are active and represent processes under execution. Processes exchange data by writing and reading data tuples to and from the tuple space.

In 2003 and 2004 there were discussions and collaborations involving Tim Berners-Lee, Dieter Fensel, Eva Kuehn, and Frank Leymann on the relationships between the Semantic Web, Web Services, and space-based computing. On the basis of those discussions and collaborations, Dieter Fensel published a technical report about *Triple Based Computing* presenting the idea of a semantically enabled, space-based communication and coordination middleware as an infrastructure for the Semantic Web and Semantic Web Services. These ideas have been adopted for two research projects, i.e., Triple Space Computing (TSC) funded by the Forschung, Innovation, Technologie – Informationstechnologie (FIT-IT), an Austrian Government research program in the line of "semantic systems," and Triple Space Communication (Trip-Com), which is a European Commission funded project under the Sixth Framework Programme, priority 2 Information Society Technologies (IST) project number IST-4-027324-STP.

Triple space computing inherits the publication-based communication model from the space-based computing paradigm and extends it with semantics [129]. Instead of sending messages back and forth among participants as in current message-based technologies, triple space computing enabled applications will communicate by writing and reading RDF triples in the shared space.

The triple space will offer an infrastructure that scales conceptually on an Internet level. Like Web servers publish Web pages for humans to read, triple space servers would provide triple spaces to publish machine-interpretable data. Providers and consumers could publish and consume triples over a globally accessible infrastructure, i.e., the Internet. Various triple space servers could be located at different paces all over the globe and hence every partner in a communication process can target its preferred space, as it is the case for Web and FTP servers. This highlights many of advantages for providers and consumers [73, 129]. The providers of data can publish it at any point in time (time autonomy), independent of its internal storage (location autonomy), and independent of the knowledge about potential readers (reference autonomy), and independent of its internal data schema (schema autonomy):

- Time autonomy. There is a only minimal time dependency between the data provider and reader, in the sense that a triple must be written first before it can be retrieved.
- Location autonomy. The triple space as a storage location is independent of the storage space of the providers or readers of data. Complete independence is achieved by ensuring that triples are passed to and from the triple space by value and in the format required by the triple space.
- Reference autonomy. The provider and the reader of data might know about each other, but *ex ante* knowledge for purposes of communication through the triple space is not required. In the simplest case, the reading and writing of data is anonymous.
- Data schema autonomy. Triple space computing provides its own schema (based on triples according to RDF) and the data written and retrieved from a triple space will follow that data model. This makes the provider and the reader independent of their internal data schemas.

In addition it is worthwhile to state further positive side effects of triple space computing [129]:

- A triple space provides a trustworthy third-party infrastructure for data communication. Its involvement can enable secure data exchange and business process negotiation and communication.
- The triple space ensures persistent data storage. It allows evolution of communication means for humans and machines in time and that the data eventually can be read by all partners involved in the data exchange.

In other words, triple spaces introduce an infrastructure that enables machines to use an equally powerful communication medium as the Web provides for humans. Triple spaces will supplement Web Services, but will not replace current technological approaches. Just as Web technology has advanced message-oriented communication means (e.g., phone or e-mail) for humans, triple space computing provides a complementary approach for machine-to-machine interaction. It is also clear that this is not the end, but just the beginning of a long and promising endeavor for a revolutionary technology. No application can quickly check the entire Semantic Web whether to determine if there is a relevant triple. And vice versa, no application may want to simply publish a triple and then wait forever until another application picks it up. Clever middleware is required that provides a virtual global triple space infrastructure without requesting each application either download or search through the entire Semantic Web. Moreover, the triple space needs to provide security and trust without neglecting scalability. However, none of these requirements are really new. They apply for any application that works at a global scale.

11.2 Triple Space Kernel

Like with the Web, the TSC project proposal aimed at building a triple space computing infrastructure based on the abstract model called representational state transfer (REST) [183]. The fundamental principle of REST is that resources are identified by URIs and accessed via a stateless protocol like HTTP in order to transfer representations, such as HTML or XML documents, of resources over the network. HTTP provides a minimal set of operations enough to model any applications domain.

Since every representation transfer must be initiated by the client, and every response must be generated as soon as possible (the statelessness requirement), there is no way for a server to transmit any information to a client asynchronously in REST. Furthermore, there is no direct way to model a peer-to-peer relationship between clients. Finally, HTTP caching based on expiration times for cached requests is not applicable in triple space computing; where a server has no preknowledge of the lifetimes of named graphs. The limitations of REST in the context of triple space computing motivated our approach of a hybrid architecture called superpeer architecture, which combines traditional client–server and peer-to-peer architectures. In this architecture there are three kinds of nodes: servers, heavy clients, and light clients. In the simplest configuration, a particular triple space is realized by a single server, which is accessed by multiple light clients, for example, via HTTP, in order to write and read named graphs and to receive notifications about graphs of interest. As the number of light clients increases, the server may become a bottleneck. To overcome this, additional servers can be deployed to provide additional access points to a triple space for light clients. As a result, a single triple space is effectively spanned by multiple servers, which use an interserver protocol to consistently distribute and collect named graphs to and from other involved servers. Servers can also be deployed to act as caching proxies in order to improve client-perceived access times. The third kind of nodes is heavy clients, which are not always connected to the system. Like servers they are capable of storing and replicating triple spaces and enable users and applications to work off-line with their own replicas. While heavy clients can join existing triple spaces spanned by servers, they are not forced to do so.

The core functionality of triple space computing servers and heavy clients is realized by a component called the triple space kernel. Heavy clients run in the same address space as the triple space kernel, and the triple space kernel is accessed by its native interface. Light clients use proxies to access the triple space kernel of a server node transparently over the network. As a variation a light client can access a triple space kernel via a standardized protocol like HTTP, as already mentioned. In this case a server side component, e.g., a servlet, translates the protocol to the native triple space kernel interface. Figure 11.1 shows the architecture of the triple space kernel. The main components of the triple space kernel are briefly described in the following subsections.

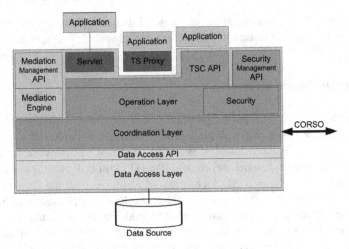

Figure 11.1. Triple space kernel architecture

11.2.1 Operations Layer

The operations layer is an important part of triple space kernel that allows clients to interact and manipulate the data in the space. It abstracts from the underlying implementation details of supported functionalities and provides a simplified view to its users. All interactions between a triple space and its participants take place through this layer. The interfaces provided by this layer to access different supported operations are described in the following subsections.

Triple Space Interface

The triple space interface is defined to provide operations specific to the usage of already existing spaces. These operations are defined and briefly described below.

The **write** operation allows the writing of an RDF graph to a triple space identified by a URI. It supports transaction. The signature of this operation is given below:

```
write (URI spaceURI, Transaction tx, Graph g): URI
namedGraphURI
```

The **query** operation allows querying over a triple space identified by a URI. It returns an RDF graph. This operation also supports transaction. The signature of this operation is as follows:

```
query (URI spaceURI, Transaction tx, Template t): Graph g
```

It is important to note that the semantics of graph and of named graph within the scope of triple space computing are different. A graph can be generated arbitrarily by taking subgraphs from different graphs, while a named graph is a complete graph having a unique name. That is, a named graph can be defined as a tuple:

```
namedGraph: (URI, Graph)
```

The **waitToQuery** operation allows querying over a triple space identified by a URI. It is similar to the query operation but waits until a given time to return an RDF graph. This is a blocking operation and supports transaction. This operation has the following signature:

```
waitToQuery (URI spaceURI, Transaction tx, Template t,
TimeOut timeOut): Graph g
```

The **read** operation allows the reading of a named graph from a triple space identified by a URI. It returns an RDF graph from the space. This operation supports transaction. Two different types of read operations, blocking and nonblocking, are supported in triple space computing. The following is the signature of the nonblocking read operation:

```
read (URI spaceURI, Transaction tx, URI namedGraphURI):
NamedGraph namedGraph
```

The signature of the blocking read operation is as follows:

```
read (URI spaceURI, Transaction tx, Template t):
NamedGraph namedGraph
```

The **waitToRead** operation allows the reading of a named graph from a triple space identified by a URI. The operation waits until some triples are available for reading. It returns a named graph. This operation also supports transaction. The following is the signature of the waitToRead operation:

```
waitToRead (URI spaceURI, Transaction tx, Template t,
Timeout timeOut): NamedGraph namedGraph
```

The **take** operation is similar to the read operation but it deletes the graph that was read. The signature of this operation is as shown below:

```
take (URI spaceURI, Transaction tx, Template t):
NamedGraph namedGraph
```

The **waitToTake** operation is similar to the waitToRead operation but with the take support. The following is the signature of the waitToTake operation:

```
waitToRead (URI spaceURI, Transaction tx, Template t,
Timeout timeOut): NamedGraph namedGraph
```

The **update** operation allows the updating of information specified on the template to the space identified by the URI. This operation supports transaction. The semantics of this operation is take and write in that order. The following is the signature of this operation:

```
update(URI spaceURI, Transaction tx, Template t):
NamedGraph namedGraph
```

The **subscribe** operation allows users to subscribe for a named graph to the triple space identified by the URI. The following is the signature of this operation:

```
subscribe(URI spaceURI, Templace t, Callback callbackReceiver):
URI subscriptionURI
```

The parameter callbackReceiver could either be a URI of the subscriber, or a remote method name or any other means of calling the subscriber. The exact nature of the callbackReceiver, however, depends on the concrete implementation of the triple space computing API.

The **unsubscribe** operation removes a previously subscribed subscription specified by the URI from the space identified by the URI. The signature of this operation is as follows:

```
unsubscribe(URI spaceURI, URI subscriptionURI): void
```

The **notify** operation delivers notification to the callback for a previously subscribed subscription identified by the URI. The signature of this operation is as follows:

```
notify(URI spaceURI, URI subscriptionURI, URI namedGraphURI):
void
```

The namedGraphURI specifies the URI of a named graph which causes this notification.

The **advertise** operation is defined for enabling the advertisement of information embedded in a template to the triple space. It could be used for space optimization, for example. The following is the signature of this operation:

```
advertise(URI spaceURI, Template t): URI advertisementURI
```

The **unadvertise** operation removes a previously advertised advertisement from the space. The signature of this operation is as follows:

```
unadvertise(URI advertisementURI): void
```

The **count** operation returns the number of RDF graphs, triples, or named graphs specified in a template available in the triple space identified by a URI. The following is the signature of this operation:

```
count(URI spaceURI, Transaction tx, Template t): long
```

In all the operations listed above the transaction parameter tx is optional. If it is not specified, the default transaction settings will be applied. The default transaction includes transaction creation followed by transaction operation followed by commit transaction. It can be seen as follows:

```
createTX(): Transaction tx
operation(Transaction tx): void
commit(Transaction tx): boolean
```

Where createTX() creates the transaction, operation(Transaction tx) will apply operations on the scope of transaction tx and commit(Transaction tx) will apply commit operation to transaction tx.

Triple Space Management Interface

The triple space management interface is defined as providing operations specific to the management of the triple space. These operations are defined and briefly described below:

1. **Space management operations**. The following space management operations are defined in triple space computing.

   The **createSpace** operation creates a triple space for a given URI with default security settings. The level of security can be changed, altered, or removed. The security in triple space computing is defined in [154]:

   ```
   createSpace(URI spaceURI):  void
   ```

   The **leaveSpace** operation enables the triple space kernel to leave the space identified by a URI. That is, the triple space kernel stops replicating RDF graphs from the space identified by a URI. The following is the signature of this operation:

   ```
   leaveSpace(URI spaceURI):  void
   ```

2. **Transaction management operations**. The following transaction management operations are defined in triple space computing.

   The **createTransaction** operation is provided to support creation of transactions in triple space computing. It creates a transaction and returns a transaction ID of this particular transaction. The following is the signature of this operation:

   ```
   createTransaction():  Transaction tx
   ```

   The **commitTransaction** operation enables execution of the transaction identified by a transaction ID. The result of this operation is boolean. That is, the transaction can either be executed successfully or it cannot be executed at all. The signature of this operation is given below:

   ```
   commitTransaction(Transaction tx):  boolean
   ```

   The **abortTransaction** operation allows the already executed transaction to be undone, which is identified by a transaction ID. The following is the signature of this operation:

   ```
   abortTransaction(Transaction tx):  void
   ```

3. **Security management operation**. The following security management operations are seen to be required for supporting basic security in triple space computing.

   The **secure** operation enforces the security policy as specified in the template. This operation can be executed at triple space level or at the named graph level. Two possible signatures of this operation follow:

   ```
   secure(URI spaceURI, Template t):  URI securityURI
   secure(URI namedGraphURI, Template t):  URI securityURI
   ```

   The **alterSecurity** operation allows the security level to be updated to the previously set security. The signature of this operation is as follows:

   ```
   alterSecurity(URI securityURI, Template t):  URI securityURI
   ```

The **validate** operation checks if the security policy has been violated while doing other operations on the triple space.

```
validate(URI securityURI, Template t): boolean
```

11.2.2 Mediation Engine

Owing to diversity in the nature of different communicating participants over triple space, the possibility of heterogeneity in the data used for communication of different participants may arise and make mediation an important issue to be resolved in triple space computing. The mediation engine [194] as part of the triple space kernel [183] is concerned with handling this heterogeneity by resolving possibly occurring mismatches among different triples. Assume two triple space computing participants using different data models for communication. Then an RDF instance in an RDF schema of one triple space computing participant is needed to be represented in the RDF schema of the other triple space computing participant without altering or losing the semantics. For this reason, a mapping language is needed that specifies how to transform the RDF triples according to different RDF schemas of different communicating participants. The mediation rules are to be specified at design time and will be processed by a mediation engine at run time.

The mediation management interface binds the mediation engine with the user interface in order to allow participants to interact with the mediation manager to turn on or off the usage of the mediation engine before template matching and to add, replace, or remove the mapping rules. The mediation manager inside the mediation engine receives and serializes the mapping rules in Abstract Mapping Language (AML) [189] as set of RDF triples on the triple space. The system interface allows the operations layer to communicate with the mediation engine in order to find any corresponding RDF schema resources using the mediation mapping rules before search for RDF triples starts. The template parser receives the template provided by a template handler in the operations layer and parses out all RDF schema resources values in there. The rule collector pulls out the appropriate set of RDF triples (mapping rules in AML serialized as set of RDF triples) and forwards it to the rule executor. The rule executor is the core component of the mediation engine and processes the mapping rules for all the RDF schema resources from the template provided by the operations layer in order to find any corresponding RDF schema resources that are to be mapped. The template generator receives a set of corresponding RDF schema resources from the mediation mapper and generates multiple templates accordingly and finally forwards them to the query engine to make a search in the triple space.

The working of the triple space computing mediation engine starts when users (i.e., triple space computing participants) add mediation mapping rules via the mediation management interface. The mediation manager takes care of serialization of the mediation rules in the triple space storage as RDF triples. The mediation engine manager also helps add, replace, and delete the mapping rules. When a triple space computing participant wants to search for something from the triple space, the operations layer generates a template which contains the information about required

RDF triples and forwards it to the system interface of the mediation engine. The template parser in the mediation engine receives the template and parses out all the RDF schema resources mentioned in the template and forwards them to the rule execution module. At the same time, the rule collector checks the triple space for any mediation mapping rules serialized as RDF triples and generates mapping expressions and forwards them to the rule execution. The rule execution being the core of the triple space computing mediation engine executes the mapping expressions against the RDF schema resources (provided by the template parser) and finds any corresponding sets of RDF schema resources. All the sets of RDF schema resources discovered from mediation mapping rules are forwarded to the template generator, which encloses the RDF schema resources in templates and sends it back to the operations layer. After all the abovementioned processes, the operations layer can forward the required triples to the coordination layer and down to the data access layer to search the required triples according to the RDF schema resources mentioned by the triple space computing participant along with the corresponding one found by mediation process and carry out data transformation from the source schema to the target schema as mentioned in the mapping expression.

Design Time

The identification of heterogeneities between different RDF schemas and instances and the process of the creation of mappings cannot be fully automated. The ontology and domain experts have to provide inputs to identify and create mappings at various stages. The creation of mapping rules requires human intervention and involves manual procedures. It makes this process a hectic and time-consuming job. Considering these issues, there is need for graphical tools that allow users to create the mappings in an easy way by providing assistance to the users and to reduce their efforts to simple choices and validations. Adaptation of this approach was inspired by related work of Web Services Execution Environment (WSMX) data mediation [149] in the WSMX Working Group [35].

The graphical interface is to be built in Java, where it should show the two particular RDF schemas of the source and target users who are to communicate with each other. The default ontology language to be supported will be AML. The graphical interface will be linked with the mediation management interface. The designer component will provide a way to identify and create the mapping rules easily and quickly, without actually knowing the internal details and syntax of AML. The users or domain experts can use the mapping tool to operate on the RDF schemas to create mapping rules. The already existing mapping rules stored in the triple space can be loaded into the graphical interface for the users to do any updates or to reuse the mapping rules.

Run Time

The run-time module of the data mediation will be the mediation engine in the triple space kernel. Based on the description of the insight details of the architecture of the mediation engine, the following is the internal API that will be developed to deal with mediation based on the mapping rules available, during the communication of users over triple space. The API will enable the mediation engine to search for the appropriate mapping rules based on the schema of the communicating participants, access any particular mapping rule, ground the mapping rule into RDF, and execute the mapping rules. The operations of the run-time API are listed below:

```
searchRule (Template ts , Transaction tx ):  Graph
```

searches the mediation mapping rules according to the template given.

```
getRule (URI ts , Transaction tx , URI g):  Graph
```

gets the particular mediation mapping rule graph.

```
groundRule (AMLrule rule ):  Graph
```

takes the mediation mapping in AML and converts it into an RDF named graph.

```
executeRule (URI ts , Transaction tx , URI g):  Templates
```

executes a particular mapping rule at the given URI.

The searchRule operation returns the set of graphs that matches with the template provided to it. Such a kind of operation is required when the particular mapping rule is not known. The requirements of the mapping rule regarding target ontology, source ontology, and a particular concept (resource) of a particular ontology (schema) can be specified in the template to find some relevant mapping rule. However, if a particular mapping rule is already known by the mediation engine, it can be accessed by its corresponding URI.

The mapping rules are specified in AML; however, the rules in mapping language cannot be stored in triple space as it is. The mapping rules in AML are grounded as a set of RDF triples with a URI to access it (i.e., named graph). New mapping rules specified in AML that have been added by users using the management API are grounded to RDF triples using the groundRule operation.

When a particular mapping rule is known and is required to be executed, the executeRule operation is used internally by the mediation engine to execute the mapping rule and to actually carry out the transformation of a particular instance from the source schema to the target schema. The mapping in RDF is basically resource to resource mapping. So, for a particular resource a search is made to find if there is some mapping rule that may exist to provide mapping to the corresponding other resource. If the resource is simple (i.e., based on simple data types like integer, float, character, string) then the mapping is also simple and straightforward. However, if the resource is based on some complex type, then mapping is also complex and it has to be specified in the mapping rule how it should be transformed from the source schema to the target schema.

11.2.3 Coordination Layer

The coordination layer has three responsibilities: (1) local triple space operations, such as reading and writing named graphs are executed by accessing the local data access layer and by consistently propagating changes to other triple space kernels involved; (2) changes of a space originating from other triple space kernels are recognized and applied to the local data access layer; and (3) remote triple space kernels involved that span a certain space are discovered automatically in the network.

Consistent concurrent access to named graphs is provided via transactions. In principle both optimistic and pessimistic transactions are applicable for triple space computing; however, they are not exchangeable owing to differences in their semantics. We decided to support optimistic transactions, because they provide a higher degree of concurrency, if read operations are more frequent than write operations, which results in a higher throughput, because they are free of deadlocks without the introduction of additional, semantically sophisticated timeout parameters and, finally, because they enable a pragmatic integration of a data access layer, which itself does not support a transaction interface.

The prototype implementation of the coordination layer is based on the Coordinated Shared Objects Spaces (CORSO) [130] middleware. CORSO is a peer-to-peer implementation of a virtual shared data space, which allows reading and writing structured, shared data objects. It has a built-in distributed transaction manager and distributes spaces via an asynchronous, primary-based replication protocol. In the triple space computing prototype, triple spaces and named graphs are mapped to distributed CORSO data structures. Triple space computing operations like reading and writing named graphs are translated to algorithms on these CORSO data structures. CORSO further provides a notification mechanism to get informed about changes in the shared space. The coordination layer uses CORSO notifications to react to inserted or removed named graphs and to asynchronously update the underlying data access layer. The discovery of triple space kernels involved in spanning a triple space is based on the Domain Name System (DNS) for wide area networks and on a new protocol based on UDP multicast and CORSO for local area networks.

11.2.4 Data Access Layer

Any triple space implementation requires a storage and retrieval framework to (1) ensure the desired persistency, (2) to support semantic template matching based on Semantic Web query languages, and (3) to provide at least a limited amount of reasoning. In order to bind arbitrary data stores and query engines to triple space kernels we define a sata access layer which defines operations for storing, retrieving, and deleting RDF graphs.

The prototype implementation of the data access layer is based on Yet Another RDF Store (YARS) [97], a lightweight persistence framework developed in Java at DERI Galway which uses optimized indexes for better query performance. Besides the noteworthy performance, the fact that the consortium has access to the source code and the implementers through STI Innsbruck has resulted in YARS in particular being chosen as it is constructed to store quads or contextualized triples instead of plain RDF triples. This allows for direct usage of the chosen data model based on named graphs [42].

One of the main tasks of the data access layer is to translate templates into N3QL queries for YARS. To keep the data access API (DAPI) as simple as possible it only defines one operation to retrieve data: retrieve(URI ts, Transaction tx, Template t):Graph. The triple space computing API, however, allows a space user to retrieve data either based on templates or by use of the graph name. As the DAPI does not directly support an interface for URI-based retrieval it is also necessary to adapt the operations layer in order to transform those requests into templates. First the URI has to be packed into a graph pattern template according to part of the operations layer processing. The request is then forwarded in the form of the template to the data access layer, where the template is transformed into a N3QL query that can be sent to the YARS servlet.

11.2.5 Triple Space Kernel Component Interaction

This section explains how each operation is executed and how components of the triple space kernel are involved in the execution of a certain operation. Components in triple space computing interact with each other either locally or remotely. To enable such interaction between components, two different types of interfaces are defined. They are native or local interface and remote interface. Before delving into the details of component interaction, the interaction interfaces are described below.

The native interface is provided by the triple space kernel. It reflects the interfaces of all the available components providing a mechanism for them to interact with each other. It is the main interface for components to interact with each other locally. That is, all the components should implement this interface.

The remote interaction between components in triple space computing can take place through any of the following proven technologies: HTTP, RMI, SOAP, and CORSO. Therefore, the triple space computing remote interface should provide interfaces that are compatible with the ones provided by the aforementioned technologies. In triple space computing, HTTP and RMI are taken into consideration at the first stage while keeping the possibility of extending it with other technologies. The remote interface duplicates and or translates operations provided by the native or local interface with the mechanisms used.

Figure 11.2 describes the involvement of components and their interaction while executing a read operation. The black arrows indicate the direction of the component interaction and the gray arrows indicate the invocation of some operation will eventually return some result. The numbers at the side of the arrows correspond to the number in the text below.

- The participant presents a read request to the operations layer by invoking the following operation through the local interface:

```
read(spaceURI, template)
```

- The operations layer invokes security internally, if needed, to check access control. If the operation is approved, the information is passed to the coordination layer.

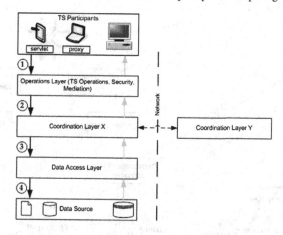

Figure 11.2. Interaction of components for a read operation

- The coordination layer uses a mediator, if needed, to resolve heterogeneity and invokes the data access layer.
- The data access layer accumulates requested data from different data sources. Through the interfaces provided by this layer, multiple data sources can be accessed.

11.3 Role of Triple Space Computing in SESA

The currently used communication paradigm in Semantic Web Services (is synchronous, i.e., users communicate with Semantic Web Services and Semantic Web Services communicate with real-world Web Services by sending synchronous messages. The problem with synchronous communication is that it requires a quick response as it makes the sender wait until the response is received, which is not possible in case of the execution process in Semantic Web Services as it involves heavy processing of semantic descriptions in terms of discovery, selection, composition, mediation, and execution. This problem has been overcome by introducing triple space computing as a semantics-based asynchronous communication paradigm for communication and coordination of Semantic Web Services. WSMX is our reference implementation for Semantic Web Services in which the triple space computing middleware is being integrated. Using triple space computing in WSMX enables support for greater modularization, flexibility, and decoupling in communication and coordination and for wide distribution and easy access. Multiple triple space kernels coordinate with each other to form a virtual space that acts as underying middleware which is used for communication by reading and writing data.

The integration of WSMX and triple space computing is being done in different ways [193]: (1) enabling management of components in WSMX using triple space computing, (2) allowing external communication grounding in WSMX, (3) providing resource management, and (4) enabling communication and coordination between

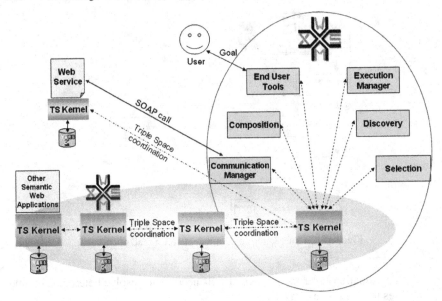

Figure 11.3. Triple space computing (TSC) as underlying communication middleware for Service-Oriented Architecture

different interconnected WSMX systems. Each of the integration aspects is described in the subsections below. In summary, triple space computing acts as middleware for WSMX, Web Services, different other Semantic Web applications, and users to communicate with each other, as shown in Fig. 11.3.

11.3.1 Intra-SESA Communication

WSMX has a management component that manages the overall execution of the system by coordinating different components on the basis of dynamic execution semantics. In this way a clear separation between business and management logic in WSMX has been made. The individual components have clearly defined interfaces and have component implementation well separated from communication issues. Each component in WSMX has a wrapper to handle the communication issues. The WSMX manager and wrappers of the individual components need to be interfaced with the triple space in order to enable the WSMX manager to manage the components over the triple space. The communication between the manager and wrappers of the components will be carried out by publishing and subscribing the data as a set of RDF graphs over the triple space. The wrappers of components that handle communication will be interfaced with triple space middleware. The WSMX manager has been designed in such a way that it can distinguish between the data flows related to the business logic (execution of components based on the requirements of a concrete operational semantics) and the data flows related to the management logic (monitoring the components, load balancing, instantiation of threads, etc.). There are two ways for WSMX components to access a triple space core, i.e., heavy clients embed the triple space core as a Java package and the application and a triple space core run in the same Java virtual machine. In this case CORSO [130] and YARS [97] run times need to be deployed together with the heavy client application. The second way is to deploy a standalone triple space kernel as a server, which may be accessed by multiple light clients via remoting. Usage of light clients in the case of communication and coordination within the WSMX system is recommended as it will keep the complexity level of the wrappers of the components and the access of the light client embedded in wrappers will be local to the triple space kernel.

There are two ways for the WSMX components to access a triple space core, i.e., heavy clients embed the triple space core as a Java package and the application and the triple space core run in the same Java virtual machine. The second way is to deploy a standalone triple space kernel as a server, which may be accessed by multiple light clients via remoting. Both scenarios can work. However, in order to ensure maximum decoupling of WSMX and triple space computing middleware, we have used the light clients. The light clients of triple space (also called as triple space proxy) have been embedded in the wrappers of each WSMX component. This will also keep the complexity level of wrappers of components to a certain limit. It will also give the flexibility that triple space light clients embedded in wrappers can either be local or remote to the triple space kernel.

The WSMX can also have the triple space kernel local to it, which will be the simplist scenario. In this case, sophisticated mechanisms for providing remote access (through RMI or HTTP) as well as distributed security and trust are not necessary. As shown Fig. 11.4, the triple space proxies (basically clients) will be embedded

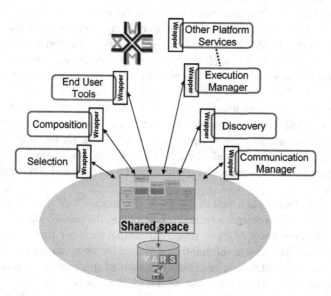

Figure 11.4. Dynamic component management in Web Services Execution Environment (WSMX) using TSC

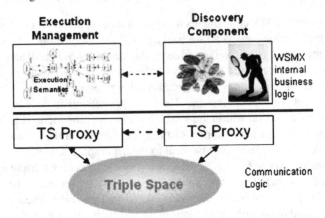

Figure 11.5. Interfacing the WSMX manager with the triple space kernel

in the wrappers of the components . The transport module of the wrapper of each component will access the triple space through simple APIs. These APIs will implement the operations provided by the triple space API [183]. WSMX components will benefit from all major aspects of the triple space kernel, i.e., publish–subscribe mechanism, RDF-based semantic template matching, data and resource handling, as well as persistent storage. Bussler [34] envisions that the WSMX manager will coordinate all the reading and writing requests received, will dispatch the request to the appropriate functional module (data module or query module), will monitor the appropriate execution of the rest of the elements of the system, and will periodically check the coherence of the information stored in the space.

Figure 11.5 shows a closer look at the interfacing of the WSMX manager with other components of WSMX (i.e., in this case, discovery component). The architecture of WSMX [95] defines a clear separation of communication issues of components and the WSMX internal business logic (it can also be called execution semantics [99]). The figure is provide to make the fact clear that adapting triple space computing for communication in WSMX will not change any of its execution semantics or WSMX internal component logic, any of the interfaces of components, nor any implementation of components. It does not define for the WSMX manager which component to invoke, and when. It rather defines how to invoke (or communicate, in general) with a particular component, by reading and writing data in the triple space.

Anytime a triple is published in the space, this module will check if related subscriptions are stored. If there are related subscriptions, the publish–subscribe module will notify the consumers of those subscriptions that there are triples available. On the basis of the management information collected by the management module, the publish–subscribe module can prioritize the order of notifications and deliver first to those components which have less workload. The query module will verify the correctness (syntax level) of the query received on the basis of a standard query language. The operation layer in the triple space kernel will execute all the operations that are related to the manipulation of data in the space (basically writing, modifying, and deleting the triples). It manages the version of the message communicated over the triple space and provides a URI to it, which can be referred to when required, rather that sending the message again. If a message or semantic description of a Web service is being communicated frequently between two or more participants, instead of sending it again and again, the URI of the message could be used to save time. Moreover, using triple space computing for component management, also brings other advantages, like complexity reduction, as the underlying triple space computing middleware incorporates features like publish–subscribe mechanisms which the WSMX manager can reuse for its intermediate even data management.

11.3.2 Distributed and Scalable Storage in SESA

WSMX contains different repositories to store ontologies, goals, mediators, and Web Services descriptions as WSML-based files. The internal repositories of WSMX are needed to be made optional and enable the storage of the WSML-based data as a set of RDF named graphs in triple space storage. This is mainly concerned with transforming the existing representation of data in the form of WSML into an RDF representation. The repository interfaces need to be interfaced with triple space middleware.

The resource manager in WSMX currently manages the persistent storage of data in the repositories. The resource manager provides a heterogeneous interface for WSMX. The component implementing this interface is responsible for storing every data item WSMX uses. The WSMO API provides a set of Java interfaces that can be used to represent the domain model defined by WSMO. WSMO4J [2] provides both the API itself and a reference implementation, but it is not a prerequisite that implementations of the resource manager use WSMO4J. Currently WSMX defines interfaces for six repositories. Four of these repositories correspond to the top-level concept of WSMO i.e., Web Services, ontologies, goals, and mediators. The fifth repository is used by WSMX for non-WSMO data items, e.g., events and messages. Finally, the sixth repository stores WSDL documents used to ground WSMO service descriptions to SOAP or SOAP/HTTP.

The first four repositories, Web Services, goals, mediators, and ontologies can be provided by grounding to triple space for the top-level entities based on some mappings that have been defined by the WSML Working Group [132]. The resource manager will be provided with RDF grounding support so that while storing data, the local repositories could be bypassed and the WSML-based data could be stored in the triple space with URIs (to identify the data afterwards). This will help make the process of persistent storage independent of WSMX. Moreover, it will help further by exploiting the large triple space storage to store the data. There will be no need to maintain local repositories as well. It will not affect the current design of components since the resource manager interface will remain the same. However, the grounding extensions will help in transforming and storing data in the triple space. Figure 11.6 shows the WSMX resource manager's bindings with triple space based storage.

The storage of WSMO top-level entities in the triple space will help in enhancing and fastening the process access of the data items afterwards. For instance, in

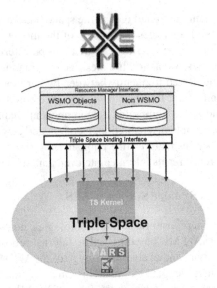

Figure 11.6. Resource management in WSMX using TSC

the current discovery mechanism of WSMX, the WSML reasoners have to reason on each and every Web service description available in the local repositories, which takes a significant amount of time. When the Web Services descriptions are stored over triple space, the template matching based simpler reasoning will be used as a first step in order to filter out the most relevant and possibly required Web service descriptions. The filtered Web Services descriptions based on template based matching over the triple space are retrieved and converted back to WSML to be reasoned over by WSML reasoners. It makes the process of discovery simpler and faster by performing the reasoning operation only on relevant Web service descriptions rather than on all. For the fifth type of repository (i.e., for events, intermediate message), data will be stored as content in simple RDF triples as there is no need to perform any kind of reasoning on events or intermediate data. For the sixth type of repository (i.e., for WSDL description), WSDL RDF mappings proposed in [128] will be used to store the WSDLs in the triple space.

11.3.3 External Communication for SESA

WSMX acts as semantic middleware between users and real-world Web Services. Currently, owing to the existence of the message-oriented communication paradigm, users communicate with WSMX and WSMX communicates with Web Services synchronously. The external communication manager of WSMX is needed to provide support to communicate over triple space. The interfaces for sending and receiving external messages by WSMX are needed to provide grounding support to alternatively communicate over triple space. This needs to be resolved by addressing several issues, i.e., the invoker component in WSMX is needed to support WSDL and

SOAP communication binding over triple space. The entry point interfaces will be interfaced with triple space middleware in order to provide the glue between existing Web Services standards and triple space computing.

The communication manager is responsible for dealing with the protocols for sending and receiving messages to and from WSMX. Its external behavior is accessed through the invoker and receiver interfaces. The WSMX receiver interface expects the contents of all messages it receives to be expressed in WSML. Each WSML message may represent a goal to be achieved or itmay be a message corresponding to a choreography or orchestration instance that already exists. The communication manager accepts the message and handles any transport and security protocols used by the message sender. The execution semantics of WSMX determines how the WSML message should be handled on the basis of the defined execution semantics of the system. The invoker is used by the execution semantics of WSMX when a Web service needs to be invoked. The invoker receives the WSMO description of the service and the data that the service expects to receive. It is responsible for making the actual invocation of an operation on a service. In the majority of existing Web service implementations, this means ensuring that the semantic description both of the data and the behavior of the Web service are grounded to the corresponding WSDL descriptions. It is anticipated that a separate grounding component to work with the invoker will be required in future versions of WSMX. The external behavior of the system is defined in a new WSMO4J interface called EntryPoint. The intent is that the EntryPoint interface be implemented by any WSMO-compliant Semantic Web Services environments to facilitate seamless runtime integration of these systems. The EntryPoint interface represents the external behaviour of the system. It is currently implemented by the communication manager.

The communication manager will also be provided with triple space based grounding support. It will help in providing an additional or alternative triple space based access interface to WSMX. It will enable triple space clients to submit goals to WSMX via triple space, which will bring a real sense of asynchronous communication of triple space because normally goal execution in WSMX (performing service discovery, selection, composition, mediation, and invocation) takes a significant amount of time. When the service requesters will be able to submit the goals to WSMX over triple space, it will not make them hang up with WSMX until the goal has been executed and will make the communication process of service requesters with WSMX more flexible and reliable. Although it is not our intention to replace the message-passing communication process which WSMX makes use of in order to invoke Web Services, we aim to provide WSMX with an alternative triple space based interface to our intelligent middleware, as required in the Enterprise Application Integration Environment described in the WSMX specifications. Having said that, it is possible that future research on asynchronous communication and scalability in open environments like the Web will eventually make our approach replace the current message-passing communication process and Web Services stack completely and will enable WSMX to invoke end-point Web Services over triple space as well. Figure 11.7, shows a big picture of the external communication with WSMX over triple space.

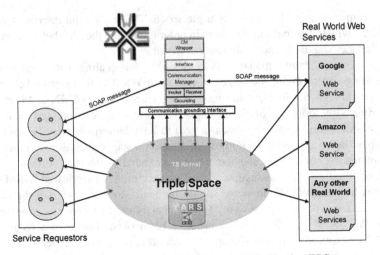

Figure 11.7. External communication in WSMX using TSC

11.3.4 Inter-SESA Communication

After enabling the WSMX manager to perform communication and coordination of components internally, the next step will be to enable the communication and coordination of different WSMXs over triple space, i.e. forming a cluster of different interconnected WSMX nodes to support distributed service discovery, selection, composition, mediation, invocation, etc. The communication model used in the current implementation of WSMX is synchronous. Synchronous communication is beneficial when immediate responses are required. Since WSMX deals with Web service discovery, mediation, and invocation, immediate responses are usually not available. In such situations, the synchronous communication will be costly as it forces the system (component) to remain idle until the response is available. In order to minimize such an overhead imposed by synchronicity, the triple space can serve as a communication channel between WSMXs, thereby introducing synchronicity between communicating parties. The triple space supports purely asynchronous communication that optimizes performance as well as communication robustness.

Figure 11.8 shows the idea of having different WSMX systems interconnected to each other over triple space. This will help the WSMX in providing distributed service discovery, selection, composition, mediation, and invocation. There can be the possibility that different WSMX systems are running at different locations over the globe and contain different information (i.e., semantic description of commercial Web Services, mediation rules, ontologies, and goals). The service requester local to a particular WSMX will not be aware of other WSMX systems and the data contained by other WSMX systems. In this case, it will enable different WSMX systems to be aware of each other and to access the data of other WSMXs over triple space, or redirect the goals to other WSMXs.

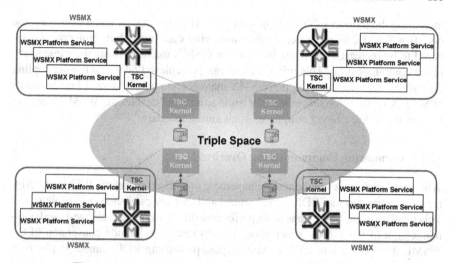

Figure 11.8. Inter-WSMX communication for WSMX using TSC

11.4 Evaluation

The integration of WSMX and triple space computing has been proposed in four major aspects, i.e., component management of WSMX, inter-WSMX communication and coordination, resource management in WSMX for providing persistent storage, and external communication. So far, the first major step of WSMX and triple space computing has been achieved by building the integrated prototype that enables WSMX to perform its internal component management using triple space computing middleware. It enables the WSMX manager to exploit the benefits provided by triple space computing middleware as mentioned in previous sections. There are certain evaluation strategies that have been planned to compare the current state of WSMX with that of integrated WSMX–triple space computing systems.

11.4.1 Comparing Resource Availability

The evaluation includes analyzing the availability of resources. While the WSMX manager schedules the goal execution by coordinating between the components, the triple space enables the WSMX manger to be released from waiting for a response and makes it available to facilitate scheduling of other incoming goal execution requests while the previous goal is already being executed. This will include the calculation of results obtained by submitting goals to WSMX and checking for availability of the WSMX manager to schedule other upcoming goal execution requests.

11.4.2 Analyzing the Performance on Concurrent Execution of Goals

The comparison is further planned to include the overall execution time taken by the WSMX manager. The performance of the WSMX manager will be analyzed by increasing the number of goals to be executed. The overall time taken to execute the goal (for WSMX using SOAP as the underlying communication protocol) is supposed to be increased more rapidly than for WSMX manager using the triple space based communication. This improvement can be achieved owing to the decoupling that will be achieved between the WSMX manager and other individual components of WSMX while communicating over triple space, and enables the WSMX manager sustain to execute a larger number of goals simultaneously.

11.4.3 Comparing Communication Overhead

While performing the component management over triple space, the WSML descriptions are converted into RDF named graphs and then are published over triple space. This involves some extra steps to be performed than for typical message-based communication of the WSML description. These extra steps include conversion of the WSML description into RDF named graphs, publishing RDF named graphs over triple space, retrieving RDF named graphs from triple space, as well as converting RDF named graphs back to WSML. Hence, these extra steps enforce some overhead on the communication of two communicating components. Some experimental tests have to be performed to get an idea of the overhead.

11.4.4 Communication Overhead Versus Time Saved in Concurrent Goal Execution

After the analysis of the behavior of the increase in availability of resources and the increase in the performance of overall goal execution by WSMX while using triple space computing for its internal components management, it is further planned to analyze the overhead caused by the required transformation of WSML data into RDF, communicated between the components of WSMX during goal execution. The idea is to compare the time saved in multiple goal execution and the increase in resource availability versus the overhead caused in serializing WSML to RDF.

11.5 Summary

In this chapter, the storage and internal communication issues of SESA were discussed. WSMX as a reference implementation of the WSMO conceptual model for Semantic Web Services, based on the principles of service-oriented computing, has been provided with a resource manager service that provides a homogenous interface to the WSMX to persistently store its data. The resource management layer separates the WSMX from the storage issues. It was further explored how the storage service can be used to bring the communication in WSMX on the basis of the persistent publication and reading of semantic data. The concept of triple space computing was also introduced, which is a semantic extension of current tuple space based communication and coordination paradigms.

Moreover, the use of the triple space computing paradigm for communication and coordination of Semantic Web Services was presented. First of all, we presented the key integration aspects of both communication and coordination, i.e., WSMX as our reference implementation of Semantic Web Services, and the triple space computing kernel. The integration is aimed in terms of using triple space computing for internal component management of WSMX, inter-WSMX communication management, resource management, and external communication management. We further proposed the interfacing of the WSMX component manager with the triple space computing kernel and described our implementation. We also listed the analysis strategies of comparison of the current state of WSMX and the WSMX–triple space computing integrated system, to analyze how WSMX can improve its resource availability and time taken in overall goal execution, by using triple space computing for management of its internal components. Moreover, using triple space computing for component management can also bring other advantages, like complexity reduction, as underlying triple space computing middleware incorporates features like publish–subscribe mechanisms which the WSMX manager can reuse for its intermediate even data management.

The next steps are to explore three proposed possibilities of integration of WSMX and triple space computing. This will include design the interfacing of the triple space kernel with the resource manager and the external communication manager of WSMX, with the assumption that it will help WSMX in improving its resource management for persistent storage of data, as well as decoupling of WSMX from external service requesters and applications. It will also include the design of a distributed coordination strategy for the WSMX system to manage and improve the inter-WSMX communication and coordination using triple space computing.

SESA Application and Compatible Systems

SESA Application

In this chapter we show how the Semantically Enabled Service-oriented Architecture (SESA) can be applied to real-world scenarios from the business-to-business (B2B) integration domain and the telecommunications domain. We describe how business services can be modeled semantically and how these services can be executed on the SESA middleware. We show how service discovery operates on the semantic descriptions of services as well as how the middleware performs the conversation between services with data and process mediation applied where necessary.

12.1 Case Scenario: B2B Integration

Interenterprise integration is an essential requirement for today's successful business. With the aim of overcoming heterogeneity, various technologies and standards for the definition of languages, vocabularies and integration patterns are being developed. For example, RosettaNet defines standardized partner interface processes (PIPs), which include standard intercompany choreographies (e.g., PIP3A4 Request Purchase Order), and the structure and semantics of business messages. Although such standards certainly enable B2B integration, they still suffer from several drawbacks. All partners must agree to use the same standard and often the rigid configuration of standards makes them difficult to adapt to local business needs.

The SESA when applied to the B2B integration can help in resolving interoperability problems between business partners and in maintaining the flexible and more reliable integration. In order to demonstrate the value of the SESA in the B2B integration domain, we implemented a scenario from the SWS Challenge.[1] The SWS Challenge aims to establish a common understanding, evaluation scheme, and testbed to compare and classify various approaches to integration of services in terms of their abilities as well as shortcomings in real-world settings.

As Fig. 12.1 depicts, the scenario introduces various service providers (such as Racer and Mueller) offering various purchasing and shipment options for various

---

[1] http://www.sws-challenge.org

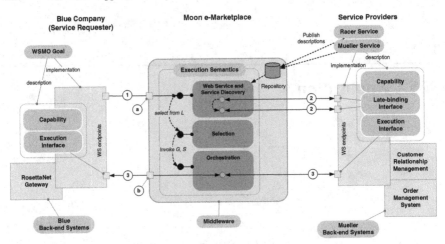

Figure 12.1. Running example

products through the e-marketplace called Moon. On the other hand, there is a service requester called Blue who intends to buy and ship a certain product for the
best possible price. The technology that Moon operates on is the middleware system
enabling the SESA. The following are basic characteristics of the scenario:

- **Back-end systems.** Service requesters and providers use various back-end systems for handling interactions in their environment. For example, Mueller uses
  a customer relationship management (CRM) system and an order management
  system (OMS), while Blue uses a system based on the RosettaNet[2] standard.
  RosettaNet is the B2B specification defining standard components called PIPs,
  which include standard intercompany choreographies (e.g., PIP3A4 Request Purchase Order), and structure and semantics for business messages. Service requesters and service providers maintain the integration with their back-end systems through Web Services (adapters for their back-end systems), while at the
  same time they are responsible for their integration with the middleware through
  semantic descriptions of services and/or through interfaces with the middleware.
- **Modeling and publishing of semantic descriptions.** Engineers on the requester's and the provider's side model services and requests using the WSMO
  model and publish them in the Moon middleware repositories. Engineers of the
  Moon define mappings between different ontologies in repositories and store
  them in the middleware.
- **Interoperability issues.** Engineers on the requester's and the provider's side
  model services independently, meaning that they use different ontologies as
  well as different descriptions of choreographies. For example, Blue models
  the request and response messages according to the RosettaNet PIP3A4 Request Purchase Order specification, while Mueller models the messages using
  proprietary information and choreography specifications of the CRM/OMS

---

[2] http://www.rosettanet.org

systems. For a request message sent by Blue, Mueller must perform several interactions with the back-end systems, such as identify a customer in the CRM, open the order in the OMS, add all items to be ordered to the OMS, and close the order in the OMS.

The scenario runs as follows. All business partners first model their business services. After that, Blue sends the purchase order request captured in the WSMO goal to the middleware system, which on reception of the goal executes the *achieveGoal* execution semantics including: (1) *discovery*, (2) *selection*, and (3) *orchestration*. During discovery, the matching is performed for the goal and potential services at abstract level as well as instance levels (abstract-level discovery allows one to narrow down the number of possible Web Services matching a given goal, while instance-level discovery carries out detailed matchmaking considering instance data of the service and the goal). During selection, the best service is selected (in our case Mueller service) on the basis of preferences provided by Blue as part of the WSMO goal description. Finally during orchestration, the execution and conversation of Blue and Mueller services is performed by processing of descriptions of choreographies from Blue's goal and Mueller's service.

12.1.1 Modeling of Business Services

In this section we show how Blue and Mueller systems can be modeled using WSMO and WSML formalisms. The modeling phase involves the following steps: (1) *Web Services creation*, when underlying services such as Web Services with WSDL descriptions are created, and (2) *Semantic Web Service and goals creation*, when semantic service and goal descriptions are created using WSMO. For our scenario, we create two services, namely, PIP3A4 and CRM/OMS service (we model both systems as one business service):

- *Web Services creation.* This step involves cthe reation of Web Services as adapters to existing systems, i.e., WSDL descriptions for these adapters, including XML Schema for messages, as well as definitions of interfaces, their operations, binding, and end point. In our scenario, we use two adapters: (1) PIP3A4 adapter and (2) CRM/OMS adapter. These adapters allow Mueller's CRM and OMS systems to connect to the middleware, and perform lifting and lowering functionality for XML Schema and ontologies according to the grounding definitions of WSMO services.
- *Semantic Web Services and goals creation.* In order to create Semantic Web Services and goals, the ontologies must be created (or reused) together with non-functional, functional, and interface description of services. In addition, a grounding must be defined from the semantic (WSMO) descriptions to the syntactic (WSDL) descriptions. Semantic Web Services and goals are described according to WSMO service and WSMO goal definitions, respectively. We create a WSMO goal as a PIP3A4 service and a WSMO service as a CRM/OMS service. Please note that WSMO goal and WSMO service have the same structural definition but differ in what they represent. The difference is in the use of defined capability

and interface – WSMO goal describes a capability and an interface required by a service requester, whereas WSMO service describes a capability and an interface provided by a service provider. In our scenario, this task is performed by domain experts (ontology engineers) using "The Web Service Modeling Toolkit". In this section we further elaborate on this step.

Creation of Ontologies and Grounding

One possible approach towards creation of ontologies would be to define and maintain one local domain ontology for Moon's B2B integration. This approach would further allow handling message-level interoperability through the domain ontology when lifting and lowering operations would be defined from the underlying message schema to the domain ontology. Another option is the definition of independent ontologies by each partner and its systems. In our case, these are different ontologies for RosettaNet and ontologies for CRM/OMS systems. The message-level interoperability is then reached through mappings between the ontologies used, which are defined during design time and are executed during run time. Although both approaches have their advantages and limitations, we will use the latter approach in our scenario. The main reason is to demonstrate mediators' aspects to integration of services which are available as independent and heterogeneous services.

Listing 12.1. Lifting from XML to WSML

```
1    /* Lifting rules from XML message to WSML */
2    ...
3    instance PurchaseOrderUID memberOf por#purchaseOrder
4    por#globalPurchaseOrderTypeCode hasValue "<xsl:value−of select←"dict:
          GlobalPurchaseOrderTypeCode"/>"
5    por#isDropShip hasValue
6      IsDropShipPo<xsl:for−each select←"po:ProductLineItem">
7        por#productLineItem hasValue ProductLineItem<xsl:value−of select←"position()"/>
8      </xsl:for−each>
9    <xsl:for−each select←"core:requestedEvent">
10       por#requestedEvent hasValue RequestedEventPo
11   </xsl:for−each>
12   <xsl:for−each select←"core:shipTo">
13       por#shipTo hasValue ShipToPo
14   </xsl:for−each>
15   <xsl:for−each select←"core:totalAmount">
16       por#totalAmount hasValue TotalAmountPo
17   </xsl:for−each>
18   ...
19
20   /* message in WSML after transformation */
21   ...
22   instance PurchaseOrderUID memberOf por#purchaseOrder
23     por#globalPurchaseOrderTypeCode hasValue "Packaged product"
24     por#isDropShip hasValue IsDropShipPo
25     por#productLineItem hasValue ProductLineItem1
26     por#productLineItem hasValue ProductLineItem2
27     por#requestedEvent hasValue RequestedEventPo
28     por#shipTo hasValue ShipToPo
29     por#totalAmount hasValue TotalAmountPo
30   ...
```

We assume that all ontologies are not available up-front and they need to be created by an ontology engineer. The engineer takes as a basis the existing standards and systems, namely, RosettaNet PIP3A4 and CRM/OMS Schema, and creates PIP3A4 and CRM/OMS ontologies, respectively. When creating ontologies, the engineer describes the information semantically, i.e., with richer expressivity as opposed to the expressivity of the underlying XML Schema. In addition, the engineer captures the logic of getting from the XML Schema level to semantics introduced by ontologies by lifting and lowering rules executed on nonsemantic XML Schema and ontologies, respectively. These rules are part of the grounding definition between WSMO and WSDL descriptions and physically reside within adapters. In Listing 12.1, an example of the lifting rules and the resulting WSML instance is shown for an extract of a RosettaNet PIP3A4 message.

Creation of Functional and Nonfunctional Descriptions

WSMO functional description (modeled as WSMO service capability) contains the formal specification of functionality that the service can provide, which is a definition of the conditions on service "inputs" and "outputs" which must hold before and after the service execution, respectively. Functional description for our back-end systems contains conditions that input purchase order data must be of a specific type and contain various information, such as customer ID, items to be ordered, etc. (this information is modeled as preconditions of the service). In addition, the service defines its output as purchase order confirmation as well as the fact that the order has been dispatched. Functional description of service is used for discovery purposes in order to find a service which satisfies the user's request. Nonfunctional properties contain descriptive information about a service, such as author, version, or information about service level agreements, quality of services, etc. In our example, we use the nonfunctional properties to describe user preference for service selection. In our case, the Blue company wants to buy and get shipped a product for the cheapest possible price which is encoded in the WSMO goal description.

Creation of Interfaces and Grounding

Interfaces describe service behavior, modeled in WSMO as (1) *choreography* describing how service functionality can be consumed by the service requester and (2) *orchestration* describing how the same functionality is aggregated out of other services (in our example we only model choreography interfaces as we currently do not use WSMO service orchestration). The interfaces in WSMO are described using abstract state machines defining rules modeling interactions performed by the service, including grounding definition for invocation of underlying WSDL operations. In our architecture and with respect to types of interactions between service requester/provider and the middleware, we distinguish two types of choreography definitions, namely, *late-binding choreography* and *execution choreography*. Listing 12.2 shows a fragment depicting these two choreographies for the CRM/OMS service. The first choreography, marked as *DiscoveryLateBindingChoreography*, defines the rule for how to get the quote for the desired product from the purchase order request (here, the concept *PurchaseQuoteReq* must be mapped to corresponding information conveyed by the purchase order request sent by Blue). This rule is processed during the service discovery and the quote information obtained is used to determine whether a concrete service satisfies the request (e.g., if the requested product is available, which is determined through quote response). The second choreography, marked as *ExecutionChoreography*, defines how to get information about the customer from the CRM system. The decision on which choreography should be used at which stage of execution (i.e., service discovery or conversation) is determined by the choreography namespace (in the listing this namespace is identified using prefixes *dlb#* for discovery late-binding and *exc#* for execution, respectively). In general, choreographies are described from the service point of view. For example, the rule in line 21 says that in order to send the *SearchCustomerResponse* message, the *SearchCustomerRequest* message must be available. By executing the action of the rule (*add(SearchCustomerResponse)*), one invokes the underlying operation with the corresponding message according to the grounding definition of the message, which in turn results in receiving instance data from the Web service.

Listing 12.2. Customer relationship management system/order management system choreography

```
1    /* late—binding choreography for service discovery stage */
2    choreography dlb#DiscoveryLateBindingChoreography
3        stateSignature
4            in mu#purchaseQuoteReq withGrounding { ... }
5            out mu#PurchaseQuoteResp withGrounding { ... }
6
7        forall {?purchaseQuoteReq} with (
8            ?purchaseRequest memberOf mu#PurchaseQuoteReq
9        ) do
10            add( # memberOf mu#PurchaseQuoteResp)
11       endForall
12   ...
13
14   /* execution choeography for service execution stage */
15   choreography exc#ExecutionChoreography
16       stateSignature
17           in mu#SearchCustomerRequest withGrounding { ... }
18           out mu#SearchCustomerResponse withGrounding { ... }
19
20   transitionRules MoonChoreographyRules
21       forall {?request} with (
22           ?request memberOf mu#SearchCustomerRequest
23       ) do
24           add(_# memberOf mu#SearchCustomerResponse)
25       endForall
26   ...
```

Creation of Ontology Mappings

Mappings between used ontologies must be defined and stored in the middleware repositories before execution. In Listing 12.3, the mapping of the *searchString* concept of the CRM/OMS ontology to concepts *cusomterId* of the PIP3A4 ontology is shown. The construct *mediated(X,C)* represents the identifier of the newly created target instance, where X is the source instance that is transformed, and C is the target concept we map to. Such format of mapping rules is generated from the ontology mapping process by the WSMT ontology mapping tool.

Listing 12.3. Mapping rules in WSML

```
1    axiom mapping001 definedBy
2      mediated(X, o2#searchString) memberOf o2#searchString :−
3      X memberOf o1#customerId.
```

12.1.2 Execution of Services

In this section we describe the execution phase run in the middleware for our example. This phase is depicted in Fig. 12.2 and implements the *AchieveGoal* execution

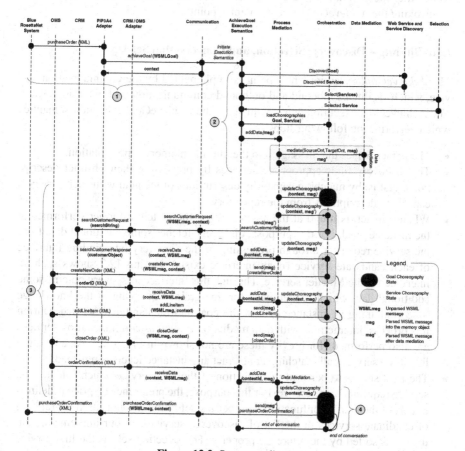

Figure 12.2. Sequence diagram

semantics. We further divide this phase into the following stages: (1) sending Request, (2) late-binding – discovery, selection, and conversation set-up, (3) execution – conversation with service provider, and (4) execution – conversation with service requester.

Sending Request

A RosettaNet PIP3A4 Request Purchase Order message is sent from Blue to the entry point of the PIP3A4 adapter. In the PIP3A4 adapter, the purchase order XML message is lifted to WSML according to the PIP3A4 ontology and rules for lifting using XSLT. Finally, a WSMO goal is created from the purchase order message, including the definition of the desired capability and choreography as well as instance data (this goal is created as an abstract goal which contains separately defined data). The capability of the requester (Blue) is used during the discovery process, whereas the goal choreography describes how the requester wishes to interact with the environment. After the goal has been created, it is sent together with the data to middleware by invoking the *AchieveGoal* execution entry point.

Late-Binding – Discovery, Selection, and Conversation Set-Up

The *AchieveGoal* execution entry point is implemented by the communication service, which facilitates inbound and outbound communication with the middleware. The AchieveGoal execution entry point starts the AchieveGoal execution semantics which performs the following steps:

- The parser parses the message into the internal memory representation.
- The discovery finds appropriate services by processing their abstract descriptions, that is, by matching capability descriptions of the goal with each service's capability descriptions from the repository.
- When a match is found at the abstract level, the match is further performed at the instance level. For this purpose, discovery fetches some additional data from the service requester through processing of the discovery late-binding interface of each candidate service (if an interface exists). Listing 12.2 shows such an interface for the Mueller service. Through this interface, discovery obtains some additional data which is then used for fine-grained querying of the knowledge base containing all instance data of the goal and the candidate service. During this process, interactions with data mediation as well as communication services are also performed (for brevity these are not shown in Fig. 12.2). As a result, a list of the services all matching at abstract and instance levels is returned.
- The next step is to perform the selection of the best service which satisfies the service requester's preference. For this purpose, the preference on price is defined as part of the goal's nonfunctional properties definition which is used for ranking of candidate services in the list of discovered services. In our implementation, the list is sorted by the reference property. The selection selects the first service from the list; in our case, it is the Mueller service.

- The final step of this stage is to set up the conversation between the service requester and the selected service. For this purpose, loading of both the requester's (goal) and the provider's (selected service) choreography in the orchestration service is performed (these choreographies are part of the goal and service descriptions). Both choreographies are then set to a state where they wait for incoming messages that could fire a transition rule. This completes the conversation set-up.
- In the next step, Blue can send the data according to Blue's goal choreography definitions. However, since our implementation is a bit simplified, all data from Blue are already in the goal description. The execution semantics extracts all the data from the goal description and passes them to the process mediation to decide which data to add to the requester's or the provider's choreographies (this decision is based on analysis of both choreographies and concepts used by these choreographies). The process mediation service first updates the memory of the requester's choreography with the information that the purchase order request has been sent. The process mediation then evaluates how data should be added to the memory of the provider's choreography – data must be first mediated to the ontology used by the provider. For this purpose, the source ontology of the requester, the target ontology of the provider, and the instance data are passed to the data mediation service. Data mediation is performed by execution of mapping rules between both ontologies (these mapping rules are stored within middleware repositories and were created during the business service modeling phase).

Execution – Conversation with Service Provider

Once the requester's and the provider's choreographies have been updated, the orchestration service processes each to evaluate if any transition rules could be fired. The requester's choreography remains in the waiting state as no rule can be evaluated at this stage. For the provider's choreography, the orchestration service finds the rule shown in Listing 12.2 (lines 8–12). Here, the orchestration service matches the data in the memory with the the antecedent of the rule and performs the action of the rule's consequent. The rule says that the message *SearchCustomerRequest* with data *searchString* should be sent to the service provider (this data has previously been added to the processing memory after the mediation – here, *searchString* corresponds to the *customerId* from the requester's ontology). The orchestration service then waits for the *SearchCustomerResponse* message to be sent as a response from the provider. Sending the message to the service provider is initiated by the orchestration service passing the message to the communication service, which, according to the grounding defined in the choreography, passes the message to the *searchCustomer* entry point of the CRM/OMS adapter. In the adapter, lowering of the WSML message to XML is performed using the lowering rules for the CRM/OMS ontology and the CRM XML schema. After that, the actual service of the CRM system behind the adapter is invoked, passing the parameter of the *searchString*. The CRM system returns back to the CRM/OMS adapter a resulting *customerObject* captured in XML. The XML data is lifted to the CRM/OMS ontology, passed to middleware, evaluated by the process mediaton service, and added to the provider's choreography memory.

Once the memory of the provider's choreography has been updated, the next rule is evaluated, resulting in the sending of a *createNewOrder* message to the Mueller service (OMS system). This process is analogous to one described before. As a result, the *orderID* sent out from the OMS system is again added to the memory of the provider's choreography. After the order has been created (opened) in the OMS system, the individual items to be ordered need to be added to that order. These items were previously sent in one message as part of order request from Blue's RosettaNet system (i.e., a collection of *ProductLineItem*) which must be now sent to the OMS system individually. As part of the data mediation in step 2, the collection of items from the RosettaNet order request were split into individual items whose format is described by the provider's ontology. At that stage, the process mediation service also added these items into the provider's choreography. The next rule to be evaluated now is the rule of sending the *addLineItem* message with data of one *lineItem* from the processing memory. Since there is more than one line item in the memory, this rule will be evaluated several times until all line items from the ontology have been sent to the OMS system. When all line items have been sent, the next rule is to close the order in the OMS system. The *closeOrder* message is sent out from the middleware to the OMS system and since no additional rules from the provider's choreography can be evaluated, the choreography comes to the end of conversation state.

Execution – Conversation with Service Requester

When the order in the OMS system is closed, the OMS system replies with *order-Confirmation*. After lifting and parsing of the message, the process mediation service first calls for the mediation of the data to the requester's ontology and then adds the data to the memory of the requester's choreography. The next rule of the requester's choreography can then be evaluated and says that the *purchaseOrderConfirmation* message needs to be sent to the RosettaNet system. After the message has been sent, no additional rules can be evaluated from the requester's choreography; thus, the choreography comes to the end of conversation state. Since both the requester's and the provider's choreographies are in the state of end of conversation, the orchestration service closes the conversation.

12.2 Case Scenario: Voice and Data Integration

Convergence of data and telecommunication networks leading to one, transparent technology promises better services, better quality, and better deals for everybody, anywhere, and anytime. Liberalization of the telecommunications market brings freedom to users, who can choose different operators for different services, enables portability of services with respect to users' needs, and enables better price and quality ratios. Convergence of networks will also bring services allowing the combination of data, voice, and video. A simple example is the integration of voice or video services such as "make a call" with data services such as "look up a phone number" or "compare prices of operators." Convergence of networks combined with the impact of liberalization will open up new opportunities for service providers. While they differ in quality, price, and offers of added value, hundreds of services available for users will be hard to use without a means of automatic service discovery, selection, and composition. A user as a subscriber of two or more operators and manually comparing their services and prices to make a call for the best possible value is likely to appear more often in the future. In order to meet users' needs and preferences in this dynamically changing environment, integration of voice and data services should be automated and transparent to users. Although practical integration of voice and data services still requires a big amount of human effort, several approaches to automate such integration already exist. These approaches are, however, based on the rigid configuration of systems and hard-wired integration. An example is a click-to-dial application allowing a caller to make a call using a callee name. In this scenario, a callee number is first selected from a preconfigured phone directory and the call is established using a predefined operator. Operators used for making a call that appear at run time can also be selected from a set of predefined, preagreed ones. Therefore, a caller will have a limited number of choices to use the best operator, to make a reliable or the cheapest call. In addition, if the operator's network fails and no alternate operator was defined when designing the application, the phone call will fail. Instead of having a rigid configuration, dynamic and reconfigurable integration is a step beyond traditional approaches. It introduces dynamics by automatically locating the best service providers for a given user request.

The SESA can significantly improve the integration of telecommunication services with services available outside the telecommunication network. In this case scenario we illustrate how the Voice over IP (VoIP) technology can be integrated with the SESA middleware and enable their seamless and flexible integration.

12.2.1 Voice over IP

In this section we briefly describe the VoIP and related technology we use in our scenario. VoIP, also known as Internet telephony or IP telephony (IPtel), refers in general to the real-time transport of voice or multimedia data between two or more parties over an IP network [191]. It presents an alternative solution to existing Public switched telephone network (PSTN) voice services enhanced with multimedia transport. VoIP by its nature enables new opportunities for integration of voice and data services native in IP networks. Since the IP network was originally designed for non-real-time services (e.g., e-mail, file transfer), supplementary technologies had to be developed to ensure quality of services (e.g., acceptable delays) with respect to real-time communication as well as *signaling* functionality. Signaling is the basis for service creation in telecommunications. It refers to the exchange of control messages in order to create, manage, and terminate communication among participants. In fact, a simple "make a call" service is initiated with an extensive exchange of signaling messages such as ensuring the location of the called party, his/her availability, as well as compatible media-type negotiation. Only after that, transport of voice data for the actual communication can start. Two standard signaling protocols have emerged to fulfill these needs in IP networks: H.323 [3] and Session Initiation Protocol (SIP) [109]. In our scenario, we will make use of the latter one.

Session Initiation Protocol

SIP is an application layer control (signaling) protocol for creating, modifying, and terminating sessions with one or more participants. Participants can be humans or machines (e.g., a voicemail server). They are identified by SIP URL addresses in the form of *sip:user@domain* or *sip:user@IPaddress*. SIP is a client–server protocol built mainly on the HTTP and SMTP principles. Its architecture includes *end system applications*, such as softphones or SIP phones and *network servers*, such as registrar, redirect, and proxy servers. They all facilitate VoIP communication in terms of looking up and keeping updates on the location of users, and redirecting or forwarding signaling requests to next-hop servers or a called party.

Asterisk

Different VoIP standards have been adopted in the telecommunications domain. Such standards include signaling protocols, different media types, or media codecs. Although they differ in quality or usability, they must often coexist together also with legacy telecommunication systems, such as PSTN. In other words, it should be possible to integrate existing VoIP technology and standards as well as legacy systems in one environment. One of the solutions addressing these requirements is called Asterisk.[3] Asterisk is a software private branch exchange (PBX) being developed under an open-source license. Although it primarily serves functionalities of PBX, it also acts as a SIP proxy server as well as middleware, connecting various telephony technologies including legacy (e.g., PSTN) as well as VoIP interfaces (e.g., SIP, H.323). On top of its fundamental functionality, Asterisk provides a set of APIs for development of new applications allowing programmers to interface with Asterisk at any stage of call set-up and teardown. Although Asterisk is not considered to be a fully fledged SIP proxy server,[4] it provides all SIP functionality required by our scenario. In addition, Asterisk with its open architecture and development interface allows us to accomplish the seamless integration with the SESA middleware.

12.2.2 Case Scenario Description

In our use case depicted in Fig. 12.3, Jana (using her standard SIP phone) intends to make the cheapest call with Tomas, of whom she only knows he works at STI. She neither knows Tomas's phone number, nor the available telecommunication operators, their services, and their prices. Instead, she is registered and connected with the *VoIP hub* provided by a third-party operator (Jana is a VoIP subscriber). The VoIP

---

[3] http://www.asterisk.org/

[4] Alternatively, other SIP proxy servers could be used for our use case, such as SIP Express Router (SER), http://www.voip-info.org/tiki-index.php?page=SIP+Express+Router.

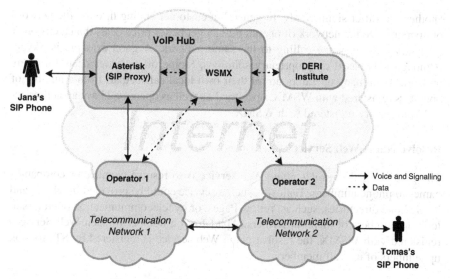

Figure 12.3. Voice and data integration use case

hub is an intermediary between Jana as a service requester, all service providers, as well as Tomas's phone. The VoIP hub comprises Asterisk and WSMX systems. Among all Web Services registered with WSMX, two types of Web Services exist. The first is a telecommunication operator Web service *authorize-call* registered by operators 1 and 2, and the second is a phone directory Web service *resolve-name* registered by DERI. We further describe these services later in this section.

In order to accomplish Jana's desire, the following steps are performed. Given Jana's request ("make a call with Tomas, who works at STI") including her preferences ("cheapest"), Web Services fulfilling this request are discovered, composed, selected, and invoked, i.e., a Web service to resolve Tomas's number, and an authorization Web service of an operator through which the call will be made. As a result, Jana's call to Tomas is authorized and established for the best possible price. In this chapter we further demonstrate this process in detail.

Authorize-Call Web Service

The purpose of the *authorize-call* Web service is to "open" an operator's gateway to which Jana's call will be redirected from the VoIP hub. We presume operators provide access to their network over the Internet using a SIP-compliant gateway; however, only authorized calls are allowed. For example, if Jana is not registered with operator 1 (in other words, if Jana is not a subscriber of operator 1) she cannot make direct calls to/over the network of operator 1 but only through another operator with which she is registered, i.e., the VoIP hub provider. At the same time, agreement and "peering" between the VoIP hub and operator 1 must exist so that calls can be made between both as well as billing. In our use case, such "peering" is built on the Internet and SIP signaling. Furthermore, prices for calling from one network to another can differ significantly. In general, a customer calling through the network of operator 1 to the network of operator 2 can get better price deals than a customer of operator 2 can when calling to the same network. A good example is Skype. Although it is based on proprietary solutions, Skype offers better deals for many networks than many operators do for their own local calls. Apart from a number of operators registered with WSMX, operator 1 as well as operator 2 have an authorize-call Web service registered with WSMX.

Resolve-Name Web Service

The purpose of the *resolve-name* Web service is to resolve people's or company's names to phone numbers. Typically, such a service could be provided by global and local phone directories, such as Yellow Pages, or by telecommunication operators to look up numbers of their subscribers. Apart from a number of such Web Services registered with WSMX, the resolve-name Web service is registered by STI to look up numbers of its staff members.

12.2.3 Voice and Data Integration Process

In this section we describe in detail the integration process of voice and data services according to the use case scenario described in Section 12.2.2. According to the sequence diagram depicted in Fig. 12.4, this process can be divided into the following phases: (1) dialing, (2) transforming desire to goal, (3) achieving goal, and (4) achieving desire.

Dialing

Jana is registered and connected over the Internet to Asterisk of the VoIP hub running at the address *voip-hub.ie* using her favorite SIP phone and her credentials (Jana is the VoIP hub subscriber). This connection is defined in the SIP phone configuration file. Using her phone, she now wants to express and send her desire "make the cheapest call to Tomas, who works at DERI." To do that, the desire must first be formalized and second it must be sent to Asterisk using SIP. There are several ways for how this can be done.

One option to formalize the desire is to use some ad hoc grammar, for example (grammar is written as the regular expression):

```
[a-zA-Z0-9]+#[a-zA-Z0-9]+#[price|quality]{0,1},
```

where terms are divided by the # character. With use of this grammar, the desire would be described as a string `tomas#deri#price`. The grammar and the meaning of each term must be known to users and at the same time the rules/program processing this string must implement them (see the next phase). The meaning of each term is as follows: (1) a callee name, (2) the name of the company that the callee works for, and (3) an optional user preference (*price* means that price for the call is preferred to the quality of the call, and vice versa). Although this approach does

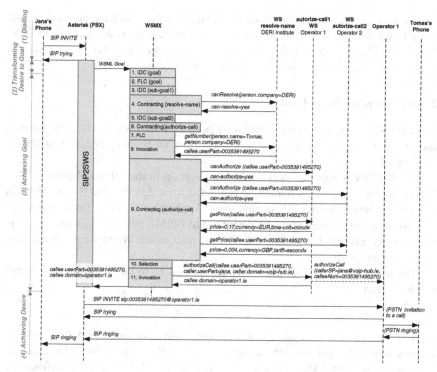

Figure 12.4. Voice and data Integration sequence diagram

not correspond with the trends of ontology engineering, it is relatively easy to use with existing SIP phones (assuming the SIP phone allows alphanumeric characters to be entered when dialing). Formalized desire is then used as a user part of the SIP address. For example, if Jana "dials" `tomas#deri#price`, the SIP phone will generate the following SIP message (note that only the first line of the message is shown):

```
INVITE sip:tomas#deri#price@voip-hub.ie SIP/2.0
```

Asterisk sends back "100 Trying" response, indicating that the INVITE has been received and is now being processed. Various extensions to SIP have already been proposed to standardize similar mechanisms, such as Control of Service Context Using SIP Request URI [39] or SIP Caller Preferences, and Callee Capabilities [190]. However, they were not aimed at the communication of a desire.

Another option to formalize the desire would be to use some standard or ad hoc ontology with a standard ontology language. Preferably, this could be done using the WSMO goal concept and WSML. However, to send such ontology through existing SIP phones would be more difficult without changing its functionality or user interface. Unlike in the first option, this ontology would not be suitable to send as the user part of the SIP address (owing to its size or possible character sets used) but rather should be sent in the SIP message body in a MIME-compliant format.

We aim for the integration of voice and data services to have minimal impact on end-user devices as well as for it to be transparent to users as much as possible. Thus, we will use the first option described; however, we admit that this approach is limited and should be improved in practical scenarios.

Transforming Desire to Goal

After the SIP message and the desire have been sent, they are received by Asterisk and processed within its *dial plan*. In the dial plan, an application called SIP2SWS is executed.

The SIP2SWS application is the key application in the SIP and Semantic Web Service integration process building a bridge between Asterisk and the WSMX. On one hand, it interfaces our SIP session using Application Gateway Interface (AGI)[5] and, on the other, it transforms the desire to the WSML goal, triggers the Semantic Web Service process by sending the WSML goal to the WSMX entry point, and receives an output from it.

The following is the dial plan entry corresponding to our desire and its formal representation:

```
exten => _.#.#., AGI(sip2sws, \${EXTEN})
```

The element `_.#.#.` defines a dial plan pattern for the user part of the SIP address (here, the pattern corresponds to the regular expression defined in the previous phase), and the element `AGI(sip2sws, \${EXTEN})` defines the AGI command to execute the SIP2SWS application on the channel. The argument `\${EXTEN}` is a placeholder for the current extension (user part, in our case formalized desire) sent by the client.

The SIP2SWS application is an external application written in Java which transforms Jana's desire "make the cheapest call to Tomas, who works at STI" formalized as `tomas#deri#price` to the goal "authorize the cheapest call between a caller Jana and a person Tomas, who works at STI." We formally describe this goal as well as its ontology further in this section. The reason why Jana's desire differs from the goal is that Asterisk redirects a channel already created by Jana to a SIP proxy to further establish the call, whereas WSMX finds the cheapest operator for the call, authorizes this call with this operator, and returns necessary information for redirecting the call (Tomas's number and the operator's SIP proxy domain name). If the goal sent to the WSMX was "make a call" instead of "authorize a call," there would be a problem with our approach to put the SIP context of the existing channel through the WSMX to another SIP proxy (in this case, the Parlay X Web Services interface [40] for telecommunications systems could be used; however, we have not investigated such an approach in our work). In our use case, we rather combine the existing SIP proxy functionality of Asterisk used for the call redirection with the WSMX functionality used for the optimal provisioning of Web Services. In other words, Asterisk and WSMX share tasks within the VoIP hub to achieve Jana's desire.

---

[5] AGI allows Asterisk to launch an external program written in any language to control a telephony channel, play audio, read DTMF digits, etc.

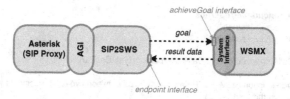

Figure 12.5. SIP2SWS and WSMX interaction

In our use case, we use a simple request–response scenario operating in the asynchronous mode as depicted in Fig. 12.5. First, the SIP2SWS application calls the following WSMX system entry point defined as part of the WSMX integration API:

```
Context achieveGoal(WSMLDocument wsmlDocument)
```

The attribute `wsmlDocument` contains data sent to the WSMX, i.e., the WSML goal and the WSML ontology. The SIP2SWS application receives a `Context` on return to identify an already established session for subsequent calls with WSMX. Result data are then sent back asynchronously from the WSMX by calling a SIP2SWS *end point* (we assume this end point is registered with WSMX). Such a scenario corresponds with the fact that no interactions between Jana and the Semantic Web Service execution process are required. In more elaborated scenarios, Jana would want to provide additional information for the selection phase of the Semantic Web Service execution process by approving, for example, terms and conditions of discovered services.

Simple VoIP ontology in WSML which describes concepts used in our scenario is shown in Listing 12.4. First, namespaces to distinguish elements of multiple resources are defined, such as for XML Schema (*xsd*), and Dublin Core (*dc*).

Listing 12.4. Voive over IP ontology

```
 1  namespace {
 2    xsd _"http://www.w3.org/2001/XMLSchema#",
 3    dc _"http://purl.org/dc/elements/1.1#"}
 4
 5  ontology _"http://www.example.org/STI/VoIPont"
 6
 7  nonFunctionalProperties
 8    dc#title hasValue "VoIP Ontology"
 9    dc#description hasValue "Ontology of VoIP concepts"
10  endNonFunctionalProperties
11
12  concept CallParticipant
13    nonFunctionalProperties
14      dc#description hasValue "Concept of a participant in a call"
15    endNonFunctionalProperties
16    userPart ofType xsd#string
17    domain ofType xsd#string
18
19  concept Person
20    nonFunctionalProperties
21      dc#description hasValue "Concept of a person"
```

```
22    endNonFunctionalProperties
23    name ofType xsd#string
24    company ofType xsd#string
25
26    relation CallAuthorized(ofType CallParticipant, ofType CallParticipant)
27    nonFunctionalProperties
28        dc#description hasValue "Relation that holds between two call participants when call is
              authorized."
29    endNonFunctionalProperties
```

The VoIP ontology contains two concepts and one relation. In particular, the *Call-Participant* concept defines a *userPart* and a *domain* attribute forming a SIP address of a call participant, the *Person* concept defines a *name* of a person and a *company* where the person works, and the *CallAuthorized* concept defines the relation which holds when a call between two call participants is authorized.

Concepts defined in the VoIP ontology are used in the goal whose definition is shown in Listing 12.5. This goal, which also includes input data values (*person.name="Tomas"*, *person.company="STI"*, *caller.userPart="Jana"*, *caller.domain="voip-hub.ie"*) as well as uer preference (*preference="price"*), is generated from the previously described desire and is sent to the WSMX by calling the WSMX system entry point.

Listing 12.5. Goal authorize call

```
1    namespace {
2    voip _"http://www.example.org/DERI/VoIPont",
3    xsd _"http://www.w3.org/2001/XMLSchema#",
4    dc _"http://purl.org/dc/elements/1.1#"}
5
6    goal _"http://www.example.org/STI/SIP2SWSgoal"
7
8    nonFunctionalProperties
9        dc#title hasValue "Authorize Call"
10       dc#description hasValue "Authorize a call between a caller and a person from a company"
11       voip#preference hasValue "price"
12   endNonFunctionalProperties
13
14   capability
15
16       sharedVariables { ?caller, ?callee }
17
18       precondition
19       definedBy
20           exists { ?person, ?caller } (
21           ?person[
22               name hasValue "Tomas",
23               company hasValue "STI"
24           ] memberOf voip#Person and
25           ?caller[
26               userPart hasValue "Jana",
27               domain hasValue "voip-hub.ie"
28           ] memberOf voip#CallParticipant
29           ).
30
31       postcondition
32       definedBy
33           exists { ?callee, ?calleeUserPart, ?calleeDomain } (
```

```
34          ?callee[
35              userPart hasValue ?calleeUserPart,
36              domain hasValue ?calleeDomain
37          ] memberOf voip#CallParticipant
38      ).
39
40  effect
41      definedBy
42          exists { ?caller, ?callee } (
43              CallAuthorized(?caller, ?callee)
44          ).
```

In our use case, we use a *preference* keyword as a nonfunctional property for the description of Jana's preference (we assume this property is defined within the *voip* namespace). Although WSMO defines nonfunctional properties such as *financial* or *quality of service*, we do not use them as there were created for the description of Web Services rather than for users' preferences. Apart from the definition of namespaces and other nonfunctional properties which are similar to those in the VoIP ontology, the goal also contains a *capability* which is requested to result from the Semantic Web Services execution process.

The *capability* description is composed of several blocks, i.e., *sharedVariables*, *precondition*, *postcondition*, and *effect*. The *sharedVariables* block is used to indicate the variables which are shared across the goal definition in all other blocks. In the *precondition* block, requested inputs are specified, i.e., a *person* and a *caller* having assigned the input values. In the *postcondition* block, requested outputs which must result from the processing of the goal are defined. In our example, we request information regarding a *callee* – his/her *userPart* and a *domain* to which a call should be redirected. Similarly, the *effect* block defines requested output corresponding to the state of the world, in our case authorized call between a caller and a callee.

The WSML goal as described in Listing 12.5 is sent to the WSMX according to the scenario depicted in Fig. 12.5. In this case, there is no need for a goal interface to be specified as all data values are sent as part of the goal definition and at the same time the output is sent back by calling the SIP2SWS end point. Such a scenario corresponds to the simple request–response interaction and reflects the latest WSMX implementation. In more elaborated scenarios requiring more interactions between a service requester and service providers during the Semantic Web Service execution process, this process will be initiated by sending an abstract goal including the requested choreography. The requested choreography defines all the requested interactions between the service requester and service providers, including definitions of input data and their "feeding" to the Semantic Web Service execution process as well as definitions of requested output data at different stages of communication. Such scenarios will be investigated in our future work.

Achieving Goal

In this section we describe the WSMX behavior according to the goal received and show the sequence of interactions between the WSMX components. The goal as shown in Listing 12.5 captures the information that the requester wants to receive (requested outputs) as well as effects of the state of the world that the requester wants to achieve (requested effects). The WSMX repository contains a number of registered Web Services; among others *resolve-name* (by STI), *authorize-call1* (by operator 1), and *authorize-call2* (by operator 2). We simplify the semantic description of the goal and the Web Services as follows:

1. **Goal:** Look up a *callee.userPart* for a *person.name* that works in a *person.company* and allow a call from the *caller.userPart@caller.domain* to the *callee.userPart* through the cheapest operator at a *callee.domain*.

   - **Requested outputs:** *callee.userPart, callee.domain*
   - **Requested effect:** *CallAuthorized(caller, callee)*
   - **Provided inputs values:** *person.name="Tomas", person.company="STI", caller.userPart="Jana", caller.domain="voip-hub.ie"*
   - **Preference:** *price*

2. **Web service:** *resolve-name*

   - **Requested inputs:** *person.name, person.company*
   - **Provided outputs:** *callee.userPart*

3. **Web service:** *authorize-call1*

   - **Requested inputs:** *callee.userPart, caller.userPart, caller.domain*
   - **Provided outputs:** *callee.domain*
   - **Provided effect:** *CallAuthorized(caller, callee)*

4. **Web service:** *authorize-call2*

   - **Requested inputs:** *callee.userPart, caller.userPart, caller.domain*
   - **Provided outputs:** *callee.domain*
   - **Provided effect:** *CallAuthorized(caller, callee)*

The following is the description of the actions of particular components within WSMX to achieve the goal, namely, discovery and composition, contracting, selection, and invocation. For discovery and composition we use the integrated approach proposed in [177]. Discovery of Web Services is called within the composition process every time a Web service needs to be discovered. In this approach, the following components are identified:

- Integrated discovery and composition (IDC).
- Functional level composition (FLC). This is used when there is no single service that can satisfy the goal. FLC refines the goal into subgoals in order to find a subset of the existing Web Services which can be combined into a composite service fulfilling the goal.
- Process level composition (PLC). This creates a workflow for the composite service with respect to choreography and orchestration constraints.

1. **IDC (goal)**
   - **Action:** Discovery component is called to match the goal with Web service descriptions in the WSMX repository.
   - **Result:** Discovery was not able to find a single Web service covering all requirements of the goal.
2. **FLC (goal)**
   - **Action:** The goal is refined into two subgoals. This refinement is based on predefined generic goals stored in the goals repository.
   - **Result:** Subgoal 1. Look up a *callee.userPart* for a *person.name* that works in a *person.company*
     - **Requested outputs:** *callee.userPart,*
     - **Provided inputs:** *person.name, person.company, caller.userPart, caller.domain*
     - **Provided inputs values:** *person.name= "Tomas", person.company= "STI", caller.userPart= "Jana", caller.domain= "voip-hub.ie"*
     - **Preference:** *price*
   - **Result:** Subgoal 2. Allow a call from *caller.userPart@caller.domain* to *callee.userPart* through the cheapest *callee.domain*.
     - **Requested outputs:** *callee.domain,*
     - **Requested effects:** *CallAuthorized(caller, callee),*
     - **Provided inputs:** *person.name, person.company, caller.userPart, caller.domain*
     - **Provided inputs values:** *person.name= "Tomas", person.company= "STI", caller.userPart= "Jana", caller.domain= "voip-hub.ie"*
     - **preference:** *price*
3. **IDC (subgoal 1)**
   - **Action:** Discovery component is called to match subgoal 1 with service descriptions in the WSMX repository.
   - **Result:** Discovery has found the *resolve-name* Web service with requested capabilities.
   - **Action:** So far, we have only considered the outputs and the effects in the service descriptions independently of input information that has to be provided to the Web service. These inputs determine whether the Web service can be actually used. Therefore, the *resolve-name* Web service will be checked for available inputs. Up to now the actions were completely internal to WSMX and they were based on abstract descriptions of goal/subgoal and Web Services. There was no interaction with the requester or service providers. For a complete guarantee that discovered Web Services can provide a concrete requested service, further communication with this Web service is necessary. Such communication is called contracting and must be called at this stage of discovery and composition.

4. **Contracting (resolve-name)**
   - **Action:** Contracting for the *resolve-name* Web service. We need to find out whether this Web service is able to provide name resolution for STI staff; thus, *canResolve(person.company= "STI")* is called.
   - **Result:** Web service *resolve-name* can provide name resolution for DERI. Before proceeding to IDC of the next subgoal 2, available inputs for subgoal 2 are extended by outputs of the already discovered and contracted Web service *resolve-name*, in this case *callee.userPart*.

5. **IDC (subgoal 2)**
   - **Action:** The discovery component is called to match subgoal 2 with Web service descriptions in the WSMX repository.
   - **Result:** Discovery has found two Web Services both satisfying subgoal 2: *authorize-call1* and *authorize-call2*.
   - **Action:** Each discovered Web service will be checked for available inputs.
   - **Result:** Both discovered Web Services need as input *callee.userPart*, which is not provided by the requester. However, thanks to the previously discovered *resolve-name* Web service which returns *callee.userPart* as its output, *authorize-call1* and *authorize-call2* can go for further processing with the restriction that they have to be invoked after the *resolve-name* Web service.

6. **Contracting**
   - **Action:** Contracting for *authorize-call1* and *authorize-call2* to find out whether each of these Web Services is able to provide the authorization for a concrete *callee.userPart* value.
   - **Result:** Contracting is not possible at this stage as all required input values are not known (*callee.userPart* value in particular). In order to contract these Web Services, the *resolve-name* Web service has to be first invoked.

7. **PLC** creates the workflow based on discovered services, *resolve-name* and *authorize-call*.

8. **Invocation**
   - **Action:** *resolve-name* is invoked, *getNumber(person.name= "Tomas", person.company= "STI")*
   - **Result:** The Web service returns *callee.userPart= "0035391495270"*. Available inputs for subgoal 2 are extended by this output.

9. **Contracting**
   - **Action:** Contracting for *authorize-call1* and *authorize-call2* to find out whether each of these Web Services is able to provide the authorization for a concrete *callee.userPart* value: *canAuthorize(callee.userPart= "0035391495270")*.
   - **Result:** Both services can provide the authorization for the requested *callee.userPart*, both services have available inputs and have been contracted. As for subgoal 2 we have discovered two possibilities; therefore, selection will be performed on the basis of the requester's preference (price). However, in order to do that, we must find out the price for calls offered by both Web Services.

- **Action:** Get information about price for *authorize-call1* and *authorize-call2* for a call to *callee.userPart*: *getPrice(callee.userPart="0035391495270")*.
- **Result:**
  - *authorize-call1* returns *price="0.17"*, *currency="EUR"*, *time-unit="minute"*.
  - *authorize-call2* returns *price="0.004"*, *currency="GBP"*, *tariff="second"*.

10. **Selection**
    - **Action:** Selection will chose between services *authorize-call1* and *authorize-call2* on the basis of the requester's preference. Since different ontologies are used by these services (e.g., different currencies, different concepts *time-unit* and *tariff*), data mediation will be called at this stage (note that mapping rules with conversions between both ontologies must be available beforehand to process this data mediation– such information is obtained during the design-time stage of the mediation process).
    - **Result:** *authorize-call1* Web service was selected.

11. **Invocation**
    - **Action:** *authorize-call1* Web service is invoked: *authorize-call1 (callee.userPart="0035391495270", caller.userPart="Jana", caller.domain="voip-hub.ie")*.
    - **Result:** *callee.domain="operator1.ie"* as well as call authorization are effected through the gateway of operator 1.

Achieving Desire

After the goal has been accomplished by the WSMX, the SIP2SWS application receives information about Tomas's number as well as the operator's SIP proxy (domain name of the SIP proxy) at which the call between Jana and Tomas has been authorized. Thus, the SIP2SWS application can now process further to achieve Jana's original desire. To do that, the following SIP message is forwarded from Asterisk to the operator's gateway (only the first line of the message is shown):

```
INVITE sip:0035391495270@operator1.ie SIP/2.0
```

Asterisk receives back 100 Trying response from the operator's gateway indicating that the INVITE has been received and is now being processed. We consider operator 1 is a VoIP operator having connection with operator 2 through some SIP/PSTN gateway. As Tomas with number 0035391495270 as a subscriber of operator 2 (hence, operator 2 is a landline operator), the SIP signaling is transformed at the SIP/PSTN gateway into the PSTN signaling in order to reach Tomas. Next, Tomas's phone starts ringing and Jana is notified by the ringing tone.

As we mentioned earlier, thanks to the liberalization and regulation of transit and termination charges for calls, the alternative operators can compete with legacy operators with regard to services offered and prices. This was also the case in our example.

12.3 Summary

In this chapter we showed the SESA and its middleware technology can be applied to integration of business services from the B2B domain and to integration of voice and data services from the telecommunication domain. The important aspect of such integration is that it must essentially build on existing technologies. In the case of B2B integration they are existing standards such as RosettaNet and related systems; in the case of telecommunications they are existing systems and standards of VoIP. In these scenarios we described how services can be modeled semantically using the WSMO framework and how the whole execution process runs in the middleware.

While the semantic technologies and the SESA in particular can facilitate the novel style of integration of services by means of semantic service descriptions and artificial intelligence methods, some people say that such an approach is not realistic today. They argue that the complexity of semantic languages and integration techniques that depend on logical reasoning is a burden for service processing and high performance. However, the logical reasoning can efficiently help resolve inconsistencies in service descriptions as well as maintain interoperability when these descriptions change. The more complex the services' descriptions are, the more difficult it is for a human to manually maintain the integration. The semantics that promote the automation is the key to flexibility and reliability of such integration. To demonstrate the value of semantics for service descriptions as well as automation in service integration, we are working on the SWS Challenge.[6] The SWS Challenge aims to establish a common understanding, evaluation scheme, and test bed to compare and classify various approaches to integration of services in terms of their abilities as well as shortcomings in the real-world settings. Although a world full of services does not exist yet, one-click integration will be desirable. The SESA and its related activities enable such a world as well as such integration.

---

[6] http://www.sws-challenge.org

13

Compatible and Related Systems

This chapter will discuss in detail the nature of one Semantically Enabled Service-oriented Arhitecture (SESA) compliant system, IRS-III, which also informs the OASIS standardization work on semantic Service-Oriented Architecture. It will also consider tools that have been independently produced to fulfill separate tasks within the architecture, specifically those which address discovery and composition. Next tools from tools from the OWL-S community will be considered from the point of view of the SESA. Finally the METEOR-S toolset, and its input into the WSDL-S standardization, will be considered.

13.1 The Internet Reasoning Service

The Internet Reasoning Service (IRS) project[1] [36] conducted in the Knowledge Media Institute at the Open University has the overall aim of supporting the automated or semiautomated construction of semantically enhanced systems over the Internet. The epistemological basis of the IRS is based on the decomposition of the system's expertise into tasks, methods, domains, and applications, usually referred to as the TMDA framework [152]. This framework, mainly influenced by extensive research on problem-solving methods, was implemented in IRS-I [46] to support the creation of knowledge-intensive systems structured according to the UPML framework [78]. IRS-II [153] continued this approach and integrated the UPML framework with Web service technology so as to benefit from the reasoning infrastructure over the Web. Finally, the current version of the IRS, namely, IRS-III [36], has incorporated and extended WSMO so that the implemented infrastructure allows the description, publication, and execution of Semantic Web Services.

IRS-III is based on a distributed architecture composed of the IRS-III server, the publishing platforms, and clients, as shown in Fig. 13.1. The server embeds an OCML [152] interpreter which includes all the reasoning machinery for manipulating definitions of ontologies and invoking Web Services in order to satisfy the

---

[1] http://kmi.open.ac.uk/projects/irs

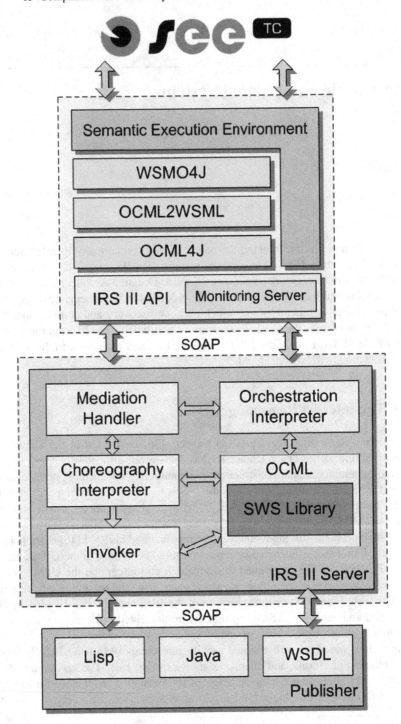

Figure 13.1. IRS-III architecture

client's requests expressed as goals. In order to support the invocation of Semantic Web Services, the core reasoning machinery is complemented with the orchestration interpreter, the choreography interpreter, the mediation handler, and the invoker.

The server provides access to client applications for creating and editing WSMO descriptions of goals, Web Services, and mediators and it also allows achieving of stored goals by invoking previously deployed Web Services. Clients communicate with the server by means of a stack of Java libraries, encapsulated in the box in Fig. 13.1. The libraries provide programmatic access to the server functionality as well performing the appropriate transformations between WSMO definitions and OCML as required. Furthermore, an implementation of the current version of the Semantic Execution Environment API is also available, so that compatible applications, like WSMO Studio or the Web Service Modeling Toolkit, can make use of the IRS in a homogeneous way.

The publishing platforms allow providers of services to attach semantic descriptions to their deployed services and allow handlers to invoke services in a specific language or platform. Currently the IRS supports four different types: WSDL, Lisp code, Java code, and Web applications. When a Web service is published in IRS-III the information about the publishing platform is also associated with the Web service description in order to be invoked. The Java and WSDL publishing platforms are delivered as Java Web applications, whereas both the Lisp and the HTTP publishers have been developed in Lisp.

In the remainder of this section we will focus on specific aspects of the IRS: firstly the basis for reasoning in OCML and an encoding of the WSMO model, then discovery, selection, and mediation, next communication, and finally support for choreography and orchestration.

13.1.1 Reasoning

OCML

The IRS has been developed entirely in Lisp and uses OCML [152] as its modeling language. The main goal of OCML is to support knowledge-level [156] modeling. Thus, it provides mechanisms for expressing relations, functions, rules, classes, and instances. It is, however, worth noting that OCML is an operational language and, therefore, as opposed to pure knowledge-level modeling languages, it aims to encompass behaviour as well. In consequence, OCML is suitable for the rapid prototyping of knowledge-level models but it does not aim to provide highly efficient execution.

OCML is intended to support the specification of problem-solving methods and the development of complete applications by reusing existing libraries. It does so by supporting the specification of domain models, tasks, and methods. OCML supports different modeling styles, i.e., formal, informal, and operational. Formal modeling is indirectly supported by the language, i.e., no formal semantics are provided for the control language, by defining mappings to formal languages [152]. Informal modeling is supported by means of a graphical notation and operational modeling is enabled by the existing interpreter for evaluating control and functional terms and for its inferencing capabilities.

OCML provides three types of constructs: functional, control, and logical expressions. Functional terms are constants, variables, strings, a function application, or can be defined by means of special constructors such as *if*, *cond*, or *setofall* to name a few. Control constructs support defining how problem-solving should occur. Among these constructors we can find *loop*, *do*, *repeat*, etc. Lastly, OCML supports defining logical expressions using the operators *and*, *or*, *not*, $=¿$, $¡=¿$ and the quantifiers *forall* and *exists*. The reader is referred to [152] for more details about this and other aspects of OCML.

The modeling language provides mechanisms for defining *relations*, *functions*, *ontologies*, *classes*, *instances*, *procedures*, and *rules* in order to support domain modeling. Relations support defining n-ary relationships between OCML entities. Functions can be characterized as relations although they cannot be queried or asserted. Instead, functions generate values. OCML supports defining hierarchies of classes and the inheritance of their slots. Typical frame-based machinery is supported for defining slots such as the type, default and fixed values, cardinality restrictions, and the inheritance mechanism to be used. OCML supports both an object-oriented approach to defining classes and a relation-oriented one by means of the *iff-def* construct. Finally, procedures support defining sequences of actions that cannot be characterized as functions between inputs and outputs.

In addition to the mechanisms presented so far, OCML provides the means for defining backward and forward-chaining rules. Backward rules are defined in terms of backward clauses that specify goal–subgoal decomposition. The OCML interpreter is implemented as depth-first search with chronological backtracking and tries to prove every subgoal in the order they are listed in the rule definition. Forward-chaining defines data-driven or goal-driven reasoning and supports defining how problem-solving should occur. Forward rules specify antecedents and a set of consequents which are treated as goals to be proven. When a forward rule is executed OCML attempts to proven each consequent until one fails.

WSMO Metamodel in the IRS

We previously mentioned that the distinguishing characteristic of IRS-III with respect to preceding versions is the incorporation of WSMO so as to support the description, publication, and execution of Semantic Web Services. IRS-III has its own internal representation of the WSMO metamodel in OCML and introduces some specific modifications and extensions, which we review next.

A first aspect that differs from WSMO is the fact that in IRS-III, goals and Web Services have an explicit declaration of input and output roles which includes the name and the semantic type. This approach contrasts with WSMO, where this information is defined in the *state signature* as part of the *choreography* specification.

A second notable feature, closely related to the previous one, comes from the fact that Web Services can inherit the goal's inputs and output roles. As a consequence, the declarations of roles in Web Services are not mandatory although they can be used to either extend or refine existing definitions of roles. This feature is in fact enabled by the fact that inputs and output roles are defined as part of goals and Web Services, as opposed to the approach prescribed in WSMO, and supports further reuse of existing definitions.

In addition to the specific extensions to WSMO included in IRS-III, further distinguishing characteristics arise from the underlying modeling support used in the IRS. WSMO is defined using the Meta-Object Facility (MOF) [160], which specifies a metadata architecture based on fours layers:

1. The *information layer*, which comprises the data described.
2. The *model layer*, where the data in the information layer is described.
3. The *metamodel layer*, which defines the structure and semantics of the metadata expressed in the model layer.
4. The *meta-metamodel* layer, where the structure and semantics of the meta-metadata are defined.

In WSML this metamodel is separate from the definitions made in the language, i.e., it is a separate metatheory. Hence, the language defining WSMO (MOF) corresponds to the meta-metamodel layer; WSMO itself represents the metamodel layer; the ontologies, Web Services, goals, and mediators defined in WSML constitute the model layer; and the actual data described by the ontologies and exchanged between Web Services belong to the information layer.

Domain- or application-specific definitions span the information and model layers where Web service, ontology, goal, and mediator are basically language constructs. Consequently, when modeling any specific domain in WSML, there is no possibility to treat Web service, ontology, goal, or mediator as concepts which could be subsumed or instantiated. This supports the execution of Web Services, since existing WSML-based software has embedded knowledge in order to deal with these concepts; however, this separation of layers has important drawbacks associated with it.

A first inconvenience is, as pointed out in [203], the fact that it is important to distinguish between prototypical goals which represent the specific static definitions and the actual instantiations of these goals which contain invocation data. The authors refer to these as goal templates and goal instances, respectively, and in fact the introduction of goal templates proposed in [203] is a way to overcome part of the limitations introduced by the MOF-based definition of WSMO.

Secondly, at the model level, goal being merely a construct, one cannot benefit from subsumption. Supporting the creation of goal hierarchies would promote and support reusing definitions. Goal achievement could be enhanced by supporting the dynamic selection of refined goals taking nonfunctional properties into account, for example. Similarly, facing situations where a specific goal cannot be achieved, systems could decide to meet part of the client requirements by achieving a more generic goal. So far, this is supported in WSMO by means of ggMediators but using these requires additional ad hoc reasoning facilities where preexisting reasoning machinery could be applied (e.g., subsumption). In fact ggMediators do not specify whether the relationship between goals is one of equivalence or refinement.

In IRS-III, these inconveniences are overcome in OCML by defining both the metamodel (WSMO) and the user models in the same language, i.e., both the WSMO metaconcept of goal and specific user goals – the previously mentioned goal templates – are both OCML classes. Being so supports the instantiation of goals and allows the defining of relationships (e.g., is-a relations) between goals.

Despite the differences described so far, the current implementation of the IRS includes a set of libraries that ensures that preexisting WSML definitions based on the official specification can be imported into IRS-III. The same way the libraries support exporting into WSML existing definitions expressed in the OCML representation of the WSMO metamodel. In the latter case, however, there is obviously some expressivity degradation, specifically because mixing levels is not supported in WSML.

13.1.2 Discovery, Selection, and Mediation

Discovery in the IRS is based on the existing ontological connection between goals and services expressed via wgMediators. This can be dynamically computed when a new goal is submitted, but the assumption is that the IRS enacts a stable broker between preexisting goals and external deployed Web Services. Having found a mediator connecting a goal to some candidate services, the IRS selects the most suitable on the basis of the preconditions and assumptions defined in their capability.

In order to support this model of discovery and selection, IRS has some extensions and differences in the interpretation of the WSMO model from that applied by WSMX. Firstly, goals are implicitly assumed to be atomic and explicitly parameterized in inputs, which are therefore all required before execution. For this reason there is no need for a behavioral part to a goal's choreography in the IRS. Secondly, a WSMO Web service is viewed as the application of an external deployed service to a particular atomic task. While this requires only the communication of inputs from the user, and return of an output, IRS as a broker may be required to carry out several interactions with the deployed service to reach this output. The prototype of this interaction is stored in the choreography of the service and is called a *client choreography*. This is different from the model of goal choreographies and service choreographies, which need dynamic process mediation in WSMX. Process mediation may be used to form client choreographies when service descriptions are added to the IRS to make deployed services available for new tasks but, like dynamic discovery, this is outside the scope of the current tool.

Data mediation in the IRS is encoded in the wgMediator, which links a goal and Web service and may take one of three forms, each allowing the inputs of the goal to be turned into the inputs required by the Web service, and the outputs provided by the Web service to be turned into the output expected by the goal. Firstly, the IRS model of the ooMediator is extended to allow OCML rules mapping between instances of concepts within the ontologies specified. In this way wgMediators can be linked to ooMediators, including a declarative specification of the data mediation. This is similar to the approach of the abstract mapping language engine described for WSMX, but explicitly attached to the mediator description. The other means to provide data mediation in the IRS are via the service abstraction and the "usesMe-diationService" attribute of WSMO's wgMediator. This can be used either to attach a service which can convert between goal and service inputs, or service and goal outputs, as described above, or to attach a goal which describes the requirements on such a *mediation service*. In the latter case, discovery and selection can be applied recursively so that the link between a goal and a candidate service may depend on the existence of such a mediation service.

The capability-driven selection mechanism provided by IRS-III has recently been extended to encompass trust-based requirements and guarantees [80]. A Web Services Trust Ontology (WSTO) has been built with which WSMO-based descriptions can be extended and a classification-based algorithm is used to discount and rank candidate services according to the "trustworthiness" of their guarantees on certain nonfunctional aspects, such as quality-of-service.

13.1.3 Communication

We previously depicted the IRS architecture as being distributed and composed of three main blocks: the server, the stack of libraries, and the publishing platform. Interactions between components belonging to the same block take place in the same execution environment and are based on direct invocation.[2] As a consequence, supporting this does not require any specific communication infrastructure or machinery. Describing the communication mechanisms implemented in the IRS therefore concerns three interactions.

The first one corresponds to the communications between clients and the IRS as supported by the libraries stack. The stack of libraries provides access to the main IRS functionality like the manipulation of knowledge models or the invocation of goals. The communication between the Java libraries and the IRS is centralized in the IRS-III API, which provides the unique access point to the IRS server as a set of methods that manipulate OCML definitions (Fig. 13.1). Additionally it embeds a server which enables run-time monitoring of the IRS server, in order to track the internal processes taking place in the server. Communication between the IRS-III API and the server, both inbound and outbound, is based on SOAP. Each client request/reply interaction is supported by SOAP and a set of fixed XML message formats. Similarly, every activity tracked in the IRS generates events expressed in terms of an events ontology which are subsequently serialized and sent to the monitoring server using SOAP.

The second communication affects the interaction between the IRS server and the publishing platforms. The IRS can currently invoke four different types of remote services: Lisp code, Java code, WSDL Web Services, and Web applications via *GET* requests. The first three types are handled by the appropriate component of the publishing platform, whereas the Web applications are directly invoked by the IRS server for it has built-in HTTP support. The remaining publishing platforms,

---

[2] Note that there is no interaction between publishers.

i.e., Java, WSDL, and Lisp publishing platforms, are external components which communicate with the server via SOAP.

An important aspect of this communication concerns the transition between the semantic world and the syntactic world, usually referred to as lifting and lowering in the Semantic Web Service community. In the IRS this functionality is provided by the invoker. The current implementation of the IRS includes lifting and lowering machinery for dealing with XML-based results. The relevant information for performing the appropriate transformations is stored as a set of Lisp macros which identify the data interchanged, the relevant Semantic Web Service and the corresponding XML element by means of an XPath expression. At run time the invoker retrieves information on how to lift or lower the data and applies it right after receiving the results or right before sending the invocation data, respectively. This way, the data sent to the publisher is always in its syntactic representation, whereas internally the IRS manipulates semantic data.

The final communication takes place between the different publishing platforms and the actual Semantic Web Service being invoked and it is therefore platform-specific. For instance, Lisp code is executed in the Lisp publishing platform; WSDL services are invoked using the protocol specified; Web applications are invoked through HTTP; and Java services are provided by a Java-based Web application deployed on a Tomcat Web server so as to be invocable.

13.1.4 Choreography and Orchestration

As discussed in Sect. 13.1.2, choreography in the IRS model consists of the attachment of client choreographies to Web Services. The choreography engine is applied to execute a client choreography when a Web service is selected in order to meet a goal. Whereas the separation of client and service choreographies, together with dynamic mediation between them, in WSMX allows the parties and communication roles in these choreographies to be implicit, a client choreography implicitly includes communications via the broker and a more sophisticated model of communication is required. The choreography model of IRS is detailed in [61].

The IRS offers two models for orchestrations attached to Web service descriptions. In both cases these models are executable and derive the required atomic behavior from a complex interaction between some number of other artifacts.

In the simple case, described in [36], control flow primitives are used to link together goals to form a complex behavior. ggMediators are used to form the data flow between these goals; when a ggMediator connects one goal to another, the input will be taken from the source goal and communicated to whichever input of the target goal matches the ggMediator's output. This may involve data mediation as described for wgMediators above. One consequence of this model is that a given goal may only be instantiated once per orchestration or the data flow is ambiguous. It is also not permitted to directly specify another Web service to be applied during the orchestration.

Both of the stated deficiencies of the simple orchestration model are addressed in the Cashew orchestration model [158]. Here both goals and Web Services can be specified in prototypical *performances*, which are the units of behavior composed in a hierarchical control flow decomposition. Data flow is unambiguously specified by a new type of mediator between performances, named a ppMediator. As described for wgMediators and ggMediators, the usual attributes may be used to specify data mediation. The second advantage of the Cashew model is the ability to represent this model in UML activity diagrams, and work has been carried out on composition in this model with execution via the Cashew orchestration implementation [158].

13.2 Other WSMO-Compatible Tools

In this section we present other tools that fit into the SESA but exist and are developed separately from WSMX and the IRS.

13.2.1 Discovery

Glue is a WSMO-compliant discovery engine produced by Cefriel [59]. Like the IRS it uses wgMediators to capture a connection between goals and Web Services and relies on a non-WSML model wherein both goal templates and goal instances may be described. Furthermore, metaclasses are used to form "classes of goals" to relate goals and aid in discovery. Glue uses Flora-2 [218] to provide reasoning over this model.

Another aspect to discovery that has been implemented separately from, but in a compatible manner with, WSMX concerns quality of service (QoS). A QoS-aware discovery component has been developed at Ecole Polytechnique Fédérale de Lausanne which codifies a description of nonfunctional service requirements and characteristics, respectively, in the "nonfunctional properties" attributes of WSMO goals and Web Services. The KAON reasoning engine [151] is used to reason over these descriptions and find those Web Services that meet the requirements expressed in the goal.

13.2.2 Composition

ILog Composer

A workflow composition tool for UML activity diagram based workflow models has been developed by ILog, based on their configurator tool, in cooperation with Ecole Supérieure d'Ingénieurs de Luminy [8]. During the DIP project[3] this composer tool was adapted and applied to WSMO-based models. A three-level framework was defined for choreography and orchestration wherein models in the Cashew workflow language could be translated into activity diagrams for composition and then back to Cashew or into abstract state machines for execution in IRS or WSMX, respectively [158]. Practically this means that from an abstract composition of goals

---

[3] http://dip.semanticweb.org

a new Web service description that contains an orchestration over Web Services that meet those goals can be automatically derived by configuration, and based on the choreographies of the candidate Web Services.

13.3 Tools Based on OWL-S

OWL-S,[4] formerly DAML-S, is an ontology for the description of Semantic Web Services now expressed in the Web Ontology Language (OWL),[5] which predates WSMO. A service description is divided into three parts:

1. The **service profile** describes "what the service does" in terms of inputs, outputs, preconditions, and effects (IOPEs).
2. The **service grounding** describes how the service can be accessed, usually by grounding to WSDL.
3. The **service model** describes "how a service works" in terms of a process model that may describe a complex behaviour over underlying services.

A comparison of the description of services using OWL-S and WSMO was undertaken in [131] and it is not the intention here to reproduce this work, but only to consider tool support. Rather than define and populate an architecture for complete tool support of Semantic Web Services using OWL-S, as has been the aim of SESA and WSMX, respectively, the community has produced a number of tools that play different roles. Consequently this section will use to SESA as the basis to survey and compare OWL-S tools.

13.3.1 Reasoning

OWL-S is an OWL ontology like any other and therefore reasoning support is provided primarily by OWL reasoners. OWL itself is divided into three sublanguages of increasing expressivity: OWL Lite, OWL DL, and OWL Full. OWL Full has no decidable reasoning and OWL Lite provides supports for only simple constraints over classification hierarchies; therefore, reasoner implementation concentrates on OWL DL, which is based in description logics. Pellet [196] and FaCT/FaCT++ [208] are two such OWL DL reasoners based on tableaux algorithms. Since, however, OWL DL is not sufficiently expressive in most cases to define all parts of the user models, for instance, defining conditions within the process model, rule-oriented extensions, or an embedding of another rule language such as SWRL,[6] are used for this purpose [167]. Consequently reasoners capable of dealing with OWL DL and rules, such as Racer [94] and Kaon2 [151], are often applied. An advantage of the OWL-S model over the expression of WSMO in WSML is that, like WSMO's expression in OCML, the same reasoner can be used to carry out metareasoning about the model and therefore the metamodel itself can be used in user models.

---

[4] http://www.daml.org/services/owl-s
[5] http://www.w3.org/TR/owl-features
[6] http://www.w3.org/Submission/SWRL

13.3.2 Discovery

The process underlying discovery in OWL-S is usually referred to as match-making and heavily relies on the explicit specification of inputs and outputs. The ontological relationships between the inputs and outputs (I/Os) of a "template" – which in this sense plays the role of a WSMO goal, but is not explicitly conceptualized as such – and a candidate service are compared. A set of five "filters" classify the structural relationships that are accepted between the template and candidate I/Os. Klush et al. [125] detailed such a matchmaker, OWLS-MX, that implements such an algorithm and combines it with syntactic match to cover those occassions when semantic matchmaking fails, for instance, when two ontologies are disjoint since there is no means for mediation to map these. The survey in this paper also affirms that there are no implementations that both offer this I/O-based approach and also consider the preconditions and effects, completing the so-called IOPE-based matchmaking that was envisioned for OWL-S. We also note that there exists no discovery approach for OWL-S that also covers the behaviour of a service, since they are simply considered to be atomic in the model.

It is worth noting one further discovery engine for OWL-S which provides an advantage not considered in the SESA. Srinivasan et al. [201] considered the addition of the OWL-S model to Universal Description, Discovery, and Integration (UDDI) descriptions and the extension of an open-source UDDI engine, jUDDI, to support semantic matchmaking based on these descriptions.

13.3.3 Choreography and Orchestration

The OWL-S model fundamentally assumes that "services" are invoked as atomic actions and therefore no model of choreography is contained. On the other hand, the *process model* allows services to be attached either to an atomic process, which is usually grounded to a WSDL operation, or to a composite process. The process model allows for a hierarchical control-flow oriented decomposition of composite processes, ultimately producing some ordering over atomic processes. When such a service is to be executed, the OWL-S virtual machine [167], formerly the DAML-S virtual machine, executes the atomic processes up to completion of the composite process description, returning the outputs just as if the invocation had been atomically carried out. In evaluating a composite process model, the virtual machine needs access to OWL DL and SWRL reasoning and this is provided by Racer [94]. In SESA terms, then, the OWL-S virtual machine fulfills the basic role of an orchestration engine, but OWL-S has no support from a choreography engine.

13.3.4 Mediation

The OWL-S model, in contrast to WSMO, provides no first-class support for mediators. Data mediation services can, of course, be described using the provision for other services. There are two notable approaches considering data mediation explicitly in OWL-S: Paolucci et al. [169] considered exactly this embedding of WSMO's mediator model into OWL-S, whereas work related to that of Szomszor et al. [206] considers mediation services as "shims," which mix, rather than isolate, the syntactic and semantic representations of data in order to efficiently apply mediation at the syntactic level. Since, as stated above, the OWL-S model treats services as invoked atomically and without choreographies, there is no notion of automated process mediation in OWL-S. If the interaction between two services requires process mediation this must be carried out as part of a composite process, though the process model has deficiencies even in this regard owing to its notion of atomic service interaction [157].

13.3.5 Composition

A great deal of work in automated service composition has been carried out in OWL-S, not least since its abstraction of service interactions to atomic ones and its simple model of composite processes are a good fit to existing techniques. Much work has been carried out using artificial intelligence planning-based techniques, for instance, resulting from [217]. A recent tool which considers the need to apply replanning during the execution of a composite service is described in [126].

13.4 METEOR-S

The METEOR-S project[7] carried out at the LSDIS Laboratory at the University of Georgia, aims to define semantics for the complete life cycle of Semantic Web processes, encompassing the annotation, discovery, composition, and enactment of Web Services. The foremost distinguishing characteristic of the research undertaken in the METEOR-S project is the strong coupling with existing Web Services standards [198]. In fact, the philosophy of METEOR-S is to incrementally extend pre-existing standards with semantics so as to better support the discovery, composition, and enactment of Web Services. This contrasts with the rest of the approaches presented in this book, which are based on the creation of brand-new languages or formalisms mostly decoupled from existing standards.

So far the METEOR-S project has focussed on the semantic annotation of Web Services, on the semantics-based discovery of Web Services, and on their composition, which also encompasses data mediation. In the remainder of this section we will focus on the specific approaches adopted in METEOR-S for each of these research topics. First, we will present, the METEOR-S Web Service Annotation Framework (MWSAF) [175] paying special attention to the language it builds upon, namely, Web Service Semantics (WSDL-S) [198] and its successor Semantic Annotations for WSDL and XML Schema (SAWSDL) [70]. Second, we will focus on the METEOR-S Web Service Discovery Infrastructure (MWSDI) [212]. Next, we will describe the METEOR-S approach to data mediation [155] and finally we will focus on the METEOR-S Web Service Composition Framework (MWSCF) [197].

---

[7] http://lsdis.cs.uga.edu/projects/meteor-s/

13.4.1 Semantic Annotation

The METEOR-S project comprises the so-called MWSAF [175], a framework for the semiautomatic annotation of Web Services. These annotations address four different aspects of Web Services's semantics. First of all, MWSAF supports including annotations about the semantics of the inputs and the outputs of Web Services. Secondly, the annotation framework supports the definition of functional semantics, i.e., what the service does. Thirdly, MWSAF allows the inclusion of execution semantics to support verification of the correctness of the execution of Web Services. Finally, the framework supports inclusion of information regarding the quality of service, such as performance or costs associated to the execution of Web Services.

Initial research on the framework was devoted to supporting the semiautomatic annotation of the XML Schema part of Web Services definitions. This work is based on the transformation of both XML Schema and ontologies into a common representation format called SchemaGraph [175] in order to facilitate the matching between both models. Once the ontologies and XML Schema have been translated into this common representation, a set of matching algorithms can be applied to (semi) automatically enhance the syntactic definitions with semantic annotations.

In a nutshell, the matching algorithm computes a "match score" between each element of the WSDL SchemaGraph and the ontology SchemaGraph. This score takes into account the linguistic and the structural similarity. After all the match scores have been computed, the "best" matching element is chosen by taking into account both the match score and the specificity of the concepts. Finally, a global matching average is computed to help in selecting the best overall match between Web Services and ontologies. Further details about the algorithm can be found in [175].

The MWSAF is composed of three main components: an ontology store, the matcher library, and a translator library. The first component stores the ontologies that will be used for annotating the Web Services. The matcher library provides different algorithm implementations for linguistic and structural matching between concepts and elements of Web Services . Finally the translator library consists of the programs used for generating the SchemaGraph representation for ontologies and Web Services.

The MWSAF assists users in annotating Web Services by browsing and computing the concordance between domain models and elements of Web Services . The last step in the annotation process is their representation for future reuse for automated processing. To cater for this the METEOR-S project makes use of WSDL-S, which we present in more detail in the following section.

WSDL-S and SAWSDL

WSDL-S was proposed as a member submission to the W3C in November 2005 between the LSDIS Laboratory and IBM [5]. In line with the philosophy of the METEOR-S project, WSDL-S is a lightweight approach to associating semantic annotations with Web Services which builds upon preexisting standards. Using the extensibility of WSDL, one can add semantic annotations in the form of URI references to external models to the interface, operation, and message constructs. WSDL-S is independent of the language used for defining the semantic models and explicitly contemplates the possibility of using WSML, OWL, and UML as potential candidates [5].

WSDL-S provides a set of extension attributes and elements for associating the semantic annotations. The extension attribute **modelReference** allows one to specify associations between a WSDL entity and a concept in a semantic model. This extension can be used for annotating XML Schema complex types and elements, WSDL operations, and the extension elements *precondition* and *effect*, which will are described below.

The **schemaMapping** extension attribute can be used for specifying mechanisms for handling structural differences between XML Schema elements and complex types and their corresponding semantic model concepts. These annotations can then be used for what we refer to as lifting and lowering of execution data (i.e., transforming syntactic data into its semantic counterpart, and vice versa).

WSDL-S defines two new child elements for the operation element, namely, **precondition** and **effect**. These elements allow one to define the conditions that must hold before executing an operation and the effects the execution would have. This information is typically to be used for discovering suitable Web Services. Finally, WSDL-S allows one to use the **category** extension attribute on the interface element in order to define categorization information for publishing Web Services in registries such as UDDI.

Recently the WSDL-S proposal was superseded by SAWSDL [70], which is a W3C Recommendation. SAWSDL is a restricted and homogenized version of WSDL-S in which annotations like preconditions and effects have not been explicitly contemplated since there is no current agreement about them in the Semantic Web Services community. It is worth noting, however, that SAWSDL does not preclude the use of these types of annotations as illustrated in the usage guide generated by the SAWSDL Working Group [7].

The main differences between SAWSDL and WSDL-S are the fact that *precondition* and *effect* have been discarded. *Category* has been replaced by the more general *modelReference* extension attribute which in SAWSDL can be used to annotate XML Schema complex type definitions, simple type definitions, element declarations, and attribute declarations as well as WSDL interfaces, operations, and faults. Finally, *schemaMapping* has been decomposed into two different extension attributes, namely, **liftingSchemaMapping** and **loweringSchemaMapping**, so as to specifically identify the type of transformation.

13.4.2 Discovery

The UDDI specification and the Universal Business Registry (UBR) are the main industrial efforts towards the automation of the discovery of Web Services. The METEOR-S Web Services Discovery Infrastructure (MWSDI) [212] attempts to enhance existing Web Services discovery infrastructure by using semantics. MWSDI is a scalable infrastructure for the semantics-based publication and discovery of Web Services.

MWSDI aims to provide unified access to a large number of third-party registries. Thus, in order to provide a scalable and flexible infrastructure it has been implemented using peer-to-peer (P2P) computing techniques. It is based on a four-layered architecture which includes a data layer, a communications layer, an operator services layer, and a semantic specification layer. The data layer consists of the Web Services registries and is based on UDDI. The communications layer is the P2P infrastructure, which is based on JXTA. The operator services layer provides the semantic discovery and publication of Web Services. Finally, the semantic specification layer enhances the framework with semantics.

MWSDI uses semantics for two purposes. Firstly, it uses the so-called *registries ontology* which stores registry information, maintains relationships between domains within MWSDI, and associates registries to them. This ontology stores mappings between registries and domains so that finding Web Services for a specific domain can be directed to the appropriate registries. Additionally the registries ontology captures relationships between registries so that searches can be made more selective on the basis of these relationships.

Secondly, MWSDI envisions including domain-specific ontologies for registries, so that Web Services can be annotated by mapping inputs and outputs to existing domain ontologies. The purpose of defining these mappings is to enable semantic discovery by allowing users to express their requirements as service templates which are expressed using concepts from the same ontology.

The semantic publication of services in MWSDI registries uses UDDI tModels for registering the domain ontologies and CategoryBags for categorizing WSDL entities according to one or more tModels. MWSDI provides both a manual and a semiautomatic mechanism for defining the mappings between WSDL elements and the concepts in the domain ontologies [212].

13.4.3 Mediation

METEOR-S deals with the inherent heterogeneity between messages exchanged by Web Services by mapping inputs and outputs of services to conceptual models. These mappings are mainly supported by means of WSDL-S or SAWSDL annotations (see Sect. 13.4.1) [155]. In particular, as we previously introduced, WSDL-S provides *schemaMapping* annotations and SAWSDL decouples these into liftingSchemaMapping and loweringSchemaMapping, where lifting is the process that transforms syntactic information into semantic data and lowering is the inverse process.[8]

Both WSDL-S and SAWSDL uniquely provide placeholders for identifying the transformations to be used for lifting and lowering data. They do so by means of URIs which point to transformation definitions. Nothing is prescribed with respect to

---

[8] METEOR-S refers to lifting and lowering as *upcasting* and *downcasting*, respectively. We here use the terminology adopted in SEE, which also coincides with the one in SAWSDL.

the transformation mechanism. Thus, the approach adopted in METEOR-S is agnostic to the mapping representation language employed. This provides total flexibility but also requires ad hoc manipulation by the execution environment at run time.

Most of the research on data mediation in METEOR-S has been devoted to identifying, categorizing, and analyzing the types of heterogeneity that can typically arise, and to providing a specific implementation based on XQuery and XSLT. In summary, message-level heterogeneity has roughly been classified (borrowing from previous work federated databases) into domain-level incompatibilities, entity definition mismatches, and differences on the level of abstraction adopted when defining concepts (see [155] for further details).

The current implementation of data mediation techniques in METEOR-S uses WSDL-S annotations pointing to mappings represented in XQuery and XSLT, which are assumed to be powerful enough in most cases. At run time these mappings are interpreted by the METEOR-S middleware in order to perform the appropriate transformations of the data exchanged between Web Services [155]. No research has, however, been devoted to the creation of a fully fledged framework capable of dealing with more complex situations where XQuery and XSLT are not convenient or even suitable, e.g., manipulation of diverse serializations of the same information in RDF/RDF Schema.

13.4.4 Composition

Semantic composition of Web Services in METEOR-S is supported by the so-called METEOR-S Web Service Composition Framework (MWSCF) [197]. In a nutshell, the composition framework aims to increase the flexibility of the composition of Web Services by making use of semantic process templates. Semantic process templates define processes in terms of semantically defined activities. Using these semantic process templates, one can generate executable processes by binding the semantically defined activities to concrete Web Services that conform to the activity specification.

MWSCF is composed of four components: the process builder, the discovery infrastructure (see Sect. 13.4.2), XML repositories, and the process-execution engine. The process builder includes a graphical user interface for defining semantic process templates and a process generator. The process generator retrieves ontologies, activity interfaces, and process templates from the XML repositories and uses MWSDI for discovering suitable Web Services, in order to transform the templates into executable processes. The executable process definitions can then be handed to the process-execution engine for the actual execution of the composition of Web Services.

In MWSCF semantic process templates are basically a set of activities connected by means of BPEL control-flow constructs. Activities can be defined with a varying degree of flexibility by using a specific Web service implementation, a Web service interface, or a semantic activity template. Implementations of specific Web Services can be specified for static compositions. Web service interfaces can be applied to gain some flexibility, allowing diverse implementations of the same interface to be inter-changeably executed. Finally, semantic activity templates provide a greater degree of flexibility by defining activities semantically in terms of their inputs, outputs, and functional semantics, e.g., preconditions and effects.

The creation of an executable process is a semiautomated process performed at design time where the user is assisted in refining the template with concrete Web Services and dataflow. In order to do so, Web Services that implement the specified Web service interfaces are retrieved from the XML repository and the MWSDI is used for discovering suitable services when semantic activity templates have been specified. After all the activities have been replaced by concrete Web Services, the user can map the outputs of Web Services to the inputs of other services in order to define the process dataflow. Once the explicit dataflow has been defined, the process generator creates the executable representation, which is a BPEL4WS process that can be executed in any BPEL execution engine.

14

Conclusions and Outlook

In the course of this book we have illustrated how to enable Semantic Web Services by means of Semantically Enabled Service-oriented Architectures (SESAs). Currently there is little or no demand for dynamic or scalable Service-Oriented Architectures (SOAs). Not only are the few SOAs in production relatively small, and thus do not yet pose scalability problems, but also current technologies are inadequate for service discovery, negotiation, adaptation, and composition. In the real (nonautomated) world, business transactions are governed by legal, regulatory, financial, tax, and other agreements or obligations. Partners who wish to automate business transactions do so after defining the terms by which automated actions must correspond to the relevant governance. At the same time, these partners establish terms of recourse or remuneration in the case of failures. Such agreements, referenced above as nonfunctional requirements, are a long way from being dynamically discovered, selected, and enacted.

14.1 Why SOA?

Web Services have become another milestone towards providing interoperability among distributed and independent software systems. But one major problem has remained unresolved. Although there is an abundance of technologies which theoretically should enable interoperability for disperse systems, from the practical perspective the process of dynamic creation of ad hoc interactions between companies, as envision by Web Services, is still fiction. So it is the interoperability issue, not the communication one, which has to be addressed next to enable dynamic collaboration of independent software entities on the Internet. Web service specifications based on commonly agreed standards and implemented in .NET and J2EE frameworks are struggling to overcome existing limitations of Web architecture. Data that is exchanged between Web servers and Web browsers remains solely dedicated for human consumption, and cannot be readily processed by automatic software agents. Similarly Web Services and their underlying XML technology still deal mainly with infrastructure, syntax, and basic representational issues, but not with the meaning of data and the processes that are used by particular systems. Adding semantics to the existing Web Services technologies is a fundamental requirement if we want to deliver workable integration solutions for the next Web generation.

The most important issue in today's design of software architectures is to satisfy increasing software complexity as well as new IT needs, such as the need to respond quickly to new requirements of businesses, the need to continually reduce the cost of IT, or the ability to integrate legacy and new emerging business information systems. In the current IT enterprise settings, introducing a new product or service and integrating multiple services and systems present unpredicted costs, delays, and difficulty. Existing IT systems consist of a patchwork of legacy products, monolithic off-shelf applications, and proprietary integration. It is even reality today that in many cases users on "spinning chairs" manually reenter data from one system to another within the same organization. The past and existing efforts in Enterprise Application Integration (EAI) do not represent successful and flexible solutions. Several studies showed that EAI projects are lengthy and the majority of these efforts are late and over budget. It is mainly costs, proprietary solutions, and tightly coupled interfaces that make EAI expensive and inflexible.

Commercial successes of SOAs are not yet apparent because the underlying technologies such as those presented in this book are still in their infancy. Available specifications and technologies will have to go through the lengthy standardization process and the real effort of consequent prototype developments, before the first commercial solutions are available on the market. There is widespread agreement and recognition that dynamic interoperability on the Internet is only possible if resources are semantically described. SESA and its underlying technologies based on Semantic Execution Environment (SEE), Web Service Modeling Ontology (WSMO), Web Service Modeling Language (WSML), and Web Service Execution Environment (WSMX) with their related specifications are the principal candidates to become the backbone of the next Web generation, enabling software entities to dynamically interoperate over the Internet.

SOA solutions are the next evolutionary step in software architectures. SOA is an IT architecture in which functions are defined as independent services with well-defined, invocable interfaces. SOA will enable cost-effective integration as well as bring flexibility to business processes. In line with SOA principles, several standards have been developed and are currently emerging in IT environments. In particular, Web Services technology provides a means to publish services in registries, describing their interfaces using the Web Service Description Language (WSDL) and exchanging requests and messages over a network using SOAP. The Business Process Execution Language (BPEL) allows composition of services into complex processes as well as their execution. Although Web Services technologies have added a new value to the current IT environments with regard to the integration of distributed software components using Web standards, they cover mainly characteristics of syntactic interoperability. With respect to a large number of services that will exist in IT environments in the interenterprise and intraenterprise integration settings based on SOA, the problems of service discovery or selection of the best services conforming to the user's needs, as well as resolving heterogeneity in services capabilities and interfaces will again be a lengthy and costly process.

As SOA technology and deployments mature over the next few years, especially scalability will become a significant issue. SOAs of large companies (for example, Verizon) currently account for less than 1% of their transactions. Implementing only one fourth of a large enterprise in a SOA would lead to many millions of simple and composite services and billions of transactions per day. Customer-facing services represent less than half of the systems of big enterprises. Supply chain, human resources, and internal operations often dwarf employee-facing systems in size and complexity. Let us imagine the number of services required to operate even 25% of such enterprises, the number of potential transactions, and then how these enterprises might work with partners via SOA-based information systems. A few large enterprises would alone scale beyond billions of services and transactions. Now let us consider how such business would operate using a SOA with no dynamic service discovery, selection, negotiation, adaptation, and composition. Manual intervention would be required to complete or approve the results of those actions. SESA provides an appealing infrastructure to deal with these kinds of issues.

14.2 Future Work

This book has outlined a comprehensive framework that integrates two complimentary and revolutionary technical advances, SOAs and the Semantic Web, into a single computing architecture that we call Semantically Enabled Service-oriented Architecture (SESA). While SOA is widely acknowledged for its potential to revolutionize the world of computing, this success is dependent on resolving two fundamental challenges that SOA does not address, namely, integration, and search or mediation. In a service-oriented world, millions of services must be discovered and selected on the basis of requirements, then orchestrated and adapted or integrated. SOA depends on but does not address either search or integration.

WSMO in its current state formalizes all the main principles that underlie our work and is now very mature. That said, we do not expect fundamental changes to the conceptual model anymore and believe that it is in suitable shape to tackle all of the main problems that we want to address in such a framework. The effort in terms of the SEE architecture, concrete language of WSML, or tools is still more dynamic. Most of the ongoing architectural effort on the WSMX has been moved to the Semantic Execution Environment Technical Committee (SEE TC) of OASIS. For the individual WSMX components outlined in this book, there is currently major progress and we have probably not been able to cover all the latest developments. Still, we can predict that we shall be able to choose between several alternative industrial-strength implementations and strategies for every task and component. Future work on WSML will include the application of the language to various use cases and the improvement of WSML tools, such as editors and reasoners (see Chap. 7).

Standardization organizations such as OASIS, OMG, and W3C have established several groups or technical committees to develop and standardize SOA and the SESA vision presented in this book. While some of these groups, such as SEE TC, directly focus on the development of SESA, other groups are working on other important related aspects. Although activities towards standardizing an overall framework for Semantic Web Services have been stalled by the W3C for the moment, other standardization groups have in the meantime established several working groups or technical committees to develop and standardize particular aspects of Semantic Web Service technologies, as presented in this book. While the SEE TC of OASIS focuses on the development of a reference execution environment for a SESA, several other groups in OASIS such as SOA Reference Model Technical Commitee (RM TC), SOA Adoption Blueprints Technical Commitee, or Web Services Resource Framework (WSRF) are working on other related aspects.

Summarizing, while SOAs are widely accepted as the next generation of computing to which most software vendors are committed, standards are still evolving. In recent years, the number and the complexity of SOA standard proposals has grown enormously, with few reference technologies. Some standards already exist, while others are scheduled for development and release within OASIS, OMG, and W3C.

14.3 Commercialization

Even when a so-called standard is in place, this is only a prerequisite for the success of a technology, and is not a guarantee by any means. The eventual criterion for success that Semantic Web Service technology has to face will be industrial adoption. While scalability and precision are the focus of current efforts related to Web Services and SOAs, the more fundamental goal of enabling Semantic Web Services is at the core of our research interests, as outlined in this book.

The challenge for the research and industrial communities over the next few years will be to collaboratively realize the concepts described in this book. This challenge involves two ongoing and complementary paradigm shifts in computing: (1) the movement to service orientation and (2) the use of semantic technologies and ontologies in industrial-scale infrastructures and applications. Achieving such a goal will require collaboration not only within the research community, but also among the global players in industry. To achieve what we consider true realization – defined not in terms of purely research prototypes but in terms of industrial-scale production applications – collaboration between the research and industrial communities is essential. In industry, SOA, or a SOA refinement, is recognized not only as the next generation of computing, but also as the technology that will largely replace or encapsulate current technologies. This will require the research community to understand the state and nature of the relevant industrial problems, products, and solutions. It will require industry to understand the relevant challenges and opportunities to which the research community can contribute. Finally, it will require researchers to collaborate with industry so that research results can be achieved and then integrated into industrial solutions.

References

1. Business process trends. http://www.bptrends.com/.
2. WSMO4J – an API and a reference implementation for building Semantic Web Services applications compliant with WSMO. http://wsmo4j.sourceforge.net.
3. ITU-T Recommendation H.323, 1999.
4. S. Abiteboul, R. Hull, and V. Vianu. *Foundations of Databases*. Addison-Wesley, 1995.
5. R. Akkiraju, J. Farrell, J. Miller, M. Nagarajan, M.-T. Schmidt, A. Sheth, and K. Verma. Web Service Semantics – WSDL-S. http://www.w3.org/Submission/WSDL-S/, Nov 2005. W3C Member Submission.
6. R. Akkiraju, R. Goodwin, P. Doshi, and S. Roeder. A method for semantically enhancing the service discovery capabilities of UDDI. In S. Kambhampati and C. A. Knoblock, editors, *Proceedings of the IJCAI-03 Workshop on Information Integration on the Web (IIWeb-03)*, pages 87–92, 2003.
7. R. Akkiraju and B. Sapkota. Semantic annotations for WSDL and XML Schema – usage guide. http://www.w3.org/TR/sawsdl-guide/, Jan 2007. Working Group Note.
8. P. Albert, L. Henocque, and M. Kleiner. Configuration-based workflow composition. In *Proceedings of IEEE International Conference on Web Services (ICWS'05)*, pages 285–292. IEEE Computer Society, 2005.
9. F. Baader, A. Borgida, and D. McGuinness. Matching in description logics: preliminary results. In M.-L. Mugnier and M. Chein, editors, *Proceedings of the Sixth International Conference on Conceptual Structures (ICCS-98)*, volume 1453 of *Lecture Notes in Computer Science*, pages 15–34, Montpelier, France, 1998. Springer, Berlin.
10. F. Baader, D. Calvanese, D. L. McGuinness, D. Nardi, and P. F. Patel-Schneider, editors. *The Description Logic Handbook*. Cambridge University Press, 2003.
11. F. Baader, R. Küsters, and R. Molitor. Rewriting concepts using terminologies. In A. G. Cohn, F. Giunchiglia, and B. Selman, editors, *Proceedings of the Seventh International Conference on Knowledge Representation and Reasoning (KR2000)*, pages 297–308, San Francisco, CA, 2000. Morgan Kaufmann.
12. F. Baader and P. Narendran. Unification of concept terms in description logics. In H. Prade, editor, *Proceedings of the 13th European Conference on Artificial Intelligence (ECAI-98)*, pages 331–335. Wiley, New York, 1998.
13. D. Bachlechner, K. Siorpaes, H. Lausen, and D. Fensel. Web service discovery - a reality check. In *3rd European Semantic Web Conference*, 2006.

14. Z. Baida, J. Gordijn, B. Omelayenko, and H. Akkermans. A shared service terminology for online service provisioning. In *ICEC04*, Delft, The Netherlands, 2004.

15. D. Beckett. RDF/XML syntax specification (revised). Recommendation 10 February 2004, W3C, 2004.

16. T. Bellwood, L. Clément, D. Ehnebuske, A. Hately, M. Hondo, Y. Husband, K. Januszewski, S. Lee, B. McKee, J. Munter, and C. von Riegen. UDDI version 3.0, Jul 2002.

17. T. Berners-Lee. The World Wide Web: past, present and future. http://www.w3.org/people/berners-lee/1996/ppf.html. Technical report, Aug 1996.

18. T. Berners-Lee. Web design issues – architectural and philosophical points. http://www.w3.org/designissues/, 1997.

19. T. Berners-Lee. *Weaving the Web*. 2000.

20. T. Berners-Lee. How it all started. http://www.w3.org/2004/talks/w3c10-howitallstarted/, Dec 2004.

21. T. Berners-Lee, R. Fielding, and L. Masinter. Uniform resource identifiers (URI): generic syntax. Standard RFC 3986, Internet Engineering Task Force, 2005.

22. T. Berners-Lee, J. Hendler, and O. Lassila. The Semantic Web. *Scientific American*, 284(5):34–43, May 2001. http://www.sciam.com/article.cfm?articleID=00048144-10D2-1C70-84A9809EC588EF21&ref=sciam.

23. P. V. Biron and A. Malhotra. XML Schema part 2: Datatypes, second edition, 2004.

24. D. Booth, H. Haas, F. McCabe, E. Newcomer, M. Champion, C. Ferris, and D. Orchard. Web service architecture. http://www.w3.org/TR/ws-arch/, W3C, Working Notes, 2003/2004.

25. E. Börger and R. Stärk. *Abstract State Machines: A Method for High-Level System Design and Analysis*. Springer, Berlin, 2003.

26. A. Borgida, R. J. Brachman, D. L. McGuinness, and L. A. Resnick. Classic: A structural data model for objects. In *Proceedings of the 1989 ACM SIGMOD International Conference on Management of Data*, pages 59–67, 1989.

27. R. J. Brachman and J. G. Schmolze. An overview of the KL-ONE knowledge representation system. *Cognitive Science*, 9(2):171–216, 1985.

28. T. Bray, J. Paoli, C. M. Sperberg-McQueen, E. Maler, F. Yergeau, and J. Cowan. Extensible Markup Language (XML) 1.1, second edition. Recommendation 16 August 2006, W3C, 2006.

29. D. Brickley and R. V. Guha. RDF vocabulary description language 1.0: RDF Schema. Recommendation 10 February 2004, W3C, 2004.

30. S. Burbeck. The tao of e-businnes services. http://www-128.ibm.com/developerworks/library/ws-tao/, 2000.

31. C. Bussler. Public process inheritance for business-to-business integration. In *Third International Workshop, TES 2002. Hong Kong, China*, 2002.

32. C. Bussler. *B2B Integration*. Springer, Berlin, June 2003.

33. C. Bussler. The role of Semantic Web technology in Enterprise Application Integration. *Bulletin of the Technical Committee on Data Engineering*, 2(4), 2003.

34. C. Bussler. A minimal triple space computing architecture. In *Proceedings of the 2nd WSMO Implementation Workshop (WIW)*, Innsbruck, Austria, Jun 2005.

35. C. Bussler, E. Cimpian, J. G. Dieter Fensel, A. Haller, T. Haselwanter, M. Kerrigan, A. Mocan, M. Moran, E. Oren, B. Sapkota, I. Toma, J. Viskova, T. Vitvar, M. Zaremba, and M. Zaremba. Web Service Execution Environment (WSMX). W3C Member Submission, Jun 2005. http://www.w3.org/Submission/WSMX, 2005.

36. L. Cabral, J. Domingue, S. Galizia, A. Gugliotta, B. Norton, V. Tanasescu, and C. Pedrinaci. IRS-III: a broker for Semantic Web Services based applications. In *Proceedings of the 5th International Semantic Web Conference (ISWC)*, Nov 2006.

37. D. Calvanese, G. D. Giancomo, and M. Lenzerini. On the decidability of query containment under constraints. In *Proceedings of the 17th ACM SIGACT SIGMOD SIGART Symposium on Principles of Database Systems (PODS'98)*, pages 149–158, 1998.

38. D. Calvanese, G. D. Giancomo, and M. Y. Vardi. Decidable containment of recursive queries. In *Proceedings of the 9th International Conference on Database Theory (ICDT 2003)*, pages 327–342, 2003.

39. B. Campbell and R. Sparks. Control of service context using SIP request-URI (RFC 3087), Apr 2001.

40. G. D. Caprio and E. Morello. OSA/Parlay lab and experiments. In *Parlay Conference*, 2003.

41. J. Cardoso and A. P. Sheth. Introduction to Semantic Web Services and Web process composition. In *SWSWPC*, pages 1–13, 2004.

42. J. Carroll, C. Bizer, P. Hayes, and P. Stickler. Named graphs. *Journal of Web Semantics*, 4(3), 2005.

43. A. K. Chandra and P. M. Merlin. Optimal implementation of conjunctive queries in relational data bases. In *Conference Record of the Ninth Annual ACM Symposium on Theory of Computing*, pages 77–90, 1977.

44. L. Chung. Non-functional requirements for information systems design. In *Proceedings of the 3rd International Conference on Advanced Information Systems Engineering – CAiSE'91, April 7-11, 1991 Trodheim, Norway*, Lecture Notes in Computer Science, pages 5–30. Springer, Berlin, 1991.

45. E. Cimpian and A. Mocan. Wsmx process mediation based on choreographies. In C. Bussler and A. Haller, editors, *Business Process Management Workshops: BPM 2005 International Workshops, BPI, BPD, ENEI, BPRM, WSCOBPM, BPS, Nancy, France, September 5, 2005. Revised Selected Papers*, volume 3812 of *Lecture Notes in Computer Science*, pages 130 – 143. Springer, Berlin, 2005.

46. M. Crubézy, W. Lu, E. Motta, and M. Musen. Configuring online problem-solving resources with the internet reasoning service. *IEEE Intelligent Systems*, 18(2):34–42, 2003.

47. M. Dahr. *Deductive Databases: Theory and Applications*. Thomson, 1996.

48. E. Dantsin, T. Eiter, G. Gottlob, and A. Voronkov. Complexity and expressive power of logic programming. *ACM Computing Surveys*, 33(3):374–425, 2001.

49. J. de Bruijn, D. Foxvog, and K. Zimmerman. Ontology mediation patterns library. SEKT Project Deliverable D4.3.1, Digital Enterprise Research Institute, University of Innsbruck, 2004.

50. J. de Bruijn and S. Heymans. A semantic framework for language layering in WSML. In *Proceedings of the First International Conference on Web Reasoning and Rule Systems (RR2007)*, pages 103–117, 2007.

51. J. de Bruijn and S. Heymans. WSML ontology semantics. Final Draft D28.3, WSML, 2007.

52. J. de Bruijn, J. Kopecký, and R. Krummenacher. RDF representation of WSML. Final Draft D32v0.1, WSML Working Group, 2006.

53. J. de Bruijn, H. Lausen, R. Krummenacher, A. Polleres, L. Predoiu, M. Kifer, and D. Fensel. The Web Service Modeling Language WSML. Technical report, WSML, 2005. WSML Final Draft D16.1v0.21. http://www.wsmo.org/TR/d16/d16.1/v0.21/.

54. J. de Bruijn, H. Lausen, A. Polleres, and D. Fensel. The Web Service Modeling Language: an overview. In *The 3rd European Semantic Web Conference (ESWC2006)*, Lecture Notes in Computer Science, pages 590–604, Budva, Montenegro, June 2006. Springer, Berlin.

55. J. de Bruijn, A. Polleres, R. Lara, and D. Fensel. OWL⁻. Deliverable d20.1v0.2, WSML, 2004. http://www.wsmo.org/2004/d20/d20.1/v0.2/.

56. J. de Bruijn, A. Polleres, R. Lara, and D. Fensel. OWL Flight. Deliverable d20.3v0.1, WSML, 2004. http://www.wsmo.org/2004/d20/d20.3/v0.1/.

57. J. de Bruijn, A. Polleres, R. Lara, and D. Fensel. OWL DL vs. OWL Flight: conceptual modeling and reasoning on the semantic web. In *Proceedings of the 14th International World Wide Web Conference (WWW2005)*, pages 623–632, 2005.

58. M. Dean and G. Schreiber. OWL Web Ontology Language reference. Recommendation 10 February 2004, W3C, 2004.

59. E. Della Valle, D. Cerizza, and I. Celino. The mediators centric approach to automated Web service discovery of Glue. In *Proceedings of 1st International Workshop on Mediation (MEDIATE 2005)*, 2005.

60. E. W. Dijkstra. Notes on structured programming. Technical report, 1972.

61. J. Domingue, S. Galizia, and L. Cabral. Choreography in IRS III: Coping with heterogeneous interaction patterns in Web Services. In *4th International Semantic Web Conference (ISWC2005), 6th - 10th November*, 2005.

62. X. Dong, A. Y. Halevy, J. Madhavan, E. Nemes, and J. Zhang. Simlarity search for Web Services. In *VLDB*, pages 372–383, 2004.

63. M. Duerst and M. Suignard. Internationalized Resource Identifiers (IRIs). Proposed standard RFC 3987, Internet Engineering Task Force, 2005.

64. S. T. Dumais, G. W. Furnas, T. K. Landauer, S. Deerwester, and R. Harshman. Using latent semantic analysis to improve access to textual information. In *Proceedings of the Conference on Human Factors in Computing Systems CHI'88*, 1988.

65. H. B. Enderton. *A Mathematical Introduction to Logic*. Academic, second edition, 2000.

66. H. Eshuis. *Semantics and Verification of UML Activity Diagrams for Workflow Modelling*. PhD thesis, University of Twente, Twente, The Netherlands, 2002.

67. J. Euzenat, F. Scharffe, and L. Serafini. Specification of the alignment format. Technical report, Knowledge Web Deliverable, 2006.

68. J. Fan and S. Kambhampati. A snapshot of public Web Services. *SIGMOD Record*, 34(1):24–32, 2005.

69. A. Farquhar, R. Fikes, and J. Rice. The ontolingua server: a tool for collaborative ontology construction. In *Proceedings of the Tenth Knowledge Acquisition for Knowledge-Based Systems Workshop*, Banff, Canada, 1996.

70. J. Farrell and H. Lausen. Semantic annotations for WSDL and XML Schema. http://www.w3.org/TR/sawsdl/, Jan 2007. W3C Candidate Recommendation 26 January 2007.

71. C. Fellbaum, editor. *WordNet: An Electronic Lexical Database*. MIT Press, May 1998.

72. D. Fensel. *Ontologies: Silver Bullet for Knowledge Management and Electronic Commerce*. Springer, Berlin, 2001.

73. D. Fensel. Triple space computing: Semantic Web Services based on persistent publication of information. In *Proceedings of the IFIP International Conference on Intelligence in Communication Systems, INTELLCOMM*, Mauritius, Nov 2004.

74. D. Fensel, J. Angele, S. Decker, M. Erdmann, H.-P. Schnurr, R. Studer, and A. Witt. Lessons learned from applying AI to the Web. *International Journal of Cooperative Information Systems*, 9(4):361–382, 2000.

75. D. Fensel and C. Bussler. The Web Service Modeling Framework (WSMF). *Electronic Commerce Research and Applications*, 1(2):113–137, 2002.

76. D. Fensel, C. Bussler, Y. Ding, V. Kartseva, M. Klein, M. Korotkiy, B. OmelayenkoS, and R. Siebes. Semantic Web application areas. In *Proceedings of the 7th International Workshop on Applications of Natural Language to Information Systems, Stockholm - Sweden*, 2002.

77. D. Fensel, H. Lausen, A. Polleres, J. de Bruijn, M. Stollberg, D. Roman, and J. Domingue. *Enabling Semantic Web Services – The Web Service Modeling Ontology*. Springer, Berlin, 2006.

78. D. Fensel, E. Motta, F. van Harmelen, V. R. Benjamins, M. Crubezy, S. Decker, M. Gaspari, R. Groenboom, W. Grosso, M. Musen, E. Plaza, G. Schreiber, R. Studer, and B. Wielinga. The unified problem-solving method development language UPML. *Knowledge and Information Systems*, 5(1):83–131, 2003.

79. M. Fitting. *First-Order Logic and Automated Theorem Proving*. Springer, Berlin, second edition, 1996.

80. S. Galizia, A. Gugliotta, and J. Domingue. A trust-based methodology for Web service selection. In *Proceedings of 1st IEEE Conference on Semantic Computing*, 2007.

81. J. Gekas. Web Service Ranking in Service Networks. In *Proceedings of the 3rd European Semantic Web Conference - ESWC'06, June 11-14, 2006, Budva, Montenegro*, 2006.

82. A. V. Gelder, K. Ross, and J. S. Schlipf. Unfounded sets and well-founded semantics for general logic programs. In *Proceedings 7th ACM Symposium on Principles of Database Systems*, pages 221–230, Austin, TX, 1988. ACM.

83. A. V. Gelder, K. Ross, and J. S. Schlipf. The well-founded semantics for general logic programs. *Journal of the ACM*, 38(3):620–650, 1991.

84. D. Gelernter, N. Carriero, and S. Chang. Parallel programming in Linda. In *Proceedings of the International Conference on Parallel Processing*, 1985.

85. M. Gelfond and V. Lifschitz. The stable model semantics for logic programming. In *Proceedings of the 5th International Conference on Logic Programming (ICLP1988)*, pages 1070–1080, 1988.

86. G. Gierz, K. H. Hofmann, K. Keimel, J. D. Lawson, M. Mislove, and D. S. Scott. *Continuous Lattices and Domains*, volume 93 of *Encyclopedia of Mathematics and its Applications*. Cambridge University Press, Cambridge, 2003.

87. J. Grant and D. Beckett. RDF test cases. Recommendation 10 February 2004, W3C, 2004.

88. B. N. Grosof, I. Horrocks, R. Volz, and S. Decker. Description logic programs: Combining logic programs with description logic. In *Proceedings of the International Conference on the World Wide Web (WWW-2003)*, Budapest, Hungary, 2003.

89. I. A. W. Group. IEEE recommended practice for architectural description of software-intensive systems, IEEE Standard 1471-2000. Technical report, IEEE, 2000.

90. T. R. Gruber. A translation approach to portable ontology specifications. *Knowledge Acquisition*, 5(2):199–220, 1993.

91. M. Grüninger and M. Fox. Methodology for the design and evaluation of ontologies. In *Proceedings of IJCAI'95, Workshop on Basic Ontological Issues in Knowledge Sharing*, Montreal, Canada, 1995.

92. N. Guarino. Formal ontology and information systems. In *Formal Ontology in Information Systems, Proceedings of FOIS'98*, pages 3–15, Trento, Italy, Jun 1998. IOS Press.

93. Y. Gurevich. Evolving algebras 1993: Lipari guide. In E. Börger, editor, *Specification and Validation Methods*, pages 9–37. Oxford University Press, Oxford, 1994.

94. V. Haarslev and R. Möller. Racer: A core inference engine for the Semantic Web. In *Proceedings of 2nd International Workshop on Evaluation of Ontology-based Tools (EON 2003)*, pages 27–36, 2003.

95. A. Haller, E. Cimpian, A. Mocan, E. Oren, and C. Bussler. Wsmx – a semantic service-oriented architecture. In *Proceedings of International Conference on Web Services (ICWS 2005), 2005, Orlando, Florida, USA.*, 2005.

96. D. Harel and B. Rumpe. Meaningful modeling: What's the semantics of "semantics"? *Computer*, 37(10):64–72, 2004.

97. A. Harth and S. Decker. Optimized index structures for querying RDF from the Web. In *Proceedings of the 3rd Latin American Web Congress*, Buenos Aires, Argentina, Nov 2005.

98. T. Haselwanter. WSMX core – a JMX microkernel, Bachelor thesis. 2005.

99. T. Haselwanter, M. Zaremba, and M. Zaremba. Enabling components management and dynamic execution semantic in WSMX. In *Proceedings of the 2nd WSMO Implementation Workshop (WIW05)*, Jun 2005.

100. S. Hawke. Rule interchange format working group charter. Technical report, Nov 2005.

101. J. Heflin. OWL Web Ontology Language use cases and requirements. Technical report, Feb 2004.

102. J. Heflin and J. Hendler. Dynamic ontology on the Web. In *Proceedings of the Seventeenth National Conference on Artificial Intelligence (AAAI-2000)*, pages 443–449, Menlo Park, 2000.

103. M. Horridge, N. Drummond, J. Goodwin, A. Rector, R. Stevens, and H. Wang. The Manchester OWL syntax. In *Proceedings of the Workshop OWL: Experiences and Directions (OWLED-2006)*, 2006.

104. I. Horrocks and P. F. Patel-Schneider. Reducing OWL entailment to description logic satisfiability. In *Proceedings of the 2003 International Semantic Web Conference (ISWC 2003)*, Sanibel Island, FL, 2003.

105. I. Horrocks, P. F. Patel-Schneider, H. Boley, S. Tabet, B. Grosof, and M. Dean. SWRL: a Semantic Web Rule Language combining OWL and RuleML. http://www.w3.org/Submission/2004/SUBM-SWRL-20040521/, May 2004.

106. I. Horrocks, P. F. Patel-Schneider, and F. van Harmelen. From SHIQ and RDF to OWL: The making of a Web ontology language. *Journal of Web Semantics*, 1(1):7–26, 2003.

107. U. Hustadt, B. Motik, and U. Sattler. Reasoning for description logics around SHIQ in a resolution framework. Technical Report 3-8-04/04, FZI, 2004.

108. C.-L. Hwang and K. P. Yoon. Multiple attribute decision making: methods and applications. *Lecture Notes in Economics and Mathematical Systems*, Mar 1981.

109. J. Rosenberg et al. SIP: Session Initiation Protocol (RFC 3261), Jun 2002.

110. I. Jacobs. Architecture of the World Wide Web, volume one. Recommendation 15 December 2004, W3C, 2004.

111. C. Kaiser. Down the gopher hole. Mar 2007.

112. M. Keen, A. Acharya, S. Bishop, A. Hopkins, S. M. C. Nott, R. Robinson, J. Adams, and P. Verschueren. *Patterns: Implementing an SOA Using an Enterprise Service Bus*. IBM Red Book, Jul 2004.

113. U. Keller, C. Feier, N. Steinmetz, and H. Lausen. Report on reasoning techniques and prototype implementation for the WSML-Core and WSML-DL languages. Deliverable d1.2v1.0, RW2, 2006. http://rw2.deri.at/pub/d1.2.pdf.

114. U. Keller, R. Lara, H. Lausen, A. Polleres, and D. Fensel. Automatic location of services. In *2nd European Semantic Web Symposium (ESWS2005), 29th May - June 1st*, Heraklion, Crete, 2005.

115. U. Keller, R. Lara, A. Polleres, I. Toma, M. Kiffer, and D. Fensel. Web Service Modeling Ontology – Discovery. Working draft, Digital Enterprise Research Institute (DERI), Oct 2004. http://www.wsmo.org/2004/d5.1/v0.1.

116. U. Keller, H. Lausen, and M. Stollberg. On the semantics of functional descriptions of Web Services. In *Proceedings of the 3rd European Semantic Web Conference (ESWC2006)*, Budva, Montenegro, Jun 2006. Springer, Berlin.

117. M. Kerrigan. WSMOViz: An ontology visualization approach for WSMO. In *10th International Conference on Information Visualization*, 2006.

118. S. Khoshafian and G. Copeland. Object identity. In *Proceedings of the ACM Conference on Object-Oriented Programming, Systems, Languages, and Applications (OOPSLA'86)*, pages 406–416, 1986.

119. M. Kifer. Rules and ontologies in f-logic. In *Reasoning Web*, pages 22–34, 2005.

120. M. Kifer, J. de Bruijn, H. Boley, and D. Fensel. A realistic architecture for the Semantic Web. In *Proceedings of the International Conference on Rules and Rule Markup Languages for the Semantic Web (RuleML-2005)*, number 3791 in Lecture Notes in Computer Science, pages 17–29, Galway, Ireland, Nov 2005. Springer, Berlin.

121. M. Kifer, G. Lausen, and J. Wu. Logical foundations of object-oriented and frame-based languages. *JACM*, 42(4):741–843, 1995.

122. M. Kifer and E. L. Lozinskii. A framework for an efficient implementation of deductive databases. In *Proceedings 6th Advanced Database Symposium*, 1986.

123. S. M. Kim and M.-C. Rosu. A survey of public Web Services. Aug 2004.

124. M. C. A. Klein, J. Broekstra, D. Fensel, F. van Harmelen, and I. Horrocks. Ontologies and schema languages on the Web. In *Spinning the Semantic Web*, pages 95–139. MIT Press, 2003.

125. M. Klusch, B. Fries, and K. Sycara. Automated Semantic Web Service discovery with OWLS-MX. In *Proceedings of 5th International Conference on Autonomous Agents and Multi-Agent Systems (AAMAS)*. ACM Press, 2006.

126. M. Klusch and K.-U. Renner. Fast dynamic re-planning of composite OWL-S services. In *Proceedings of 2006 IEEE/WIC/ACM International Conference on Web Intelligence and Intelligent Agent Technology*, pages 134–137. IEEE Computer Society, 2006.

127. G. Klyne and J. J. Carroll. Resource description framework (RDF): concepts and abstract syntax. Recommendation 10 February 2004, W3C, 2004.

128. J. Kopeck, D. Roman, M. Moran, and A. Mocan. WSMO grounding, WSMO working draft v0.1. http://wsmo.org/tr/d24/d24.2/v0.1/. Technical report, 2005.

129. R. Krummenacher, M. Hepp, A. Polleres, C. Bussler, and D. Fensel. WWW or what is wrong with Web Services. In *Proceedings of the 2005 IEEE European Conference on Web Services (ECOWS 2005)*, Vxj, Sweden, Nov 2005.

130. E. Kühn. Fault-tolerance for communicating multidatabase transactions. In *Proceedings of the 27th Hawaii International Conference on System Sciences (HICSS)*, Wailea, Maui, Hawaii, USA, Jan 1994.

131. R. Lara, D. Roman, A. Polleres, and D. Fensel. A conceptual comparison of WSMO and OWL-S. In *Proceedings of 2004 European Conference on Web Services*, volume 3250 of *Lecture Notes in Computer Science*, pages 254–269. Springer, Berlin, 2004.

132. H. Lausen, J. de Bruijn, A. Polleres, and D. Fensel. WSML – a language framework for Semantic Web Services. In *Proceedings of the W3C Workshop on Rule Languages for Interoperability*, Apr 2005.

133. D. L. Lee, H. Chuang, and K. Seamons. Document ranking and the vector-space model. *IEEE Expert*, 14(2):67–75, 1997.

134. B. M. Leiner, V. G. Cerf, D. D. Clark, R. E. Kahn, L. Kleinrock, J. P. Daniel, C. Lynch, L. G. Roberts, and S. Wolff. A brief history of the internet. Dec 2003.

135. D. B. Lenat. CYC: A large-scale investment in knowledge infrastructure. *Communications of the ACM*, 38(11):33–38, 1995.

136. U. Leser. *Query Planning in Mediator Based Information Systems*. PhD thesis, Technical University Berlin, 2000.

137. A. Y. Levy and M.-C. Rousset. Combining Horn rules and description logics in CARIN. *Artificial Intelligence*, 104:165–209, 1998.

138. L. Li and I. Horrocks. A software framework for matchmaking based on semantic web technology. In *Proceedings of the Twelfth International Conference on World Wide Web*, pages 331–339. ACM Press, 2003. http://www.cs.man.ac.uk/ horrocks/Publications/ download/2003/p815-li.pdf.

139. H. Lin, T. Risch, and T. Katchaounov. Adaptive data mediation over XML data. *Journal of Applied System Studies*, 2001.

140. Y. Liu, A. Ngu, and L. Zheng. QoS computation and policing in dynamic Web service selection, 2004.

141. J. Lloyd and R. Topor. Making Prolog more expressive. *Journal of Logic Programming*, 3:225–240, 1984.

142. A. Malhotra, J. Melon, and N. Walsh. XQuery 1.0 and XPath 2.0 functions and operators. Recommendation 23 January 2007, W3C, 2007. http://www.w3.org/TR/xpath-functions/.

143. M. E. Maron and J. L. Kuhns. On relevance, probabilistic indexing and retrieval. *Journal of the ACM*, 7:216–244, 1960.

144. D. L. McGuinness. Ontologies come of age. In D. Fensel, J. Hendler, H. Lieberman, and W. Wahlster, editors, *Spinning the Semantic Web: Bringing the World Wide Web to Its Full Potential*, chapter 6, pages 171–194. MIT Press, 2003.

145. R. Meersman. Semantic ontology tools in IS design. In *Proceedings of the ISMIS'99 Conference*, Warsaw, Poland, Jun 1999.

146. G. Miller, R. Beckwith, C. Felbaum, D. Gross, and K. Miller. Introduction to wordnet: an on-line lexical database. *International Journal of Lexicography*, 3(4):235–244, 1990.

147. R. Miller, M. Hernandez, L. Haas, L. Yan, C. Ho, R. Fagin, and L. Popa. The Clio project: managing heterogeneity. *SIGMOD Record*, 30(1):78–83, 2001.

148. A. Mocan and E. Cimpian. Mapping creation using a view based approach. In *Proceedings of the 1st International Workshop on Mediation in Semantic Web Services (Mediate 2005)*, Dec 2005.

149. A. Mocan and E. Cimpian. An ontology-based data mediation framework for semantic environments. *International Journal on Semantic Web and Information Systems (IJSWIS)*, 3(2):66–95, 2007.

150. A. Mocan, E. Cimpian, and M. Kerrigan. Formal model for ontology mapping creation. In *Proceedings of the 5th International Semantic Web Conference (ISWC 2006)*, Nov 2006.

151. B. Motik, U. Sattler, and R. Studer. Query answering for OWL-DL with rules. In *Proceedings of 3rd International Semantic Web Conference (IWSC 2004)*, volume 3298 of *Lecture Notes in Computer Science*, pages 549–563, 2004.

152. E. Motta. *Reusable Components for Knowledge Modelling. Case Studies in Parametric Design Problem Solving*, volume 53 of *Frontiers in Artificial Intelligence and Applications*. IOS Press, 1999.

153. E. Motta, J. Domingue, L. Cabral, and M. Gaspari. IRS-II: a framework and infrastructure for Semantic Web Services. In *2nd International Semantic Web Conference*, 2003.

154. M. Murth and J. Riemer. Security and privacy models in triple space. Austrian FIT-IT TSC Project Deliverable D2.1, TUW, 2006.

155. M. Nagarajan, K. Verma, A. P. Sheth, J. Miller, and J. Lathem. Semantic interoperability of Web Services – challenges and experiences. In *ICWS '06: Proceedings of the IEEE International Conference on Web Services (ICWS'06)*, pages 373–382, Washington, DC, USA, 2006. IEEE Computer Society.

156. A. Newell. The knowledge level. *Artificial Intelligence*, 18(1):87–127, 1982.

157. B. Norton. Experiences with OWL-S, directions for service composition. In *Proceedings of OWL: Experiences and Directions Workshop (OWLED-2005)*, 2005.

158. B. Norton, C. Pedrinaci, L. Henocque, and M. Kleiner. 3-level behaviour models for Semantic Web Services. *International Transactions on Systems Science and Applications*, 2007. In press.

159. N. F. Noy and M. A. Musen. Evaluating ontology-mapping tools: requirements and experience. *Workshop on Evaluation of Ontology Tools at EKAW'02(EON2002)*, pages 1–14, 2002.

160. Object Management Group Inc. (OMG). Meta Object Facility (MOF) Specification v1.4, 2002. http://www.omg.org/technology/documents/formal/mof.htm.

161. B. Omelayenko and D. Fensel. An analysis of integration problems of XML-based catalogs for B2B electronic commerce. In *Proceedings of the 9th IFIP 2.6 Working Conference on Database Semantics (DS-9)*, Hong Kong, Apr 2001.

162. B. Omelayenko and D. Fensel. A two-layered integration approach for product information in B2B E-commerce. In *Proceedings of the Second International Conference on Electronic Commerce and Web Technologies (EC WEB-2001)*, Munich, Germany, Sep 2001.

163. T. O'Reilly. What is Web 2.0? Sept 2005. http://www.oreillynet.com/pub/a/oreilly/tim/news/2005/09/30/what-is-web-20.html.

164. J. O'Sullivan, D. Edmond, and A. H. ter Hofstede. Formal description of non-functional service properties. Technical report, Queensland University of Technology, Brisbane, 2005. http://www.service-description.com/.

165. L. Page, S. Brin, R. Motwani, and T. Winograd. The PageRank citation ranking: bringing order to the Web. Technical report, Stanford Digital Library Technologies Project, 1998.

166. J. Z. Pan and I. Horrocks. OWL-E: Extending OWL with expressive datatype expressions. IMG Technical Report IMG/2004/KR-SW-01/v1.0, Victoria University of Manchester, 2004. http://dl-web.man.ac.uk/Doc/IMGTR-OWL-E.pdf.

167. M. Paolucci, A. Ankolekar, N. Srinivasan, and K. Sycara. The DAML-S virtual machine. In *Proceedings of 2nd International Semantic Web Conference (ISWC 2003)*, volume 2870 of *Lecture Notes in Computer Science*, pages 290–305. Springer, Berlin, 2003.

168. M. Paolucci, T. Kawamura, T. Payne, and K. Sycara. Semantic matching of Web Services capabilities. In I. Horrocks and J. Handler, editors, *Proceedings of the 1st International Semantic Web Conference (ISWC)*, pages 333–347. Springer, Berlin, 2002.

169. M. Paolucci, N. Srinivasan, and K. Sycara. Expressing WSMO mediators in OWL-S. In *Proceedings of Semantic Web Services: Preparing to Meet the World of Business Applications*, 2004.

170. M. P. Papazoglou. Extending the Service-Oriented Architecture. Business Integration Journal, Feb 2002.

171. M. P. Papazoglou. Service-oriented computing: Concepts, characteristics and directions. Web Information Systems Engineering, 2003. WISE 2003. Proceedings of the Fourth International Conference on, December 2003.

172. M. P. Papazoglou and P. Ribbers. *e-Business: Organizational and Technical Foundations*. Addison-Wesley, Reading, 2006.

173. M. P. Papazoglou, P. Traverso, S. Dustdar, and F. Leymann. Service-oriented computing research roadmap, Mar 2006.

174. M. P. Papazoglou and W.-J. van den Heuvel. Service Oriented Architectures: approaches, technologies and research issues. *VLDB Journal*, 2007.

175. A. A. Patil, S. A. Oundhakar, A. P. Sheth, and K. Verma. METEOR-S Web service annotation framework. In *WWW '04: Proceedings of the 13th international conference on World Wide Web*, pages 553–562, New York, 2004. ACM Press.

176. M. Pistore, F. Barbon, P. Bertoli, D. Shaparau, and P. Traverso. Planning and monitoring Web service composition. In *Workshop on Planning and Scheduling for Web and Grid Services (held in conjunction with the 14th International Conference on Automated Planning and Scheduling*, page 7071, 2004.

177. M. Pistore and P. Roberti. D2.4.6 – a theoretical integration of Web service discovery and composition. Technical report, University of Trento, Italy, Jun 2005.

178. C. Preist. A conceptual architecture for Semantic Web Services. In S. A. McIlraith, D. Plexousakis, and F. van Harmelen, editors, *The Semantic Web – ISWC 2004: Third International Semantic Web Conference, Hiroshima, Japan*, volume 3298 of *Lecture Notes in Computer Science*, pages 395–409. Springer, Berlin, Nov. 2004.

179. E. Prud'hommeaux and A. Seaborne. SPARQL query language for RDF. Working Draft 26 March 2007, W3C, 2007.

180. R. Ramakrishnan, Y. Sagiv, J. D. Ullman, and M. Y. Vardi. Proof-tree transformation theorems and their applications. In *PODS '89: Proceedings of the Eighth ACM SIGACT-SIGMOD-SIGART Symposium on Principles of Database Systems*, pages 172–181, New York, 1989. ACM Press.

181. S. Ran. A model for Web Services discovery with QoS. In *ACM SIGecom Exchanges*, Lecture Notes in Computer Science, pages 1–10. Springer, Berlin, 2003.

182. R. Richardson and A. F. Smeaton. Using WordNet in a knowledge-based approach to information retrieval. Technical Report CA-0395, Dublin, Ireland, 1995.

183. J. Riemer, F. Martin-Recuerda, Y. Ding, M. Murth, B. Sapkota, R. Krummenacher, O. Shafiq, D. Fensel, and E. Kuehn. Triple space computing: adding semantics to space-based computing. In *Proceedings of 1st Asian Semantic Web Conference (ASWC 2006)*, Beijing, China, September 2006.

184. D. Roman, U. Keller, H. Lausen, J. de Bruijn, R. Lara, M. Stollberg, A. Polleres, C. Feier, C. Bussler, and D. Fensel. Web service modeling ontology. *Applied Ontology*, 1(1):77–106, 2005.

185. D. Roman, H. Lausen, and U. Keller. Web service modeling ontology (WSMO). Working Draft D2v1.2, WSMO, 2005. http://www.wsmo.org/TR/d2/v1.2/.

186. D. Roman, J. Scicluna, and J. Nitzsche. Ontology-based choreography. Deliverable D14v1.0., WSM0, 2007. http://www.wsmo.org/TR/d14/v1.0/.

187. G. Salton and M. J. McGill, editors. *Introduction to Modern Information Retrieval*. McGraw-Hill, New York, 1986.

188. F. Scharffe and J. de Bruijn. A language to specify mappings between ontologies. In *IEEE Conference on Internet-Based Systems SITIS6*, Yaounde, Cameroon, Dec 2005.

189. F. Scharffe and A. Kiryakov. OMWG – mapping and merging tool design, DERI OMWG Working Draft, Oct 2005.

190. H. Schulzrine and J. Rosenberg. SIP caller preferences and callee capabilities (internet draft), Nov 2000.

191. H. Schulzrinne and J. Rosenberg. Internet telephony: architecture and protocols - an ietf perspective. *Computer Networks*, 31(3):237–255, 1999.

192. N. Shadbolt, T. Berners-Lee, and W. Hall. The Semantic Web revisited. *IEEE Intelligent Systems*, 21(3):96–101, 2006.

193. O. Shafiq, R. Krummenacher, F. Martin-Recuerda, Y. Ding, and D. Fensel. Triple space computing middleware for Semantic Web Services. In *Proceedings of 2006 Middleware for Web Services (MWS 2006) Workshop at the 10th International IEEE Enterprise Computing Conference (EDOC 2006)*, Hong Kong, Oct 2006.

194. O. Shafiq, F. Scharffe, R. Krummenacher, Y. Ding, and D. Fensel. Data mediation support for triple space computing. In *Proceedings of the 2nd IEEE International Conference on Collaborative Computing (CollaborateCom 2006)*, Atlanta, Nov 2006.

195. M. P. Singh and M. N. Huhns. *Service-Oriented Computing: Semantics, Processes, Agents*. Wiley, New York, 2005.

196. E. Sirin, B. Parsia, B. C. Grau, A. Kalyanpur, and Y. Katz. Pellet: a practical OWL-DL reasoner. *Journal of Web Semantics*, 5(2):51–53, 2004.

197. K. Sivashanmugam, J. A. Miller, A. P. Sheth, and K. Verma. Framework for Semantic Web process composition. *International Journal of Electronic Commerce*, 9(2):71–106, Jan 2005.

198. K. Sivashanmugam, K. Verma, A. P. Sheth, and J. A. Miller. Adding semantics to Web Services standards. In *ICWS*, pages 395–401, 2003.

199. L. Sjberg. Gopher: underground technology. Apr 2004.

200. F. Sørmo and J. Cassens. Explanation goals in case-based reasoning. In P. Gervás and K. M. Gupta, editors, *Proceedings of the ECCBR 2004 Workshops*, number 142-04 in Technical Report of the Departamento de Sistemas Informáticos y Programación, Universidad Complutense de Madrid, pages 165–174, Madrid, 2004. http://www.idi.ntnu.no/ cassens/work/publications/download/2004-ECCBR-WS-goals.pdf.

201. N. Srinivasan, M. Paolucci, and K. Sycara. Adding OWL-S to UDDI: implementation and throughput. In *Proceedings of 1st International Conference on Semantic Web Services and Web Process Composition (SWSWPC 2004)*, 2004.

202. M. Stollberg, U. Keller, H. Lausen, and S. Heymans. Two-phase Web service discovery based on rich functional descriptions. In *4th European Semantic Web Services Conference, 3–7 June*, Innsbruck, Austria, 2007. Springer, Berlin.

203. M. Stollberg and B. Norton. A refined goal model for Semantic Web Services. In *The Second International Conference on Internet and Web Applications and Services*, Mauritius, May 2007. In press.

204. R. Studer, V. R. Benjamins, and D. Fensel. Knowledge engineering: principles and methods. *Data and Knowledge engineering (DKE)*, 25(1-2):161–197, 1998.

205. K. Sycara, S. Widoff, M. Klusch, and J. Lu. Larks: Dynamic matchmaking among heterogeneous software agents in cyberspace. *Autonomous Agents and Multi-Agent Systems*, pages 173–203, 2002.

206. M. Szomszor, T. Payne, and L. Moreau. Automated syntactic mediation for Web Services integration. In *Proceedings of IEEE International Conference on Web Services (ICWS 2006)*, 2006.

207. I. Toma and D. Foxvog. Non-functional properties in Web Services. Working draft, Digital Enterprise Research Institute (DERI), Aug 2006. http://www.wsmo.org/TR/d28/d28.4/v0.1/.

208. D. Tsarkov and I. Horrocks. Fact++ description logic reasoner: System description. In *Proceedings of the International Joint Conference on Automated Reasoning (IJCAR 2006)*, 2006. http://www.cs.man.ac.uk/ horrocks/Publications/download/2006/TsHo06a.pdf.

209. J. D. Ullman. *Principles of Database and Knowledge-Base Systems, Volume I*. Computer Science Press, 1988.

210. M. Uschold. Where are the semantics in the semantic web? *AI Magazine*, 24(3):25–36, 2003.

211. M. Uschold, M. King, S. Morale, and Z. Y. The enterprise ontology. *The Knowledge Engineering Review*, 13(1):31–89, 1998.

212. K. Verma, K. Sivashanmugam, A. Sheth, A. Patil, S. Oundhakar, and J. Miller. METEOR-S WSDI: a scalable P2P infrastructure of registries for semantic publication and discovery of Web Services. *International Journal of Information Technologies and Management*, 6(1):17–39, 2005.

213. T. Vitvar, M. Zaremba, and M. Moran. Dynamic service discovery through meta-interactions with service providers. In *Proceedings of the 4th European Semantic Web Conference (ESWC 2006)*, June 2007.

214. L.-H. Vu, M. Hauswirth, and K. Aberer. QoS-based service selection and ranking with trust and reputation management. Technical report, EPFL, 2005. http://dip.semanticweb.org/documents/Manfred-Hauswirth-CoopIS-SemanticDiscovery.pdf.

215. L.-H. Vu, M. Hauswirth, and K. Aberer. Towards P2P-based Semantic Web Service discovery with QoS support. In C. Bussler and A. Haller, editors, *Business Process Management Workshops, BPM 2005*, volume 3812 of *Lecture Notes in Computer Science*, pages 18–31, Nancy, 2006. Springer, Berlin.

216. S. Weibel, J. Kunze, C. Lagoze, and M. Wolf. Dublin Core metadata for resource discovery. RFC 2413, IETF, Sep 1998.

217. D. Wu, B. Parsia, E. Sirin, J. Hendler, and D. Nau. Automating DAML-S Web Services composition using SHOP2. In *Proceedings of 2nd International Semantic Web Conference (IWSC 2003)*, volume 2870 of *Lecture Notes in Computer Science*. Springer, Berlin, 2003.

218. G. Yang and M. Kifer. Implementing an efficient DOOD system using a tabling logical engine. In *Proceedings of 1st International Conference on Computational Logic*, 2000.

219. A. Zaremski and J. Wing. Specification matching of software components. In *3rd ACM SIGSOFT Symposium on the Foundations of Software Engineering*, Oct 1995.

220. L. Zeng, B. Benatallah, H. Lei, A. Ngu, D. Flaxer, and H. Chang. Flexible composition of enterprise Web Services. In *Electronic Markets - Web Services 13*, pages 141–152, 2003.

221. L. Zeng, B. Benatallah, A. H. Ngu, J. Kalagnanam, and H. Chang. QoS-aware middleware for Web service composition. *IEEE Transactions on Software Engineering*, 30(5):311–327, 2004.

Index

A2A Integration, 81
Abstract State Machines (ASM), 50, 104, 129
Adaptation, 69, 80, 88
Application Programming Interface (API), 71
ARPANet, 3
Asynchronous Communication, 247
Attribute, 47
Axiom, 48

B2B Integration, 28, 80, 261
Behavior Semantics, 31, 33
  Conditional Exchange Sequence, 34
  Data Granularity Mismatch, 34
  Data Mismatch, 34
  Exchange Sequence Mismatch, 33
Business Process Execution Language (BPEL), 71, 92, 119, 300, 304
Business Process Execution Language for Web Services (BPEL4WS), 73

Capability, 49, 265
  Assumption, 49
  Effect, 49
  Postcondition, 49
  Precondition, 49
Choreography, 50, 79, 104, 225, 229, 265, 288, 290, 292
  in IRS, 292
  in OWL-S, 295
Choreography Engine, 90, 104, 129, 292
Closed World Assumption, 142, 143
Communication Mismatches, 224

Solvable Mismatches, 225
Composition, 27, 69, 80, 89, 105, 293
  ILog Composer, 293
  in METEOR-S, 300
  in OWL-S, 296
Concept, 46
Concurrent Goal Execution, 256
CORSO, 245

Data Semantics, 31
Datalog, 144, 158
Description Logic, 54, 56, 137, 141, 145, 150, 177, 294
Discovery, 27, 40, 69, 79, 87, 101, 111, 129, 155, 167, 268, 293
  Abstract State Spaces, 183
  in IRSIII, 290
  in METEOR-S, 298
  in OWL-S, 295
  Keyword-based discovery, 169
  Levels of Abstraction, 168
  Matching, 176
  QoS-Enabled Discovery, 102
Dublin Core, 45

Enterprise Application Integration (EAI), 28, 80
Execution Management, 79, 96
Execution Semantics, 44, 120
  achieveGoal, 125, 127
  getWebServices, 123
  invokeWebService, 124
External Communications Manager, 107

F-Logic, 19, 56
Fault Handling, 79, 92
Function, 47

Goal, 51, 105, 288, 290, 295
Gopher, 4
Grounding, 80, 92

Heterogeneity, 211
HTML, 7
HTTP, 6, 71

Instance, 48
Instance Transformation, 215, 216, 222
Interface, 50
Internationalized Resource Identifier (IRI),
    54, 58
Internet Engineering Task Force (IETF), 8
Internet Reasoning Service, 99, 285
    Architecture, 285
    IRS-I, 285
    IRS-II, 285
    IRS-III, 285
Invocation, 69

Japanese Emperor Date, 38

Knowledge Interchange Format (KIF), 23

Linda, 235
Logic Programming, 54, 56, 137, 143, 149,
    151, 163
Logical Expression, 48

Mash-ups, 32
Mediation, 33, 40, 80, 91, 211
    Behavioral Mediation, 211, 223
    Data Mediation, 69, 102, 111, 130, 155,
        211, 215, 222, 290, 295, 299
    in METEOR-S, 299
    in OWL-S, 295
    Process Mediation, 69, 111, 129, 156,
        211, 223, 225, 229, 290
Mediation Service, 52, 212, 214
Mediator, 51, 213
    GGMediator, 52, 213, 292
    OOMediator, 52, 213, 290
    WGMediator, 52, 213, 290, 292
    WWMediator, 53, 213
Meta-Object Facility (MOF), 44

METEOR-S, 296
    MWSAF, 296, 297
    MWSCF, 296, 300
    MWSDI, 296, 298
    WSDL-S, 296, 297, 299
MOF, 289
Monitoring, 69, 79, 93
Mosaic, 4

N-Triples, 55
Negation-as-failure, 143
Negotiation, 69
NESSI, 70
Non Functional Properties, 45, 49, 194, 265
Non-monotonicity, 143

OASIS, 37, 70
OCML, 285, 287
    Constructs, 288
    Modeling, 287
Ontology, 33, 45, 139
ontology, 12
Ontology Mapping, 215, 217, 218, 266
    Mapping Process, 221
    Perspective, 218
    Suggestion Algorithms, 220
Open World Assumption, 142
Orchestration, 50, 105, 265, 292
    in IRS, 292
    in OWL-S, 295
Orchestration Engine, 104
OWL, 23, 55, 65, 160
OWL-S, 294
    Process Model, 295

Parameter, 47
Persistent Publication, 233, 256
Process Compatibility, 224
Prolog, 144

Quality of Service, 195

RDF, 11, 55, 233
RDF Schema (RDFS), 16, 55
Reasoner, 111
Reasoning, 39, 75, 80, 95, 137
    Deductive reasoning, 138
    in OWL-S, 294

Reasoning Tasks, 144, 159, 162
  Logical Entailment, 144, 154
  Query Answering, 145, 149, 154, 159
  Satisfiability, 146, 162
  Subsumption, 146, 162
Relation, 47
Relation Instance, 48
Resource Manager, 111
REST, 35
RosettaNet, 104, 261
Rule Interchange Format (RIF), 55, 162

SAWSDL, 36, 296, 298, 299
Security, 79, 97
SEE, 37
Selection, 40, 88, 155, 206, 268
  in IRSIII, 290
  Multi criteria ranking, 205
  Non Functional Properties Ontologies, 195
  Service Ranking, 201
Semantic Computing, 27
Semantic Mediation Patterns, 212
Semantic Mediators, 212
Semantic Web, 27
Semantic Web Services, 138
Semantic Web Services (SWS), 27, 37, 69
Semantically Enabled Service Oriented Architecture (SESA), 233
Semantically Enabled Service Oriented Architectures (SESA), 69
  Middleware Layer, 79
    Base Layer, 80
    Broker Layer, 79
    Vertical Layer, 79
  Problem Solving Layer, 78
  Service Providers Layer, 80
  Service Requesters Layer, 79
  Stakeholders Layer, 78
Semantics, 10, 30
Service directories, 170
Service Oriented Architecture (SOA), 69
Service Oriented Computing (SOC), 70
Simple Object Access Protocol (SOAP), 73
SOAP, 35, 71, 107
Space Based Computing, 235
SPARQL, 55
Storage, 80, 95
SWRL, 19

Syntax, 30
System Behavior Modeling, 120

TCP/IP, 3
TMDA, 285
Triple Based Computing, 235
Triple Space, 235
  advertise, 240
  count, 240
  notify, 240
  query, 238
  read, 239
  subscribe, 239
  take, 239
  update, 239
  write, 238
Triple Space Computing, 233, 235
Tuple Space, 115, 132
Tuple Space Computing, 233

UDDI, 170, 299
UML, 101
Unified Modeling Language (UML), 121
  Activity Diagrams, 121
Uniform Resource Identifier (URI), 54
Uniform Resource Identifiers (URI), 5
Unique Name Assumption, 142
Universal Resource Locator (URL), 28

Web 2.0, 24
Web Service, 48, 73, 105, 288
Web Service Execution Environment, 277
Web Service Execution Environment (WSMX), 41, 70, 99, 112
Web Service Modeling Framework (WSMF), 43
Web Service Modeling Language (WSML), 41, 43, 53, 140, 152, 263
  Design Principles, 54
  Identifiers, 58
  Syntax, 57
    Conceptual Syntax, 58
    Logical Expression Syntax, 62
    OWL, 65
    RDF Syntax, 64
    XML Syntax, 64
  WSML-Variants, 56, 64
    WSML-Core, 56
    WSML-DL, 56

WSML-Flight, 56
WSML-Full, 57
WSML-Rule, 57
Web Service Modeling Ontology (WSMO),
    41, 43, 263, 288
  Importing Ontologies, 46
  Using Mediators, 46
Web Service Modeling Toolkit (WSMT), 82,
    103, 218, 264
Web Services, 27, 34
Web Services Programming Model, 71

World Wide Web, 4
World Wide Web Consortium (W3C), 8
WSDL, 71, 263
WSML2Reasoner Framework, 156
WSMO4J, 109

XML, 10, 54, 71, 74
  Namespaces, 15
XML Schema, 16, 265
XMLRPC, 35
XQuery, 16, 54